BRING ME THE HEAD OF JOAQUIN MURRIETA

ALSO BY JOHN BOESSENECKER

Badge and Buckshot: Lawlessness in Old California

The Grey Fox: The True Story of Bill Miner, Last of the Old-Time Bandits (with Mark Dugan)

Lawman: The Life and Times of Harry Morse, 1835–1912

Against the Vigilantes: The Recollections of Dutch Charley Duane

Gold Dust and Gunsmoke: Tales of Gold Rush Outlaws, Gunfighters, Lawmen, and Vigilantes

Bandido: The Life and Times of Tiburcio Vasquez

When Law Was in the Holster: The Frontier Life of Bob Paul

Texas Ranger: The Epic Life of Frank Hamer, the Man Who Killed Bonnie and Clyde

Shotguns and Stagecoaches: The Brave Men Who Rode for Wells Fargo in the Wild West

Ride the Devil's Herd: Wyatt Earp's Epic Battle Against the West's Biggest Outlaw Gang

Wildcat: The Untold Story of Pearl Hart, the Wild West's Most Notorious Woman Bandit

Gentleman Bandit: The True Story of Black Bart, the Old West's Most Infamous Stagecoach Robber

Joaquin Murrieta, by the San Francisco artist Charles Christian Nahl, 1868.
Greg Martin collection

BRING ME THE HEAD OF JOAQUIN MURRIETA

THE BANDIT CHIEF WHO TERRORIZED CALIFORNIA AND LAUNCHED THE LEGEND OF ZORRO

JOHN BOESSENECKER

HANOVER
SQUARE
PRESS

ISBN-13: 978-1-335-00703-2

Bring Me the Head of Joaquin Murrieta

Hanover Square Press
22 Adelaide St. West, 41st Floor
Toronto, Ontario M5H 4E3, Canada
HanoverSqPress.com

HarperCollins Publishers
Macken House, 39/40 Mayor Street Upper,
Dublin 1, D01 C9W8, Ireland
www.HarperCollins.com

Printed in U.S.A.

In memory of William B. Secrest (1930–2019)

CONTENTS

	Prologue	1
CHAPTER 1	A Legend Is Born	3
CHAPTER 2	The Wickedest Man in California	17
CHAPTER 3	El Dorado, the Land of Gold and Gunfire	30
CHAPTER 4	The Birth of a Bandit Gang	51
CHAPTER 5	Claudio Feliz, the Brigand Chief	67
CHAPTER 6	Kill the Yankees!	84
CHAPTER 7	A Bullet for Sheriff Buchanan	105
CHAPTER 8	Seduced by the Devil	119
CHAPTER 9	The Battles of Sawmill Flat and Salinas River	140
CHAPTER 10	Murder in Los Angeles	166
CHAPTER 11	Joaquin, the Mountain Robber	190
CHAPTER 12	Marauders of the Mines	215

CHAPTER 13 No Man Takes Me Alive 234

CHAPTER 14 Captain Love and the Rangers 252

CHAPTER 15 I Am the Leader of This Band 271

CHAPTER 16 Bring Me the Head of Joaquin Murrieta 299

CHAPTER 17 End of the Trail 326

CHAPTER 18 Last of the California Rangers 361

CHAPTER 19 The Widow of Joaquin 389

CHAPTER 20 An Outlaw's Legacy: Procopio Murrieta 407

CHAPTER 21 From Joaquin to Zorro: The Launching of Legends 434

Acknowledgments 461

Notes 463

Index 485

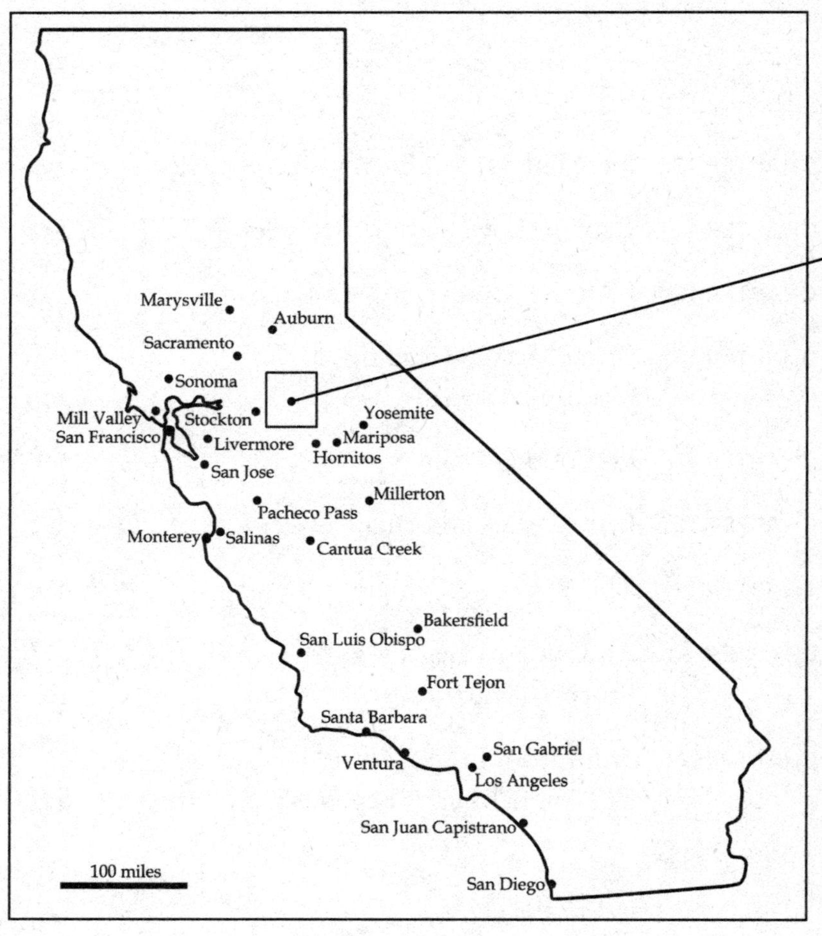

The California of Joaquin Murrieta.

Maps by Robert Boessenecker

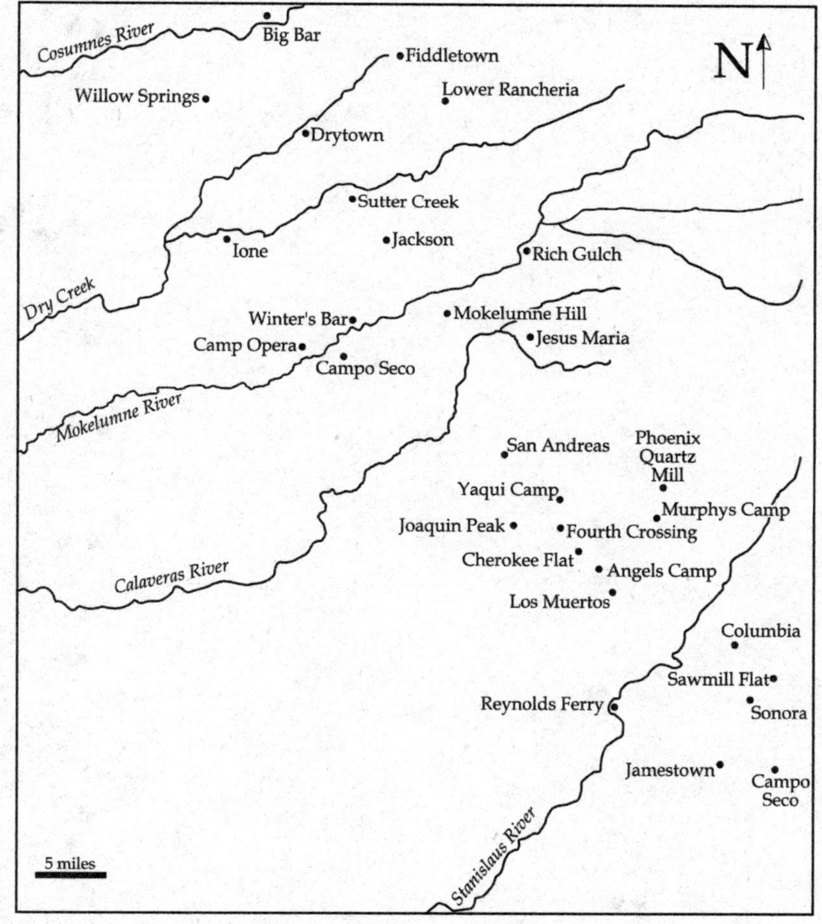

The gold rush mining camps of the Sierra Nevada foothills that feature in the bloody raids of Joaquin Murrieta.

Maps by Robert Boessenecker

PROLOGUE

Joaquin Murrieta. His name is one of the most famous in the annals of the American frontier, and his popular myth is seductively compelling. He was a Mexican Robin Hood and the real-life inspiration for Zorro. He was both bandit and rebel, a horseback avenger who battled injustice and fought to protect the rights of Latinos in the Wild West. Joaquin first came to California during the gold rush of 1849 and worked for two years as an honest and peaceable miner. But Anglos falsely accused the young man of theft and flogged him mercilessly. They drove him from his mining claim, raped his teenage wife, and lynched his half brother. Forced into a life of banditry, he raided the gold camps in revenge, robbing and killing those who had abused him and his family.

For more than one hundred seventy years, Joaquin Murrieta has been America's most renowned Latino outlaw. He remains a folk hero, not only in the American West, but also in Mexico and South America. He became the subject of *corridos*, or ballads, and of poetry, books, and Hollywood films. Numerous academic historians have described Murrieta as a man who resisted Anglo American economic, social, and political domination, a warrior who rebelled against Western imperialism and colonialism. Other historians describe how he engaged in social banditry, defined as a form of class struggle and resistance in preindustrial and frontier societies. Scholars write that Latino social bandits were primitive rebels who struck out in self-defense against the conquering Anglos.

Murrieta's life has been portrayed in, and obscured by, generations of myth, fiction, and folktales. Men like Joaquin—shadowy bandits and elusive outlaws—did not leave diaries, correspondence, or memoirs to record their thoughts, their experiences, and the details of their violent careers. But fortunately the true story of Joaquin Murrieta is not lost in the murky fog of legend and folklore. It lives on in obscure, long-forgotten contemporary sources—newspaper accounts, court records, pioneers' journals, and the written recollections of those who lived through the turbulent gold rush years.

Was Joaquin Murrieta a frontier Robin Hood? Was he Zorro, the Fox? Was he a freedom fighter, an avenger who battled for social justice for Mexican Americans? Perhaps a ride back through the mists of time—through the blood, thunder, and gunsmoke to a long forgotten and much misunderstood era—will lead us to the answers.

CHAPTER 1

A LEGEND IS BORN

The boy bolted upright in bed, awakened by loud shouts that echoed through the early dawn. He heard his mother's screams as a band of shadowy strangers smashed through the front door and burst into his parents' bedroom. One held a cocked pistol to his father's head and pulled the trigger, but the hammer snapped down harmlessly, and the gun misfired. The youth, shaking with fright, rushed to the front room in time to see three men grappling with his father and dragging him toward the front door. He, with the rest of his roused family, looked on helplessly as the intruders forced his father out the door and into the yard. Glancing outside, the boy spotted more than twenty armed men mounted on horses and surrounding the house. Several of them wrestled his father to the ground, while another drew a long-bladed knife and plunged it repeatedly into his body. The youth's mother rushed past him toward her husband, but several of the mob brandished rifles and pistols and forced her back into the doorway. As the terrified boy gaped openmouthed, the men picked up the limp, bloodied body and threw it into the air. His father landed heavily on the dirt. Then the mob lined up single-file, and each man stepped forward and stomped the torso with his boots. Incredibly, his father was still alive, and his mother rushed out again and embraced him. He tried to speak, but he could only sputter blood. Moments later, as the killers rode off, his father died in her arms.

The boy's name was John Rollin Ridge, and fifteen years later, he would write a hugely popular book that launched the legend of Joaquin Murrieta. Young Ridge hailed from Georgia, where he was born in 1827, the second eldest child of John Ridge, a prominent Cherokee leader, and Sarah Bird Northrup, an educated white woman from Connecticut. His parents gave him the Cherokee name of Cheesquatalawny, or Yellow Bird. His father was a lawyer and farmer who owned a ferry, cropland, and eighteen black slaves. In 1835, Ridge's father, grandfather, and uncle were among the signers of a controversial treaty in which they sold Cherokee lands and moved to Indian Territory, now Oklahoma. Most Cherokees opposed the treaty, and the result was that US soldiers forced thousands of Native Americans in the southern states to march more than seven hundred miles to Indian Territory. So many Indians died during the long trek that it went down in infamy as the Trail of Tears.

Four years later, when Ridge was twelve, a band of vengeful Cherokees who had resisted the treaty rode up to the family home. As Ridge recalled, "On the morning of the 22nd of June, 1839, about daybreak, our family was aroused from sleep by a violent noise. The doors were broken down, and the house was full of armed men. I saw my father in the hands of assassins. He endeavored to speak to them, but they shouted and drowned his voice for they were instructed not to listen to him for a moment for fear they would be persuaded not to kill him. They dragged him into the yard, and prepared to murder him. Two men held him by the arms, and others by the body, while another stabbed him deliberately with a dirk twenty-nine times." On the same day, another band of Cherokee assassins murdered Ridge's grandfather by shooting him from ambush, and a third group of killers stabbed his uncle to death.[1]

His father's murder traumatized the boy, who later said, "It has darkened my mind with an eternal shadow." And it left him with a burning desire for vengeance. As he wrote when still a teenager, "Although I have always been taught never to harbour feelings of revenge, it is impossible for me to control them." His mother, widowed and terrorized, fled to safety in Arkansas with her seven children. There, despite the family trauma, young Ridge received a good education, and he learned to enjoy writing, especially poetry. In 1843, when he was sixteen, his mother sent him to a boarding school in Massachusetts, and two years later he returned to Arkansas to study law. But he did not follow the legal profession, and at age nineteen, Ridge bought a farm in what is now Delaware County near the northeastern corner of Oklahoma. The following year, 1847, he married a young white woman, Elizabeth Wilson. They soon had a daughter, and John Rollin Ridge seemed destined for a simple and happy domestic life.[2]

That all changed in May 1849, when Ridge learned that his prized stallion was missing from his homestead. He tracked the animal to the nearby farm of David Kell, a Cherokee judge who supported the side that, ten years earlier, had killed his father, grandfather, and uncle. Ridge had made open threats of vengeance against that faction, and Kell apparently took the horse in order to antagonize him. Ridge rode into Kell's farmyard and asked if he had seen the stallion.

"There is a *gelding*," Kell responded with a sneer.

Ridge spotted his stolen mount nearby. The animal had been castrated and was standing in a pool of blood.

"Who made him so?" he demanded.

"I did, and am willing to stand by my deeds with my life," Kell taunted.

At that, Ridge leaped down from his saddle. He then paused, realizing that Kell was a bigger and stronger man. According to a newspaper report, "Ridge remarked that the disparity of their strength forbade that they should fight in close contest." But Ridge instead jerked out his pistol, thumbed back the hammer, and covered Kell.

"If you approach me," Ridge warned, "you will lose your life."

Kell paid no heed, and stepped toward Ridge.

"Stand back, Kell! Advance any further, and you die."

Kell continued straight toward Ridge, who squeezed the trigger. The pistol ball slammed into Kell, killing him. Then Ridge, having little faith in Cherokee tribal courts, fled east into Missouri. In the spring of 1850, he joined the gold rush. Leaving his wife and daughter behind, he traveled overland by wagon train to California. Like most gold seekers, Ridge failed to strike it rich, and he soon turned to a career as a writer, poet, and newspaperman. He sent for Elizabeth, and she and their little girl joined him in California. Despite his skill as a journalist, Ridge struggled to earn a living. Eventually he realized that the story of Joaquin Murrieta could make a fascinating and financially successful book. And because of Ridge's own tumultuous background, the saga of the young Mexican outcast and outlaw resonated deeply within him.[3]

Like everyone else in California, he was fascinated by the career of the gold hunter turned murderous bandit, whose gang

John Rollin Ridge, from a daguerreotype taken about 1853. *John McWilliams collection.*

had terrorized the new state, plundering the mining camps and killing prospectors with abandon. For more than a year, the band rode roughshod across gold rush California, robbing and murdering at will, then vanishing into the pine forests and the chaparral-covered hills. Ridge had closely followed the many newspaper reports, and listened to countless tales, about Joaquin and his daring raids. On a wintry day late in 1853, he hunched over a writing desk in his room in the Tremont House, a popular hotel in the rowdy gold rush town of Marysville.[4]

John Rollin Ridge knew that he could spin the dramatic tale with flourish and passion. The outlaw's story, as Ridge reimagined it, had strong parallels with his own violent life. He dipped his pen into an inkwell, and the saga of the notorious bandido poured out.

> The first that we hear of him in the Golden State is that, in the spring of 1850, he is engaged in the honest occupation of a miner in the Stanislaus placers, then reckoned among the richest portions of the mines. He was then eighteen years of age, a little over the medium height, slenderly but gracefully built, and active as a young tiger. His complexion was neither very dark nor very light, but clear and brilliant, and his countenance is pronounced to have been, at that time, exceedingly handsome and attractive. His large black eyes, kindling with the enthusiasm of his earnest nature, his firm and well-formed mouth, his well-shaped head from which the long, glossy, black hair hung down over his shoulders, his silvery voice, full of generous utterance, and the frank and cordial manner which distinguished him made him beloved by all with whom he came in contact. He had the confidence and respect of the whole community around him, and was fast amassing a fortune in his rich mining claim. He had built him a comfortable mining residence in which he had domiciled his heart's treasure—a beautiful Sonorian girl, who had followed the

young adventurer in all his wanderings with the devotedness of passion which belongs to the dark-eyed damsels of Mexico.

It was at this moment of peace and felicity that a blight came over the young man's prospects. The country was then full of lawless and desperate men, who bore the name of Americans but failed to support the honor and the dignity of that title. A feeling was prevalent among this class of contempt for any and all Mexicans, whom they looked upon as no better than conquered subjects of the United States, having no rights which could stand before a haughtier and superior race. They made no exceptions. If the proud blood of the Castilians mounted to the cheek of a partial descendant of the Mexiques, showing that he had inherited the old chivalrous spirit of his Spanish ancestry, they looked upon it as a saucy presumption in one so inferior to them. The prejudice of color, the antipathy of races, which are always stronger and bitterer with the ignorant and unlettered, they could not overcome, or if they could, would not, because it afforded them a convenient excuse for their unmanly cruelty and oppression.

A band of these lawless men, having the brute power to do as they pleased, visited Joaquin's house and peremptorily bade him leave his claim, as they would allow no Mexicans to work in that region. Upon his remonstrating against such outrageous conduct, they struck him violently over the face, and, being physically superior, compelled him to swallow his wrath. Not content with this, they tied him hand and foot and ravished his mistress before his eyes. They left him, but the soul of the young man was from that moment darkened. It was the first injury he had ever received at the hands of the Americans, whom he had always hitherto respected, and it wrung him to the soul as a deeper and deadlier wrong from that very circumstance.

He departed with his weeping and almost heart-broken mistress for a more northern portion of the mines, and the next we hear of him, he is cultivating a little farm on the banks of a beautiful stream that watered a fertile valley far out in the seclusion of the mountains. Here he might hope for peace—here he might forget the past, and again be happy. But his dream was not destined to last. A company of unprincipled Americans—shame that there should be such bearing the name!—saw his retreat, coveted his little home surrounded by its fertile tract of land, and drove him from it, with no other excuse that he was "an infernal Mexican intruder!"

Joaquin's blood boiled in his veins, but his spirit was still unbroken, nor had the iron so far entered his soul as to sear up the innate sensitiveness to honor and right which reigned in his bosom. Twice broken up in his honest pursuit of fortune, he resolved still to labor on with unflinching brow and with that true moral bravery, which throws its redeeming light forward upon all his subsequently dark and criminal career. How deep must have been the anguish of that young heart and how strongly rooted the native honesty of his soul, none can know or imagine but they who have been tried in like manner. He bundled up his little movable property, and again started forth to strike once more, like a brave and honest man, for fortune and for happiness.

He arrived at Murphy's Diggings in Calaveras County, in the month of April, and went again to mining, but, meeting with nothing like his former success, he soon abandoned that business and devoted his time to dealing "monte," a game which is common in Mexico, and has been almost universally adopted by gamblers in California. It is considered by the Mexican in no manner a disreputable employment, and many well-raised young men from the Atlantic States have resorted to it as a profession in this land of luck and chances. It was then in much better odor than it is now, although it is at present a game which may be played on very fair and honest principles, provided, anything can be strictly honest or fair which allows the taking of money without a valuable consideration in return.

It was therefore looked upon as no departure from rectitude on the part of Joaquin, when he commenced the business of dealing "monte."

Having a very pleasing exterior and being, despite of all his sorrows, very gay and lively in disposition, he attracted many persons to his table, and won their money with such skill and grace, or lost his own with such perfect good humor that he was considered by all the very beau ideal of a gambler and the prince of clever fellows. His sky seemed clear and his prospects bright, but Fate was weaving her mysterious web around him, and fitting him to be by the force of circumstances what nature never intended to make him.

He had gone a short distance from Murphy's Diggings to see a half-brother, who had been located in that vicinity for several months, and returned to Murphy's upon a horse which his brother had lent him. The animal proved to have been stolen, and being recognized by a number of individuals in town, an excitement was raised on the subject. Joaquin suddenly found himself surrounded by a furious mob and charged with the crime of theft. He told them how it happened that he was riding the horse and in what manner his half-brother had come in possession of it. They listened to no explanation, but bound him to a tree, and publicly disgraced him with the lash. They then proceeded to the house of his half-brother and hung him without judge or jury.

It was then that the character of Joaquin changed, suddenly and irrevocably. Wanton cruelty and the tyranny of prejudice had reached their climax. His soul swelled beyond its former boundaries, and the barriers of honor, rocked into atoms by the strong passion which shook his heart like an earthquake, crumbled around him. Then it was declared to a friend that he would live henceforth for revenge and that his path should be marked with blood. Fearfully did he keep that promise, as the following pages will show.

It was not long after this unfortunate affair that an American was found dead in the vicinity of Murphy's Diggings, having been cut to pieces with a knife. Though horribly mangled, he was recognized as one of the mob engaged in whipping Joaquin. A doctor, passing in the neighborhood of this murder, was met, shortly afterward, by two men on horseback, who fired their revolvers at him, but, owing to his speed on foot, and the unevenness of the ground, he succeeded in escaping with no further injury than having a bullet shot through his hat within an inch of the top of his head!

A panic spread among the rash individuals who had composed that mob, and they were afraid to stir out on their ordinary business. Whenever any one of them strayed out of sight of his camp or ventured to travel on the highway, he was shot down suddenly and mysteriously. Report after report came into the villages that Americans had been found dead on the highways, having been either shot or stabbed, and it was invariably discovered, for many weeks, that the murdered men belonged to the mob who publicly whipped Joaquin. It was fearful and it was strange to see how swiftly and mysteriously those men disappeared. "Murieta's revenge was very nearly complete," said an eyewitness of these events, in reply to an inquiry which I addressed him. "I am inclined to think he wiped out the most of those prominently engaged in whipping him."

Thus far, who can blame him? But the iron had entered too deeply in his soul for him to stop here. He had contracted a hatred to the whole American race, and was determined to shed their blood, whenever and wherever an opportunity occurred. It was no time now for him to retrace his steps. He had committed deeds which made him amenable to the law, and his only safety lay in a persistence in the unlawful course which he had begun. It was necessary that he should have horses and that he should have money. These he could not obtain except

> by robbery and murder, and thus he became an outlaw and a bandit on the verge of his nineteenth year.
>
> The year 1850 rolled away, marked with the eventful history of this young man's wrongs and trials, his bitter revenge on those who had perpetrated the crowning act of his deep injury and disgrace; and, as it closed, it shut him away forever from his peace of mind and purity of heart. He walked forth into the future a dark, determined criminal, and his proud nobility of soul existed only in memory.[5]

With those opening words from John Rollin Ridge, the legend of Joaquin Murrieta was born. Ridge went on to describe the principal members of Joaquin's gang and recounted in gory detail their many murderous bandit raids. He based much of his book on the plentiful reports of Joaquin's forays that were published in California newspapers. But authentic details about Murrieta, his early life, and his pivot into banditry were hard to come by, so Ridge used his imagination to fill in the gaps with invented scenes and fictitious dialogue. He finished his book in the spring of 1854 and titled it *The Life and Adventures of Joaquín Murieta, the Celebrated California Bandit*. Ridge, hugely proud of his heritage, authored it under his Cherokee name, Yellow Bird. Released that August in San Francisco, it was the first novel by a Native American author, and the first novel written and published in California. The dramatic, compelling story of an innocent young Mexican miner—his claim stolen by Yankees, his bride raped, his half brother murdered, and his subsequent quest for vengeance—captivated audiences and, at the same time, justified and glorified Joaquin's campaign of banditry against the gringos. It also reflected Ridge's own experiences as a Cherokee outcast, and allowed him, vicariously, to satisfy his thirst for revenge against the assassins who had stabbed his father to death.

Ridge's book unleashed a century-long torrent of newspaper accounts, magazine articles, novels, poems, and purported historical works that were eagerly devoured by readers. It helped make Joaquin one of the most famous outlaws of the Wild West. Hollywood seized on the story and featured Joaquin Murrieta in such films as *The Robin Hood of El Dorado* in 1936 and *The Mask of Zorro* in 1998. Writers crowned him with titles that he had never known in real life: El Famoso, El Patrio, and the Ghost of Sonora. During the Chicano movement of the 1960s and '70s, when social reformers sought equal rights for Latinos, Joaquin was acclaimed as a Mexican hero, a great avenger.

The legend created by John Rollin Ridge was an epic one—but was it true? The fact is that the authentic life of Joaquin Murrieta was so dramatic, so violent, and so tragic that it needed no novelization and no embellishment. The real story was far more exciting, and far more nuanced, than any fiction could ever be.

The birth of the bandido's legend is clear, but Joaquin's actual origins are elusive and remain obscure. Even the correct spelling of his name—Murieta, Murrieta, or Murietta—has long been a matter of dispute. The surname is a relatively common one in Mexico, where it is spelled Murrieta. It was customary for Mexican children like Joaquin to be baptized in the nearest Catholic church soon after birth. However, a number of researchers since the 1930s have sought in vain to find his baptismal record, which was probably lost over the years. According to an old Murrieta family tradition, his father was Juan Carrillo and his mother was Eduviges Hipolito. He was born Joaquin Carrillo in 1829 or 1830 in the town of Alamos, situated in the southern part of the Mexican state of Sonora. Juan Carrillo and Eduviges Hipolito had several other children, among them a daughter, Vicenta, who was several years older than Joaquin. His father, Juan Carrillo, died when Joaquin was quite young, and his mother then married a man named Murrieta. Their union produced several more children, including a son, Jesus Murrieta. Joaquin Carrillo and his siblings all took the Murrieta surname.[6]

Joaquin's hometown of Alamos was a picturesque adobe village and silver mining center nestled in the western foothills of the Sierra Madre Mountains. Alamos traced its beginnings to 1630 when Jesuit missionaries built an adobe church. Fifty years later, the village prospered when silver mines were discovered nearby in the Sierra Madre Mountains. By the time of Joaquin's birth, Alamos was home to about 5,000 people, but during his youth, the silver boom began to decline. Murrieta's boyhood years in Alamos are as obscure as his birth. According to John Rollin Ridge, he was "born in the province of Sonora, of respectable parents, and educated in the schools of Mexico. While growing up, he was remarkable for a very mild and peaceable disposition, and gave no sign of that indomitable and daring spirit which afterwards characterized him. Those who knew him in his school-boy days speak affectionately of his generous and noble nature at that period of his life." However, in 1891, a Mexican *vaquero*, or cowboy, who said he was related to the

Joaquin Murrieta's boyhood home of Alamos, in Sonora, Mexico.
John Boessenecker collection.

Murrieta family, declared that "the boy had from his birth always been cruel and vicious in his tendencies. When he could scarcely walk he was in the habit of lassoing chickens and cats with small pieces of cord and then dragging them to death. The child was so very sly. It was seldom that his parents could detect him in the cruel sport." The truth, of course, was probably somewhere in the middle.[7]

One thing is clear about Joaquin's youth: he became an expert horseman, hunter, and vaquero, skilled with knife and leather *reata*, or lariat, and a dead shot with rifle and pistol. And he was certainly not educated, for as we will see, Murrieta was illiterate and could not even sign his own name. Like many young men in Alamos, Joaquin gained some experience as a silver miner. When still a youth, he spent time in Baroyeca, a silver mining town situated in the Sierra Madre Mountains about fifty miles north of Alamos. Joaquin met a girl, Rosa Feliz, in Baroyeca, and the teenage couple wed in 1848. However, according to some early accounts, they eloped without benefit of marriage. Either way, their lives changed permanently in October of that year when they heard breathtaking news: gold had been discovered in far-off California, formerly a territory of Mexico. In that era before the telegraph, communication was extraordinarily slow, with news delivered by horseback or by ship. As a result, it had taken nine months for word to arrive in Sonora. Many Sonorans were experienced miners, and the lure of distant riches was more than they could resist. During the next ten months, about 10,000 Mexicans emigrated to California from Sonora. The men journeyed, many with wives and children, in large caravans for protection from Indian attacks. The number of emigrants was so great that Mexican officials feared their northern frontier would be depopulated.

Joaquin Murrieta, like so many of his fellow Sonorans, was swept up by gold fever. He and his wife Rosa joined one of the many caravans headed north. They were accompanied by his half brother, Jesus Murrieta, and by Rosa's three brothers: Claudio Feliz, aged about sixteen, Jesus Feliz, also in his teens, and Reyes Feliz, about thirteen years old. All would play prominent roles in the violent events to come. Their journey to California across a vast and barren desert was a long and dangerous one, with a lack of water and the constant danger of Indian attack. They followed the trail first blazed in 1774 by Lieutenant Colonel Juan Bautista de Anza, a Spanish frontiersman, Indian fighter, and the last of the conquistadors. The twelve-hundred-mile Anza Trail began in San Miguel de Horcasitas, the adobe capital of Sonora. From there it proceeded two hundred miles north to the frontier settlement of Tubac, now in southern Arizona. The Murrieta group continued through the pueblo of Tucson, then followed the Santa Cruz and Gila Rivers north and west to the Colorado River, crossing near present day Yuma, Arizona.[8]

In late November 1848, a US Army officer watched the caravans of Mexicans crossing the Colorado River and flocking into California's Mojave Desert. He was stunned by their number, and also by the riches found by those who were returning from the mining region. "Mexicans, from Sonora, are passing us daily on their way to the abundancia, the gold mines. This is all we can hear, 'The Mines!'" he wrote. "The whole state of Sonora is on the move, are passing us in gangs daily, and say they have not yet started. Naked and shirttailed Indians and Mexicans or Californians go and return in fifteen or twenty days with over a pound of pure gold each, per day, and say 'they had bad luck and left.'"[9]

One of those bands of eager gold seekers included young Joaquin Murrieta, his bride, and their family. As they trudged north into the promised land of California, none could have foreseen the tumult and bloodshed that awaited them.

CHAPTER 2

THE WICKEDEST MAN IN CALIFORNIA

They called him Three Fingered Jack. He would become Joaquin Murrieta's lieutenant, as well as one of the most infamous desperadoes of the American frontier. His life is inextricably tied to the story of early California. He was violent, even demonic, and above all, he was a *Californio*—a native-born Californian of Mexican ancestry. Long before Murrieta arrived in Alta, or Upper, California, the Californios had been masters of their own land. The future US state was a distant and isolated province, first of Spain, then of Mexico. Mexico was a Spanish colony in 1775 when the explorer Juan Bautista de Anza and his leather-jacketed troops led the first caravan of Mexican settlers into California. They followed the trail that de Anza had blazed a year earlier, from Sonora to the Mission San Gabriel, near present-day Los Angeles, and finally north to Monterey. For the first time, an overland route was opened from northern Mexico to Alta California. The new province of California was a remote, rugged frontier, and the Spanish government, fearing it would be claimed by Russia or England, wanted colonists to settle it.

Two hundred years earlier, Spanish explorers had first arrived in California in ships they sailed up the Pacific Coast. They discovered a fertile, sun-drenched landscape, peopled only by Native Americans. Beginning in 1769, a series of twenty-one Catholic missions was built along the coast from San Diego in the south to Sonoma, six hundred miles north by primitive roads and trails. Each mission was about thirty miles—a one-day ride—from each other. The missions were connected by *El Camino Real*—The King's Highway. Despite that lofty title, it was a dusty trail that roughly followed the route of modern-day US Highway 101. At each mission, the Catholic priests worked to convert the Native Americans to Catholicism and to train them in trades and farming skills—often against their will. The *padres* wanted to save their souls, but the government wanted to make the Indians loyal subjects of the Spanish empire. Small villages of Mexican settlers soon appeared near the missions, and they later became cities like San Diego, Los Angeles, Santa Barbara, San Luis Obispo, Monterey, San Jose, and San Francisco, then called Yerba Buena.

Numerous Mexican pioneers followed de Anza and flocked into California from northern Mexico. But immigration stopped abruptly as a result of the Yuma Massacre of 1781. Yuma Indians, who had been mistreated by the Spanish, retaliated by attacking the missions and settlements near the Colorado River, killing all adult males and capturing women and children. The Yuma Massacre largely closed the Anza Trail, and California became even more isolated. The Mexican settlers began calling themselves Californios and grew increasingly distant from Mexico. At the same time, a pastoral society emerged, supported by ranching and cattle raising. Most Californios were expert horsemen. California *mestenos,* or mustangs, were sturdy animals, and unlike American horses, they fed on grass instead of grain. That meant they could cover long distances, and the rider did not have to carry feed on his saddle. The *vaquero,* or cattle herder, swinging his *reata,* or lariat, later became the prototype of the American cowboy.

In Mexican California, class lines were strictly drawn. At the top were the *ricos*—the rich rancheros, as well as families who claimed pure Spanish blood. At the next class level were *mestizos,* those of mixed Spanish-Indian heritage, and finally, at the bottom of the social scale, were Christianized Native Americans. However, many mestizos and even some *mulatos* achieved economic and social prominence by receiving land grants due to distinguished military or government service. Because of California's remoteness from Mexico, its settlers became self-reliant and independent. They called themselves *hijos del pais*, or native sons, and Californios instead of *Mexicanos*.

Cattle raising made many Californios prosperous. The beeves provided food, and the hides provided leather for boots, saddles, and reatas. Fat from butchered cattle was boiled into tallow, which was used to make soap and candles. Californios engaged in regular trade with merchant ships from the East Coast of the United States, selling cowhides and tallow to the Americans. Yankee merchants came to call a steer hide a "California bank note," with a value of a dollar. Because few of the Anglos spoke Spanish, they referred to Californios as Californians. After Mexico won its independence from Spain in 1821, the Californios grew to dislike the Mexican government due to its neglect and also to its custom of sending *cholos*, or convict soldiers, to police the frontier pueblos. Cholos enraged Californios by stealing chickens and livestock and sexually harassing the young women. Some Californio leaders believed they would be better off under the US government.

Due to the hide trade, numerous Yankees settled in California, and some married Californio women and obtained Mexican land grants. But during the 1840s, relations between Mexico and the US rapidly deteriorated, even in California. "We find ourselves suddenly threatened by hordes of Yankee emigrants, who have already begun to flood into our country and whose progress we cannot arrest," declared Pio Pico, the last governor of Mexican California. "Shall we remain supine while these daring strangers are overrunning our fertile plains and gradually outnumbering and displacing us? Shall these incursions go on unchecked, until we shall become strangers in our own land? We cannot successfully oppose them by our own unaided power; and the swelling tide of immigration renders the odds against us more formidable every day."[1]

The Mexican War erupted on the Texas border in May 1846. The war was hugely unpopular in the Northern states, where many, like Abraham Lincoln, believed that it would result in the country acquiring new territories in the Southwest, resulting in the expansion of slavery. General Ulysses S. Grant later called the Mexican War "one of the most unjust ever waged by a stronger nation against a weaker nation." Even before the declaration of war, trouble had already spread to the Pacific Coast. In December 1845, Captain John C. Fremont, the famed American explorer, rode into California at the head of sixty mounted men, among them the legendary mountain man and guide Kit Carson. Captain Fremont claimed that they were on a scientific expedition, but Californios did not believe him, because most of his men were scouts and soldiers, not scientists. In Monterey, the capital of Mexican California, Fremont received permission to spend the rest of the winter on the coast. He and his company then rode twenty-five miles east to Gavilan Peak. There, in defiance of the Mexican government, they constructed a log fort that overlooked the Salinas Valley and hoisted the American flag. Finally, under threat of attack by a Californio force, Fremont and his riders retreated north toward Oregon, which was then claimed jointly by the US and Great Britain.

Those Californios who were inclined to favor American rule over Mexican rule quickly changed their minds in the face of Fremont's aggression. In early June 1846, Californios rushed to defend their homeland when the Bear Flag Revolt broke out. During the previous few years, dozens of American fur trappers, mountain men, and border ruffians had drifted into the Sacramento Valley. They made their headquarters at Sutter's Fort in modern-day Sacramento, built in 1840 by John Sutter. He was a Swiss immigrant turned Mexican citizen who had received an enormous land grant from the Mexican government and established Sutter's Fort as a trading post. The Yankees, inflamed by rumors of pending war with Mexico, organized themselves into a military force. They then captured the headquarters of General Mariano Vallejo in the adobe village of Sonoma, fifty miles north of San Francisco. This action was extraordinarily foolish, for Vallejo, a prominent soldier and leader of the Californios, strongly supported American rule. The rebels came to be called the Bear Flaggers, or Bears, because they adopted a battle flag emblazoned with a crude image of a grizzly bear—though the Californios thought it looked more like a pig. One of the men who helped make the flag was a young Missourian named Thomas Cowie, who would figure prominently in the violent events to come.[2]

Today tourists flock into the idyllic plaza in downtown Sonoma, a center for fine dining and wine tasting—and a far cry from the drama and bloodshed of the Bear Flag Revolt. On June 14, 1846, the Bears raised their banner over the Sonoma plaza and declared a new "California Republic." Word of the conflict quickly spread, and many Californios joined local militia units. One of them was a young man named Bernardino Garcia. He was descended from a typically large Californio family, born on November 10, 1821, near what is now San Jose, at the southern end of San Francisco Bay. Like most young Californios, he became a skilled vaquero. At nineteen, Garcia enlisted in the Mexican army and was stationed for two years, from 1841 to 1843, at the San Francisco *presidio*, a military fort. Garcia then returned to herding cattle, and at some point he lost one finger from his right hand, a fairly common injury for a vaquero. Californios called him "Juan de Tres Dedos," and to Anglos he was known as "Three Fingered Jack" or "Four Fingered Jack," depending upon whether one counted a thumb as a finger. According to a San Francisco journalist of the era, "Jack derives his soubriquet from the mutilation of one of his hands, caused by its having been caught under a lariat against the pommel of his saddle, while lassoing a bullock." [3]

Another pioneer newspaperman who met Garcia in the late 1840s recalled, "Jack came into Monterey, and then I first saw him. He appeared to be about twenty-eight years of age, and had a very disagreeable, doggish cast in his features." In November 1845, just seven months before the Bear Flag Revolt, Garcia married Hilaria Sanchez Reed, the widow of John Reed, a respected ranchero and lumber dealer. Hilaria came from a prominent family, daughter of the commandant of the San Francisco presidio, and Reed was an Irish sailor who had arrived in California in 1826 at the age of twenty-one. John Reed operated the first ferry on San Francisco Bay, became a Mexican citizen, and received a large land grant just north of the Golden Gate. Reed's heavily wooded rancho rested in the shadows of majestic Mount Tamalpais and consisted of much of the modern-day suburban towns of Mill Valley, Tiburon, and Corte Madera. The prosperous Reed raised thousands of cattle, logged and sold redwood, and built the water-powered sawmill for which Mill Valley is named. His mill, still standing today, is situated in a grove of redwoods and built next to a creek that drains the south slope of Mount Tamalpais. In 1836, Reed wed the twenty-two-year-old Hilaria Sanchez in San Francisco, which was then a tiny adobe village of a few hundred people. The couple made their home in a small wood cabin in Mill Valley, where they raised four children.

John Reed died of illness in 1843, and a distraught Hilaria and her children moved back to San Francisco. She was alone, with young children to feed and no one to run her ranch and lumber business. Two years later, she married Bernardino Garcia—eight years her junior—in San Francisco. The couple welcomed a daughter and then a son, but as it turned out, Hilaria's second husband proved much different than John Reed. He was combative, brutal, and even bloodthirsty. General Vallejo, who was

Hilaria Garcia, the wife of Three Fingered Jack, and her son John Reed, in a daguerreotype taken about 1850. *Lucretia Little History Room, Mill Valley Public Library*

a personal friend of Reed, may not have approved of Hilaria's marriage to a man like Garcia. Vallejo later explained that Garcia had been a desperado long before the Bear Flag Revolt, writing that he "had already been the terror of the Sonoma frontier for years." After Garcia married Hilaria, the couple moved back with the children to Mill Valley, where they lived in a large, two-story adobe that John Reed had started building prior to his death. Three Fingered Jack would soon become even more notorious in the area north of San Francisco Bay, today known as Marin and Sonoma Counties.[4]

In June 1846, while Sonoma was occupied by the Bear Flaggers, Garcia joined a militia group of about twenty-five Californios led by Juan N. Padilla and Jose Ramon Carrillo. Padilla, though only twenty-three, had already served as *alcalde*, or mayor, of San Francisco, and not long before, he had been granted a large rancho near Sonoma. Carrillo, twenty-five, was the son of a well-known ranchero family in Santa Rosa, twenty miles northwest of Sonoma. Like Three Fingered Jack Garcia,

Carrillo would reappear conspicuously in the story of Joaquin Murrieta. So too would a Californio named Blas Angelino, who also joined the militia company. Angelino was older than the other men. He had lived in San Francisco in the 1830s, then moved north to Sonoma, where he became a ranchero. Angelino, Three Fingered Jack, and their fellow Californios were armed with antiquated and inaccurate *escopetas*, or muskets, as well as their favorite weapon, the lance. It consisted of a long willow pole mounted with an iron blade at the tip. Its advantage was that, unlike a musket, which could take up to a minute to prime with powder and ball, a lance never had to be reloaded.

By this time, the leader of the Bear Flaggers in Sonoma recognized the danger of attack from local Californio militias. The Bears were also low on ammunition. Their commander ordered Thomas Cowie and another young volunteer, George Fowler, to ride to the home of Moses Carson, brother of Kit Carson, and fetch a keg of gunpowder for their rifles. On June 18, 1846, Cowie and Fowler mounted their horses, trotted out of Sonoma, and headed toward Carson's home on the Fitch Ranch. Moses Carson was the ranch foreman, and it was located thirty-five miles north, on the Russian River near modern-day Healdsburg. Cowie and Fowler ignored warnings to avoid the enemy forces by taking side trails. Instead they rode boldly up the main wagon road toward Santa Rosa. They never got there. The Californios led by Padilla and Carrillo were patrolling the road, and they spotted the two Yankees approaching. The militiamen quickly surrounded Cowie and Fowler, then captured and disarmed them.

Padilla and Carrillo could not decide what to do with their captives, whom they held prisoner for more than a day. Some of the Californios, including Three Fingered Jack and Blas Angelino, wanted to kill them. But as General Vallejo later wrote, "Neither one of the two impromptu leaders believed it was right to take the lives of the young captives who were found to be carrying letters that proved without a doubt that Moses Carson and certain others of the Americans employed at the Fitch rancho were siding with . . . others who had proposed to put an end to Mexican domination in California. So they decided to tie the young men to some trees while they determined what to do with the captives, whose fate would be decided at the meeting that night. All the rancheros who had voted to entrust the command of the Californian forces to the wealthy citizens Padilla and Carrillo were summoned to that meeting."[5]

But that night, while the meeting was going on inside a small adobe on the Padilla rancho, Three Fingered Jack, Blas Angelino, and a number of other Californios took matters into their own hands. Stepping up to the two trees to which Cowie and Fowler were bound, they first began stoning the young men in the body and face. The rocks broke Fowler's jaw, so the attackers drew their knives and carved a hole under his chin, then tied a lariat around the jawbone and yanked it from his skull. Cowie was now unconscious, and Three Fingered Jack and his men used their poniards, or daggers, to strip the flesh from his arms and shoulders. They did the same with Fowler, and crammed pieces of flesh into their victims' mouths. Then the Californios slashed the pair's chests and abdomens, cut out their bowels, and sliced off their penises. Finally they put Cowie and Fowler to death by slitting their throats, then tossed their bodies into a ditch. Having committed one of the most brutal murders in California history, Three Fingered Jack returned to the adobe and announced proudly, "I thought you here were going to decide to free the prisoners, and since that action is not good for my country, I beat you to it and took the lives of the Americans who were tied to the trees."

As General Vallejo later explained, "Yet not one of them dared to condemn his actions, because they knew such a step would risk their falling prey to the knife of the feared Bernardo [Bernardino] Garcia." When Cowie and Fowler failed to return to Sonoma with the keg of gunpowder, their comrades began searching for them. On the night of June 20, five Bear Flaggers galloped up to the Fitch Ranch and learned that Cowie and Fowler had never arrived. They picked up the gunpowder and then rode back toward Sonoma. But Three Fingered Jack, Blas Angelino, and several Californios spotted them riding south near Santa Rosa. They attacked the better-armed Bears, who returned the fire, wounding one Californio and capturing Three Fingered Jack and Blas Angelino.

When the two were questioned about Cowie and Fowler, Garcia brazenly admitted that they had brutally butchered the two Americans. He said that they "tied them to trees, then stoned them, one of them had his jaw broken, a riata [reata] was made fast to the broken bone and the jaw dragged out, they were then cut up, a small piece at a time, and the pieces thrown at them, or crammed in their throats and they were eventually despatched by cutting out their bowels." Three Fingered Jack also revealed where the remains were. One of the Bear Flaggers who found the two corpses was Alexis Godey, a twenty-eight-year-old mountain man. Godey was a famous frontiersman, a friend of both Kit Carson and the celebrated mountain man Jim Bridger, and one of Fremont's most trusted scouts. Godey later said, "Their bodies presented a most shocking spectacle, bearing the marks of horrible mutilations, their throats cut, and their bowels ripped open; other indignities were perpetrated of a nature too disgusting and obscene to relate."[6]

The Bear Flaggers, instead of immediately executing Garcia and Angelino, held them as prisoners in Sonoma, where threats of lynching were made. Meanwhile news of the outbreak of the Mexican War finally reached California in July, when American warships captured the ports of Monterey and San Francisco. The commanding naval officer proclaimed that California was now part of the United States. US Marines from the ships were joined by Bear Flaggers and John Fremont's company, which had returned from Oregon. At the same time, Californio fighting men flocked to join militias to oppose the Americans. Soon the US Navy commander in San Francisco heard rumors that Three Fingered Jack would be lynched by the Bear Flaggers. On July 20, 1846, he reported to his superior that "Bernardino Garcia (Four-fingered Jack, as he is called) is now a prisoner at Sonoma, and in danger of receiving summary punishment for his participation in the murder of two Americans of the Sonoma party, unless prevented." The commander sent a written order to the Bear Flaggers in Sonoma: "Your prisoner Four-fingered Jack, who is said to have been concerned in the murder of the two Americans, you will keep safely in your charge until an opportunity for his trial may be afforded, or until the commander-in-chief shall give directions concerning him. No man should be punished without trial."[7]

According to a story that became popular a few years later, Three Fingered Jack managed to escape and then fled south. He joined a Californio militia from Monterey and played a prominent role in the Battle of Natividad, killing one of the American leaders, Captain Charles Burroughs. But that was impossible. The Battle of Natividad took place near modern-day Salinas on November 16, 1846—the same time that Garcia was a prisoner of the US Navy. In fact, due to the vigilante threats, Garcia had been removed to the Yerba Buena Marine Barracks in San Francisco on October 3. As the lieutenant in charge reported to his captain, "A man by the name of Bernardino Garcia was brought to the barracks yesterday and placed in confinement. This man is more generally known as five [sic] fingered Jack . . . The place has been quiet and orderly and the guards have been vigilant in the discharge of their duties."[8]

The Yerba Buena Marine Barracks held a number of other prisoners. Most of them were Anglo civilians, along with a few Californios and US soldiers who had committed civil crimes like assault and theft. Garcia remained locked up in the barracks for more than a month, his ankles shackled with iron chains to prevent escape. He demanded to see an attorney, and on December 9, 1846, the barracks officer reported, "At the request of Mr. Green, a lawyer, I allowed him to have conversation with Bernardo Garcea [sic]." As was customary at that time, Anglos frequently misspelled Spanish names or used phonetic spellings. Three Fingered Jack was not satisfied with being allowed to meet with an attorney, and he became angry and disruptive. Five days later, the barracks officer wrote, "The prisoner Garcia has created great noise during the night." The naval officers became concerned that Garcia would escape, and on December 20, he was locked in the brig aboard the USS *Savannah*, a frigate anchored in San Francisco Bay. As the naval surgeon on the *Savannah* noted in his diary, "Today, the two or three Californians who were prisoners on shore were brought on board. Three Fingered Jack had the irons taken from his ankles—he is the man who shot [stabbed] the two Americans before the United States Flag was hoisted here . . . I suppose that the reason the prisoners have been brought on board is their better

The adobe home of Bernardino Garcia and his wife Hilaria was in ruins by the time this photo was taken in Mill Valley about 1890.
Lucretia Little History Room, Mill Valley Public Library

security. They might have escaped in the confusion of a night attack on Yerba Buena."[9]

But the Californio forces never attacked San Francisco. Only one major battle and several skirmishes took place in California, and in January 1847 the Californios surrendered to John C. Fremont, thus ending the war in California. With the cessation of hostilities, Bernardino Garcia and Blas Angelino were granted parole and released on their promise not to take up arms against the US. The fighting continued in Mexico, and a year later, on February 2, 1848, Mexican officials signed the Treaty of Guadalupe Hidalgo, which ceded its northern territories, including Alta California, to the United States.

After the Californios' surrender in 1847, Three Fingered Jack returned to his wife, Hilaria, and the children. Apparently they lived, alternately, in San Francisco and Mill Valley, but Garcia seems to have been often away from home. Probably unknown to Hilaria, he was riding with several Anglo and Latino desperadoes. Then, within a few months, a shocking event would change his life forever.

On a bitterly cold morning in January 1848, just nine days before the signing of the Treaty of Guadalupe Hidalgo, a worker named James Marshall was inspecting the tailrace at John Sutter's lumber mill in the foothills of the Sierra Nevada Mountains. Marshall was Sutter's foreman, in charge of a crew of lumbermen. As he walked along the ditch that diverted water from the South Fork of the American River to the sawmill, Marshall saw something glitter in the gravel. He reached down into the foot-deep water and picked up a piece of yellow rock the size of a small pea. Turning it over carefully, he placed it on a larger rock and struck it with a stone. It was soft and did not crack. Marshall then walked back to the millhouse and uttered nine words that would rock the world.

"Boys, I believe I have found a gold mine."

CHAPTER 3

EL DORADO, THE LAND OF GOLD AND GUNFIRE

The long caravan of Mexican gold seekers, some on foot and others on horseback, trudged slowly in the bright sunshine across the Mojave Desert. A chilly December wind stirred up great clouds of dust as the riders swayed in their saddles and struggled to control the burros and pack mules. The men wore large straw sombreros and baggy white *pantalones*, while the brightly attired women wrapped their *rebozos* tightly around their heads for protection from the sun and the wind. Like everyone else in the caravan, Joaquin Murrieta, his half brother Jesus, his wife Rosa, and her teenaged brothers were overcome with gold fever and filled with anticipation of the riches that awaited them.

Their thirteen-hundred-mile journey from Mexico to the California gold fields took more than three arduous months. After crossing the Mojave Desert, they continued west to the pueblo of Los Angeles, then a small collection of adobe houses clustered around the old mission church. There the gold seekers rested and obtained supplies, then headed north three hundred miles, across the Tehachapi Mountains and through the San Joaquin Valley to the Southern Mines. The mining region—known to Latinos as El Dorado and to Anglos as the Mother Lode—covered much of the western foothills of the Sierra Nevada Mountains, more than two hundred miles from north to south. The country south of the Mokelumne River, including the hills drained by the Calaveras, Stanislaus, Tuolumne, and Merced Rivers, was called the Southern Mines. The area north of the Mokelumne River—the Cosumnes, American, Bear, Yuba, and Feather River drainages—was the Northern Mines. Because the Southern Mines were the first gold fields to be encountered by Mexican emigrants, they were largely settled by experienced miners from the state of Sonora. Thus the principal mining camp of the Southern Mines was called Sonora, also known to Anglos as Sonorian Camp.

Joaquin Murrieta and his party arrived in Sonora early in 1849. It was situated in a beautiful valley of creeks and rocky ravines ornamented with live oaks. But in that pastoral setting, they gazed upon a scene that beggared description. Heavily armed prospectors, their belts bristling with pistols and bowie knives, swarmed across the grassy hills. As smoke from countless campfires wafted through the air, two thousand Mexicans, and about two hundred Anglos, clustered along the nearby streams and gullies, feverishly panning for gold. Shouts of glee rang out from those who struck pay dirt. Their labors were back-breaking. The miners used *bateas*, or pans, to scoop sand from the streambeds, swirling the water in a circular movement that left small nuggets of gold at the bottom of the pan. Others diverted running stream water into gold rockers, in which they mixed sand and water in a box that looked like a child's cradle. The box was rocked back and forth, which allowed the mud and sand to pass out through a sieve at one end, thus separating the gold. Those gold hunters not fortunate enough to stake a streamside claim worked the *placer seco*, or dry diggings. They engaged in "coyoting," with each miner, armed with picks and shovels, digging and burrowing into the earth. Still others employed "winnowing," in which they placed gravel and sand in a blanket, then tossed it in the air to separate the gold flakes and nuggets.

A prospector who arrived in the Southern Mines in 1849 described the excitement that consumed the gold seekers, Anglo and Latino alike. "We began to smell the precious ore. Here were even real live miners; men who had actually dug out the shining metal, and who had it in huge buckskin pouches in the pockets of their pantaloons. Men who spoke jestingly, lightly, of chunks of gold weighing one, five, or ten pounds! Of 'pockets' where a quarter of a bushel of gold dust had been washed from! These men were awful objects of our curiosity. They were the demi-gods of the dominion of Plutus. Their long rough boots, red shirts, Mexican hats; their huge uncombed beards, covering half the face; the Colts' revolver attached to its belt behind, the *cuchillo* [knife] stuck into the leg of the boot—all these things were attributes belonging to another race of men than ourselves; and we looked upon them with a certain degree of respect, and with a determination soon to be ourselves as little human-like in appearance as they were."[1]

At first the only Anglos in the mining region were those who had already settled in California. Word of the great gold strike did not reach the East Coast until the fall of 1848. The accounts, published in newspapers, were widely disbelieved. But then in December of that year, President James Polk, in his annual message to Congress, announced that the reports were true, and had been verified by government officials in California. These words electrified the American public, and hordes of adventurous young men quickly joined the gold rush. Those on the Eastern Seaboard eagerly booked passage on sailing vessels for San Francisco, while people in the Midwest joined wagon trains across the plains to California. They began arriving in the Mother Lode in the spring of 1849 and quickly became known as gold hunters, placer miners, prospectors, gold washers, Argonauts, and forty-niners. By that time word had reached China, and thousands of aspiring Chinese miners quickly boarded ships and crossed the Pacific to the California gold fields.

The gold seekers who flooded into the Mother Lode came from across the globe—from the East Coast, Latin America, Europe, and Asia. One forty-niner described them vividly: "The Mexicans were very numerous, and wore their national costume—the bright-coloured serape thrown gracefully over the left shoulder, with rows of silver buttons down the outside of their trousers, which were generally left open, so as to show the loose white drawers underneath, and the silver-handled bowie-knife in the stamped leather leggings. Englishmen seemed to adhere to the shooting-coat style of dress, and the down-east Yankees to their eternal black dress-coat, black pantaloons, and black satin waistcoat; while New Yorkers, southerners, and Frenchmen, came out in the latest Paris fashions. Those who did not stick to their former style of dress, indulged in all the extravagant license of California costume, which was of every variety that caprice could suggest. No man could make his appearance sufficiently bizarre to attract any attention. The prevailing fashion among the rag-tag and bobtail was a red or blue flannel shirt, wide-awake hats of every conceivable shape and colour, and trousers stuffed into a big pair of boots. Pistols and knives were usually worn in the belt at the back, and to be without either was the exception to the rule."[2]

In Sonora, Joaquin, with his half brother, Jesus, and his three Feliz brothers-in-law, Claudio, Jesus, and Reyes, quickly joined the feverish hunt for gold in the surrounding hills and gullies. The mining camp was then home to about 1,500 prospectors, with hundreds more in the nearby hills. Sonora was a collection of canvas tents and brush huts clustered along a stream that became known as Woods Creek, a tributary of the Tuolumne River. As was common throughout the mining region, gambling places known as monte parlors, dance houses called fandango halls, and saloons, or cantinas, had quickly sprung up. One pioneer in Sonora recalled, "Hordes of gamblers kept in the wake of the industrious miners, accompanied by rum-sellers and abandoned females; and no sooner was a camp laid out by the miners, than a large rough tent was erected by the outcasts. A plank, resting on two empty barrels, served for a counter; and in lieu of the 'fixins' of a regular bar, a barrel of whisky, with a tin cup or two, and we had a first-class hotel and gambling saloon, from which issued the din of cracked fiddles and the chink of money, from early morn until late at night; and not infrequently would the sun find the gambling tables crowded and the game and the dance as lively as ever."[3]

Sonora was then more than 90 percent male, and all the women in camp were Latina. At first they were as scarce as large gold nuggets, but then more and more females arrived in town, many from northern Mexico. The miners, both Anglo and Latino, were fascinated by them. "There are a large number of Mexican women now in Sonora, and many of them rather pretty," wrote one Anglo gold hunter in his journal. "Like the men they are all addicted to gambling. Last night I sat down beside a couple of young girls, richly dressed, who were playing

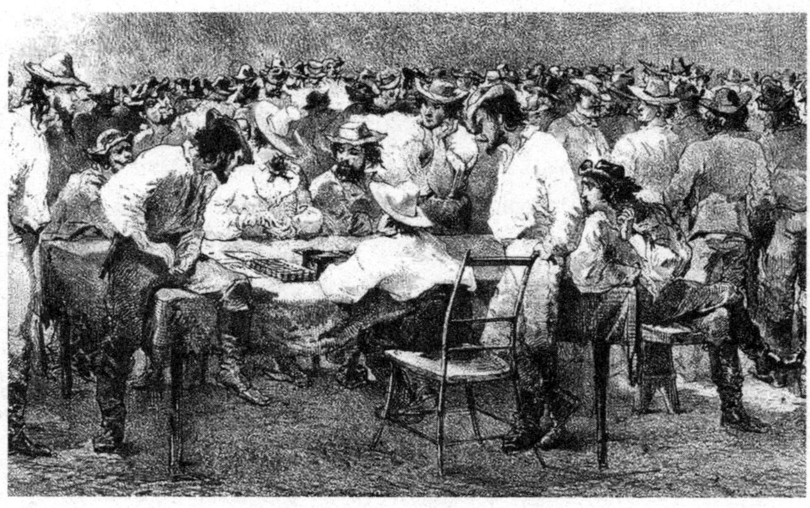

A monte table in a gold rush gambling hall.
John Boessenecker collection.

at a monte table in one of our handsome saloons. They commenced with one dollar each, and had such an immediate run of luck that in a half an hour they were the possessors of a considerable pile of silver dollars. They continued betting, flirting, and smoking cigaritos, winning almost always, when the devil tempted them both at the same moment to stake all their money on one card. The card lost! But the *sang froid* of this people is sublime. Not a sign of discontent was to be noticed in the faces of the olive beauties. Rising from their seats, they gracefully drew their *rebosas* over bosoms that had heretofore been somewhat exposed in the excitement of the game, and with a soft and sweet '*Buenas noches, senores*,' they glided away. Yes, *glided*; that is the word. A Mexican woman never *walks*; she floats rather, over the ground, such is their natural grace."[4]

Joaquin, with Claudio, Jesus, and Reyes Feliz, worked alongside American prospectors in Sonora, and each learned to speak a little English. Many knew him simply as Joaquin, while to some he was Joaquin Murrieta. Still others, primarily those who were acquainted with him or his family in Mexico, called him by his birth name, Joaquin Carrillo. And as we will see, he was also known as Joaquin Muliati. Murrieta's last name, and Anglos' difficulty in pronouncing and spelling Spanish surnames, would later become an important issue in the bandit's saga.

In addition to Joaquin, other members of the extended Murrieta clan settled in Sonora and in the nearby camps that sprang up in the Southern Mines. As was customary, their names were often misspelled in Anglo census returns and court records. Two men in Sonora were identified as Merettia and Muretha, the latter of whom was both deaf and mute. Another, Jose Moretta, was a miner, while Rafaela Moretto was a twenty-eight-year-old woman from Mexico. Felipe Marietto of Mexico was a merchant in Campo Seco, or Dry Camp, five miles from Sonora. And Jose M. Murrieta, also from Mexico, owned a store in the trading center of Stockton, sixty miles due west. Some or all of them were undoubtedly related to Joaquin, and he became well-known to many Latinos in the Southern Mines.[5]

During that first year of the gold rush, rich claims were many, and a spirit of camaraderie and cooperation prevailed among the Anglo and Latino miners. As one Anglo pioneer said of Sonora and its Mexican miners in 1849, "The whole neighborhood abounded in rich diggings and for a few months they were left to pursue their labors in undisturbed peace. Bullfights, fandangos, and other Spanish amusements took place almost every evening and the people lived quite happily, gathering their ounces during the day from the rich placers and spending them at the monte table or fandango at night. At this time it was computed that they numbered some five or six thousand. But this happy state of things was limited to but a short duration. In a little while the Americans learned that very rich diggings existed in the neighborhood and they flocked in by hundreds. Feuds, quarrels, disputes and contentions were the result."[6]

There was little to no law in the Mother Lode in 1849. At that time, American law enforcement was in its infancy. Prior to 1845, there were no professional, organized police departments anywhere in the United States, let alone on the frontier. Policing in the eastern states had been performed by constables in the daytime and by watchmen, many of them volunteers, at night. As villages on the East Coast became cities, that traditional system could no longer cope with the increasing crime, social unrest, and rioting that took place in the 1830s and 1840s. Philadelphia and New York City were among the first cities to establish full-time police forces manned by paid officers. However, due to the transient and unstable nature of frontier communities, law enforcement developed far more slowly in the American West. This was especially true in remote, rowdy California. Its native-born Californios reasonably expected legal protections. Under the Treaty of Guadalupe Hidalgo, they became US citizens and retained their property rights under Mexican law. The Mexican governmental position of the *alcalde*, a combination mayor and judge, was adopted by the Americans, and remained in effect until California achieved statehood in 1850.

Because in 1849 California had very little law enforcement, no secure jails, and no state prison, California miners turned to vigilantism, known as Judge Lynch, for safety and protection. Yet not all gold hunters supported lynch law. That spring an Anglo miner wrote a letter of warning to a friend. "Don't go to the mines on any account. They are . . . loaded to the muzzle with vagabonds from every quarter of the globe, scoundrels from nowhere, rascals from Oregon, pickpockets from New York, accomplished gentlemen from Europe, interlopers from Lima and Chile, Mexican thieves, gamblers of no particular spot, and assassins manufactured in Hell for the express purpose of converting highways and byways into theaters of blood; then last, but not least, Judge Lynch with his thousand arms, thousand sightless eyes, and five hundred lying tongues, ready under the banner of justice to hang, half, and quarter any individual who may meet his disapprobation."[7]

The reasons for California's widespread violence were multifold. Most forty-niners were overwhelmingly young, male, and heavily armed with Colt six-shooters, "pepperbox" revolvers, and large bowie knives, popularly known as Arkansas toothpicks. Many had left their homes, wives, mothers, and sisters for the first time. Too much testosterone, too many repeating firearms, and too much alcohol led to extraordinary levels of violence. Without the settling influences of women and family, they engaged in behavior that would have disgraced them back home. The Argonauts openly carried guns, gambled, drank, brawled, and consorted with prostitutes. And the Mother Lode held many temptations. As one pioneer declared, "I have seen purer liquors, better segars, finer tobacco, truer guns and pistols, larger dirks and bowie knives, and prettier courtezans here, than in any other place I have ever visited; and it is my unbiased opinion that California can and does furnish the best bad things that are obtainable in America."[8]

And racism soon became a principal cause of violence. As American gold hunters flooded into the mining region in 1849, they were outraged to discover that Mexicans, as well as miners from Chile and Peru, were already in the placers and had staked out the most lucrative claims. Even worse for the Anglos, the many Mexicans who were skilled miners had better success in finding gold. Numerous forty-niners were veterans of the Mexican War, and they had strong antipathy toward their recent enemy. Because California was now American territory, and would soon become a state, Anglos believed that "foreigners"—especially Mexicans and even Californios who were US citizens—had no right to dig for American gold.

In July 1849, San Francisco's principal newspaper, the *Alta California*, described the level of envy in the Sonorian Camp. "The emigration from Sonora [Mexico] this season, consisting of that class of men to which the placer is scarcely a novelty, and numbers of friendly Indians of the Yakee [Yaqui] tribe, expert washers all, will probably amount to about 8,000 souls. They are well armed, and the appearance of such a vagabond army of intruders on American soil has, very naturally, excited American jealousies and not a little bitter feeling. Their movements are closely watched and their neighborly encroachment viewed with some suspicion. About eighty miles distant from Stockton, situated a few leagues from the Stanislaus River, is a settlement styled in that region, the Sonorian camp. Here are congregated not less than 2,500 of this people."[9]

Serious trouble soon erupted. During the summer of 1849, Anglos forcibly expelled numerous Mexicans and South Americans from the diggings. A miner from Chile described how the Mexicans were driven from their claims. "A Yankee would invade the claim of a Sonoran with his revolver in hand. He would watch the Mexican panning gold for a while until he was sure it

The gold camp of Sonora in 1853. It was a favorite haunt of Joaquin Murrieta and his brother-in-law Claudio Feliz.
Huntington Library, San Marino, CA

was a good claim. Then he would go up to the poor Mexican, put his pistol to his head and order him off in language which was half-English, half-Spanish: 'You largo de aqui, mi quiere you Sonoreim. Vamos de rancho.' The Sonoran did not even take time or trouble to ask in sign language why he was being attacked and his claim taken away. Instead he would shoulder his tools and leave the place, fully confident that he could find an even richer location."[10]

Even Californios were envious of the Mexican miners' success, and some disparaged them as *calzoneros blancos*, or white trousers. Many Anglos referred to Mexicans derogatorily as greasers, and in return Mexicans called them *gringos*. The Anglo xenophobia reached a pinnacle in 1850, months before the territory of California became a state. The territorial legislature passed the Foreign Miners' Tax Act, which provided that all noncitizen miners had to pay a license fee of $20 a month. This created such an uproar that a year later, the monthly fee was reduced to $4. Nonetheless, efforts to enforce the racist law led to a great deal of violence, especially in the Southern Mines.[11]

These ethnic troubles would soon profoundly affect Joaquin Murrieta, though not as described by John Rollin Ridge. As we have seen, his book detailed how Joaquin was driven from his mining claim by Yankees, his wife raped, and his half brother—Jesus Murrieta—lynched. Those injustices supposedly drove him to seek vengeance against the Anglos. But Ridge's account of Joaquin's pivot into banditry is largely fictitious. Most lynchings during the gold rush were reported in the California newspapers, but there is no record of the hanging of a Jesus Murrieta—by that or any similar name—during the years 1849 through 1852. As we will see, Joaquin's half brother Jesus most likely ended up at the end of a lynch rope—but not until 1853 and well after Murrieta had turned to banditry. And the claim that Rosa was raped by Anglos is also hugely improbable. No such rape was recorded in the newspapers, and reported cases of sexual assault during the gold rush were exceptionally rare. Women were so few in those years that even the most racist Anglo ruffian revered Latina women and treated the lowest prostitute with respect. And as early as 1879, knowledgeable pioneers of the Southern Mines, including William T. "Billy" Henderson, Caleb Dorsey, Samuel Seabough, William J. Howard, and others, declared that the story of Rosa's rape was untrue.[12]

Yet there can be little doubt that Murrieta, like so many of his fellow Mexicans, was abused by Anglos and that he developed a profound hatred for them. Joaquin himself would later tell a Californio that he had "been driven from a piece of land which he was working with an American companion," that he "had been insulted and grossly maltreated without justice," and "had been flogged." But he said nothing about his wife being raped. Joaquin's account was largely confirmed by Billy Henderson, who later played an important part in the Murrieta story. Henderson, who knew Murrieta in the Southern Mines, explained, "The stories that have been told about the capture of Joaquin and the causes that led to his following the life of a bandit are incorrect, in a great measure. Joaquin used to live in Sonora in early days with Colonel Acklin. Joaquin found a very rich claim in the town of Sonora, but was driven out of it by the Americans. He gave it up with a struggle. Subsequently he found another claim nearby, and was working in it one day when a couple of Irishmen came to it and ordered him off. Joaquin refused to go, when one of the men, who had a bottle of whisky, struck him a fearful blow in the face, opening a frightful wound, and stunning him. They then took possession of the claim. Joaquin was taken by Colonel Acklin to his home, and his wounds dressed and attended to by that gentleman. From that day Joaquin seemed a changed man."[13]

"Colonel Acklin" was actually Captain William M. Acklin of Alabama, a loyal friend to the Mexican miners. He was not the only Anglo acquainted with Murrieta. Joaquin became well-known to a number of Anglos in the newly formed counties of Tuolumne and Calaveras. Samuel Seabough, a pioneer journalist in the rowdy mining camp of San Andreas, described Murrieta in colorful detail. "He was of middle stature, Indian complexion, lithe, active, strong, and in brute courage brave to recklessness. Like all of his race, who ride at all, he rode well and always a good horse, with rich trappings and the inevitable 'reata' hung to the pommel of his Spanish saddle. His hands and feet were small and admirably formed; his head large, low in front and covered with a mass of coarse, long black hair, and his face, the features of which were regular and not unhandsome, was lit up by eyes as dark as night and lustrous in their blackness, and as full of warning of danger as those of an enraged serpent. From top to toe and in his whole appearance and demeanor he had nature's stamp as a man not to be fooled with and a leader of his class." Seabough, however, was wrong in one detail, for Joaquin actually had a fair complexion.[14]

Murrieta, like many Argonauts, roamed from one gold camp to another, hoping to strike pay dirt. In Quartzburg, about fifty miles south of Sonora, Billy Henderson first became acquainted with Joaquin, who was then an honest miner. Henderson and two partners owned a small ranch on a wagon road near Quartzburg. There they also ran a hotel and general store, along with a rudimentary banking operation in which they traded in gold. Henderson later told a friend, "Joaquin Murrieta in the early days [1849] worked in the diggings near Quartzburg and visited occasionally . . . to make small purchases of milk, eggs, and other supplies." As Henderson's comrade explained, "During his stay in the mines near Quartzburg, Joaquin seemed to be both industrious and peaceable, and his gentlemanly deportment had attracted the notice of Henderson."[15]

Despite Murrieta's mistreatment by Anglos, it was actually his brother-in-law, Claudio Feliz, who first turned to robbery soon after they arrived in the camp of Sonora. And Claudio was motivated by greed, not by racial injustice. He was short in stature, only five-feet-four, with dark brown hair and a light complexion, and looked older than his sixteen or seventeen years. Claudio was well-liked by the Yankee gold seekers whom he knew in Sonora, and was able to converse with them in English. And from forty-niners from France, he picked up a little of the French language. In the summer of 1849, Claudio fell in with a group of Anglo miners who had been crewmen on a steamship in the Pacific. At that time, the crews of many vessels, on arriving in San Francisco and hearing of the gold strike, promptly jumped ship and headed for the mines. Claudio joined the Anglo seamen in hunting gold near Sonora. One of them was Charles Bassett, who spoke fluent Spanish. Another was an Irish sailor named Boyd, and a third man was the ship's cook. The group was walking to Mormon Creek, about five miles from Sonora, when they stopped to rest at a nearby gulch, now called Sonora Creek. After Claudio playfully rolled over some large rocks in the creek, Bassett thought he spotted gold in the streambed. He grabbed a washing pan and quickly flushed out two ounces of pure gold.

Bassett demanded that the group stay and work the stream, but the rest insisted on proceeding to Mormon Creek. They argued over which location was a better prospect. In the end, most of the sailors left for Mormon Creek and left Bassett, Boyd, the ship's cook, and Claudio to work the Sonora Creek gulch alone. Some days later, a party of American prospectors arrived and began panning for gold close by. At first the two groups got along well, but then the Americans complained that someone in Bassett's group had stolen their gold dust. Suspicion fell on the ship's cook, and Sonora's alcalde arrested him. The alcalde organized a trial before a jury of miners. Bassett acted as defense counsel for the cook, and Claudio also attended the trial. The testimony showed that the cook not only had the opportunity to steal the gold but also possessed gold specimens that were similar to those that had been stolen.

At one point during the trial, Claudio whispered to Bassett in Spanish, "What will they do with our cook if they find him guilty?"

Bassett responded, "They would probably hang him."

At that, Claudio blurted out, "But perhaps he did not steal the gold, but someone else."

Bassett, alarmed by Claudio's comments and by the tone of his voice, promptly addressed the spectators and translated the youth's words. Bassett then sent Claudio to fetch a pair of balance scales, which the alcalde used to weigh the cook's gold. The gold specimens taken from the cook weighed less than those nuggets that had been stolen. That evidence, combined with Claudio's suspicious remark, raised a reasonable doubt among the jury of miners. As one pioneer later explained, "The jury, in bringing in their verdict, found the prisoner guilty of robbery, but recommended him to mercy." The alcalde sentenced the cook to a flogging by whip, but the punishment was apparently never carried out.

There was no solid evidence that Claudio Feliz had stolen the gold, and he was not arrested. He wisely left Sonora and headed to Stockton, sixty miles west. There lawmen found him in possession of a stolen chunk of gold, which was identified by a unique hole in the center of the nugget. Claudio told the officers that his former mining partner, Charles Bassett, could prove that the gold was not stolen. A Stockton lawman accompanied young Feliz to Sonora so they could interview Bassett. In Sonora, Claudio managed to speak privately to Bassett and offered him a bribe if he would testify that they had found the nugget while prospecting together. But Bassett had never seen the gold piece before, and he refused to lie. The officer returned with Claudio to Stockton, where the youthful thief was jailed. Before long, however, Claudio managed to escape.[16]

By this time, in late 1849 or early 1850, Joaquin Murrieta had been driven from his mining claim. He first drifted into Calaveras County, just north of Tuolumne County. Joaquin found the gold towns of Calaveras, among them Mokelumne Hill, San Andreas, and Murphys Camp, to be just as dangerous as those in Tuolumne. As one Argonaut recalled, "Mokelumne Hill was one of the worst camps in California. 'Who was shot last week?' was the first question asked by the miners when they came in from the river or surrounding diggings on Saturday nights or Sundays to gamble or get supplies. It was very seldom that the answer was, 'No one.' Men made desperate by drink or losses at the gambling table, would race up and down the thoroughfares, in single file, as boys play the game of 'follow my leader,' each imitating the actions of the foremost. Selecting some particular letter in a sign, they would fire in turn, regardless of everything but the accuracy of the aim. Then they would quarrel over it as though they were boys playing a game of marbles, while every shot was likely to kill or wound some unfortunate person." The pioneer added, "I remember that one night in West Point, Calaveras County, a party of roughs 'cleaned out' the leading saloon because the proprietor would not furnish them free whisky."[17]

Murrieta tried his hand at mining in San Andreas, one of the principal camps in Calaveras County. It had a large Latino population, which made Joaquin feel at home. The settlement was described by a gold seeker a few years later: "In the winter of 1848, a few Mexicans encamped at the forks of the Gulch (since called San Andreas), about one-fourth of a mile above where the town now stands, and commenced working in the bed of the gulch, by sinking holes and washing out with *bateas*. In the fall of '49, their numbers considerably increased, but the place was not looked upon as worthy of any great note as a mining locality. But in the winter of 1849, or spring of '50, a few Americans came in, and commenced operations in the main gulch, which soon had a tendency to bring in others. In the meantime the Spanish population continued to increase, until, in the fall and winter of 1850, they numbered some twelve or fifteen hundred. At this time, the principal part were encamped on the hillside, on which is now located the town of San Andreas, and on all sides were seen small tents, such as usually designated any important mining locality, in the palmy and prosperous days of 1849–50. The mines were rich, every person was doing well, and of course, during these 'flush times,' a number of fandango houses and gambling shops, were the necessary concomitants of a large Spanish population—and on every night might be seen numbers of brave *caballeros* and comely *senoritas* capering nimbly 'on light fantastic toe.'"[18]

Joaquin found that gold mining was becoming increasingly competitive and sophisticated. By 1850 the gold rocker had been replaced by the "long tom," basically a huge rocker up to fifteen feet long, placed next to a stream so water could be fed into it by a flume at the top. Later that year, sluice boxes began to appear. Each box was a wooden trough, a foot wide and from

Typical Forty-Niners at their mining claim in the gold rush.
Nelson Atkins Museum of Art, Kansas City, MO

thirty to sixty feet long, and open at the top. At the bottom of the sluice box were a series of step-like slats, or riffle bars. Water was diverted into the sluice while miners shoveled sand and gravel into the top of the sluice. As the water rushed down, the dirt and rock washed away, leaving particles of gold collected on the riffle bars. The work was hard and back breaking, and the use of streamside sluice boxes became known as placer mining. Because of the labor involved, groups of miners organized into companies, sharing the work and the gold.[19]

At the end of a long day of shoveling dirt, miners like Joaquin looked for relaxation and entertainment. He soon found that gambling was hugely popular in rowdy San Andreas. As one pioneer explained, "It was certainly the most out-at-elbows and disorderly-looking camp I had yet seen in the country . . . The Mexicans formed by far the most numerous part of the population. The streets—for there were two streets at right angles to each other—and the gambling-rooms were crowded with them, loafing about in their blankets doing nothing. There were three gambling-rooms in the village, all within a few steps of each other, and in each of them was a Mexican band playing guitars, harps, and flutes. Of course, one heard them all three at once, and as each played a different tune, the effect, as may be supposed, was very pleasing."[20]

One Anglo gold hunter later recalled mining with Murrieta in San Andreas Gulch and called him "a beardless boy—a good boy and a good looking boy." But Joaquin had little success as a prospector. He was too independent to join a mining company and too restless to stay in one place more than a few months. Whether Rosa accompanied him is unknown. He soon turned to dealing cards to support himself. Another forty-niner who knew Murrieta in Calaveras insisted that by that time, he was primarily a gambler, not a gold miner. "During his four years' residence in California his labors as a miner were trifling, and he never owned a claim that was worth working or jumping. He was not even skillful with the horn [gold scoop] and batea, as were the most of his countrymen, and was in no sense a miner by occupation." Murrieta began drifting through the mining camps, from Sonora in the south to Jackson Gate, in what is now Amador County, forty-five miles to the north, dealing monte as he went.[21]

Joaquin soon became well-known to Latino and Anglo card sharps alike in Calaveras and Tuolumne Counties. His dislike of Anglos did not extend to fellow gamblers, for several of them befriended him. One was Henry V. McCargar, twenty-five, who hailed from upstate New York. A few years later, McCargar declared that he had been "well acquainted with Joaquin" and "drank frequently and rode often with him." Another friend was William W. Byrnes, who dealt cards with the future bandit in the Southern Mines. The hard-drinking, heavily bearded Byrnes had fought in the Mexican War and claimed that he once rode the border as a scalp hunter, killing Apaches for the bounty offered by the Mexican government. Byrnes, like Billy Henderson, would later play an important part in the saga of Joaquin Murrieta.[22]

Joaquin acquired skill in playing Spanish monte, also known as monte bank, which was very popular in Mexico. American veterans of the Mexican War brought monte home to the US, where it rapidly gained favor. It was different from the confidence game of three-card monte. As one forty-niner explained, "The Spanish game of monte, which was introduced into California by the crowds of Mexicans who came there, was at this time the most popular game, and was dealt almost exclusively by Mexicans. It is played on a table about six feet by four, on each side of which sits a dealer, and between them is the bank of gold and silver coin, to the amount of five or ten thousand dollars, piled up in rows covering a space of a couple of square feet. The game is played with Spanish cards, which are differently figured from the usual playing-cards, and have only forty-eight in the pack, the ten being wanting. At either end of the table two compartments are marked on the cloth, on each of which the dealer lays out a card. Bets are then made by placing one's stake on the card betted on; and are decided according to which of those laid out first makes its appearance, as the dealer draws card after card from the top of the pack. It is a game at which the dealer has such advantages, and which, at the same time, gives him such facilities for cheating, that any one who continues to bet at it is sure to be fleeced."[23]

In the spring of 1850, Joaquin drifted into Murphys Camp, an unruly mining town in Calaveras County, eighteen miles north of Sonora. Murphys Camp was situated in a broad valley in the foothills, surrounded by pine-studded knolls and watered by gold-rich Angels Creek. The camp was described by an Argonaut who visited Murphys Camp at about the same time as Joaquin. He said that it "consisted of one regularly built and main street—tents of course—with only one frame shed (and how respectable it looked among its cotton comrades!) between them; but every tent a grog shop, and in some of them gambling tables as well. Behind this street, and farther on in the flat, other tents were wildly scattered about, just as they had found the shade of a tree or a cluster of little bushes to shelter them against the wind, and in these the miners lived. The landscape was beautiful, and the little place, surrounded by high, wooded hills, with the American stars and stripes waving over it, was as romantically situated in the wide valley as the heart could wish."[24]

But it was the gold and the card tables, not the landscape, that interested Murrieta. As Leonard Noyes, a pioneer settler in Murphys Camp, recalled, "One street was half a mile long, lined on both sides with cloth houses with an occasional house built of splits. Gambling there was no limit to. Every store had its game . . . Every night the gambling houses were in full blast, and generally shooting done by one or more men each night." Joaquin and his friend Bill Byrnes became partners in one of the monte tents. Byrnes and his brother, Mike, were well-known in Murphys. Leonard Noyes noted in his journal that in 1850, Bill Byrnes "gambled [and] was a shooter from Texas and inclined to quarrel." He wrote—ungrammatically—that Mike Byrnes "delighted in swagering around town with a big six-shooter and Boey knife . . . usually half drunk and aching for a quarel," and added that Bill Byrnes "was a dandy compared with Mike."[25]

Murrieta and Byrnes seemed to have little in common, other than their mutual passion for monte. Byrnes, however, had picked up Spanish when he was on the Mexican border, and coupled with Joaquin's rudimentary English, the two were able to converse and develop a camaraderie. But Murrieta's willingness to befriend some Anglos would not last.

At the same time, his experiences in the Southern Mines were crucial in shaping his violent character and his bloody career. For the first time, he had been exposed to racial abuse, as well as to the wild swings of success and failure that were part and parcel of a gold hunter's life. He came of age in a time and place of extraordinary violence, where heavy drinking and reckless gambling were commonplace; when disputes were routinely resolved by fisticuffs, bowie knives, and six-shooters. And unlike many Anglo miners, Murrieta was born to the saddle. He knew horseflesh and could guide a mustang over the rockiest terrain, or pace his animal to cover fifty miles in a day. As he roamed the mining camps, he learned the travel routes, from well-graded wagon roads to the narrowest of mountain trails. He became acquainted with many in the Latino community, including numerous desperadoes and *pistoleros*, or gunmen. And whether he was wielding a shovel on a placer claim or a deck of cards on a monte table, he learned that in the Mother Lode, easy riches were always within reach.

CHAPTER 4

THE BIRTH OF A BANDIT GANG

The old mining town of Columbia is nestled in the heavily wooded, pine-scented Sierra foothills, four miles north of Sonora. First settled in 1849, it was originally known as American Camp. Columbia boasted a population of about seven thousand miners who, after laboring each day with pick and shovel, spent evenings and nights in its many watering holes and gambling dens. Today it is one of the best preserved gold camps in America, and many of its stone and brick buildings from the 1850s are still intact. Columbia is a state park, and the streets of its historic district are closed to automobiles. The town's blacksmith shop, express office, stores, and saloons remain just as they were during the gold rush, and tourists flock in to experience the life of the forty-niners. But as visitors wander along the board sidewalks, few recognize that Columbia was once the scene of violent racial strife as well as a favorite haunt of Joaquin Murrieta.

Late in the spring of 1850, Joaquin left Murphys Camp and returned to the area around Columbia and Sonora, frequenting the camps' gambling houses and monte tents. Trouble soon found him. Sonora had recently become the county seat of newly formed Tuolumne County. Two months later, the legislature passed the Foreign Miners' Tax Act, and efforts to enforce it quickly began in the mining region. George Work, the Tuolumne County sheriff, was charged with collecting the highly controversial license fee. Mexican, Chileno, and French prospectors were outraged by the new tax, and rumors spread among Anglos that they were planning a rebellion. On May 19, 1850, Murrieta was in Columbia when most of the Anglos fled town, fearing they would be killed by the Latino and French miners. One of the few Anglos who stayed behind was Claudio Feliz's sailor friend, Charles Bassett, who had built a general store, restaurant, and butcher shop in Columbia. Bassett thought that there was no truth to the rumors. When the throng of fleeing Anglos arrived in Sonora without Bassett, another story quickly spread that he had been murdered.

Because Anglos were greatly outnumbered in Tuolumne County, many more rushed into Sonora from the surrounding camps, seeking protection. That evening, Sheriff Work began forming a large armed force to confront the supposed threat to the neighboring camps. The danger became real when a Mexican miner approached Work and demanded to know "if he was not an officer, or the officer who intended to enforce payment of the license." When Work answered that he was, the Mexican yanked out a knife and tried to ram it into the sheriff's body. It was his last move. One of Work's friends leaped forward, bowie knife in hand, and slashed it across the assailant's throat, almost severing his head from his body. Sheriff Work had no time to reflect on his close brush with death, and he continued making preparations for a march on Columbia in the morning.[1]

One member of Work's posse later described what happened next. "Many and various were the reports circulated on that eventful night. According to some, the town was to be attacked and set fire to at different points. Rumors of assassination and massacre were fearfully rife; but at length morning dawned, and the country was discovered to be safe. Breakfast was spread out for us at the same hospitable board, and then all were assembled on the main street, and divided into companies, headed each by its own captain and lieutenant. A column of some three hundred armed men, in all, was thus formed, which, headed by the [tax] collector and sheriff of the county, commenced its march through the disaffected camps.

"Alas, as we marched along, what a scene of confusion and terror marked our way! Mexicans, Chilenos, *et id genus omne*—men, women and children—were all packed up and moving, bag and baggage. Tents were being pulled down, houses and hovels gutted of their contents; mules, horses and burros were being hastily packed, while crowds upon crowds were already in full retreat. What could have been the object of our assembly, except as a demonstration of power and determination, I know not; but if intended as an engine of terror, it certainly had its desired effect, for it could be seen painted upon every countenance and impelling every movement of the affrighted population. However, on we marched, through this dire confusion, peacefully pursuing our way, until we reached what was deemed to be the headquarters of malcontent—a camp [Columbia] containing some thousand Spanish Americans—about four miles from the county seat. Here we halted for the last time (liquored up, of course, for it was the month of June [May], and the roads were dry and dusty), and, after being paraded through the main street, and held for an hour or more in readiness, awaiting the report of certain officials dispatched to inquire into the truth of a rumor that a foreign flag had been hoisted somewhere in the vicinity, were finally discharged. Every man then fired his rifle in the air, reloaded his piece, and started homeward."[2]

Joaquin Murrieta was one of the many Latinos who fled Columbia that fateful spring day in 1850. It was the second time he had been driven from the mines, and it helped ignite a deep, abiding hatred of Anglos. But for many of the Anglo gold hunters, the ethnic frenzy soon calmed down, and displaced Latino miners returned to the diggings around Sonora. Joaquin was one of them, and he and his brothers-in-law spent much of their time in Sonora and the nearby camps of Martinez and Sawmill

Flat. Then, two months later, more racial strife erupted. On Wednesday morning, July 10, 1850, a Mexican rushed toward a group of Anglo miners who were camped at Green Flat Diggings, about eight miles from Sonora. He breathlessly announced that two Americans had been murdered in their tent nearby. The miners raced to the spot and caught four men red-handed, burning the victims' bodies. The Anglos arrested one Mexican and three Yaqui Indians and marched them into Sonora. They turned the prisoners over to the justice of the peace, and word of the killings swept the town. "The excitement was intense," one Argonaut wrote in his journal. "I could not help in joining it. The murders daily committed are heart sickening, and leave no room for a feeling of mercy."

A huge crowd of Anglos quickly gathered, and loud shouts rang out in the summer heat: "String 'em up! Hang them!"

The mob seized the four prisoners, bound their hands, and dragged them to a large oak tree just outside Sonora. Ropes were draped over tree limbs and the nooses looped around their necks. But just before the men were launched into eternity, Sheriff Work and a small posse galloped up on horseback. They seized the lynch ropes, ordered the four men to run with them, and raced back toward Sonora. The mob roared in anger, and several lynchers fired off their pistols. As one witness said, "The prisoners knew they were running for their lives, and each one taking hold of the rope, one end of which was around his neck and the other lashed around the pommel of the officer's saddle, to ease the strain on his throat, kept pace with the rapid flight of the horses."

Sheriff Work safely reached the jail in Sonora, where he locked up the Mexican and the three Yaquis. Their court hearing was scheduled for the following Monday. Meanwhile Sonora was in an uproar, and wild rumors spread that the prisoners were part of a large Mexican bandit gang that was holed up in a mining camp a few miles distant. Sheriff Work raised a twenty-man posse, rode to the camp, rounded up a hundred Latino miners, and marched them into Sonora. The suspects were placed inside a corral, under a heavy guard. But it turned out that most of them were recent arrivals and had nothing to do with banditry. The sheriff released them all. Then, on the day of the court hearing, hundreds of armed Anglos flocked into Sonora from the surrounding camps. Waving an American flag, they marched up Washington Street, the main thoroughfare, accompanied by the sound of fife and drum. The mob stopped in front of the courthouse, a crude wood building just opposite the historic, and still standing, City Hotel.

Sheriff Work, the county judge, and other officials faced the crowd and ordered them not to interfere with the court. Then the preliminary hearing began inside the packed courthouse. The evidence against the four accused men appeared conclusive, until the county coroner testified that he had examined the corpses. He said that they were infested with maggots, meaning that the men had been dead at least four to five days before they were burned. The defendants swore that they had accidentally stumbled upon the two badly decomposed bodies and tried to dispose of them by burning, according to the custom of the Yaqui Indians. It was now obvious that they were innocent, and the judge ordered their release.

The mob gradually drifted away, much to the relief of Joaquin Murrieta, his brothers-in-law, and the other Latinos in Sonora. However, many Anglos, blinded by racism, were furious with the result. The editor of the newly founded *Sonora Herald*, the first newspaper in the gold region, pleaded for calm. "Far better would it be that a hundred guilty men should escape than the lives of four innocent men be sacrificed," he declared. "Let no blind passion determine them to hang a man before he is proved guilty." But within a few days, reports of fresh murders reached Sonora, along with claims that a force of a hundred armed Mexicans was preparing to attack the town. The Anglo

Two vaqueros in a daguerreotype, about 1850. Both wear *calzoneras*, with silver buttons down the sides, and the young man on the left carries a huge Colt Walker revolver with its butt protruding from a flap holster. *John McWilliams collection*

miners held a mass meeting and issued several resolutions: "That all foreigners in Tuolumne County except persons engaged in permanent business and of respectable character, be required to leave the limits of said county within fifteen days." They were also ordered to surrender their firearms and deadly weapons.

At first, many Latino prospectors complied with the order. As one Sonora pioneer recorded in his journal, "Two hundred Mexicans with their pack animals marched through this place on their return home, poor and dispirited. They had come here, many of them with their families, for the purpose of becoming good citizens and settling in the country. They thought, and very justly, too, that they should all have to suffer because a few bad men were among them, and sooner than be the cause of disturbances, they would return to the homes which they had so recently left." But the committee of Anglo miners had no authority to expel anyone from the diggings, and most Latinos, including Joaquin Murrieta and the Feliz brothers, stayed put.[3]

Joaquin continued to eke out a living as a monte dealer in Sonora, Columbia, Martinez, and Sawmill Flat. During the early years of the gold rush these settlements were extraordinarily rowdy and violent. In 1850, Sonora, which had boomed to about five thousand people, saw nineteen murders. That equates to a homicide rate of 380 per 100,000 people—more than fifty times higher than the modern US national rate. Sonora was just as violent in 1851 when eighteen murders took place, resulting in an equally high rate of homicide. And that number does not include the 1851 lynchings of four men who were accused of murder. The editor of the *Sonora Herald* declared, "That firearms are necessary in a country like this, no one living here can doubt. It would not be prudent to travel without them, nor should they be thought useless under the pillow at night."[4]

The astronomical murder rates led inevitably to a rise in vigilantism. Law officers and judges of the gold rush were often untrained, incompetent, and overwhelmed by violent crime. California's criminal justice system was rudimentary, its handful of jails were notoriously flimsy, and no state prison would be built until 1854. The state's few prisoners were held in a primitive prison brig anchored in San Francisco Bay. As a result, many criminals escaped punishment. Gold seekers, including those in Sonora, formed vigilance committees, known as miners' courts or popular tribunals, to deal with the threat to public safety. Those early vigilantes acted openly, holding public trials, and they made no attempt to disguise themselves. They hanged murderers and flogged those who were found guilty of stealing. Some thieves were branded with an *R* for robber or *HT* for horse thief, not to shame or humiliate them, but to publicly identify felons because there were no secure jails to hold them. The vigilantes did not see themselves as in conflict with the established legal system, but rather in support of it.

As Sonora's vigilance committee declared, "We are not opposing ourselves to the courts of justice already organized. We are simply aiding them or doing work which they should do, but which under the imperfect laws of the State, they are unable to accomplish." Between 1849 and 1853, more than two hundred lynchings took place in California, most in the Mother Lode region. And in the coastal counties, from Santa Cruz south to Los Angeles, Californios often played prominent roles in vigilantism, because it was they who were frequent victims of livestock theft and violent crime.[5]

Despite the levels of violence in Tuolumne County, there is no evidence that Joaquin took part in any criminal activity until later that year. The same could not be said of Claudio Feliz. He later boasted that he joined a large bandit gang composed of Mexicans, Californios, and Anglos. Some of the last were ex-convicts from the Australian penal colonies. In the slang of the era, they were known as Sydney Ducks, so-called because they were jailbirds from Sydney, Australia. The leaders of the gang were Salomon Pico, Mariano Hernandez, and Joaquin Valenzuela, who were destined to become three of California's most infamous bandits. The only known Anglo member of the band was a desperado who called himself Robert Scott. He was one of the frontier's bloodiest robbers, and would later confess to a whopping eighteen murders during the gold rush.[6]

Young Feliz was hugely impressed with his new compadres. Salomon Pico and Mariano Hernandez were older than Claudio and Joaquin, and both came from very different backgrounds. The twenty-eight-year-old Pico was born to a distinguished Californio family. One of his first cousins was Pio Pico, the last Mexican governor of California. Another cousin, General Andres Pico, was a Californio hero who, in 1846, had defeated the American forces at the Battle of San Pasqual, north of San Diego. Salomon Pico married at the age of nineteen, and he and his wife had three children. In 1844 he received a vast land grant from the Mexican government. During the Mexican War, he fought with the Californios and developed a profound enmity for the Yankees. Pico later claimed that he had been "cheated out of his property by Americans" and declared that he "would kill every American falling into his hands." He was suspected of robbing and murdering numerous travelers on the wagon road between Monterey and Los Angeles, and once boasted of having slain thirty-nine Anglos. Numerous witnesses said that Pico carried the severed ears of his murdered victims on a leather strap hanging from his saddle horn. In California, during the Spanish and Mexican eras, soldiers in punitive expeditions against Native American horse thieves often sliced off their ears as proof that they had slain their quarry. Pico, as a former soldier, may have obtained his string of ears from dead Indians, or perhaps they indeed came from his Anglo victims. Many Latinos of the era saw Salomon Pico as a patriot and hero. However, most Anglos, as well as the landed Californios—rancheros and ricos—were terrified of him. One pioneer said that in Monterey, "the very adobes of the ancient capital trembled at the mention of his name."[7]

Like Salomon Pico, Mariano Hernandez was also a Californio. He was born in San Francisco in 1810, the son of a soldier. At age twenty-four, Hernandez married into a prominent family; he and his wife raised four children. In 1844 the Mexican government granted him the 13,000-acre Rancho del Puerto in what later became San Joaquin County. But Mariano Hernandez had a larcenous streak, and as early as 1843—well before the gold rush—fellow Californios charged him with stealing cattle. After the discovery of gold, Yankees squatted on his rancho, inducing his deep hatred for all Anglos. Hernandez became an infamous livestock rustler and highway robber. When not riding the outlaw trail, he lived with his wife and children in an adobe house in the center of San Jose, unsuspected of any wrongdoing. One of his most brutal crimes occurred in May 1850 when he and a companion robbed and stabbed to death two Anglo gold miners in the Southern Mines. Hernandez was arrested and jailed in San Jose, but he posted bail and fled.[8]

The last of this deadly trio was Joaquin Valenzuela, who would become a partner of Joaquin Murrieta and play an important role in the career of the future bandit chieftain. Valenzuela was a Mexican who hailed from Sonora, where he had worked as a vaquero. A notorious horse thief, he was known by the nickname of Joaquin Nacomoreno, or Naco Moreno, which was Mexican slang for "the dark Indian." His brother, Jesus, known as Chiquito, "the little boy," always rode with him. After joining the gold rush, Joaquin Valenzuela lived, off and on, with a woman he called his wife. During the summer of 1850, while Claudio and Joaquin were in Sonora, the Valenzuela brothers drifted into San Diego County. They were accompanied by Mariano Hernandez and another desperado named Martinez, and hid out at a rancho near the Mission San Luis Rey. There they happened to meet the bloodthirsty Robert Scott. Literate and educated, Scott was a young man from a respectable family. He later said that this name was an alias, and he steadfastly refused to reveal his true identity. Scott admitted that his mother and sisters lived on the East Coast, and he plainly wanted to spare them the shame of his murderous career.

Robert Scott stood five-feet-eight—an average height for that era—with curly brown hair and a powerful build. He was surly and had a short temper. A contemporary remarked, "In his movements and speech he is slow, and not inclined to be sociable in his habits." Scott later said that he had arrived in San Francisco by ship in July 1849. After spending a few weeks in the boomtown by the bay, he met a Sydney Duck, and the pair traveled to the Stanislaus River. They tried mining for two months, without success, and then hired on as drovers for an American who was on his way to Monterey County to buy cattle for sale in the gold camps. After learning that their employer had $4,500 in gold, Scott and the Australian showed their true colors. One night as the cattle buyer slept in their camp near the Mission Soledad, forty miles southeast of Monterey, they shot him to death and looted his body.[9]

This was but the first of the eighteen cold-blooded murders that Scott would commit in California. He was already a hardened robber and killer by the time he encountered the Valenzuela brothers, Mariano Hernandez, and their compadre Martinez near the Mission San Luis Rey in the summer of 1850. For a few days, Scott and the four bandidos loitered about the rancho north of San Diego. As was typical with Anglos who spoke little to no Spanish, Scott garbled Jesus Valenzuela's nickname of Chiquito and called him "Jackatone." Scott later described their sojourn at the rancho: "While we were there two Americans came along and stated that they wanted to buy a ranch. We supposed they had money, and prevailed on them to stay all night with us. We gave them a room in the house, and that night Joaquin, Jackatone, and myself entered their room and killed them with axes. We searched them and found only the small sum of sixteen dollars in [gold] dust and three dollars in silver. This was a sad disappointment to us, for we thought we had a rich prize. We took their revolvers and packed their bodies off and buried them and turned their five mules out."[10]

Scott, with the Valenzuelas, Mariano Hernandez, and Martinez, and accompanied by a few other desperadoes, rode north to Santa Barbara. They made camp in the nearby mountains and watched the wagon road, El Camino Real, for cattle buyers on their way to Los Angeles. The outlaws soon spotted two travelers, a Californio and an American named Young, who had stopped to make camp. As Scott later said, "We discovered their campfire very late at night, and surrounded them before they were aware of our presence and completely riddled them with bullets. We got from them seven thousand dollars, five thousand from Young and two thousand from the Californian. We tied reatas to their bodies and dragged them off the road and left them, took their animals, and returned to our camp. Some short time after that we killed three Spaniards [Mexicans] who were traveling south and took five thousand dollars and four mules from them. We had an Indian with us, whom we kept for the purpose of stealing horses, and he was very expert at the business, and in that capacity was of great service to us, but he got to know too much, and we were fearful that he would leave us and blow on us, so we just took a revolver and blew out his brains, which we concluded was the best way to silence his tongue."[11]

Scott explained that he, Joaquin Valenzuela, and the rest of the gang agreed to split up and ride east across the Coast Range, which runs north and south and separates California's coastal region from the San Joaquin Valley. First they would proceed to French's Ranch, situated in the southern San Joaquin Valley between the Tehachapi Mountains and modern-day Bakersfield. There they would meet up and ride together to Pacheco Pass, two hundred miles to the north. Later, both Joaquin Murrieta and Claudio Feliz would become more than familiar with Pacheco Pass. Located on the main route from the Southern Mines to San Jose, it was and still is one of the main passages through the Coast Range. A wagon road into the remote pass would not be built until 1857. During the gold rush, the route was a primitive trail that had long been used by Native Americans and Spanish soldiers. The trail crossed the basin that is now flooded by the San Luis Reservoir and then wound its way up the steep hills into Pacheco Pass. It was an ideal place for bandits to ambush and rob Argonauts returning to San Francisco from the gold mines.

Pursuant to their agreement, Scott and several Anglo companions rode to the rendezvous at French's Ranch and waited for Joaquin Valenzuela and the other bandidos to arrive. Their plan was to ride up a trail that ran along the base of the Coast Range through the barren, waterless west side of the San Joaquin

Alexis Godey, the famed mountain man, as he looked about 1865. He and a group of Mexican miners were robbed in Pacheco Pass by the gang that Claudio Feliz joined. *Wild West History Association, Robert G. McCubbin Collection*

Valley, from Tejon Pass in the south to Pacheco Pass in the north. The 250-mile trail meandered through tule swamps and barren alkali desert, across dry creeks, and past occasional *aguajes*, or watering holes. It was also an area that Joaquin Murrieta would come to know well. Scott later described their dangerous journey north: "When we got to French's the Spaniards had not arrived, and after staying there some time in wait for them, and not hearing anything from them, we started with only five days' rations for Pacheco's Pass. We suffered everything but death. We all came near starving, and had to kill and eat our horses, and after a trip of twenty-five days we arrived at the Pass in a most destitute condition. We remained at this point some two weeks for the purpose of recruiting ourselves, and whilst here we were joined by our Spanish friends . . . We here divided ourselves off into small parties and scoured the whole country between this point and Livermore's Pass one way and Pacheco's on the other."

It was at this point that Claudio Feliz joined the band. Where Claudio first met Salomon Pico and the other highwaymen is unknown, but he was now being trained by the best of the bandidos. Mariano Hernandez, on the other hand, decided to return to his family in San Jose with his share of the gang's loot. He was so brazen that he did not fear capture for jumping bail on the charge of murdering the two miners three months earlier. But soon after, on August 8, 1850, Hernandez was arrested at his San Jose adobe. His accomplice had confessed to the murders and led law officers to the dead bodies. Hernandez did not remain in jail long. A month later, he escaped from the sheriff in San Jose and then rejoined Robert Scott and the growing gang. By then it was a multiethnic, multinational group of Mexicans, Californios, Yankees, and Sydney Ducks, bound together by a mutual passion for plunder. Claudio Feliz was one of them. Robert Scott later said that they hid out in the mountains near Pacheco Pass and rode out to make raids. On one occasion, he and two of the band, whom he refused to name, "killed the old man Swift, who had settled twelve miles from Pacheco's Pass, and robbed him of sixteen hundred dollars." On the evening of October 5, 1850, the bandits were at a lookout high in the Coast Range, near Pacheco Pass. They spotted a party of forty Mexican miners riding west from the San Joaquin Valley into the pass. The gold seekers were accompanied by Alexis Godey, the famed mountain man who had discovered the butchered bodies of Thomas Cowie and George Fowler during the Bear Flag Revolt.[12]

Godey, born in St. Louis, Missouri, to French parents, spoke Spanish fluently. When only sixteen, he became a fur trapper with Kit Carson and Jim Bridger in the Rocky Mountains. After many adventures with Carson, Bridger, and John C. Fremont, both before and during the Mexican War, he joined the hunt for gold in the Mother Lode. Godey and his Mexican companions had worked together in the diggings, accumulating a small fortune of $18,000 in gold dust and nuggets. By comparison,

$1,000 in 1850 is worth $40,000 today. He and the other miners were on their way to the coastal settlements, and as they rode leisurely through the ten-mile-long Pacheco Pass, they drifted apart into small groups of three to six horsemen each. Suddenly, according to a contemporary account, "They were met by a gang of Sydney convicts, armed to the teeth with six-shooters, rifles and double-barreled guns, and immediately robbed by these desperadoes." The bandits rampaged eastward through the pass, holding up each approaching group of unsuspecting Argonauts. Godey and a few others were at the rear of the caravan when the highwaymen stopped them at gunpoint, stripped them of their gold, and galloped away. Though darkness was gathering, Godey easily tracked the outlaws to their camp in the hills. He hid nearby until they fell asleep, then drove off all their horses. But realizing that he was outnumbered and outgunned, the mountain man gave up in despair.

Five days later, the same gang, including Robert Scott, approached the adobe ranch house of Francisco Pacheco, for whom the pass was named. The sixty-two-year-old Pacheco was a wealthy Californio, former soldier, and the owner of several ranchos. The lavish hacienda, home to his large family, was situated on the west side of Pacheco Pass, seven miles north of modern-day Hollister. Pacheco, ever friendly and hospitable, often treated travelers to food and drink. Claudio later claimed that he was not then with the band and had returned to the Southern Mines. A pioneer in Monterey described what happened when the gang rode up to Pacheco's hacienda: "Fifteen to twenty Americans presented themselves at his home in broad daylight and demanded to drink. The good man hastened to satisfy their desires; but they had hardly entered than these bandits grabbed him and his family (women without defense), bound them, locked them up and, pistol on throat, ordered the old man under penalty of death to hand over his money. It was only common sense to submit to such a formulated request. In an instant

Francisco Pacheco, the ranchero of Pacheco Pass. Claudio Feliz belonged to the gang that robbed him and his rancho in 1850.
Santa Clara University Archives

trunks, chests, boxes, everything was looted, broken into and the band disappeared." Robert Scott later said that they escaped after "robbing old Pacheco of *mucho oro* [much gold]." The desperadoes galloped off with more than $11,000 in gold and valuables. Claudio Feliz, however, later said that the amount stolen was actually $7,000. Either he was there, or he heard that number from the other bandits.[13]

Claudio had developed a strong taste for stolen gold, and he wanted more of it. Feliz had learned his profession well from men like Joaquin Valenzuela and Salomon Pico, and now he was ready to form his own band. He had also surely boasted to Joaquin Murrieta about the gang's successful bandit raids. But Joaquin, at least for a time, did not join him, and rode a different trail.

CHAPTER 5

CLAUDIO FELIZ, THE BRIGAND CHIEF

Joaquin Murrieta was fed up with the ill treatment he had suffered in the mining camps. He left Sonora and rode sixty-five miles west to Stockton, then a wild and woolly boomtown of about three thousand people, the gateway to the Southern Mines. Stockton's port on the San Joaquin River connected it by steamboats to San Francisco Bay. Gold miners flocked into town, buying food, clothing, shovels, picks, and gold pans, then continued on their way to the Mother Lode. One of Stockton's pioneers described its rapid development that winter of 1849 to 1850: "The town is growing very fast; there were only two wooden buildings when I arrived here in June [1849], and there are now about three hundred wooden buildings and five hundred tents, some of them very large . . . The buildings are generally rough and of small dimensions. The town is regularly laid out into squares, but not much can be said of its beauty as yet, as no regard is made as to the manner of finish, owing to the great expense of building. Stores, eating houses, gambling and drinking shops take up all the buildings. Gambling and drinking are indulged in to great excess."[1]

Joaquin was attracted by Stockton's numerous gambling halls that catered to its transient populace. He loved the excitement of the gaming dens, especially the lavish saloons and card parlors. As another Stockton pioneer explained, "On entering a first-class gambling room, one found a large well-proportioned saloon sixty or seventy feet long, brilliantly lighted up by several very fine chandeliers, the walls decorated with ornamental painting and gilding, and hung with large mirrors and showy pictures, while in an elevated projecting orchestra half-a-dozen Germans were playing operatic music. There were a dozen or more tables in the room, each with a compact crowd of eager bettors around it, and the whole room was so filled with men that elbowing one's way between the tables was a matter of difficulty. The atmosphere was quite hazy with the quantity of tobacco smoke, and was strongly impregnated with the fumes of brandy. If one happened to enter while the musicians were taking a rest, the quiet stillness was remarkable. Nothing was heard but a slight hum of voices, and the constant chinking of money; for it was the fashion, while standing betting at a table, to have a lot of dollars in one's hands, and to keep shuffling them backwards and forwards like so many cards.

Stockton, as Joaquin Murrieta saw it in the early 1850s.
Library of Congress

"The people composing the crowd were men of every class, from the highest to the lowest, and though the same as might be seen elsewhere, their extraordinary variety of character and of dress appeared still more curious from their being brought into such close juxtaposition, and apparently placed upon an equality. Seated round the same table might be seen well-dressed respectable-looking men, and, alongside of them, rough miners fresh from the diggings, with well-filled buckskin purses, dirty old flannel shirts, and shapeless hats; jolly tars [sailors] half-seas over, not understanding anything about the game, nor apparently taking any interest in it, but having their spree out at the gaming-table because it was the fashion, and good-humouredly losing their pile of five or six hundred or a thousand dollars; Mexicans wrapped up in their blankets smoking cigaritas, and watching the game intently from under their broad-brimmed hats; Frenchmen in their blouses smoking black pipes; and little urchins, or little old scamps rather, ten or twelve years of age, smoking cigars as big as themselves, with the air of men who were quite up to all the hooks and crooks of this wicked world (as indeed they were), and losing their hundred dollars at a pop with all the nonchalance of an old gambler; while crowds of men, some dressed like gentlemen, and mixed with all sorts of nondescript ragamuffins, crowded round, and stretched over those seated at the tables, in order to make their bets."[2]

For Murrieta, gambling proved an uncertain occupation. He had ill luck at the monte tables, and one day he found himself short of cash. The result was his first recorded crime, and it did not involve banditry, murder, or wreaking vengeance against the Yankees. On November 28, 1850, Murrieta stepped inside a general store in Stockton owned by two Jewish brothers, Hyman and Levi Mitchell. His visit was a brief one, and after he left, the storekeepers discovered that a pair of boots had disappeared. Hyman Mitchell soon spotted Joaquin with the stolen boots, and he asked local officers to place him under arrest. The lawmen collared Murrieta and hauled him into court for a preliminary hearing. The purpose of the hearing was to determine whether there was sufficient evidence to hold him for trial.

The court clerk entered his name in the docket as "Joaquin Muliati." Then the judge began questioning him, with the clerk taking down every word.

"What is your name and age?"

"Joaquin Murieta, age eighteen," he responded. He was able to understand the questions, and some of his answers were in imperfect English.

"Where have you been?"

"In Placers Seco and mile of American Camp."

"Where do you reside and how long have you resided there?"

"In Stockton, in the street, been there about five months."

"What is your business or profession?"

"A miner."

"Give any explanation you may think proper of the circumstances appearing in the testimony against you and state any facts which you think will tend to your exculpation."

"Another man gave me the boots," Joaquin responded. "I didn't take them myself."

Placers Seco meant Dry Diggings, and American Camp was the alternate name for Columbia. Joaquin's statement meant that he had been living at one of the mining camps a mile from Columbia, which was either Martinez or Sawmill Flat. And in an apparent effort to seek sympathy, he subtracted several years from his age. After Joaquin's testimony was written down, the court clerk had him sign his name at the bottom of the document. Murrieta was illiterate and could not write his name, so he signed it with an X. The judge then found that there was enough evidence to bring him before a jury. Murrieta's case came up for trial a week later, on December 8, 1850. The six male jurors did not believe his claim of innocence. They found him guilty and sentenced him to three months in the county jail. Apparently Joaquin was known in Stockton as both Muliati and Murrieta, because after he testified, the court clerk crossed out the surname "Muliati" from the court record and replaced it with "Murieta."[3]

Three days before Joaquin's trial, his brother-in-law Claudio Feliz began the first of a long series of bandit raids that would eventually bring Murrieta almost two centuries of notoriety. But Joaquin, languishing in the Stockton jail, took no part in the planning of the gang's first robberies, and the name of Claudio Feliz—the band's original chieftain—would soon vanish into the mists of the past. Feliz gathered together a large gang of Mexican and Californio bandits. Other than Claudio, the only identified member of his initial band was a ruffian named Miguel Luches, destined to meet a bloody death in San Francisco.

The bandidos, a rough and hardscrabble lot, looked nothing like modern depictions in television and film. In the popular mind, inspired by the silver screen, Mexican outlaws of the 1850s and 1860s carried repeating rifles and wore leather bandoleers, filled with rifle cartridges, draped over their shoulders. Such wildly inaccurate depictions are based on widely distributed photographic postcards of fighters in the Mexican Revolution of 1910 to 1920. During the gold rush era, lever-action rifles like the Winchester had not yet been invented. Pistols and longarms that fired metallic cartridges also did not exist, nor did bullet-laden bandoleers. Instead, bandits like Claudio Feliz carried percussion firearms, known as cap-and-ball guns—the heavy .44-caliber Colt Model 1848 Dragoon, the smaller and lighter .31-caliber Colt Model 1849 Pocket Revolver, and inexpensive pepperbox revolvers.

These weapons, including double-barrel shotguns and single-shot rifles, were hard to load. To reload a Colt revolver, its cylinder first had to be removed. Then gunpowder was poured from a flask into each chamber, followed by a lead ball. The cylinder was then replaced and the loading lever, under the barrel, pulled down to ram the bullet into place. Finally a percussion cap was

Three of the most widely used firearms of the gold rush. Top, a Colt Model 1848 Dragoon revolver; middle, a Colt 1849 Pocket Model; and bottom, an 1845 Allen & Thurber pepperbox revolver.
John Boessenecker collection

affixed to each nipple on the other side of the cylinder. Because this process was so slow, bandits, lawmen, and gold miners often carried two loaded pistols on their belts. Also popular were pommel holsters, each of which held a revolver in a leather flap holster draped from the side of a horseman's saddle. A well armed pistolero might have one or two six-shooters on his belt and two more in pommel holsters. Joaquin Murrieta would later carry four revolvers, two on his gun belt and two on his saddle. And last, all fighting men carried a long-bladed bowie knife, because it never had to be reloaded.

At noon on December 5, 1850, Claudio and a pair of compadres rode up to the isolated adobe ranch house of John Marsh, situated in the foothills of Mount Diablo, midway between Stockton and San Francisco. It was a crude affair, long and narrow, with dirt floors, a roof made of thatched tule reeds, and a portico stretching across the front door. The four-room house was sparsely furnished with a few tables, benches, and beds for Marsh and his vaqueros. The adobe is no longer there, but nearby is a large stone house that the newlywed Marsh built for his bride in 1855. It is still standing, situated in Marsh Creek State Historic Park in eastern Contra Costa County. The fifty-one-year-old Marsh was a Harvard-educated physician who had come to California in 1836 and received an expansive land grant from the Mexican government.

Claudio stepped up to the adobe and told Dr. Marsh and his two vaqueros that he was hunting for stray horses. Marsh had no idea who Claudio was and invited the trio inside. According to a witness, "They spent the afternoon in pleasant conversation, and left the house about three o'clock." He added that the leader, who later turned out to be Claudio, "stated that he was a native of the Argentine Republic, that he had traveled in Europe, and had resided for some time in Mexico. He speaks Spanish fluently, and French and English imperfectly. He is a young man, of short stature, very fair complexion, and black eyes and hair. His manners are pleasing and his appearance rather prepossessing."[4]

Though Claudio was then no more than nineteen, Dr. Marsh thought he was older. The budding outlaw and his two partners then bid Marsh *adios*, swung into their saddles, and rambled away. Marsh thought little of their visit until that night. "At about 8 o'clock this evening, this house was surprised by a band of robbers, and completely plundered," he wrote to an army general who was the former military governor of California. "The robbers are Mexicans, and I think about twenty in number. But it was so totally dark that the numbers who remained outside and surrounded the house could only be conjectured. The first notice we had was both doors were at the same moment burst open, and the passage filled with pistols and other arms. The people within the house were knocked down and bound, and the house coolly and deliberately rifled. The leader of the party is a man of twenty-five or twenty-eight years of age, short stature and exceedingly fair complexion; the others were all with blackened faces or otherwise disguised. They went off in the direction of my other house at the ranch, with the declared intention of robbing it. . . . They took from here some twelve or fourteen hundred dollars, and a valuable gold watch."[5]

Claudio himself later boasted of the raid to one of his compadres, who explained what the bandido had told him: "Dr. Marsh asked what number the robbers were; they answered him that they were a hundred and fifty in number. Dr. Marsh then said that they were enough to destroy California. They responded that it was none of his business, and demanded him to be quick and deliver their money."

John Marsh, who was robbed by Claudio Feliz and his gang in 1850.
Bancroft Library

At the same time as the attack on the house, other members of the gang surrounded a canvas tent not far from Marsh's adobe. It was occupied by a young man from Missouri, William Harrington, and two other Anglos. Some of the bandidos carried revolvers, and others were armed with lances. The lancers were probably Californios, because that was their favorite weapon. Inside the tent, Harrington and his comrades heard the sound of approaching hoofbeats. Before they could react, the robbers riddled the tent with pistol balls. Harrington and his companions fled from the tent and raced on foot to the nearby woods. Harrington never made it. Two bandits pursued him on horseback, and one shot him through the shoulder. He landed face down in the dirt. The robbers charged forward and drove their lance blades again and again into his prone body. Claudio and his men then rounded up about forty of Marsh's horses and mules and galloped away. At daybreak Harrington's corpse was found where he died, pierced by eight lance wounds. John Marsh was fortunate to have escaped with his life, but his good luck would not last. Six years later, he was ambushed and murdered by three of his own vaqueros.[6]

Claudio and his gang fled south twenty miles to the Livermore Valley, located between the Coast Range and the East Bay hills. Today it is home to vast housing tracts, shopping centers, vineyards, and traffic-clogged freeways, but then it boasted little except herds of grazing cattle and the scattered adobes of rancheros and their vaqueros. From the Livermore Valley, the desperadoes made a hard ride sixteen miles southwest to the Mission San Jose. Confusingly, it is not located in San Jose, but twenty miles north in what is now the suburban city of Fremont, at the southeastern tip of San Francisco Bay. Because it was situated on one of the main trails from San Francisco Bay to the gold mines, a small settlement had sprung up around the old mission, featuring several shops, hotels, and saloons.

Claudio's band arrived at Mission San Jose one night after their raid on the Marsh ranch. The hungry outlaws rode up to the Chamberlain & Musser general store and called for its proprietors to bring them bread. According to a local settler, the storekeepers refused to give anything to the riders: "They were told by one of the firm within that they had no bread to give to marauders, and were advised to seek farther." Claudio and his men then surrounded the store, but fearing that the merchants inside were armed, they instead stole three horses and rode off. Next the bandidos approached a nearby hotel and tavern, the Tulare House. They stormed the place at gunpoint, tied up all the victims, and took everything of value. Finally the gang rode south to San Jose, which was then a village of adobe houses, home to about a thousand people. Despite its small size, San Jose had plenty of fandango halls, bordellos, and cantinas, all of which catered to outlaws and working men alike. Due to the slow and primitive communications of the era, no one there suspected Claudio and his pistoleros of the recent bandit raids.[7]

Claudio spent his stolen loot carousing in San Jose with Salomon Pico and another bandit named Domingo Hernandez. One of the most dangerous outlaws of the California gold rush, Hernandez was a thirty-five-year-old Californio and former militia soldier in the Mexican War. Often confused with Mariano Hernandez, to whom he was not related, Domingo Hernandez was suspected of numerous robberies and murders on the wagon roads between San Jose and the coastal village of Monterey. A contemporary described him as having "medium stature, bronze complexion, with large head and broad shoulders . . . His mouth was enormous, and the teeth set wide apart, so that however horrible might be his frown, his laugh was worse." Another said, "He boasted of the way he used to kill travelers who had the appearance of foreigners. He would ask the victim for a cigar, or a light, and pretending to be occupied with the cigar, he would let the traveler advance a few steps, and then shoot him from behind." Like Salomon Pico, Hernandez carried a string of severed ears, cropped from his victims and draped across his saddle horn.

Domingo Hernandez's most infamous exploit occurred in Monterey in 1849. He was arrested for stealing horses and cattle, convicted, and sentenced to be hanged. On the fatal day, a large crowd gathered, including numerous Californio and Anglo desperadoes who were his friends. After a frayed old rope was draped around his neck, the trap was sprung. Hernandez plunged toward the ground. To the astonishment of the gawkers, the hanging rope snapped in two, and the bandido landed with a thud, unhurt. A huge cheer erupted from the ruffians. At the same time, many of the Californios, including a Catholic priest, declared that it was a miracle and that his life had been spared by the Virgin Mary. Monterey's alcalde, convinced that Hernandez would soon be lynched anyway, ordered his release. That night a fandango was held to celebrate his escape from death. The bandido got roaring drunk, knifed a man in a fight, and escaped from Monterey.[8]

In San Jose, Claudio Feliz and Domingo Hernandez began planning another bandit foray. On the chilly evening of December 15, 1850, just ten days after the attack on the John Marsh ranch, they rode out of the little pueblo with Miguel Luches and several other desperadoes. Claudio later said that Salomon Pico did not accompany them. The outlaws followed the lush foliage along Los Gatos Creek southwest for about three miles until they reached the hundred-acre farm of Digby Smith. The forty-seven-year-old Smith lived quietly in his ranch house, a rustic wood cabin near the creek, situated in what is now the affluent Willow Glen neighborhood of San Jose. Smith had joined the gold rush in 1849 from his native New Jersey, but like so many Argonauts, he found that farming was more profitable than mining.

Claudio and his gang, just as they had done in the John Marsh raid, quietly surrounded the cabin. Inside, the occupants—Digby Smith, his friend Edgar Barber, and a cook named Wood—were relaxing and warming themselves by the fire. Suddenly Claudio, with Domingo Hernandez, Miguel Luches, and their compadres, burst through the door, revolvers in hand. Without any warning, they opened fire, putting two pistol balls each into Smith and Barber. As the pair sprawled on the floor, wounded and writhing in pain, one of the outlaws charged forward. Swinging an axe, he crushed their skulls and killed them both. At the same time, another bandido whipped out a knife and began hacking Wood's neck until he sliced the head from his shoulders. Claudio and the rest then ransacked the farmhouse, stealing $1,500. Finally, before galloping off in the blackness, they set the cabin on fire.

The robbers, in their haste to escape the flames, failed to notice a valuable keg of gunpowder stored inside. Just minutes after they rode away, a terrific explosion ripped through the house. The family of a farmer who lived some distance away heard the blast and rushed outside, only to see Smith's house engulfed in flames. They rushed to the scene, but the raging fire prevented them from entering the house. The farmer sent word into San Jose, and at daybreak, a crowd descended on Smith's place. Onlookers searched the rubble and found the charred remains of the three victims. A newspaperman who visited the scene wrote, "In one corner of the room lay a body, supposed to be that of Mr. Digby B. Smith, with the legs and arms nearly burnt off, the entire abdomen destroyed, and the top part of the skull appeared to have been crushed, and was lost. In a parallel line with this body lay another, supposed to be Mr. Wood, the cook, with the legs and arms similarly burnt, and the entire skull wanting. Between these two bodies lay the blade of a sheath dirk about six inches in length. Nearer to the door, just below the body last referred to, lay another, since recognised to be Mr. E. G. Barber's. The skull was also broken as by the blow of an axe. At the feet of this body lay an open jack-knife, the blade of which had the appearance of being corroded with blood."[9]

San Jose townsfolk were shocked by the gruesome murders. They quickly organized a posse to find the culprits, but their manhunt proved fruitless. Although one of Edgar Barber's friends offered a $1,000 reward "for the apprehension and conviction of the murderer, or murderers," it was never claimed. Claudio and his men had succeeded in committing one of the most barbarous crimes of the gold rush. But they were only getting started. Seven weeks after the triple murder–arson, they replicated that raid. Claudio, with an eighteen-year-old Mexican bandit named Jose Cheverino and four other desperadoes, rode thirty-five miles due north from San Jose, retracing their route back to the Livermore Valley. The outlaws cantered their horses across the valley and into Altamont Pass, then and now the main connecting route between the San Francisco Bay Area and the San Joaquin Valley. On the night of February 7, 1851, the bandidos rode up to a tavern and store called the Blue Tent. It was also known as the Mountain House, situated sixteen miles east of Livermore on the eastern edge of Altamont Pass. The location today is where the Mountain House Bar now stands, north of the West Grant Line Road exit from Interstate 580. Originally the tavern was housed in a blue canvas tent erected in 1849 to serve miners on their way to the Mother Lode. However, by the time of Claudio's visit, the name remained, but the tent had been replaced by a wood-and-adobe structure that is no longer standing.

The pistoleros dismounted in front of the Blue Tent and ordered supper from the owners, one an elderly man, and the other a youth named Starr. A young Native American boy worked as their helper. The names of the old man and the Indian boy are unknown. Starr thought the Mexicans looked suspicious, but he didn't believe that he and his companions were in any danger. That all changed in thirty minutes. Claudio, Cheverino, and the rest, after finishing their meal, suddenly attacked all three with their knives. They slashed to death the elderly man and the Indian youth, and almost killed Starr. The bandits threw the old man's body into a nearby ditch and left Starr weltering in his own blood. After looting the place, they set it afire, and the body of the Indian boy was consumed by the flames. Claudio and his men, thinking that Starr was also dead, mounted their horses and thundered off. The next day, two travelers came upon the scene and discovered the still smoking ruins. They also found young Starr, treated his wounds, and brought him to the nearest ranch, eight miles distant. Then they raised a fifteen-man posse of ranchers and vaqueros and started in pursuit. Their quarry, however, had vanished, and Claudio remained unsuspected, at least for a time.[10]

Claudio Feliz and his men rode back to San Jose, still thirsting for loot. Three days later, on February 10, 1851, he and a dozen other mounted bandits rode up to the rancho of Antonio Chabolla, two miles east of San Jose. Claudio later said that the gang included Jose Cheverino and another young desperado, Jesus Sanate, plus a mixture of Anglo, Mexican, and Californio outlaws. Sanate, who also used the first name of Gabriel, hailed from Sonora, Mexico, and was a prolific gambler and robber. Dismounting, Claudio's band silently crept up to the hacienda. But after watching the adobe, the robbers became convinced that the place was too heavily guarded, and they rode off empty-handed. The outlaws returned the following night and again lost their nerve. Finally, on the third night, February 12, they stormed the adobe house. It turned out that Chabolla and his wife were not present, and the only occupants were a number of children. The desperadoes tied up a boy, then ransacked the place, breaking open trunks and stealing everything of value. Several neighbors heard the commotion. Grabbing their guns, they rushed to the adobe. Claudio, Cheverino, Sanate, and the rest opened fire on them, but the neighbors immediately shot back with a volley of lead. After a brief exchange of gunfire, the bandidos leaped onto their horses and fled, leaving their booty behind. Had it not been for the quick action of the Chabollas' friends, the children would surely have met the same fiery deaths as the gang's other victims.[11]

By this time, news of the forays had spread, causing a public uproar. One young man suspected of belonging to the gang was Jose Pacheco, the twenty-year-old son of a landed Californio, Antonio Pacheco. The family's large rancho was located in Contra Costa County, across the bay from San Francisco. Its spacious adobe hacienda, built by Antonio's older brother, is still standing in the city of Concord. On February 17, 1851, five days after the Chabolla raid, Jose Pacheco stepped into a general store in the village of Martinez, seven miles north of Concord. Located on the Carquinez Strait, where the Sacramento and San Joaquin Rivers flow into San Francisco Bay, it had, confusingly, the same name as the mining camp of Martinez, near Sonora. Young Pacheco, after entering the store, tried to steal a pair of boots. Just like Joaquin Murrieta a year earlier, he was promptly caught. But unlike Joaquin, Pacheco suffered a much harsher punishment. An Anglo mob accused him of taking part in the recent bandit raids near Mount Diablo and Pacheco Pass. They seized the youth and dragged him to a nearby tree. Pacheco managed to break loose, but the vigilantes chased him down. The enraged mob dragged him back to the tree, stripped off his shirt, and bound him with rope.

Meanwhile Antonio Pacheco, who happened to be in Martinez, rushed to the scene and pleaded with the mob to release his son. He even offered them $2,000 for the youth's freedom, but the vigilantes rejected it. Instead of hanging Pacheco, however, they stripped off his shirt and flogged him with a hundred lashes from a rawhide whip. Antonio Pacheco then took his bloodied son home. He eventually recovered from his flayed back wounds. The Pacheco clan was large and prominent, and a few days later, a group of eighty Californios gathered at the family rancho. They directed their anger at the Anglos in Martinez and threatened "to ride into the town and burn it." Some of the townsfolk rushed to the state militia arsenal at Benicia, just across the Carquinez Strait from Martinez. There, according to a newspaperman, they "procured arms from the arsenal, for the defence of the beautiful little town of Martinez." But in the end, Antonio Pacheco and his fellow rancheros proved far more responsible than either his son or the vigilantes, for the Californios refrained from seeking vengeance against the Anglos in Martinez.[12]

By this time, Claudio Feliz and most of his gang had fled the Bay Area and returned to the Southern Mines. Within a few weeks, Joaquin Valenzuela, with his partner Martinez and the murderous Robert Scott, showed up in Mariposa County. Scott later said that he and an unnamed accomplice encountered a lone miner mounted on a mule. The rider was on his way to Coarse Gold Gulch, now called Coarsegold, about thirty miles south of the gold town of Mariposa, the gateway to modern-day Yosemite National Park. "We traveled with him for some distance, when my partner ordered him to dismount from his mule," Scott recalled. "This he refused to do, and attempted to draw his revolver, whereupon my partner shot him. We got from him six hundred dollars in gold dust and three hundred dollars in coin, and then packed his body off from the road about a quarter of a mile and left it." Scott took the dead miner's pistol and then joined up with members of the big gang, whom he vaguely described as "some others of the old boys"—apparently including Joaquin Valenzuela, his brother Jesus, and their compadre Martinez.

"We formed ourselves together and committed a great many murders in a short time, mostly Mexicans," Scott said. "At last I came very near being caught. I had lost all my money one night gambling and pawned my revolver, which was the one I had taken from the man we killed on his road to Coarse Gold Gulch, and the number of the pistol was noticed by the man to whom I pawned it, he having seen it advertised soon after the murder." The pawnbroker promptly sent a message to the mining camp of Agua Fria, then the Mariposa County seat, reporting his discovery to the law officers. Fortunately for Scott, his partner Martinez got wind of what the pawnbroker had done.

Martinez warned both Robert Scott and Joaquin Valenzuela. As Scott recalled, "Joaquin gave me a horse and two hundred dollars, and I left for Diamond Springs by the way of Stockton and Sacramento."[13]

Joaquin Valenzuela's participation in these murders would not come to light for several years. He first achieved a measure of notoriety in 1852, when he was living with his wife on the Merced River in the San Joaquin Valley. His neighbors suspected him of theft and searched his house, but found only the woman and a six-year-old American girl who spoke no English and called herself Anita. Valenzuela's wife insisted that the girl "had been given to them in Marysville some two years before." However, Anglos said that Valenzuela had kidnaped the child and killed her father, and that "he and his Mexican female partner brought her up to learn Spanish and hate the gringos." The girl had no memory of her real parents, so the citizens took her from the house, and a county judge placed her with a local family. She was later identified as Ann Smith and was returned to her mother in Stockton. Whether Valenzuela actually murdered her father is unknown, but no report of such a killing appeared in the newspapers.[14]

Joaquin Valenzuela's camaraderie with Robert Scott resulted from their mutual appetite for robbery and murder. And Scott would not be the last Anglo to ride with Claudio Feliz, nor with Joaquin Murrieta. But Joaquin was then just a petty thief, languishing in the Stockton jail.

CHAPTER 6

KILL THE YANKEES!

Joaquin Murrieta found the Stockton jail rickety and overcrowded. It was a two-story wood frame building, situated on Commerce Street between Main and Market, a few hundred feet south of the town's riverfront. Today this is the heart of the city's business district. As one Stockton journalist succinctly remarked, "The jail is a mere wooden shell." The building was so decrepit it later became a livery stable. The stench was foul, with slop buckets in the cells overflowing with human waste. Although the windows were barred, the lockup was far from secure, and to prevent escape, the jailers forced Joaquin and his fellow inmates to wear chains, made of soft iron, around their ankles. They occupied cells on the top story, while the rooms and offices of the San Joaquin County sheriff and his jailer were on the ground floor. During the daytime, Murrieta and the others were marched outside to work on a chain gang, making repairs to the nearby San Joaquin River levee.

In February 1851, while Claudio Feliz and his gang were raiding the Blue Tent and the Chabolla rancho, Joaquin's cellmates began planning a jailbreak. A dozen prisoners—two of them murderers and the rest horse thieves—carefully chose the mode and the time. At ten o'clock on the night of February 24, they snapped a leg off a table, then used it to pry loose their flimsy chains. But some prisoners were ironed better than others, and they could not remove all the chains. The escapees, using the table leg, pried open the bars on a front window, climbed onto the veranda, and dropped heavily to the ground. Because some still were in irons, the jailer downstairs heard their chains rattling. He rushed outside and captured one prisoner, but the rest fled into the blackness. The county sheriff organized a manhunt and caught two of the fugitives the next day, but nine succeeded in making their escape. As it turned out, Joaquin stayed in his cell and did not join the jailbreak, probably because he had less than two weeks left to serve of his sentence.[1]

After his release, Murrieta returned to the Southern Mines. There, according to a tradition dating to the 1850s, he rode with "Mountain Jim" Wilson, a noted desperado. Wilson's true name was Noah James. He was born to a respectable family in Indiana in 1830. His father, a Baptist minister, died when he was nine, and his mother then settled near her parents' family home at Springfield, Illinois. There Noah's first cousin, William H. Herndon, became Abraham Lincoln's law partner in 1844. Two years later, sixteen-year-old Noah hired on as a teamster for the Donner and Reed families, who were about to embark on an epic journey by wagon train to distant California. They left Springfield in April 1846, crossed the plains, and then took a supposed shortcut through the Utah and Nevada desert, which instead added two weeks to their trip. At the end of October, they finally reached a gap in the Sierra Nevada Mountains, known ever since as Donner Pass. Heavy snow trapped them in the mountains, and many died from cold and starvation. In one of the most infamous episodes of the Old West, members of the Donner Party resorted to cannibalism to stay alive. Of the eighty-nine people in the wagon train, almost half perished.

Noah James was one of the fortunate ones. In February 1847, a relief expedition rescued him and several others and brought them to safety in the Sacramento Valley. By then the Mexican War had ended in California, and later that year, the impressionable teenager began riding with Bernardino Garcia—the veritable Three Fingered Jack. James's other partner was a German ruffian named "Dutch Fred" Salkman who claimed to have been a US Army veteran. Noah James, probably to protect his family's reputation, adopted the alias of Mountain Jim Wilson. One day in 1847, he, with Three Fingered Jack and Dutch Fred, rode through the adobe-lined streets of the seaside village of Monterey. To onlookers, the trio displayed a number of buttons made from silver. They said that some Indians had discovered silver deposits on the nearby Carmel River and had traded the precious metal to US soldiers in exchange for army food rations. Three Fingered Jack and his two compadres claimed that they had in turn obtained the pieces of silver from the soldiers. Yet it was more likely that they had stolen the silver. Either way, Noah James, alias Mountain Jim, never struck it rich in the gold rush. It was his ill luck to be in Southern California when James Marshall discovered the Mother Lode in January 1848.

A typical group of well-armed men during the gold rush era.
Heritage Auctions, Dallas, TX

News of the big gold strike had not yet arrived in the Southland, and a few weeks later, the unknowing Mountain Jim enlisted in the US Army in Los Angeles under his true name. He served just seven months. Then, overcome with gold fever, he deserted and headed for the gold fields. After more than a year of back-breaking work in the mines and failing to strike pay dirt, Mountain Jim turned to crime.[2]

In 1851, Mountain Jim and Dutch Fred joined an organized band of thieves, burglarizing buildings and stealing horses in San Francisco, Stockton, and Sacramento. According to one early account, Joaquin Murrieta was a member of their gang. Two years earlier, San Francisco's citizens had founded a well-organized police department—the first in the Far West. It would quickly develop into one of most effective and professional law enforcement agencies in America. In March 1851, alert San Francisco police officers captured Dutch Fred and several Anglo accomplices red-handed as they burglarized a house. But the following month, they broke out of the city jail and fled San Francisco. Dutch Fred rejoined Mountain Jim, and a few weeks later, the pair drifted through the Southern Mines to Sonora. There, on May 24, 1851, they stole seven horses and drove them to Stockton, where Murrieta reportedly joined them. Unfortunately for the outlaws, one of the stolen horses belonged to Billy Owen, a noted gambler and gunfighter who did not take kindly to victimhood. One pioneer later said of Owen, "He is a handsome young man, rather effeminate in his appearance, with long, black, silken, curling hair, which he wears falling over his shoulders." He added that Owen's feminine looks were deceiving. "He is one of the bravest men in California. Nothing intimidates him; he will attack ten men with the same nonchalance as he would one. He has been in dozens of fatal affrays, and has always been victorious."[3]

In Sonora, Billy Owen began hunting his stolen horse, and he managed to trace the animal out of the foothills and down to

Stockton. There he got a tip that one of the thieves was Mountain Jim Wilson. On the night of May 28, four days after the theft, Owen and three comrades captured Mountain Jim in a Stockton bordello. They marched him to the town gallows, situated not far from the county jail—the same lockup from which Joaquin had been released two months earlier. Owen and his men tried in vain to get Mountain Jim to confess. Then they stripped their captive to his waist and flogged him with a bullwhip, but still he would not talk. Finally they draped a rope around his neck and hoisted him up and down several times. That was enough for Mountain Jim, and he gasped out a confession. He admitted stealing the horses and revealed where the rest of the band was hiding out.

Mountain Jim led Billy Owen and the others to his camp in a field half a mile outside of town. The posse searched it and found several stolen horses and saddles, plus a supply of burglars' tools. They soon captured Dutch Fred and three Anglo horse thieves, one a hulking, thirty-year-old Irishman named Jerome Boland. Joaquin Murrieta, however, had vanished, his connection with the gang still undetected. Like Mountain Jim, all three captives proclaimed their innocence, but a savage whipping soon brought out the truth. They confessed to the horse theft and disclosed where the other stolen animals were. Then Billy Owen brought the outlaws to the Stockton jail, where they were locked up for the night. The next day, an angry crowd gathered for their court hearing. The city marshal—as a chief of police was then called—and his deputy were the only officers available to guard the prisoners. After numerous witnesses testified about their guilt, Owen addressed the throng. According to an eyewitness, Owen announced that the "evidence was clear against the prisoners and that he moved that they now proceed to hang them . . . A scene of uproar and confusion now commenced that baffles description. In an instant, fifty revolvers were drawn."

The mob quickly overpowered the judge, the city marshal, and his deputy. But before the vigilantes could seize Mountain Jim, the hulking Jerome Boland tore loose from his guards. He charged through the crowd and fled out the back door of the courthouse. Billy Owen, armed with a five-shooter, was close on his heels. He fired four times as Boland raced toward the San Joaquin River levee. Finally Boland, realizing he could not escape, raised his hands in surrender. Owen marched him back to the jail, which was now surrounded by a mob of several hundred, shouting, "Hang 'em! Hang 'em!"

By then the county sheriff had arrived on the scene. He climbed the stairs to the jail's second-floor veranda, where he pleaded with the mob to disperse. He promised that a strong guard would be posted and that the prisoners could not escape. Finally the infuriated vigilantes calmed down and began to drift away. Several members of the gang then stood trial for horse theft and were convicted. Jerome Boland received a ten-year term in the state prison brig in San Francisco Bay. Mountain Jim and Dutch Fred were not so lucky. A new state law had been enacted that made grand larceny punishable by one to ten years in prison, "or by death in the discretion of the jury." The jurors sentenced Mountain Jim and Dutch Fred to death by hanging. On November 28, 1851, they climbed the Stockton gallows in front of a crowd of three thousand, including numerous women. The scaffold stood under a tree near the jail; it was the same upon which Mountain Jim had been whipped and choked into confessing.

Dutch Fred, a cigar in his mouth, jauntily mounted the gallows and declared in his German accent, "I take my place to the right, as a good soldier always should."

Then, addressing the crowd, Dutch Fred exclaimed, "I wish to die like a man, and not like an old woman."

He gave a long speech, providing details of his life and repeating his claim that he had served in the US Army during the

Mexican War. Mountain Jim, on the other hand, made a few somber remarks, declaring that he forgave all his enemies and insisting that he was innocent. The two then took their positions under the nooses. The hangman bound their hands and feet and looped a rope around each man's neck, with the large knot under one ear. With a proper drop from the scaffold, the knot would break the prisoner's neck and cause instant death. If done improperly, the condemned man would slowly strangle until dead, something a hangman considered both a failure and an embarrassment.

When all was ready, Dutch Fred called out to the women in the throng, "Here we go, gals!"

The hangman released the trap door, and the pair plunged through it. The drop broke Mountain Jim's neck, and he died almost instantly. Dutch Fred, on the other hand, slowly strangled to death. Their bodies were left dangling for more than an hour as a warning to evildoers.[4]

Mountain Jim and Dutch Fred left behind a bloody legacy, for it was most likely through them that Joaquin Murrieta had first met Three Fingered Jack. Murrieta and Garcia would become close compadres. Three Fingered Jack, after the Mexican War, seems to have followed a quasi-respectable life for several years. Although at times he rode with Mountain Jim and Dutch Fred, at other times he worked on his wife Hilaria's rancho, headquartered at the family adobe in Mill Valley. After the discovery of gold, there was a huge demand for lumber in San Francisco, both for ship building and construction of houses. From the rancho, Garcia supplied timber that was floated along the bayfront to a steam-powered sawmill in nearby Sausalito. In September 1850, he received $2,600 for delivering lumber, a significant sum at the time.

That era was marked by extensive litigation in California over Mexican land grants, because many ranchos had vaguely described parameters. Disreputable lawyers and "land sharks" often targeted property-rich but cash-poor Californios with lawsuits over the title to their ranchos. In 1850, Hilaria sold her holdings to an Anglo investor for $30,000, but when he failed to pay, she and Bernardino Garcia filed a lawsuit, which was eventually successful, to set aside the deal. However, under California's law, derived from Mexican law, the rancho, and any money it produced, belonged solely to Hilaria and her children fathered by John Reed. No part of the property belonged to Bernardino Garcia. For a violent ex-vaquero, that must have been a bitter pill to swallow. That same year, 1851, Garcia abandoned Hilaria and the children and rode to the gold country. Although there is no evidence that they formally divorced, Hilaria was thereafter known as "the widow Reed," and she never used Garcia's surname again.[5]

During the summer of 1851, while Mountain Jim and Dutch Fred were in jail and awaiting trial, Murrieta continued to visit Stockton. His connection with their gang of horse thieves was still unknown. Joaquin stayed at the Hotel de Minas, or Hotel of the Mines, where he became acquainted with Father Dominique Blaive. A former captain in the French army, Father Blaive later became a Catholic priest. He arrived in San Francisco from France in 1850 and settled in Stockton, where he established its first Catholic church in May 1851. He and Joaquin both boarded for a time at Hotel de Minas, and the latter—not yet a wanted man—made no attempt to conceal his identity. Father Blaive later said that he knew him in Stockton as "Joaquin Muriatta."[6]

By this time, Rosa Feliz, the wife of Joaquin and sister of Claudio, was no longer in the mining country. What happened to her is a mystery. According to John Rollin Ridge, she left Joaquin and returned to her parents in Mexico. True or not, Joaquin soon had a new, and beautiful, paramour. Her name was Maria Ana Andrada, but she was variously called Ana and Mariana. She was born in Mexico in 1830, and as we shall see, in Los Angeles she was known as Ana Benites. A vaquero who

A gold rush fandango, by the noted California artist Maynard Dixon.
Bancroft Library

knew her in later years said that she first arrived in California as a teenage girl in 1849. She later became widely known in the far-flung Californio and Mexican community of central California as Mariana Murrieta, although there was no evidence that she and Joaquin ever legally married. Because her personality was erratic and her mental status unstable, Latinos called her Mariana la Loca—Crazy Mariana.[7]

In old age, Mariana was very frank in describing her early life in California. "When I came to womanhood of plenty knowledge, I liked a lot of money," she told a friend. "I gave myself to the streets giving service to men. In time I became one woman of strength. I made a lot of money. I came to Los Angeles, San Diego, and I had intentions to go back to my land of birth but I like so much the drinking and I stayed. With this money I made, I returned to the camp of Sonora, in [the] placers. I arrived walking. When I arrived [in] camp Sonora, since I liked drinking a lot, I would fight with anybody, man or woman."[8]

Mariana first encountered Joaquin in Sonora, though another account claims they met in Coulterville, twenty-five miles south. According to her story, she was drinking in a saloon when Joaquin and several compadres stepped in. Just as they entered, Mariana pointed a pistol at one of the patrons and ordered, "You drink with me or I will kill you!"

Joaquin was hugely impressed. He later told her that it was love at first sight, and that he said to himself, "This woman will be very useful to me."[9]

A journalist who met Mariana in 1874 wrote that she claimed to have been married to Joaquin. He described her as "a woman of medium height, and though rather stout, is of finely developed proportions. Despite her age, her loose mode of life, her present fondness for aguardiente [brandy], and a scar extending across her face, from nose to ear, she is not by any means a homely or repulsive-looking woman. Her lips still retain their fine curves and her teeth are a marvel of perfect preservation. It required no very strong draughts on the imagination to believe that twenty years ago she possessed a figure which was a model of grace, and that then, arrayed in the brilliant-hued garments her husband admired, with her magnificent eyes, either sparkling at the daring deeds of her protector or looking with defiance at his hunters, she was the woman of rare beauty and witchery who could maintain her supremacy in the robber's ardent affections, even after his discovery of her infidelity to himself. Then, too, more in harmony with her appearance was her soft, musical name, Mariana Murrieta.

"She makes no secret of the story of the scar. Tired, she says, of the continual fear and danger in which the visits of Joaquin's pursuers kept her, and at the same time pleased with the attentions of one Charlie Baker, who occasionally visited her in the husband's absence, she gradually transferred to Baker the whole treasure of her love. Joaquin, upon discovering this, upbraided her but little, forgiving her upon her promising reformation.

She, finding no cessation of the perils to which she was exposed, soon fled to her paramour, in whose camp the robber chief afterwards found her. Baker being absent, Joaquin vented his rage on the woman, and shooting her twice through the arm, slashing her breasts, and cutting her across the thighs, he finished by drawing the keen edge of his knife from her nose to the left ear, and leaving her for dead, burned the camp and departed."[10]

But it seems evident that Mariana and Joaquin were lovers before he became a bandit. And the incident in which Joaquin assaulted her may have taken place during a night of violence at Melones Camp, on the Stanislaus River. The camp, situated ten miles west of Sonora and now covered by the New Melones Lake reservoir, was home to about eight hundred miners. The trouble started on the evening of June 12, 1851, when two Mexican prostitutes began quarreling. Soon the fight was taken up by their gambler paramours, one Yankee and the other Mexican. That erupted into a larger brawl between the camp's Latino miners on one side and Anglos on the other. Several Mexicans began yelling, "Kill all the Americans!"

Five Mexicans opened fire with Colt revolvers, and the Anglo men scattered for cover. Joaquin's friend, Captain William Acklin, happened to be present. He quickly stepped to the forefront and pleaded for calm. It was no use. As one man in Melones later reported, "At the moment of assault a number of Mexicans cried out not to kill the captain, but a Mexican ran him through the body with a long knife. The fight now became general, the Americans fighting in self defense."

Suddenly a pistol-toting American gambler appeared in the midst of the fray. He was none other than Billy Owen. The gunfighter had just arrived in Melones Camp, having ridden in from Stockton after his capture of Mountain Jim. As soon as the Mexican pistoleros saw Owen, they began yelling, "Kill the curly-headed man!"

They fired a barrage with their revolvers at him. Owen, unscathed, jerked his six-shooter and returned the fire, badly wounding one of the Mexicans. A number of Anglos then joined the fray, shooting rapidly. Two Mexicans were wounded, and their leader dropped with three bullets in his body. As the man sprawled on the ground, one Yankee snatched away his long bowie knife and drove the blade clean through his torso, pinning him to the dirt. The skewered Mexican lay writhing in the throes of death.

"*Mata! Mata a los chingados Yanquis!*" he cried out in rage. "Kill! Kill the fucking Yankees!"

But by then, most of the bloodshed was over. The peaceable Latinos in Melones Camp later said that the entire affray was a plot by a group of Mexican robbers. The bandidos hoped that by inciting the violence and causing everyone to flee, they could loot the miners' tents while their occupants were gone. Sure enough, a monte dealer found $1,200 missing from his tent, and another miner lost his trunk and a pocket watch. While all that was going on, an enraged Mexican burst into the tent of his mistress. As a witness explained, "A Mexican cut open a tent and attacked a woman who had deserted him because of his abusive treatment. He cut her in the face and stabbed her through the arm, but before he could complete the murder her cries frightened him out of the tent." That incident may well have been Joaquin Murrieta's knife assault on Mariana. And fortunately for Joaquin's friend, Captain Acklin, his stab wound soon healed.[11]

Mariana also recovered, but the attack left the jagged scar on her face. Like so many abused women before and after, she stayed loyal to Joaquin. They drifted through the mining camps in Tuolumne and Calaveras Counties as he pursued his luck at the monte tables. In the gold towns, she was known as Joaquin's woman and sometimes as Joaquina or Mariana Joaquina. In 1878 a pioneer doctor in San Andreas recalled her vividly, replete with the racist terms so common in that era: "She was a tall, fine looking Greaser woman, who would have been remarkably handsome if a long scar, extending nearly the whole length of her face from the left temple, had not disfigured it. It was the result of one of her lover's blows, rumor said. Joaquina had frequent attacks of hysteria and I was called to see her in my professional capacity. These attacks, people said, always followed an interview [argument] with Joaquin, but she persistently asserted he was not in the vicinity, nor had been." Mariana would feature prominently in the events to come.[12]

By the time of the Melones gun battle, Claudio Feliz had returned to Sonora, flush with loot from his raids near Livermore and San Jose. No one suspected him as the leader of that rampaging band. In Sonora he associated with David Hill, a notorious robber and horse thief. Hill, also known as Charles May, was about twenty-three and hailed from upstate New York. Just a week after Billy Owen captured Mountain Jim in Stockton, Claudio and Hill, with several other Anglo outlaws, began planning the robbery of a general store in Campo Seco, five miles south of Sonora. Notably, Joaquin Murrieta was not one of the gang. Campo Seco is situated near the modern-day Railtown 1897 State Historic Park. Though little of the old mining town is left, in 1851 it was a bustling camp of about sixty wood frame buildings, with two hotels and several businesses that catered to the gold hunters. The general store was owned by George Gleason, whom Claudio called "Don George," and his partners Benjamin Mardis and Charles Lippincott.

On June 6, 1851, David Hill and an accomplice rode up to the store. Pretending to be customers, the two ruffians stepped inside, and Hill pawned his six-shooter in exchange for half an ounce of gold. Gleason unlocked a 150-pound iron safe, removed and measured the gold dust, and handed it to Hill. Then Hill and his comrade left, having learned exactly where the storekeepers kept their gold. Early the next morning, the three shopkeepers were sound asleep when Claudio, Hill, and five Anglo robbers crept inside their store. Each was armed with a Colt six-gun and a bowie knife. A slight noise jarred the merchants awake, as a local journalist reported: "On opening their eyes, they found that a man was standing over each with a cocked revolver and bowie knife, threatening upon the least attempt to create an alarm, to blow out their brains." Mardis started to reach for his pistol, but stopped when he remembered that it was not loaded. As one of the outlaws grabbed it, Lippincott closed his eyes and pretended to be asleep. But his ruse did not work, for the bandits argued loudly whether to kill their three victims. Lippincott, terrified, got a good look at David Hill and recognized him, later saying that Hill "had a bad name."

Claudio and the others stole three pistols and then hoisted up the iron safe, which held several thousand dollars in gold, and carried it from the store. As soon as they left, Mardis leaped from his bed, seized an axe, and rushed into the street, yelling for help. Instantly the entire camp was aroused, and armed miners started in pursuit. Claudio later said that the miners shot and wounded one of his fellow robbers. He and the other freebooters carried the treasure box to a nearby hill, but they were pressed so hard by the manhunters that they were forced to drop the unopened safe and run for their lives. The band scattered, and David Hill, unaware that he had been recognized, returned to Sonora. For the next three weeks, he lay low in Sonora and managed to avoid its law officers.[13]

On the night of June 27, Hill was visiting a Mexican bordello on the outskirts of Sonora when he quarreled with another patron over the favors of a prostitute. Hill jerked out a five-shooter, struck the man over the head, and pulled the trigger. Fortunately for his rival, the hammer snapped on a defective percussion cap, and the gun misfired. Word was sent to the county sheriff, George Work, who rushed to the brothel with one of his deputies. Work, as we have seen, was an able lawman who opposed vigilantism. He had married a Latina woman and gained a reputation for fairness to all. The sheriff and his deputy searched the entire bagnio without finding the suspect. They were about to leave when Work decided to look under one of the beds. Lying underneath was a heavily armed Anglo, covered with a pile of clothes. Work hauled the man out and relieved him of two Colt revolvers, a bowie knife, and a double-barrel shotgun. Taking his prisoner outside, the sheriff looked him over carefully and realized that he matched the description of the robber at Campo Seco. Work soon identified the man as David Hill and lodged him in the Sonora jail.

In the morning, a dozen vigilantes entered the jail, removed Hill, and took him to Campo Seco. As a huge crowd gathered, a vigilance committee was quickly organized. It was headed by Colonel Benjamin F. Cheatham, a veteran of the Mexican War who later became a prominent Confederate general in the Civil War. The vigilantes appointed a prosecutor, a defense lawyer, and twelve jurors. The three storekeepers, Gleason, Mardis, and Lippincott, testified about the robbery. Mardis was unable to identify Hill, but Gleason and Lippincott swore that he was one of the robbers and that he had also pawned his revolver in the shop. The jury deliberated for fifteen minutes before finding Hill guilty. The crowd of spectators then voted that he be hanged in the next ninety minutes.

While the vigilantes began preparing a scaffold and a coffin, five others met privately with Hill to try to get him to confess. Hill, hoping for mercy, admitted his guilt and named seven Anglos and two Latinos whom he said were horse thieves. Notably he did not include Claudio Feliz, because some of the names he provided were most likely fictitious. One of the men on his list, Ned Ward, was real, and had actually been in the mob of onlookers watching the trial. The vigilantes began hunting Ward and captured him that night. In the morning, they brought him to trial. But there was no evidence against Ward other than Hill's confession, and the jury of vigilantes found him not guilty and set him free.

At six that evening, the vigilance committee prepared to hang David Hill in Campo Seco in front of a throng of hundreds of miners. Sheriff Work was present with several of his men, but this time he made no effort to interfere. According to a Sonora journalist who looked on, some of the unidentified men in Hill's gang were also there, but whether Claudio was reckless enough to view the lynching is unknown. The newspaperman later described the excitement in his journal: "Since early morning, people from the various camps had been on their way to Camp Seco and an immense number of accomplices and other villains had collected. After the prisoner was placed on the stand [scaffold], he made a few remarks describing his life as one of crime, and warning others against following his course. He also said that he had robbed and stolen and done other acts of crime, but had never shed blood, and he threw himself upon the mercy of the people. This appeal to the people caused the question to be put amongst them, 'Shall he be hung?' A large number answered aye, but an equal number responded in the negative. Immediately some hundreds of pistols were drawn and a universal stampede occurred. Horsemen plunged through the crowd and over them, and the people ran in every direction."

At that, Sheriff Work called out for calm. The newspaperman later said, "He pledged his own life that the prisoner should be forthcoming at the District Court, if the people would deliver him into the hands of the civil authorities." As the crowd debated what to do, David Hill waited nervously on the makeshift gallows, his hands bound behind him. Suddenly Work sprang forward, seized Hill, and with the aid of his deputies, bundled him into a wagon. Then, before the crowd could react, they whipped up the team and raced off toward Sonora. While Work and his men headed for town on the wagon road, a vigilante horseman took a shortcut over the hills and arrived in Sonora first. He raised the alarm, and another huge crowd, many armed with revolvers, gathered to confront the sheriff,

Colonel Benjamin F. Cheatham, leader of the mob that lynched Claudio's partner, David Hill, in Sonora in 1851.
Heritage Auctions, Dallas, TX

who arrived soon after. By then it was dark, and Sheriff Work, to avoid the mob, raced his team through the dusty streets toward the jail. But the wagon suddenly crashed into a hitching post. The sheriff jumped down, one hand holding Hill's collar and the other his six-gun. The two ran for the jail, pursued by the armed lynchers. By this time, Colonel Cheatham and other vigilantes had galloped into town from Campo Seco.

"Stop him in front," one vigilante yelled at a group of bystanders. "We are afraid to shoot, lest we may kill our friends. Stop him in front!"

A pioneer storekeeper in Sonora watched the scene and recalled, "I was standing in front of the store when they passed. The form of the prisoner I shall never forget. His body was bent, probably to escape a bullet, and his head pushed forward as he strained every nerve in the fearful race. The people were deterred from firing, although a hundred revolvers were in steady and determined hands, from a fear of killing the sheriff, who, after all, was bravely performing the duty of his office, and nothing more. One young man overtook the officer and threw himself upon the prisoner, clasping him in his arms. Work raised his pistol, but a dozen men were close upon him, and shouts of 'Don't fire, George, or we will cut you to pieces!' made him drop his arm, and wresting the prisoner from the grasp of his assailer, he redoubled his speed, and gained the door of the jail ahead of the crowd."

Just as Work reached the jail, Colonel Cheatham appeared in the doorway. He pointed a cocked revolver at the sheriff and declared, "George, you have a pistol and I have a pistol. Yours is cocked and so is mine. Blow away. I can kill too—but let this man go!"

As Work leveled his own six-shooter at Cheatham, one of his deputies exclaimed, "It is no use, George. We have done all we can. Give him up!"

Sheriff Work, completely outnumbered, lowered his gun, and the mob seized Hill.

"We have got him! We have got him!" they yelled, while others shouted in unison, "Hurrah!"

Two men draped a rope around Hill's neck. Then the mob marched him a short distance to an oak tree behind the El Dorado saloon. To prevent any interference, they formed a large circle around the tree, with each man brandishing a pistol. Hill asked to see a clergyman, but he was just trying to delay the inevitable. When the minister arrived, Hill refused to speak to him. The Sonora storekeeper described what happened next: "The rope was put around his neck, the other end thrown over the branch of a tree. A couple of score of men ranged themselves alongside the long rope, each having hold of it. The words, 'All ready! Now then! Haul up!' and in a moment a black object shot up, and loomed in obscure relief against the bright starlit heavens. The body spun 'round as its weight untwisted the coil of the rope, but no other movement was visible. Death, or at least entire insensitivity, was almost simultaneous with the act of running the man up."[14]

The sudden demise of David Hill had no salutary effect on Claudio Feliz. He continued his raids, and eventually led Joaquin Murrieta into his even bloodier career of robbery and murder. Claudio's younger brother, Reyes Feliz, then about fifteen, also followed in his footsteps. Reyes later confessed to murdering a man in Sonora that same year, 1851. "The man I killed was called Anselmo Marias. I killed him with a shot at the camp of Sonora," he said. "I had a dispute with Anselmo. He was going to kill an American, a night previous, who was a 'padrino' [mentor] of mine." Reyes insisted that Anselmo Marias was the only man he killed. "I do not own but one murder," he declared. Claudio, however, later admitted that after the fatal robberies by his gang near San Jose, he had returned to Columbia and met up with Reyes. He and his brother then rode thirteen miles south to Camp Salvado, where, as Claudio boasted, they "murdered a Sonoran and robbed him of all the gold he had." He added that they then joined up with an American desperado and raided the tent of an Anglo miner on the Tuolumne River, killing him and taking $500.[15]

By this time, the bandido Miguel Luches, who had taken part in the triple murder at Digby Smith's farm near San Jose, had left Claudio's gang. He was arrested in Sacramento and lodged in its county jail, which, like the state prison, was a ship outfitted with cells and anchored in the Sacramento River. Luches soon broke out of the brig and fled to San Francisco. On the night of October 8, 1851, he was carousing in a fandango hall owned by a Mexican woman in Murderers' Alley. Murderers' Alley intersected Dupont Street (now Grant Avenue), in what later became the city's Chinatown. According to a San Francisco journalist of the 1850s, Murderers' Alley acquired its name as "the theater of many dark and midnight deeds of blood." During the fandango, Luches quarreled with a Mexican desperado known as Marcelino, and the two agreed to settle the affair in a knife duel. The pair stepped outside into the bright moonlight and walked a short distance north to the sand dunes of North Beach. Today North Beach is a dense neighborhood, built on landfill and situated blocks from the bay. Then, however, before the bay shoreline was filled in, it was an actual beach on the city's waterfront. There were no witnesses to the duel, but as a San Francisco journalist remarked, "The usual manner of fighting among the Mexicans is to wrap their serape in many folds around their left arm, thus forming a kind of guard or shield, and dagger in hand, strike with the right."[16]

Miguel Luches flashed his knife for the last time. Unlike Luches's unarmed and unsuspecting victims near San Jose, Marcelino was ready for a fight. Their duel lasted only a few moments, as Marcelino quickly stabbed Luches to death. Marcelino then returned to Murderers' Alley, where he boasted to several Mexican women and a monte dealer that he had slain Luches in a duel. The bandido's blood-soaked corpse was discovered a day later in North Beach, covered with eighteen stab wounds. Some of the cuts were in his back, showing that Marcelino had finished Luches off after he was down. The San Francisco police soon heard of Marcelino's boasts and began hunting for him. Several days later, they arrested two Mexicans, one of whom had a fresh knife wound. Part of his Panama hat had been sliced off. But it proved to be a case of mistaken identity, and the killer of Miguel Luches was never captured.[17]

It was at this time—in the fall of 1851—that Joaquin Murrieta finally joined Claudio's band. It was a risky decision, but he had learned to take risks at the monte tables. While Joaquin was undoubtedly motivated in part by his mistreatment at the hands of American ruffians, a significant reason was his thirst for gold. He knew that Claudio and his men had made numerous bloody raids, stealing significant sums, and little effort had been made to pursue and capture them. Joaquin could not resist the temptation, and it was an opportunity he could not pass up. The gang first gathered in Sacramento, and its members included Murrieta, Claudio Feliz and his brother Reyes, a robber named Miguel Sasuelta, and three desperadoes known only as Trinidad, Gabriel, and Soliz. Several Anglos and one Chileno also rode with them; their names are unknown, with the exception of an American ruffian named Bellamy. Claudio later said that the gang, eleven in number, rode southeast toward San Jose. On the way, they stopped at the farm of a man named Gee and stole a herd of forty-five horses and mules. Apparently realizing that they could not sell the stolen animals locally, they retraced their route and headed north to Marysville, the gateway to the Northern Mines. In Marysville they sold the herd, then rode south to Campo Seco in Calaveras County. There, at the camp's monte tables, Murrieta and the rest lost every cent of their ill-gotten gains.[18]

Joaquin and the Feliz brothers decided to head back to the rich diggings of the Northern Mines. It would mark a new and even more violent chapter in the gang's bloody reign of banditry, one that would change Joaquin Murrieta's life forever.

CHAPTER 7

A BULLET FOR SHERIFF BUCHANAN

A cold November wind swept across the Sacramento Valley as four gaudily attired horsemen swayed easily in their saddles. Each boasted a wide, flat-brimmed sombrero and fancy *calzoneras*, or trousers, with slits that ran down the sides of the legs, buttoned with a seam of silver *conchas*. They were the perfect picture of well-dressed, well-mounted young rancheros. The riders spurred their animals along the Sacramento River road, lined with tule plants, and north toward Marysville. Situated forty miles above Sacramento, Marysville was a port on the Yuba River near its confluence with the Feather River. It was a center of trade, because sailing vessels and small steamers could reach the town from the Golden Gate by proceeding across San Francisco Bay and then up the Sacramento River. From Marysville, goods, food, and other cargo were carried by mule trains, driven by Mexican packers, to the mountain camps of the Northern Mines. Marysville was bustling and booming, home to about four thousand people, and like most gold rush towns, it was 95 percent male. Its occupants were served by four churches, nine hotels, two newspapers, and, inevitably, dozens of saloons, gambling houses, and bordellos.[1]

Claudio Feliz, accompanied by his brother Reyes, Joaquin Murrieta, and a fellow Sonoran desperado named Manuel Pena, cantered leisurely into town. As they dismounted to rest and refresh themselves, the banging of hammers and sawing of wood echoed through the streets. The townsmen were then rebuilding. Just two months earlier, a devastating fire had swept through the center of town, destroying three city blocks. Many gold rush communities experienced such conflagrations, caused mainly by the careless use of open fires, oil lanterns, and candles. Most of the Marysville buildings had canvas walls and false fronts made of wood. Canvas awnings provided shade from summer and fall heat, but the structures were highly flammable.

Although the town's saloons and brothels were going full blast, Murrieta and his compadres did not stay long in Marysville. The outlaws continued another three miles northeast to a Latino settlement of cabins and tents situated on the west bank of the Yuba River, called Sonoran Camp. According to several early accounts, Joaquin's sister—apparently Vicenta—lived there. Six years before the gold rush, Vicenta had a relationship with a man named Tomas Bustamante. They were not married, and their union produced a son, Procopio, in 1843. After Bustamante died, Vicenta emigrated from Mexico to California with her son. Young Procopio would grow up idolizing his infamous uncle, Joaquin Murrieta, and yearning to emulate his bloody exploits.[2]

Sonoran Camp near Marysville was a perfect hideout for Claudio and his band, replete with fandango halls, cantinas, and monte parlors. An Argonaut who regularly visited Sonoran Camp recalled, "It is a regular Mexican town, some 3,000 people and about forty houses and a number of Mexican families engaged in packing mules." The forty-niner explained how everyone was welcome at the dances in Sonoran Camp: "Well, I heard of the fandango and I went. It was held in a good sized room with a bar on one side, of course, and crowded with men and women, all smoking. The orchestra consisted of two fiddles and guitars and made pretty good music. The men were dressed in sky-blue velvet pants, open at the sides and [with] rows of buttons, with white drawers, red sash and a fancy shirt. The senoritas, with white muslin dresses, stretched so stiffly that you could not get very near, and silk stockings, looked very pretty. We had cotillions and waltzes and one senorita danced a fancy dance and made more noise with her little feet and slippers than I could with thick boots . . . The fandango went off well. I was very much amused and came away without being stabbed, which was lucky as such things often happen."[3]

Claudio and Joaquin, after dallying with the senoritas of Sonoran Camp, began planning a series of raids in the mountainous mining country in Butte County, north of Marysville. They met a Mexican desperado in Sonoran Camp and invited him to join them. He agreed, but by the time they were ready to ride, the man had fallen ill and was unable to accompany them. In the first week of November, Joaquin Murrieta, the Feliz brothers, and Manuel Pena rode out of Sonoran Camp and headed northeast into the Sierra Nevada foothills. A forty-mile ride over rough trails brought them to Bidwell Bar, a gold camp on the Middle Fork of the Feather River. It was then home to about two thousand gold seekers, but today the town is submerged under Lake Oroville, where it is spanned by the 1,100-foot-long Bidwell Bar suspension bridge. During their horseback journey, Joaquin, the Feliz boys, and Pena lost two of their mounts. Whether the horses were injured or strayed off into the hills is unknown, but the bandidos were forced to ride double.[4]

The four outlaws trotted their mustangs into Bidwell Bar on the evening of November 9, 1851. Like so many gold camps, it was a cluster of wood frame houses and canvas tents perched next to the river, in the shadow of a tall, bare hill. The town had half a dozen hotels, plus a theater, a bakery, a livery stable, and numerous saloons and gambling halls. A pioneer later recalled what happened that November day: "One evening a party of Mexicans stopped at [Bidwell] bar and, as usual, spent a part of the night in gambling. This was so common an event as to excite no comment. One of the men with whom the Mexicans played

Bidwell Bar in a daguerreotype taken in 1856.
Meriam Library, California State University, Chico

was a butcher named Robbins, who had with him a considerable sum of money. Robbins left the bar at a very early hour the following morning on his rounds among the miners with some mules loaded with beef. He was accompanied by a very stout and powerful colored man who had long been in his employ.

"Shortly afterwards the Mexicans saddled their horses and followed the two men. They were overtaken about two miles above the bar in a narrow canyon leading to Miner's Ranch, and the butcher was shot down by one of the Mexicans. When the party attempted to take what money Robbins had upon his person, they were met by a sturdy resistance on the part of the colored man, though he had no firearms with which to defend himself. One of the murderers threw a lariat over the man and, wheeling his horse, attempted to drag him away from the dead body. The negro, however, caught hold of some bushes by the trail, and so powerful was he that the utmost efforts of the Mexican's horse could not dislodge him or break his hold. Another of the party dismounted and, rushing upon the negro with a long, sharp knife, cut great gashes on the back of his hands till the cords were severed, and the poor fellow was dragged through the bushes and over the rocks until he was nearly dead. Not satisfied with this, however, they ended their job by stabbing him several times till life was extinct. Taking what money Robbins had upon his person, this gang of cutthroats then rode on."[5]

The bandits left both bodies under the roadside brush, with the blood trails easily visible in the dirt. Later that day, a group of Argonauts came down the trail on their way to Marysville. They spotted the blood and quickly found two dead bodies. From the evidence at the scene, it was readily apparent how the victims had died. The gold hunters first identified the white man as a miner named Gallagher, and said that he and his black servant were known to have been carrying $10,000 in gold. However, it turned out that the dead man had the name "C. Miller" tattooed on one of his arms. After stories of the murders appeared in the newspapers, Gallagher quickly surfaced and announced that he "is not dead, but liveth." Whether the white man's true name was Robbins or Miller was never determined, nor was the identity of his African American companion. Claudio, who later boasted of the killing, said merely that the white man was "a poor, unhappy fellow, whom we murdered and robbed of two ounces."[6]

Joaquin and his compadres fled the death scene on their two horses and rode ten miles south to a hotel and general store known as the Kentucky Ranch. No longer standing, it was located four miles south of Wyandotte, on one of the main roads to Marysville. The bandidos, posing as honest travelers, ate supper, then mounted up and started for Marysville, thirty miles to the south. By then a hue and cry had been raised, and a small posse tracked the outlaws from Bidwell Bar to the Kentucky Ranch.

The tracks were easy to follow because one horse was unshod and the other had shoes on its right feet only. At the Kentucky Ranch, the unsuspecting hotelkeepers told the possemen that "four well-dressed Mexicans, riding two on a horse, had stopped to dinner, but being in a great hurry did not feed their animals. Immediately after refreshing themselves they mounted two on each horse, and rode off with great rapidity." The manhunters followed the killers' trail south to a spot five miles outside Marysville. By then it was so dark that they could no longer see the tracks. The possemen raced into Marysville and reported the murders to Yuba County Sheriff Robert "Buck" Buchanan and Constable Ike Bowen. Buchanan, twenty-nine, was a capable and energetic lawman. He and his adventurous young wife were newlyweds when they joined the gold rush in 1849. Like many gold washers, Buchanan had little success, and the following year, he became the new county's first sheriff. He and Constable Bowen raised a small posse and began scouring the area just north of Marysville. They also visited Sonoran Camp and searched its tents and houses, with no luck. Finally Sheriff Buchanan and his men rode back to Marysville empty-handed.[7]

Joaquin, the Feliz boys, and Manuel Pena had managed to outwit their pursuers by backtracking up the road toward Bidwell Bar. Instead of returning to the Kentucky Ranch, they stopped that night at another inn, Miller's House, situated about eight miles south of Bidwell Bar. As a Marysville journalist later reported, "About an hour after supper, four Mexicans rode up to the house, and going immediately into the kitchen, asked for supper to be got ready in a hurry, as they wanted to go to Marysville that night. While their supper was preparing, they laid hold of the fragments of the regular supper, and devoured them like wolves, as if they had not recently eaten. A person in the kitchen, who had been interpreting between them and the cook, asked them where they had been, and they replied that they had been on Feather River selling cattle. They manifested great haste, continually hurrying the cook, and would not go out into the public apartment to eat their supper, insisting upon doing so in the kitchen. All four of them were young men, well dressed, two of them in blue pantaloons, open at the side, with bright buttons, and were of light complexion. Their appearance excited the remark from the cook that he had never seen Mexicans so well dressed and so 'bright' and gentlemanly."

As Joaquin and his compadres devoured their meal in Miller's House, a teamster named George Mather was camped outside, sound asleep in the bed of his wagon. In conversation with the innkeepers, the outlaws learned that Mather had brought a load of goods to the mines and was on his way back to Marysville. One of the gang, while eating in the kitchen, stepped out twice and walked around Mather's wagon, then returned to the hotel. After finishing their dinner, Joaquin and the rest mounted their two horses and rode off into the darkness. However, just half an hour later, one of them returned and purchased a large supply—several pounds' worth—of crackers, sardines, and onions. The hotelkeeper thought that was odd because all four had declared that they were in a hurry to leave and had to reach Marysville that night.

Joaquin and the gang had different plans, and they made camp in the woods downhill from Miller's House. At daybreak they lay in wait for the teamster, George Mather. When his wagon approached, the bandits wasted little time. They forced him to stop, then dragged him from the seat. As he fell to the ground, several clubbed him over the head with their pistols. Then they stabbed Mather in the right arm and slashed his throat. Finally the outlaws slipped a lariat around his neck and hauled his dead corpse into the trailside bushes. Claudio later said that they stole $500 from the teamster. The desperadoes then mounted up and trotted off, taking Mather's horses and leaving his wagon in the road. They had gone only a hundred yards when they spotted two unarmed young men on foot following behind them.

They were a pair of miners, John Gardner and Andrew Jinkerson, on their way to Marysville. Gardner and Jinkerson had stumbled upon the abandoned wagon. As the two gold hunters approached Joaquin and his compadres, they asked the horsemen if they knew what had become of the driver of the wagon. Claudio later described what happened: "After we left the cart, we fell in with two Americans who enquired of us for the one with the wagon. After sending them away we went back to them and asked for fire [matches] and murdered and took from them two ounces of gold and a watch, which was all they had."

But "murdered" was an understatement. Claudio, Joaquin, and the other bandidos stabbed Jinkerson seventeen times, including seven punctures in his chest, any of which would have been fatal. They cut Gardner's throat not once, but twice, then slashed open and rifled the dead men's pockets. Finally they pulled their victims off the trail with their lariats. A passerby approached on foot and spotted the desperadoes dragging a body into the brush. He was unarmed and stayed out of sight, then ran back up the road to spread the alarm. Soon a mounted posse of miners thundered out in pursuit. As Claudio recalled, "After finishing the murder of these men, we saw a company of ten Americans coming. We then ran away to the mountains, where we remained a whole day." The outlaws wisely abandoned their horses, which made them easy to spot, and took to the heavy brush on foot. Meanwhile other possemen searched the road and found Mather's body. Using lanterns, they continued to hunt after dark and finally discovered the bloody corpses of Gardner and Jinkerson a hundred yards down the road. While they were loading the bodies into a cart, a bay horse wandered up. The animal was tired, well lathered, and had marks on its back showing that a saddle had been recently removed. The manhunters brought the horse to Miller's House, where it was immediately identified as one of the two animals that had been ridden by the four Mexicans.[8]

As news of the killings spread like wildfire, Joaquin and the band walked south toward Sonoran Camp. Their spree of murder quickly created an uproar in the nearby mining towns. Wild rumors spread that six more dead bodies had been found; another report claimed that seventeen men had been slain. Though the stories were false, the gang was responsible for murdering one more victim while on their way to Sonoran Camp. Robbers waylaid and killed a young man named Isaac Pray six miles north of Marysville. The bandits' method was almost identical to the other killings. Pray was shot once and stabbed multiple times, one of his pockets sliced open, and his body dragged off the trail. The place he was killed was on the route taken by Joaquin and the gang, and even more damning, Claudio later boasted that he and the gang had murdered six men in the area. Though Isaac Pray's decomposed corpse was not discovered until a few weeks later, he was undoubtedly their sixth victim.[9]

Meanwhile the bodies of Mather, Gardner, and Jinkerson were taken to the nearby settlement of Natchez and buried. A vigilance committee quickly formed in Natchez, and posses rode out to hunt the killers. But Joaquin and his compadres managed to avoid the manhunters, and they made their way on foot back to Sonoran Camp, arriving on November 12. The same day, Marysville officers picked up a suspicious Mexican in Sonoran Camp and brought him into court. He turned out to be the same desperado who had agreed to take part in the raids but had taken sick and was unable to ride with the gang. Probably in exchange for leniency, the man told what he knew and said that the four killers were hiding out in a house in Sonoran Camp.[10]

At ten o'clock that night, Sheriff Buchanan and Constable Bowen mounted their horses and rode out to Sonoran Camp. Joaquin, Claudio, and one of the gang were outside, watching the trail. Seeing two Anglos approaching, and not knowing who they were, the three bandidos stepped into the road. Brandishing their revolvers, they ordered the Yankees to leave. The two lawmen wheeled their horses and rode away. But as soon as they were out of sight, Buchanan directed Bowen to go back to Marysville and raise a posse. Then he dismounted and crept back to the spot where they had encountered the Mexicans. Joaquin and Claudio were waiting for him. As Sheriff Buchanan bent over to slip through a corral fence, the outlaws fired four times. Three of their pistol balls missed, but one tore into Buchanan's lower back, ripped through his bowels, and exited near the navel. The sheriff was a tough character and yelled out that he had been shot. Bowen heard the gunfire, and then the shout, and galloped back. He found Buchanan desperately wounded and his attackers gone. Constable Bowen waved down a passing buggy and brought the sheriff to a doctor in Marysville. Meanwhile Joaquin and his fellow pistoleros rounded up fresh horses and prepared to flee Sonoran Camp.[11]

Fevered accounts of the shooting quickly arrived in Marysville. One pioneer recalled, "I was stopping at the United States Hotel when, between ten and eleven o'clock, word came into town that Sheriff Buchanan had been shot and was dead at the Mexican camp on the Yuba River. The news spread rapidly through the city, and every saddle horse or conveyance of any kind that could be used was in demand. It was a wild night in Marysville." As citizen posses quickly formed, a storekeeper provided pistols and rifles to those volunteers who were unarmed. The possemen surrounded and searched Sonoran Camp, then scoured the brush along the west side of the Yuba River. Soon they were joined by reinforcements from Marysville, and they crossed the river and began beating through a dense thicket of chaparral. Joaquin and his compadres were concealed in the brush, and when two possemen closed in, the bandidos fired a single shot. The manhunters quickly retreated, and the outlaws vanished.[12]

A Marysville newspaper editor who took part in the manhunt was quick to criticize the actions of the posse. "It was then

Marysville, with the Yuba River in the foreground, as it looked when Joaquin Murrieta and Claudio Feliz saw it in 1851. *Library of Congress*

deemed futile to enter the chaparral with so few men, as the Mexicans had a decided advantage from its extent and thickness. It was determined therefore to keep a strict guard on the outskirts of the wood, and wait for morning, and a reinforcement from the city sufficient to scour the whole chaparral. Matters continued in this state until some time after sunrise, when an express came into town for more men. Our citizens did not by any means turn out in the strength they should have done, though it was just as well as it happened, for when the reinforcement of about twenty-five men arrived at the chaparral, they found that those left to guard it had come away! Thus, when we might have had this desperate band of cutthroats in our grasp, they were allowed to escape from their hiding places. We do not hesitate to say that this business has been managed in the most boy-like and ridiculous manner, and we only regret, for ourself, that we were out all night and a large portion of the next day, without a moment's rest, only to find upon returning to the chaparral, after coming with a friend into town for more assistance, that all our labor and trouble had been in vain, because those who should have had control of the actions on the ground, had by mismanagement frittered away their and our time."[13]

Murrieta and the gang did not know that the man they shot was the sheriff, but they were sure that they had murdered him. As Claudio later related, "By killing an American, we made our escape, by swimming the river Yuba with our horses—followed by the Americans. At the Sacramento River we abandoned our horses, to secure our escape. As soon as we had passed the Sacramento, we went to a stable and stole seven horses. On the road we met a cart with provisions; we took what we wanted and then destroyed a great portion. Farther on the road we fell in with another wagon, which had [gun]powder, of which we took and laid a train and blew up the wagon, together with what was in it; the owner was not present."[14]

While Joaquin and the rest fled south, Sacramento officers arrested four suspects—three Mexicans and one Native American—in the town's El Dorado Saloon. They brought the four men into court and accused them of the Yuba County murders. However, the local judge, known as the recorder, found that the evidence against them was weak, and he released one of the men. The other three were taken to Marysville, where Sheriff Buchanan, from his sickbed, said that he recognized them as the desperadoes who had shot at him. The editor of the *Marysville Express* complained, "The leader of the bloody gang was turned loose by the recorder of Sacramento. He was the bloodiest villain of the crowd. We trust he will yet be caught by those who know how to keep him." But one Anglo in Sacramento who knew the arrested suspects sent an outraged letter in response, which was published in the *Sacramento Union*. "Those Spaniards are the most harmless looking set of men that could possibly be got together, and the 'bloodiest villain' of them all is one of the most quiet citizens of this city. He has been and is now living in quiet felicity with his senorita, and he can be found at any time after five minutes notice. The Indian is nothing more than a simple vaquero . . . which fact was communicated to the police here by several gentlemen, two of whom saw him engaged there at his business at the very time those murders were committed. Of the others, one is so nearly dead with the consumption that the vigilantes, in suspending him to a limb, would only rob the grave of its legitimate prey."[15]

Sheriff Buchanan, whose wounds were thought to be fatal, began to recover. His doctor announced, "You may bet on Buck now." A Marysville journalist reported, "His recovery will come nearer a miracle than anything we have heard of . . . He still lives to lend his efficient aid in ridding this community of the bands of murderers, cutthroats, robbers, and thieves which at present infect it." Buchanan was able to go to Butte County, where the arrested men were held on murder charges. After looking them over again more closely, he decided that his identification was wrong. The four prisoners were released. By that time, the real killers were long gone.[16]

Claudio said later that he and the gang rode south to Calaveras County. There a bloody raid took place at Turnersville, near Campo Seco—not to be confused with the mining town of the same name in Tuolumne County. A band of Mexican outlaws, knives flashing and pistols flaming, attacked a tent occupied by four American miners. Not long before, one of the Yankee gold seekers had foolishly boasted of striking pay dirt. The robbers killed two of the miners and wounded the other two, then looted the tent. One of the bandidos was quickly caught. Before he died at the end of a lynch mob's rope, he confessed and declared that an American had put them up to it the day before. He said that the American had then watched the murders from his hiding place in the nearby brush. Newspapers would later repeatedly accuse Joaquin Murrieta and his gang of the Turnersville murders. But Joaquin's participation was impossible. The raid took place on the night November 14, 1851, just two days after the shooting of Sheriff Buchanan. The band could not have traveled on foot to Sacramento, stolen horses, robbed two wagon drivers, and then ridden horseback, all on a hundred-mile journey from Marysville, in time to plan and carry out the Turnersville raid.[17]

A few years later, Three Fingered Jack would often be described as the most bloodthirsty member of Murrieta's gang. According to myth, he reveled in stabbing and clubbing his victims, then slitting their throats. But in the mountains above Marysville, it was Joaquin, the Feliz brothers, and Manuel Pena who robbed and murdered the six victims, all of whom they repeatedly stabbed to death. Such butchery is consistent with Three Fingered Jack's violent mutilation of Thomas Cowie and George Fowler during the Bear Flag Revolt. But Three Fingered Jack had nothing to do with those six murders. The butchery in the mountains north of Marysville showed that Joaquin Murrieta, Claudio Feliz, and Reyes Feliz were just as murderous as Three Fingered Jack.

Joaquin had participated in his first known murders, and he and his compadres had succeeded in committing one of the bloodiest bandit raids of the Western frontier. They knew better than to linger in the Northern Mines. The four desperadoes made a long ride, through driving winter rains in the San Joaquin Valley and snow flurries in the Sierra foothills, to their old haunts in the Southern Mines. Joaquin Murrieta had taken his first and inexorable steps down the outlaw trail.

CHAPTER 8

SEDUCED BY THE DEVIL

Claudio Feliz enjoyed boasting of the gang's violent exploits. Of their return to the Southern Mines, he declared, "We then went to the Calaveras, where we were attacked by the Americans. One of our party, Manuel Pena, a Sonoran, was wounded, who we brought away with us on horseback. We then went to the camp of Sonora, but were driven off by the Americans." In Sonora the band split up. Joaquin Murrieta stayed behind in the mining country, probably to wager his share of the loot on the monte tables. Claudio, accompanied by several other desperadoes, rode across the Coast Range to San Francisco Bay. "We then came to San Jose," Claudio later recalled. He felt comfortable returning to San Jose, for no one suspected him of leading the violent raids there earlier that year. [1]

The future capital of Silicon Valley was a thriving adobe town with many Latino residents, located just south of San Francisco Bay and surrounded by the vast Santa Clara Valley. The Coast Range stood to the east, the Santa Cruz Mountains to the west, and the foothills of both were blanketed with wild oats and grazing cattle. Well-cultivated vineyards and orchards—for which the Santa Clara Valley would later become famous—had started to appear, and the town was connected to San Francisco by stagecoaches and bay steamboats. San Jose was growing quickly and served as a supply center for gold seekers on their way to the mines.

For Claudio and his fellow bandidos, San Jose's social life was just as engaging as that of the mining camps. One Anglo who visited by steamship from San Francisco remarked, "The town was more than usually thronged with visitors, either to witness or to mingle in the sports of the native Californians and Mexicans. Feats of horsemanship, in the main street, occupied the early part of the evening. Graceful evolutions, dashing leaps through bonfires, impetuous speed and almost instantaneous halts, performed by expert caballeros, and well worthy of 'the ring'—amused the lookers-on until the hour came for the commencement of the fandangos. Of those there were several in various parts of the town, and we visited two of them, rather in the capacity of auditors than as actors. They were singular medleys of old and young: dark eyed and gaily dressed senoritas, brisk but rustic looking 'sparks' [beaus], girls and boys of ten and twelve, elderly dons with broad sombreros, mothers with babes in their arms, seated around the room, and encouraging the merry dancers by their glances of approval . . . The rooms, though large, were redolent with the perfume of the delicate cigaritos, smoked by both sexes, and by the senoritas of sweet sixteen as well as those of riper age. Orchestras of violins, flutes, harps, lutes, and guitars enlivened the hour with some of the most sweetly flowing and plaintive Spanish airs we have heard, and completed the impression of freshness and novelty to which the scene gave rise."[2]

But Claudio Feliz was not in the pueblo just to enjoy the fandangos and the music and the senoritas. "We hovered about San Jose for the purpose of trying to murder the marshal, Mr. Whitman," he later admitted. Two months earlier, on October 5, 1851, George N. Whitman, San Jose's city marshal, had led a five-man posse to the New Almaden quicksilver mine to serve an arrest warrant. The New Almaden, situated in the tall hills fifteen miles south of San Jose, was one of the biggest in California. It employed more than two hundred miners, most of them Latino. They mined quicksilver, or mercury, essential in gold mining because it was used to separate gold from ore. The New Almaden and its adjacent miners' village, then and for several decades afterward, would serve as the hideout for many desperadoes. The New Almaden was described by a journalist who visited in 1851. "At this mine a large number of furnaces are in operation. These furnaces resemble in appearance a long steam boiler, set in brick, with fires underneath. The cinnabar, or quicksilver ore, is thrown into the boiler, where it is left from thirty to forty hours, by which time it is smelted, and the quicksilver, in a fluid state is drawn off in vessels . . . The mine is worked by Mexicans and Chileans, who carry the ore in rawhide sacks, upon their shoulders, from the bottom of the vein to the opening above, a distance of between three and four hundred feet."[3]

City Marshal Whitman and his posse had galloped up to the New Almaden mine on horseback. Their sudden arrival alarmed some of the desperadoes and their miner friends. As the possemen approached, a band of gun-toting Latino miners opened fire on them, but their shots went wild. Other miners, from perches on the hilltops, pelted the posse with stones, bloodying Whitman and one of his men. But the marshal refused to retreat. The man they wanted finally surrendered to Whitman's posse, and they took him to jail in San Jose. The possemen, probably because they were outnumbered, did not try to arrest the assailants who shot at them.[4]

Claudio apparently knew some of the New Almaden miners. At the fandango halls in San Jose, he heard their story of the affair and sympathized with them. Though not involved in the scrape with the posse, the young bandido thirsted for revenge against Marshal Whitman. His gang members in San Jose included the Anglo ruffian, Bellamy, and the Mexican desperado known as Trinidad, both of whom had taken part in the theft of the large herd of horses and mules that the band had sold in

Marysville. Claudio began planning the murder of Whitman, but Trinidad told them that he wanted nothing to do with killing a law officer. As Claudio later declared, "He threatened to deliver us to the authorities." Instead of attacking Marshal Whitman, Claudio turned his vengeance on Trinidad. On the night of December 14, 1851, Claudio and Bellamy found Trinidad at a fandango in the United States Saloon in San Jose. They killed him on the spot and fled, but a Californio named Julian revealed the outlaws' hiding place. Claudio and Bellamy were promptly captured and lodged in San Jose's jail.[5]

Known to Latinos as the *calabozo*, and to Anglos as the calaboose, the jail was a crumbling adobe building that dated from the Mexican era. It was located on Market Plaza, now called Plaza de Cesar Chavez, in downtown San Jose. Numerous prisoners had escaped from it over the years. The inmates were kept in a single room, which had a long chain that ran along the floor and was bolted to opposite walls. They were guarded by a deputy sheriff who was the sole jailer. At night the prisoners were each manacled to the long chain. Claudio found himself ironed to a young man named Teodor Vasquez. He had emigrated from Sonora, Mexico, earlier that year, leaving his wife and children behind in the city of Hermosillo. Before long, young Vasquez found himself riding with several dangerous bandidos, among them the notorious Francisco "Pancho" Daniel and his brother, Bernardo. The Daniel brothers, both in their early twenties, also hailed from Sonora, and were two of the deadliest outlaws of the gold rush. The leader of the two was Pancho—tall, handsome, and light-complected. His nickname was El Guero—"the Blonde."

Teodor Vasquez later confessed that he had first met the Daniel brothers in San Jose. He said that they "invited me in their company to pass the winter with them. They told me that if I would join them, I should not be lacking in anything necessary for my subsistence. They asked me to join them in stealing, to which I consented." Vasquez explained that Pancho and Bernardo Daniel boasted of robbing an Anglo in Los Angeles, taking $7,000 and nine horses. Hugely impressed, young Vasquez accepted the Daniels' offer and began riding with them. He later revealed that the brothers stole mules in San Juan Bautista and tried to rob the nearby rancho of Francisco Pacheco, but, as he recalled, they "were driven away by the force of arms." Finally Bernardo Daniel robbed and murdered a fellow Mexican in the Livermore Valley, east of San Francisco Bay. Vasquez said that when Pancho Daniel learned what his brother he had done, "he became angry, and reprimanded Bernardo, and separated from his company." Pancho Daniel rode back to Los Angeles, where he was destined to have misadventures with both Joaquin Murrieta and Salomon Pico.[6]

Teodor Vasquez stayed behind in San Jose, where he began stealing horses. The youth was captured twice, but each time, he managed to escape. Then, late in 1851, Vasquez entered a store in Santa Clara, just north of San Jose, and purloined a coat and a serape. He was arrested and sentenced to a $15 fine and twenty-five lashes with a rawhide whip. The court interpreter, however, falsely told him that he would get two hundred lashes. While in jail awaiting his punishment, Vasquez met another prisoner, Jose Cheverino. He was the same young desperado who had ridden with Claudio in the Blue Tent and Chabolla raids earlier that year. Cheverino had been jailed in San Jose for knifing a man. As Vasquez recalled, "He told me that if my case was for two hundred lashes, his punishment would certainly be death—that he would be hung for having stabbed a man with a knife. He then wished me to break jail with him. I asked if it could be done. He told me he had a knife in his boot, and with it we misplaced the windows and escaped."[7]

Vasquez later said that Cheverino bragged of robbing and murdering an Indian, and after their jailbreak, Cheverino tried to get him to rustle livestock. "He also advised me to go with him to San Francisco, steal horses, and sell them there, when I escaped with him from prison, which I would not consent to. I told him my intention was to return home as quick as possible." Vasquez, however, did not go to back to Mexico, and instead hid out in San Jose. At the same time, Cheverino continued down the outlaw trail. Six months later, in May 1852, he and another desperado appeared in the Mother Lode country. They attacked two Frenchmen while they slept in their tent near the mining camp of Jackson. Cheverino and his partner stabbed the men to death, then looted the tent. The pair was quickly captured, and an enraged mob dragged them to a large oak tree on Jackson's main street and lynched them both. Two men had already been hanged there a year earlier, and the big oak was destined to become the most famous hanging tree of the California gold rush.[8]

Teodor Vasquez, for his part, soon found himself back in the San Jose calaboose. In mid-December 1851, he was arrested for horse theft. He was only behind bars a day or two before Claudio and Bellamy, charged with murdering Trinidad, joined him in the adobe jail. Claudio became friendly with Vasquez and openly boasted of his many thefts and murders. Once again young Vasquez was impressed, and he listened carefully to all the gory details. One day a lawman came to the jail and looked over Vasquez carefully. As the young outlaw later recalled, "During the time I was in prison, there was a person [who] came to see me. He took my measure and looked at my hands to see if any of my fingers were cut, and into my face to see if it was cut. He became satisfied that I was not the person he was looking for. Claudio told me afterwards that I was measured in a mistake, thinking I was his brother Reyes, because on the river Yuba we murdered six Americans." Claudio, of course, was referring to the men they had robbed and killed in Yuba and Butte counties.[9]

Claudio Feliz was in the old jail less than two weeks before he saw a chance to escape. He used a concealed knife to saw through his chains, which were made of the soft iron so common in that era. As Vasquez explained, "Claudio, at the time he was cutting his chains off, said that it would be well to kill the sheriff, which I, Teodor, would not consent to. I told him I would not take away the life of anyone, but if I could make my escape I would. Claudio had a club and a pocket knife. He said he would stun him and afterwards cut his throat." The iron bars in the jail windows were loosely inserted into the adobe wall, and Claudio easily dug them out with his knife. The bandido then climbed through a window and vanished while Vasquez remained behind. Whether Vasquez was unable to remove his chains or decided to stay and seek mercy from the court, only he knew.[10]

A few days later, on Christmas Eve, Teodor Vasquez stood trial for horse theft. He was defended by two Anglo attorneys, and the jury deliberated only twenty minutes before finding him guilty of grand larceny. The jurors, applying the same new law that had condemned Mountain Jim and Dutch Fred, sentenced him to death. As Vasquez stood solemnly in court, the judge intoned, "It is therefore considered by the court that the said defendant be taken to the jail of this county, from whence he came, and from there be taken to the place of execution on the 31st day of January, A.D. 1852, between the hours of ten o'clock a.m. and three o'clock p.m. and there be hanged by the neck until dead."[11]

Vasquez broke down. A San Jose newspaperman who covered the trial reported, "The prisoner was deeply affected when the verdict was interpreted to him." He later asked that some money be sent to his wife and children in Mexico, and requested paper and pen so he could write a letter to his brothers. Vasquez also dictated a long confession, not only admitting his own crimes with Pancho Daniel and other outlaws but also providing a detailed and accurate rendering of the many thefts and murders of which Claudio Feliz had boasted. His confession received very

San Jose's main business street in 1851, with modern two story buildings near the old adobes. *California Historical Society*

little publicity, published in the San Jose newspaper and one other California journal and then quickly forgotten.

During the gold rush era, there was no automatic right of appeal to the California Supreme Court from a sentence of capital punishment. As a result, on the fatal day of January 30, 1852, the county sheriff took Vasquez from jail and marched him to the nearby gallows in Market Plaza. A large crowd gathered to watch his execution. As a San Jose newsman observed, "Whilst on the scaffold he spoke for nearly half an hour, advising his friends and all others to take example from his early and ignominious death, and pursue a more honest and upright course than he had." The sheriff then fastened the noose around his neck, tied his hands behind his back, and released the trap. Vasquez plunged down, and within five minutes, he was dead.[12]

Claudio Feliz was hardly fazed by the public hanging of Teodor Vasquez. Instead of fleeing from San Jose's rough justice, he stayed for a brief time in the Santa Clara Valley and avoided detection. His goal was simple: he wanted to find Julian, the

Californio who had given him up to the law officers. As Vasquez explained in his confession, "Claudio told me that as soon as he got clear I should hear of the murder of a Californian named Julian, the one that informed on him. He was determined to kill him." Claudio found Julian a few miles outside San Jose, murdered him, and concealed the body. The dead man was not discovered until three months later. After the coroner held an inquest, a San Jose journalist reported that "the body found is the person mentioned in the confession of Vasquez." But by then, Claudio Feliz had fled back to the Southern Mines.[13]

Meanwhile Joaquin Murrieta may have engaged in bloodletting of his own in San Jose. According to a story from John Rollin Ridge, Joaquin showed up in the adobe pueblo and got into a brawl at a fandango. A deputy sheriff named Clark arrested Murrieta and took him to court, where the judge fined him $12. When the deputy walked him home to get the money, Joaquin whipped out a concealed knife and stabbed the officer to death. Ridge's account was based on an actual event, but he got the names wrong. On March 4, 1852, a month after Vasquez was hanged, San Jose officers arrested a Mexican who called himself Pedro Montemayor for assaulting a woman in San Jose. The town mayor, who doubled as judge, found him guilty and ordered Montemayor to pay a fine. Charles H. "Buckskin" Smith, a deputy city marshal, or police officer, escorted the prisoner out of the court to a nearby house, where Montemayor said he could get his money. In the era of rudimentary pioneer policing, Smith failed to handcuff his man or to search him for weapons.

The two walked a short distance toward the adobe homes near the town's *acequia*, or irrigation ditch. It was lined with willow trees and situated just west of modern-day St. James Park in downtown San Jose. As they stepped along the ditch, Montemayor suddenly whipped out a knife and plunged it into Smith's heart. Nearby, three stunned Latina women looked on as Montemayor fled into the willows and vanished. Buckskin

Smith, bleeding heavily, lived but a minute. A large posse rode out in search of the killer, but they never found him. The women testified before the grand jury, which issued a murder indictment in the florid legal language of the era: "The said Pedro Montemayor, not having the fear of God before his eyes, but being moved and seduced by the instigations of the Devil, on or about the 4th day of March, in and upon one Charles H. Smith then and there feloniously, willfully, and of malice aforethought" killed Deputy Marshal Smith. Later, as we will see, evidence surfaced that the man who called himself Pedro Montemayor may well have been Joaquin Murrieta. Either way, his victim was the first San Jose police officer killed in the line of duty. Today Buckskin Smith's murder is totally forgotten, and his name does not appear on any California law enforcement memorial. And if his killer was indeed Joaquin, given the assault in San Jose, it was not the first time Murrieta had abused a woman.[14]

A month later, Murrieta first appeared as the chief of his own robber band in the gold fields. Instead of partnering with Claudio and Reyes Feliz, he was accompanied by two other desperadoes whose names are unknown. On April 4, 1852, the trio stole several horses near Ione, a small mining camp in what later became Amador County. One of the animals was a valuable saddle horse taken from the pasture of Judge Henry A. Carter, a lawyer and gold seeker. Then Joaquin and his compadres rode eight miles north through the brush-covered hills to the small settlement of Willow Springs. It was situated in a cluster of scrub oak on the wagon road, now State Highway 16, that led through a broad valley from the mines to Sacramento, thirty-five miles west. Several stagecoach lines had been established from Sacramento into the Mother Lode, and Willow Springs boasted a stage stop and hotel owned by James Clark. That evening Joaquin and his bandidos dismounted in front of the hotel. They hitched their horses to a fence, stepped inside, and ordered supper.

By this time, Judge Carter and a comrade, James Corcoran, had tracked the outlaws and the stolen animals north to Willow Springs. As Carter and Corcoran approached the stage stop, they spotted the judge's horse hitched in front. Carter stepped inside and asked the station keeper, James Clark, to point out the man who had been riding his stolen mount. Clark gestured toward the dining room where Joaquin and the other two were eating. All three were armed with pistols. According to an early account, Clark "was a powerful and daring man." He immediately volunteered to arrest the culprits, then strode boldly into the dining room. At the same time, James Corcoran took up a position at the back door, armed only with an axe.

Clark walked up to Joaquin Murrieta, put one hand on his shoulder, and announced, "You are my prisoner."

"I think not," Joaquin declared in English. At the same time, one of his men, sitting across the table, jerked his six-shooter and fired at Clark. The bullet missed, and the hotelkeeper dove for cover. Inside the kitchen, the hotel's African American cook, B.F. Moore, was busy at work. Moore reacted instantly to the gunfire. He grabbed a rifle inside the kitchen and burst into the dining room. The Mexican spotted him and fired a second time, directly at Moore. But the outlaw was a poor shot and missed his man. It was a fatal mistake. Moore swung up his rifle, and with its muzzle just five inches from the target, squeezed the trigger. The heavy slug tore off the top of the pistolero's head. He crumpled to the floor, instantly killed.

Joaquin and the other desperado raced out of the hotel and took cover behind a tree. At the same time, Judge Carter and two bystanders fled in terror. Clark and Corcoran were made from a different cloth, and they burst out the front door in pursuit of the bandidos. From the cover of the tree, Joaquin and his compadre opened a volley of fire, striking the hotelkeeper James Clark in the head and killing him instantly. B.F. Moore rushed to their aid, but his single-shot rifle was empty. Joaquin's partner whipped out his knife and charged at Moore, who responded by clubbing the ruffian in the shoulder with his rifle butt. The desperado staggered and dropped his knife. At that, Moore raced back into the dining room and grabbed a six-shooter from the body of the dead bandit. Just as Moore exited the building, the outlaw swung into his saddle and started to spur his horse. Moore raised the pistol, thumbed back the hammer and took dead aim. He squeezed the trigger, and the heavy slug ripped into the bandido's back, tearing him out of the saddle. But Joaquin Murrieta was still game. He immediately returned the fire, emptying his revolver at Moore and Corcoran and wounding the latter man in the thigh. This left Joaquin with only one weapon—his trusty reata. As Moore took cover behind the corner of the house, Joaquin rushed forward, swinging his reata and attempting to lasso him. But fearing Moore's pistol, Murrieta then retreated, loaded his wounded partner onto a horse, and galloped off.

A large manhunt was quickly organized, but no trace of the outlaws could be found. When a San Francisco newspaper gave an incorrect account of the affair and failed to give credit to Moore for his courage, a local Anglo wrote to the *Sacramento Union* in defense of the black cook: "Had the other men shown the bravery displayed by Moore, the Spaniards would both have been caught. Moore having acted in such a manner, it is due to him to make a correct statement of the facts." Two weeks later, a man named Joaquin was arrested in Jackson and accused of being one of the outlaws who killed James Clark. The local newspaper, the *Calaveras Chronicle*, reported, "He was taken to the Willow Springs where it was thought summary punishment would be dealt out to him." But the suspect was not Joaquin Murrieta, and there was no report of anyone being lynched, so the arrest was most likely a case of mistaken identity.[15]

By then rumors had begun to spread in Sonora and Columbia that Claudio Feliz was the leader of a bandit gang. One day after the murder of James Clark, Claudio and his brother Reyes "smelt powder" near the mining camp of Humbug, three miles west of Sonora. The brothers, with several other pistoleros, were loitering in Humbug when Constable John Leary rode in with a small posse from Columbia and nearby Sawmill Flat. Leary was a highly capable and popular lawman; six years later, he and a fellow officer would be murdered by outlaws in Columbia. Leary and his posse were apparently hunting for Claudio, but the ever alert constable soon spotted Reyes Feliz wearing a distinctive pair of pistols that had been reported stolen a year earlier. He placed the teenaged Feliz under arrest, then mounted up and started toward Columbia with his prisoner. Constable Leary was accompanied by several armed Anglos, including Caleb Dorsey, a Harvard-educated lawyer who ran a lumber mill at Sawmill Flat. Claudio quickly learned of the arrest. Determined to free his brother, Claudio and his men leaped onto their horses and galloped across the brush-covered hills. They managed to circle around Leary's posse and waited to ambush them. As the possemen approached, Claudio and the rest opened fire, but they were outgunned. Constable Leary and his riders returned the shots with a barrage of six-gun fire, killing one of the desperadoes and badly wounding Claudio with several bullets to his midsection.

The bloodied young bandit chieftain reeled in his saddle, then spurred his horse up a nearby hillside in an effort to escape. Constable Leary and Caleb Dorsey followed closely, revolvers in hand. Claudio managed to swing up a brace of six-shooters and open fire, but he was so weak, he fell from his horse. Sprawling on the brushy ground, he emptied both pistols at the manhunters. His wounds prevented him from shooting straight. Leary, seeing that the outlaw's weapons were now useless, rushed toward the prostrate pistolero. He slammed the barrel of his cocked revolver against Claudio's head. As Dorsey later said, "The constable was about to blow the youth's brains out." But before Leary could fire, Dorsey shoved the gun away and saved

Caleb Dorsey in later years. He helped capture Claudio Feliz near Columbia in 1852. *Lynn Roberts at www.pcgenweb.com*

Claudio's life. During the excitement and confusion, Reyes Feliz managed to escape.

Leary and his posse brought the gutshot Claudio into Sonora for medical treatment. His wounds were patched up, and the next day, they took him to Columbia for a court hearing before Joseph Carly, the town's justice of the peace. Carly, who was notorious for the poor grammar and spelling in his court records, dipped his pen and scribbled the title of the case: "The Peapple of the State of California vs. Claria Farlia." He may have butchered Claudio's name, but he got the facts right. "The above named Defendant was brought before me this 6th day of April, 1852, by John Leary, Constable, charged with Stealing two Pistols. The said Pistols was stolen about one year since. And also an Attempt to rescue a Prisoner from a Publick officer, and Shooting at Said officer. The said Defendant is in my charge. I would further request the Court of Sessions to Order the said Prisoner before the Grand Jeury as soon as Convenient. The Defendant is Badly Wounded."

Claudio was held in the Sonora jail pending action by the grand jury. He had a strong constitution and began to recover from his gunshot wounds. On May 3, the county sheriff noted in his fee book that he had paid $100 for Claudio's medical care. Because communication in the gold rush was so slow and rudimentary, the law officers in Sonora had no idea that Claudio was wanted for murder and jailbreaking in San Jose. Nor did they know about the published confession of Teodor Vasquez, with the details of Claudio's many robberies and murders. As a result, the teenage bandit chieftain stayed locked up in the county jail to await his trial. If Sonora's vigilantes had known his history, they surely would have tried to lynch him.[16]

Years later, Caleb Dorsey claimed that Joaquin Murrieta was one of the men who attacked Constable Leary and his posse. As Dorsey related, "Joaquin himself took a hand in the fight, and although shot at repeatedly, made his escape." However, that was most improbable, because just a day earlier, Murrieta was more than fifty miles north, taking part in the murder of James Clark at Willow Springs. He did return to the Southern Mines, however. Only three weeks after Claudio was shot, Joaquin became the main suspect in yet another robbery-murder.[17]

Two brothers, Allen and John Ruddle, had a cattle ranch in the San Joaquin Valley, on the Merced River about six miles west of the town of Snelling, and forty-five miles south of Sonora. The Ruddles were both forty-niners from Missouri, and when they failed to find gold, they took to ranching. Allen, the eldest, was twenty-seven, and John was five years younger. Their parents had also emigrated to California and settled on a nearby ranch with several adult children and three black slaves. Allen Ruddle loved the gold rush frontier. In an 1850 letter to another brother in Missouri, he offered both caution and praise for California. "I should not advise you to attempt to reach it with your family by the overland route. No, if you are to start for California and do not want your patience worn threadbare or more so, do not embark on the plains with a wagon. Such a journey will do for the old men and adventurous ladies to talk of, but it takes young men to perform it without considerable risk of dying. It is our opinion, we may be wrong, that no country ever held out such inducements to emigrants as California does. Its famous gold mines, its fertile valleys, its very healthy climate, and its commercial position are advantages never so admirably combined with so few objections by any new country ever yet discovered."

The ranch house of Allen and John Ruddle was a primitive cabin with old shipping crates serving as table and chairs. On the morning of April 26, 1852, Allen announced to his brother that he was "tired of sitting on boxes," and he intended to go to Stockton, sixty miles north, to buy some real furniture. He hitched up a team of oxen to his wagon and, carrying several hundred dollars in gold dust, started out. But Ruddle didn't get far. Four miles north of Snelling, he was waylaid. Bandits swung a lasso around his neck, shot him in the head and the chest, and robbed him of his gold. The killers drove his wagon off the road, unhitched the oxen, and galloped away with their booty.[18]

About an hour later, a forty-niner named Sam Ward, mounted on horseback, came trotting down the road on his way to Stockton. As he recalled, "Shortly after striking the main road, about four miles beyond Snelling's, I noticed the track of a wagon, which had been abruptly turned off from the highway into the grass on the left towards the river. There were also marks of horses' hoofs in the turf, which grew into a hillock some twenty feet high on the right, its summit not more than thirty yards from the roadside. It struck me as a capital spot for an ambuscade, and I intuitively loosened the revolver in my belt, and kept 'my eyes skinned' until I again reached level ground." Ward continued a few miles up the road, then stopped to eat at a wayside inn. He said that while sitting at the dinner table, "A rider

Allen Ruddle. Joaquin Murrieta, Reyes Feliz, and Pedro Gonzales were the prime suspects in his murder.
William B. Secrest collection

dashed up to the house and announced the startling news that a teamster had been shot upon the road that afternoon, robbed of six hundred dollars in gold dust, and his wagon driven into a clump of brushwood two miles from the road and there left with his corpse in it."[19]

Soon the team of oxen was found, and then Allen Ruddle's body. Local settlers formed a posse and began hunting the killers. They followed their tracks forty miles west to Hills Ferry, where the Merced River flows into the San Joaquin. Just as the possemen rode up, they spotted their quarry—three Mexicans—swimming their horses across the San Joaquin River. The manhunters' animals were exhausted from their hard ride, so the posse obtained fresh mounts from a nearby rancher. But by that time, the outlaws had vanished. Because there were no witnesses to Allen Ruddle's murder, the killers could not be positively identified. Soon, however, Joaquin Murrieta, Reyes Feliz, and a desperado named Pedro Gonzales became the prime suspects. Claudio Feliz could not have participated, because he was still recovering from his wounds in the Sonora jail. A large reward, probably posted by Ruddle's father, was offered for the unknown culprits.[20]

Joaquin and his compadres occasionally hid out at the camps of the *mesteneros*, or mustang hunters, in the San Joaquin Valley. Prior to the gold rush, herds of wild horses roamed the vast and fertile plains of the great valley, which spans Central California from the Sierra Nevada foothills west to the Coast Range. Following the discovery of gold, enterprising Mexicans and Californios began rounding up the animals and selling them in the horse markets at Stockton, Sacramento, and Marysville. Because so many forty-niners had journeyed west by ship, they had no saddle animals. This created a huge market for horses in the mining region. Some of the mesteneros were simply horse thieves, but most were honest men who worked hard to catch, break, and sell the wild mustangs.

The first news of the Ruddle killers came on May 5, 1852, nine days after the murder. A correspondent at Fort Miller on the San Joaquin River reported, "There is a body of Mexicans down the river about thirty miles, in a very secret camp, almost invisible, who have a large number of tame animals, report says nearly a hundred. They number between twenty and thirty, and no doubt their scouts are out continually, and that is the grand depot of stolen animals in all this section of country. It is also supposed that the two Mexicans who shot young Ruddle, a week ago, have taken refuge in this camp. There are about thirty men, in different parties, in pursuit of the murderers, and they will not escape apprehension, as they are known."[21]

But Joaquin, if he was indeed one of the killers, returned to his old stomping grounds in Stockton. On May 22, 1852, three weeks after the Allen Ruddle murder, Murrieta attended a Saturday night dance in a Stockton fandango hall. He was accompanied by one of his gang, Jose Barrillo, a twenty-six-year-old *mestizo*—part Californio and part Native American. Barrillo, who later confessed to three murders, was a dangerous ruffian whose body was covered with scars from knife and bullet wounds. Inside the fandango house, Murrieta and Barrillo paid little attention to the guitars, the singing, and the dancing senoritas. They scanned the crowd and soon spotted a Mexican desperado with whom Barrillo had quarreled the night before. He and Barrillo confronted each other and exchanged heated words. Barrillo later said that the Mexican insulted him, and Joaquin then ordered him to kill the man. Barrillo needed no encouragement. He stepped into the front doorway so that he could easily make an escape. Then, pulling his pistol, he fired one shot at his enemy. But Barrillo's aim was as bad as his judgment. The ball crashed into the skull of William W. Janes, an inoffensive Canadian who was sitting on a bench near the targeted Mexican. Barrillo sprang from the doorway and fled down the street with several bystanders in pursuit. They fired six times at him, without effect. A manhunt swung into action, but Barrillo escaped. The next day, William Janes died from his wound.[22]

Joaquin slipped away, unsuspected, and his involvement in this murder would not become public for another year. He left Stockton and rejoined Reyes Feliz and Pedro Gonzales. Feliz later admitted that they rode to a Mexican's ranch on Orestimba Creek, near its confluence with the San Joaquin River, about fifty miles south of Stockton. There the outlaws stole a herd of twenty horses and headed south for Los Angeles, where they intended to sell them. During the next week, they rode down the San Joaquin Valley, stopping regularly at creeks and watering holes so the grass-fed mustangs could drink and graze on the lush tule growth. After a 230-mile ride, they finally reached Tejon Pass, the gateway to Southern California. Today known as Old Tejon Pass, it was situated about twenty miles northeast of modern-day Tejon Pass on Interstate 5 where it cuts through the Tehachapi Mountains. The Grapevine route that passes through current Tejon Pass was not surveyed until 1853 and would not become widely used until the construction of Fort Tejon, a US Army post, in 1854.

During the gold rush, the Stockton–Los Angeles wagon road was the main route into Southern California. It crossed the Tehachapis on winding trails and through deep canyons in Old Tejon Pass. From the 5,300-foot-high pass, the road dropped down into San Francisquito Canyon and then proceeded another fifty miles to Los Angeles. Near Old Tejon Pass was the home of Jose Zapatero, chief of the Tejon Indians. Chief Zapatero and his tribe lived in a village of dome-shaped houses made of willows and thatched with tule reeds.

Joaquin and his riders did not know that they were being followed. The Mexican ranchero at Orestimba Creek had discovered the loss of his horses, and he tracked Murrieta's little band south. Suspecting that the outlaws were trying to reach Los Angeles, he headed them off and rode directly to Old Tejon Pass, where he warned Chief Zapatero. It was early June when Joaquin, Feliz, and Gonzales drove their stolen herd into the pass. Zapatero and his men were waiting for them. As Murrieta and his compadres approached, Zapatero's warriors covered them with bows, arrows, and rifles. The desperadoes found themselves outmanned and outgunned.

The Indians quickly captured the three horse thieves and seized the stolen animals. As Reyes Feliz later said, "There the Indians took some of them from us; others, the owner took, who went in pursuit of us. I don't know his name, he was a Mexican." After retaking the horses, Chief Zapatero let the three outlaws go free. Joaquin Murrieta and Pedro Gonzales continued on to Los Angeles. Reyes Feliz, however, did not accompany them. He recalled, "I was then ill in the Tulares of the effects from bites of a bear." At that time, grizzly bears were common in the Coast Range and even in some parts of the Sierra Nevada, and "the Tulares" was a common name for the San Joaquin Valley. Apparently the grizzly had attacked Feliz after he separated from

Murrieta and Gonzales. His injuries could not have been very severe, for he was soon able to ride back to the camp of Sonora, where he quickly recovered.[23]

By this time, the posses hunting the Allen Ruddle killers had all abandoned the search and returned home, with one exception. A single pair of manhunters simply refused to give up.

CHAPTER 9

THE BATTLES OF SAWMILL FLAT AND SALINAS RIVER

The two riders urged their mustangs forward as they made their way up the long climb into Old Tejon Pass. The leader was burly and physically imposing, with fierce brown eyes, a well-trimmed mustache, and long black hair falling from under his slouch hat. Strapped to his waist was a large bowie knife and a holstered .44-caliber Colt Dragoon revolver, carried butt-forward for a cross-draw. He sported two more six-shooters in a pair of pommel holsters slung down each side of his saddle. Tough and agile, he was in his early forties, an old man by gold rush standards. The pair rode through the grassy hills that towered over the pass, the hot June sun beating down mercilessly on them. The horsemen followed the rough wagon road down San Francisquito Canyon, then into the San Fernando Valley, and finally toward the little adobe pueblo of Los Angeles.

Harry Love rested his right hand on the pommel of his bowie knife as he swayed in the saddle, the Tehachapi Mountains gradually disappearing in the distance behind him. The hundred-mile ride from Old Tejon Pass to Los Angeles was nothing to Love, for he was used to horseback rides many times that distance. But as a boy in New England, he never dreamed that one day he would be a frontiersman, tracking some of the most

Harry Love in 1854.
John Boessenecker collection

dangerous outlaws of the American West. The journey that led him to California had been a long one. He had earned experience as a sailor on distant seas, then won acclaim as a soldier, tracker, express rider, and explorer in Texas and on the Mexican border. After joining the gold rush, Love had prospected with little success in Mariposa County in the Southern Mines. Then he learned that a large reward had been offered for the killers of Allen Ruddle.

In the Southwest, Harry Love had been an expert tracker of Indian warriors and raiders. As one Texas pioneer recalled, "He seemed to know the trail almost intuitively. A crushed blade of grass, or some other slight signal, led him on their track for miles." Soon after the Ruddle murder, Love and a comrade—whose name was never recorded—began hunting the assassins. They heard reports that the killers had been seen at the mustang hunters' camp thirty miles south of Fort Miller. After a long manhunt, they finally picked up the trail of Joaquin Murrieta, Reyes Feliz, Pedro Gonzales, and the stolen horses and followed it into Old Tejon Pass. Love and his partner did not know the names of the thieves they were tracking. They were also unaware that Feliz had split off and returned north after Chief Zapatero seized the herd of horses. Love and his comrade tracked Murrieta and Gonzales into Los Angeles. The manhunters arrived about June 10, 1852, and after several days of searching the adobe pueblo, they learned that Gonzales and another Mexican had left for the picturesque mission town of San Buenaventura, now called Ventura. Love and his companion trailed the two horsemen eighty miles west to the Pacific Coast and caught up with the fugitives at a roadhouse near the Mission San Buenaventura. All four men went for their guns, and a shootout erupted. After a brief exchange of gunfire, Love captured Pedro Gonzales unharmed. His compadre, who may have been Murrieta, fled the scene and vanished.[1]

To prevent Gonzales from escaping, Love forced him to walk on foot toward Los Angeles. Love and his posseman followed on horseback, leading Gonzales's horse behind them. A nine-mile journey brought them to the Santa Clara River, which they crossed. Then they proceeded on toward the old pueblo. Gonzales repeatedly complained of fatigue, but that did not stop him from trying to escape into the brush. Several times he fled off the road, but in each instance, Love and his partner caught the outlaw and resumed their march. They continued another eight miles from the river until they reached a spot below Conejo Mountain, near modern-day Camarillo. Conejo ("Rabbit") Mountain today overlooks Highway 101 and is part of a high ridge situated a mile to the south of the freeway. Tens of thousands of motorists pass by daily, commuting to and from Los Angeles, totally oblivious to the dramatic events that occurred there more than 170 years ago.

Conejo Mountain, where Harry Love shot and killed Pedro Gonzales, partner of Joaquin Murrieta. *Photograph by the author.*

As the riders passed Conejo Mountain, the desperado began complaining of thirst and pointed to a nearby ravine. According to Love, Gonzales told him, "There is plenty of water a little way up."

Harry Love consented to the outlaw's request. He swung down from the saddle and followed Gonzales up the ravine, but the pistolero suddenly broke into a run toward the thick brush. Love tried to give chase, but his heavy riding boots and jangling spurs slowed him down. He drew his heavy Colt .44 and fired once. The bullet slammed into Gonzales's head, and he plunged to the rocky ground, dead. Love and his partner then carried his body back to their horses. The manhunters draped Gonzales's corpse across the saddle of his mustang, then rode into Los Angeles, where they reported the shooting to local officials. Soon after, on June 18, the county coroner held an inquest. Love testified that he had killed Gonzales. He said that "in endeavoring to knock him down with his pistol, [I] accidentally discharged it and shot him through the head, killing him instantly." However, Love's weapon was a single-action revolver, meaning that he had to pull back and cock the hammer with his thumb before it could be fired. That would have required him to strike Gonzales over the head with a cocked revolver, an unlikely scenario. In that era, law officers were allowed to shoot and kill unarmed fleeing felons, a rule that the US Supreme Court did not declare unconstitutional until 1985. Whether or not Love killed Gonzales by accident, the coroner found the shooting to be justifiable. The connection between Pedro Gonzales, Joaquin Murrieta, and Reyes Feliz would not become publicly known for another six months. The two manhunters rode back to Mariposa County, but that would not be the last encounter between Harry Love and Murrieta's gang.[2]

A week after the inquest, a man named Captain William Wilson rode into Los Angeles from his home in Santa Barbara. He knew about Harry Love's manhunt, and of the reward for the killers of Allen Ruddle. Wilson had also learned, probably from Love, that one of the men that Love had been hunting was a Mexican who called himself Jose Botero, and that he was the same man who had killed the deputy city marshal, Buckskin Smith, in San Jose. Harry Love later said that Jose Botero was actually Joaquin Murrieta.

Late on Saturday night, June 26, 1852, Captain Wilson and a friend went to an Indian camp on the outskirts of Los Angeles to watch a game of peon, popular with Native Americans in Southern California. In peon, two teams of four men each held small sticks or bones concealed in one hand, and the opposing team had to guess which fist they were in. The game was often accompanied by singing, as well as wagering on the outcome. A large crowd of Indians and Mexicans, plus a handful of Anglos, were present. As Wilson and a friend wandered through the gathering, illuminated by campfires, he explained that he was on the lookout for the fugitive Jose Botero. At about 1:30 in the morning, Wilson spotted a Mexican, mounted on an iron-gray horse, just outside the crowd. Wilson looked him over carefully for several minutes and saw that he matched Botero's description. The horseman saw Wilson staring at him, and cautiously backed his animal into the darkness. Wilson then turned away, and his friend asked why he was so interested in the rider.

"No matter," Wilson replied. "Only I thought . . ."

He did not finish the sentence, and his friend did not bother to inquire further. About ten minutes later, Wilson was chatting with another acquaintance when the horseman suddenly reappeared and guided his animal through the crowd. Drawing his pistol, the rider took aim and fired once at Wilson. The barrel of his gun was so close to the crowd that the muzzle flash gave one man powder burns in his face. The lead ball slammed into Wilson, who plunged to the ground.

"Gentlemen, I am shot!" he gasped. "I am a dead man."

He then propped himself up with one arm, at the same time pulling his own revolver. Wilson fired one shot at his assailant, but missed. The Mexican wheeled his horse and galloped off into the night. Moments later, Captain Wilson died. Later that day, an inquest took place, and the coroner's jury determined that the killer's name was Jose Botero. Despite the fact that the shooting happened in front of a large crowd, many of the witnesses claimed—probably due to fear—that they did not see the shooter. The *Los Angeles Star* remarked, "It is one of the strangest occurrences of which we have ever heard, and it seems to us that the Indians present should be brought before a Justice, and interrogated in relation to it. It is hardly possible that a man should be shot down in a crowd of persons, and not one among them know it." The *Star* explained that Wilson "had said that if he should find a certain man, he would apprehend him for the sake of the reward. That man was Jose Botero, accused of murder in Mariposa County, and of killing the deputy sheriff [marshal] in San Jose." Whether or not Harry Love was right about Wilson's killer being Joaquin, his surname Botero, albeit misspelled, would later become a major point of controversy in the Murrieta saga.[3]

Although Joaquin was not immediately suspected of Wilson's murder, he nonetheless wasted no time in shaking the dust of Los Angeles from his boots. He started a long, three-hundred-mile ride back to his old stomping grounds near Sonora. By that time, trouble had erupted in the camps of Martinez and Sawmill Flat. Not surprisingly, Claudio Feliz was at the bottom of it. Claudio had remained safely locked in the Sonora jail, where he fully recovered from his gunshot wounds and faced a charge of assault with intent to kill Constable John Leary. Years later Caleb Dorsey, the Tuolumne County pioneer, recalled that Claudio asked him to be his defense attorney and promised that if he won the case, "the whole band should leave the country and go to Mexico, never to return." Dorsey claimed that when he asked for proof that this promise would be kept, Claudio declared, "Sir, you have the word of honor of a highwayman!"

Dorsey also asserted that Claudio sent word of the agreement to Murrieta, who was hiding out near Sonora, and Joaquin agreed to abide by it. Dorsey said that he persuaded the grand jury to dismiss the case against Claudio. But that is not what happened, because Joaquin was then in Southern California. According to the original court record, which does not identify Dorsey or any of the lawyers involved, Claudio stood trial in Sonora on June 8, 1852. The jury consisted of twelve Anglos, and the sole witness against Claudio was Constable Leary. His trial lasted less than a day, including deliberation by the jurors. Then the judge's clerk entered the result into the court minutes: "After the argument of counsel the cause was submitted to the jury, who retired and brought into court the following verdict: We the jury find the prisoner not guilty." Claudio was promptly set free. Though many Anglo jurors of the gold rush harbored racist sentiments against Latinos, it appears that these twelve were not governed by those prejudices. The court record does not reflect why they acquitted Claudio, but perhaps they believed that his painful gunshot wounds were punishment enough.[4]

Claudio, after his release, made his headquarters in Sawmill Flat and began gathering a band of almost a dozen desperadoes. Both he and Murrieta had been long familiar with Sawmill Flat. According to one account written a few years later, Joaquin had frequented Sawmill Flat, where he "was a monte dealer and had a number of villainous scamps connected with him in fleecing his less informed countrymen and others out of their daily earnings." Sawmill Flat was a gold camp with two lumber mills that provided timber for the nearby mines. Home to about a thousand laborers, most of them Latino, it was served by three general stores, three "grog shops" or saloons, a billiard hall, a ten-pin bowling alley, and numerous fandango houses. Just a few hundred yards to the east was the settlement of Martinez, also a favorite haunt of the Feliz brothers and Murrieta. Claudio was eager to exact revenge on the settlers in Sawmill Flat, because some of the possemen who had shot him were from the little gold camp.[5]

Caleb Dorsey was part owner of a lumber mill in Sawmill Flat. He later claimed that he and several others, including a prominent merchant named Ira McRae, decided to capture Joaquin Murrieta. Acting on a tip that he was attending a fandango in Martinez, they stormed inside and ordered a stop to the music. The dancers insisted that Joaquin was not there. Dorsey said that he then "fell into conversation with an ordinary looking Mexican, upon the subject of Joaquin's whereabouts, and was informed with the most charming innocence that it was very foolish to attempt to arrest the brigand, as he would never be taken alive." Dorsey and the others left the fandango empty-handed, but upon returning to Sawmill Flat they were told that the "ordinary looking Mexican" was Joaquin himself. But as we have seen, at that time, Murrieta was still in Southern California. Well-known as a gambler, not a robber, he was not yet a wanted man. The only notorious member of the bandit gang was its leader, Claudio Feliz, and Ira McRae's posse most likely was searching for him.[6]

In Sawmill Flat, Claudio was joined by his brother Reyes, who had recovered from the wounds inflicted by the grizzly bear. They spent much of their time at the card tables inside a pair of large monte tents. Suspicious Anglos quickly concluded that they were part of a band of "Mexican guerrillas." In late June 1852, just two weeks after Claudio's release from the calaboose, and while Joaquin was in the Southland, trouble started. Someone, probably Claudio or one of his men, poisoned the water well in Sawmill Flat, and a number of miners fell ill. One pioneer recalled rumors spreading that the "gang of gamblers had thrown poison in the spring" and that they "contemplated making an attack on Mr. Ira McRae." McRae owned a general store in Sawmill Flat, and his opposition to Claudio's band was well-known. Things came to a head on June 29 when a Mexican woman who lived with an Italian miner in Sawmill Flat received a written warning from one of Claudio's gang: "In some seven or eight days or nights from the present time, should you hear any disturbance, you and yours keep to your house, as we at that time intend visiting the flat for the purpose of taking our revenge; and the advent of our visit will be a greater scourge to the persons on the flat than if they were visited by the cholera, in its worst form."

The Italian turned the letter over to Ira McRae and William Stacey, a lumber mill owner. Stacey, in a letter written from Sawmill Flat, detailed what happened: "The letter came from one of a guerrilla band that infest the country and range between Mariposa and Mokelumne Hill, having their haunts and spies along the whole line. The day after this, an old man, a trustworthy, respectable Mexican, called upon the same storekeeper [McRae] and myself, and after making us give a pledge of secrecy as to his name (as he stated that, should it be known that he had given information, his life would be taken by the band), he informed us that this same band or guerrilla party had sworn to take the lives of some four or five persons on the flat, and also to fire and rob the house of the same storekeeper and one other house here—whose it was he could not say. He advised us to be on our guard, and to arm; and stated that the gang consisted of from thirty to forty. Another person gave us the same information, and advised caution, declaring that mischief was intended us. It is easy to account for the hostility of this gang. Some three months since, the officers of Columbia arrested one of them [Reyes Feliz] for stealing a pistol. Whilst taking him over to Columbia, another portion of the gang, who had secreted themselves in the chaparral by the roadside, opened a brisk fire upon the officers, who were thereby compelled to let their prisoner escape, though some of the assailants were wounded. One of them [Claudio Feliz] was taken prisoner the same night by a party from the flat, who also, at the time of the attack, hastened to the support of the law and the law's officers. Hence their hatred for the inhabitants of the flat, and their seeking our lives."[7]

McRae and Stacey did not take the threats seriously, because it seemed outlandish that a bandit gang of thirty to forty men would attack a mining town. But by July 8, news of the threats had spread to the adjacent mining camps. One report claimed that the outlaws were going to rob McRae's store. In nearby Columbia, Anglo hotheads began shouting, "Let's go and clean out the greaser population!"

A crowd of two hundred, including miners and local militia members, gathered at a Columbia hotel, and a group of them prepared to march on Sawmill Flat. They grabbed rifles and revolvers, plus a small brass cannon, sixteen inches long with a two-inch bore, mounted on a wagon. One witness thought the expedition was foolish, observing sarcastically, "A patriotic lady cocked the soldiers' hats and put feathers in them, urging the braves on to deeds of valor. The little army, after much preparation, made a start of the scene of war, at which place they arrived at quite a late hour." As the men approached Sawmill Flat, they fired warning shots from their little cannon. It was dark when the band marched into the camp. McRae and other residents were more than surprised to see them.

"Boys, what the thunder is up?" McRae called out from the front porch of his store. "And what are you doing here?"

The commander of the group responded that an invasion by the bandit gang was to take place that night, and they had come to protect Sawmill Flat. At that McRae laughed and said, "Boys, come in and take something to drink, and then go home. The greasers or no one else is going to trouble me."

Despite McRae's seemingly unconcerned response, it turned out that Claudio and his compadres, apparently alerted by the firing of the cannon, had mounted their horses and fled into the mountains. Then the militiamen turned their efforts against the law-abiding Latinos in Sawmill Flat. As one Mexican miner wrote to a friend in Stockton, "Yesterday I was notified that I must leave the camp forthwith, [and] I did not consider that the order emanated from a source authorized to give it. But this morning they have commenced carrying their intentions into effect, and have stopped the Mexican miners from working." The Mexican gold seeker promptly rode into Sonora and complained to the justice of the peace, who in turn sent the sheriff to Sawmill Flat to stop the militia's actions. But by that time, the militiamen had drunk all the whiskey in town, sobered up, and returned to their homes in Columbia. Ever after, the affair was facetiously known as the Battle of Sawmill Flat.[8]

William Stacey, the sawmill owner, angrily denied that any honest Latinos had been targeted. "There were two tents owned by Mexicans on this flat, who harbored this set of guerrillas when they were here. On last Sunday, one individual only, the storekeeper [McRae], warned these parties to leave, and no others . . . As to the Mexicans being prevented working in a single instance, I pronounce it a base, groundless fabrication, and it could only have been written by some evil disposed person to give wrong information and raise a false sympathy. The honest foreigner, let him be Mexican or what he might, is just as much protected in his rights and privileges on this flat, around Columbia, and in Tuolumne County, as he is in any place in the mines, and my private opinion is more so." Despite Stacey's protestations, there is no question that the Columbia militia marched through Sawmill Flat, striking terror in Latinos—desperadoes and honest miners alike. Six weeks later, the local newspaper, the *Sonora Herald*, identified Claudio as the leader of the outlaws and declared, "Most of these scoundrels are known to belong to the same gang of Mexican miners that were lately driven from Sawmill Flat. This is not mere assertion, but actual testimony."[9]

By this time, Joaquin Murrieta had rejoined Claudio. He had also permanently abandoned his career as a gambler in favor of one as a highwayman. At five in the evening of August 27, 1852, Joaquin, with the Feliz brothers and an anonymous bandido, stopped three Chinese gold-seekers who were walking down the wagon road between Sonora and the busy camp of Jamestown, located three miles below Sonora. The route, lined with a lush growth of live oak and California buckeye, wound its way through the hills, and today is part of historic Highway 49, which runs north-south and passes though many principal gold rush towns. One of the Chinese miners was carrying a holstered revolver, which was unusual because in 1852, prospectors from China were only just beginning to become familiar with American guns. Joaquin and the other bandidos were unswayed by the fact that he was armed with a pistol. And unknown to the desperadoes, he may not have been experienced in drawing and firing the weapon quickly. Before the miner could reach for it, one bandit put a knife to his throat, while another slashed the holstered revolver from his belt. Murrieta and his compadres then robbed the three Chinese men of their gold and, sparing their lives, galloped away. The victims immediately raised an alarm, but the highway robbers disappeared.[10]

The next day, the band rode seven miles south to Camp Salvado, situated just east of Chinese Camp. Camp Salvado had first been settled by Chinese miners in 1849, but within a couple of years, they had all moved to Chinese Camp. By the summer of 1852, the miners in Camp Salvado were all Latino, with the exception of a lone American gambler. Joaquin and his compadres quickly looted the camp, and Claudio shot one of their victims to death. The robbers did not bother to wear masks, and some of the townsfolk recognized Claudio Feliz. The *Sonora Herald* reported, "On Saturday evening last a band of Mexican scoundrels, under the lead of the same man—called Claudio—who was shot some time since by officer Leary and who has lately been released from jail, entered the old Chinese Camp, back of the hill from the present village of that name, and made an indiscriminate levy upon all the money . . . that could be found there. There was but one American in camp, a monte dealer, who was lucky enough to elude them. The rest of the inhabitants, all Spanish Americans, were laid under contribution. To add to the atrocity, one man—a Chileno—was shot dead by the leader of the band."[11]

Two days later, on August 30, Claudio, Joaquin, and their compadres galloped into the camp of Sullivan Creek, just south of Sonora. They held up and robbed the town's general store, then thundered away on their mustangs. Three days afterward, a large posse rode out of Sonora to hunt the bandits, but once again, Murrieta and the rest had vanished. By this time, Claudio's leadership of the gang was becoming common knowledge. A correspondent in Sonora wrote to a Stockton newspaper, "There is no doubt of the existence of a formidable band of guerrillas in the mountains around Sonora. We have received several communications from which we learn that the party is guided by one 'Cloudy,' a noted Mexican guerrilla chief. Two daring robberies have been committed, and they number some forty strong." Although there was no evidence that the gang was so large, newspapers would frequently repeat this number. And "Cloudy" was an Anglo mispronunciation of Claudio.[12]

On the morning of September 2, 1852, the same day the posse left Sonora, Judge John G. Marvin, a noted political figure and editor of the *Sonora Herald*, mounted his mule at a roadhouse near Chinese Camp. Like almost all men in the gold fields, he carried a pistol for self-protection, especially after the recent bandit raids. Judge Marvin followed the wagon road north toward Sonora. He was two miles from town when a Mexican mounted on a fine horse approached at a gallop. The judge was immediately suspicious because Western horsemen—unlike modern depictions in film and television—did not race at full speed to their destinations. Riders covered long distances in the arid West by walking or trotting their horses. Marvin blocked the horseman's approach, forcing him to halt, then asked him where he was going. The Mexican responded simply, "I am taking a *pasea*," meaning that he was out for a ride.

But Marvin saw that the man's shirt was covered with blood. The judge later said that he "believed that he was one of the murderous gang, and asked him if he knew anything relative to the matter, and remarked that it was generally thought the murders were committed by Mexicans. The Mexican replied that they were committed by five Mexicans and five Americans, and exhibited a great desire to escape." The blood-soaked suspect put spurs to his horse, which was exhausted and foaming with sweat. Marvin's mule was still fresh, and he wheeled it about and pursued the man for a mile and a half back down the road and into Jamestown. Halfway through town, the judge pulled his pistol and threatened to fire. At that, the Mexican, realizing he could not escape, surrendered. Then Marvin and several citizens took him to jail in Sonora. As the judge reported, "There did not seem to be much doubt in the minds of the people present, that this Mexican belonged to a band of guerillas now infecting Tuolumne county, and that he had probably been frightened from his cover that morning, and was trying to make his escape when he was fortunately arrested."[13]

Though the name of the bloodied outlaw is unknown, his capture had no salutary effect on Joaquin or the Feliz brothers. A newspaper correspondent in Tuolumne County promptly reported that "at Yorktown Gulch, near Campo Seco, a lawless band of fifty Mexicans have started for the lower country on a plundering expedition. They have stolen about eighty animals in that part of the country, committed several robberies and two or three murders, and are now on the way to Los Angeles to join a party who are waiting for them at that place. They are headed by a Mexican named Cloudy who was in jail in Sonora last winter, and who is represented as one of the most desperate villains in the country. He has a brother named Reyes now in jail in Monterey, and it is said that Cloudy and his party have it in view to release him by force." However, contrary to the report, the gang numbered nowhere near fifty, and Reyes Feliz was never jailed in Monterey. But the correspondent got the most important facts correct: Claudio was headed for the coastal region, while Joaquin Murrieta and Reyes Feliz were on their way back to Los Angeles.[14]

As posses of armed miners hunted in vain for the robbers, Claudio led six of his men out of the Sierra Nevada foothills. Among the gang were Esteban Alvarado Silva, a twenty-two-year-old Californio from Los Angeles, and a Mexican named Mateo Andrade, twenty-one, who had lost his left eye. An acquaintance described Silva as a "broad-chested, powerful-made man, about six feet high." Silva had reportedly killed two men, one in Los Angeles and another at the Mission Soledad in Monterey County. In November 1851, Silva had been convicted of horse theft in Los Angeles and was sentenced to two years in prison. He remained in jail so he could be tried on a second charge of stealing horses. But two months later, in January 1852, Silva, with two other prisoners, escaped the Los Angeles calaboose. Although the three prisoners had been heavily ironed, their friends managed to break them out in the middle of the night. Silva fled to the mining region, where he fell in with Claudio Feliz. He accompanied Claudio and his pistoleros as they rode out of the Sierra and across the San Joaquin Valley, then up the Coast Range. From atop the mountains, they looked down into the Livermore Valley, with vast fields of wild oats and ryegrass swaying in the breeze, and populated only by a handful of rancheros and their herds of grazing cattle. Claudio, because of his raids in and near the valley a year earlier, including his attack on the John Marsh ranch, knew the area well.[15]

Claudio and his six compadres rode west across the Livermore Valley to the adjacent Amador Valley. There, in what is now the suburban city of Pleasanton, at a spot a few hundred feet south of the stream named the Arroyo Valle, or Valley Creek, a settler named John W. Kottinger had built a substantial house of adobe and redwood. The house is no longer extant, for it was torn down in 1930. However, the Kottingers' adobe barn is still standing at 200 Ray Street, the oldest building in Pleasanton. John Kottinger was a thirty-two-year-old Austrian forty-niner who in 1850 had married Maria Bernal, fifteen, the daughter of a prominent Californio rancher. Given the scarcity of women in the gold rush—California was then 90 percent male—such unions between teenage girls and older men were common. Kottinger and his young wife had acquired a cattle ranch from her father, who lived in a large hacienda a mile distant.

On Thursday evening, September 9, Maria and several female relatives were socializing in the adobe while her husband rode the cattle range. Just before dark, Claudio's band arrived at

The adobe home of John and Maria Bernal Kottinger in what is now the city of Pleasanton. It was raided by Claudio Feliz and his gang in 1852. *Library of Congress*

the Arroyo Valle and tethered their horses in the creek. Claudio and two of his men cautiously walked a hundred yards to the adobe. There they encountered Kottinger, who had just ridden in, covered with dust. Claudio, thinking that he was a vaquero and not the ranch owner, asked, "Is the *patron* in?"

"Yes," Kottinger replied. Then, to his surprise, Claudio and another of the strangers abruptly brushed past him and burst into the adobe without knocking. Seeing Maria and the other startled women in the room, Claudio and his compadre rudely ordered them to fetch some bread. An alarmed Kottinger stepped into the doorway in time to see Claudio reach inside his coat, supposedly for money to pay for the bread. As the bandido put his hand into his breast pocket, Maria spotted the gleam of a knife blade. She screamed in terror and fled the front room. Kottinger reacted instantly. Before Claudio could raise his knife, he charged both outlaws and shoved them out the front door. Then he slammed the door shut and barred it. At the same time, Maria and the other women rushed to the side door and locked it. Kottinger suddenly realized that a bedroom window was open. As he raced to close it, the other members of the gang ran up to the house. Kottinger got to the window just as four pistoleros attempted to climb over the sill. Kottinger swung the heavy shutter in their faces and bolted it shut. Claudio and the rest, enraged that they had been outwitted, pulled their pistols and fired a volley of gunfire though the wood shutter. Then, realizing that they had no cover and that Kottinger would surely return their fire, the bandits ran back to the Arroyo Valle, mounted their horses, and galloped away. John and Maria Kottinger would remember their close brush with death for the rest of their lives.[16]

Claudio and his raiders then headed for the Salinas Valley, eighty miles to the south. They undoubtedly skirted San Jose, because Claudio was too well-known there due to his arrest for murder and his subsequent escape from jail. Today the Salinas Valley, situated east of Monterey, is famed for its lush farmland and endless acres of crops and lettuce fields. But in 1852 it was isolated, remote, and thinly populated by rancheros, including a number of Anglos who had married into Californio families. The rancheros resided in spacious haciendas, while their vaqueros and laborers occupied *jacales*, or brush-covered adobe huts. They raised cattle, which vaqueros drove in large herds to the butcher markets in San Francisco, Stockton, and Sacramento. The cows were sold to feed the hungry miners and adventurers who flocked daily into the burgeoning new state. The Salinas Valley was different from the gold fields because it had been well settled by Californios decades before, and most people in the valley knew each other. Californios in Monterey County, as well as in most of the coastal region south of San Jose, were then in the majority. They wielded significant political power and often took an active hand in law enforcement.

On the afternoon of September 12, 1852, three days after the raid on the Kottinger ranch, Claudio and his men rode south through the Salinas Valley and crossed the Salinas River. They were headed toward Monterey, the picturesque coastal village where clusters of adobes looked out upon the Pacific Ocean. A few miles north of Monterey, Claudio spotted a lone horseman approaching. He was a Mexican named Agapito, on his way to Alisal, now the city of Salinas. The bandidos stopped Agapito, stealing his mustang, his serape, and what little money he had. But the gang allowed him to walk away with his life, unlike so many of their other victims. Then they wheeled their horses around and rode back north toward the Salinas River.

Agapito ran back to Monterey, where he borrowed a horse. He raced north through the sand dunes along the coast and then inland to Salinas, covering the eighteen-mile distance in record time. Hitching his mount in front of the house of Henry Cocks, the justice of the peace of Alisal Township, he rushed inside and gasped breathlessly that he had been robbed. Cocks, a twenty-eight-year-old Englishman, was the right man in the right place. He had served as a US Marine on a Navy warship and came to Monterey in 1848. There he married Miguela Garcia, the daughter of a ranchero, and several of her brothers lived with them. Cocks and his family listened closely to Agapito's description of the bandidos and quickly recognized the diminutive Claudio Feliz from the description provided of the gang's leader. The older Garcia brothers, like many Californios, had rushed to the gold mines in 1848. They had known Claudio at Sonora in 1849 when he was first suspected of gold theft.

Henry Cocks and his brothers-in-law also knew that Claudio was wanted for many crimes in the mining country, and they had heard a rumor that a $3,000 reward had been placed on his head. Cocks promptly raised a posse that included Agapito and three of the Garcia brothers. They rode west to the Salinas River, where their friend, James Anthony, an African American pioneer, owned a lodging house and ferry across the river. Thirty-two-year-old Anthony had arrived in California from

New England with his wife before the gold rush and settled in Monterey. To Californios he was known as Antonio. In 1848 he and a small party of miners from Monterey explored the area that became Calaveras County. When Anthony discovered gold, the spot was named after him as San Antonio. He was apparently the only African American to have a California mining camp named after him. Anthony returned to Monterey and then acquired his property on the Salinas River. Despite the fact that he had a wife and young son, Anthony ignored the danger posed by Claudio's band. He readily agreed to join Cocks's posse.[17]

Each justice of the peace had one or more constables to enforce his rulings. In this case, Henry Cocks also recruited his constable, a Californio named Anastacio Garcia. He lived nearby with his wife and young children in an adobe house situated close to the modern-day intersection of Cooper Road and Blanco Road. Garcia was a close friend of Cocks, and during the Mexican War, he had sided with the Americans. Ironically enough, Anastacio Garcia would soon become a noted outlaw himself. Before dying at the end of a lynch mob's rope in Monterey, he would lead Tiburcio Vasquez, the infamous bandit chieftain of the 1870s, into a life of crime. Garcia, tall and muscular, an expert horseman and a deadly shot, was a valuable addition to the posse. Henry Cocks rounded off his nine-man posse with his three brothers-in-law, the robbery victim Agapito, and four Californio neighbors, all armed to the teeth.[18]

Cocks and his possemen heard rumors that several strangers had been stopping at the adobe of Manuel Espinosa, located two miles southeast on the south bank of the Salinas River. Cocks decided to investigate, for he knew that Espinosa had a checkered history. He was a petty thief and had been released from the Monterey jail just four days earlier. Espinosa lived with a couple of compadres, Antonio Valenzuela and Juan Alvitre, and they had allowed Claudio and his men to hide out at the house. One of the band was a twenty-seven-year-old from Sinaloa,

Mexico, named Pablo Valdez. Surprisingly enough, Valdez, unlike the other bandidos, was married, and he had been staying at Espinosa's adobe with his wife and small child. Apparently he would leave his family periodically to ride with Claudio's gang on their raids.

That evening Claudio made himself at home in the isolated house, which was surrounded by a dense thicket of willow trees and brush. Manuel Espinosa kept several guard dogs on watch outside. Claudio relaxed with his gang members Esteban Silva and Mateo Andrade, along with Espinosa, Antonio Valenzuela, Juan Alvitre, and Pablo Valdez and his wife. The group enjoyed the pleasant evening weather, with the wood window shutters open and the interior of the adobe illuminated by candles and lamps. Their horses—most of them stolen—were picketed nearby, and Espinosa's guard dogs provided protection from any unwanted intruders. Claudio, in conversation with the occupants of the adobe, claimed that his brother Reyes was imprisoned in San Luis Obispo, 125 miles to the south, and he declared that he was on his way to break him out of jail. Perhaps he had heard a rumor that his brother had been arrested, but in fact, Reyes Feliz was not charged with any crime in San Luis Obispo County.[19]

As dusk gathered, Cocks and his posse splashed their mustangs across the Salinas River and rode the two miles to Espinosa's house. It was nine o'clock that night when the possemen cautiously approached the adobe. As they rode in through the thicket, Espinosa's dogs began barking wildly. Claudio and his bandidos, ever alert, blew out the lights and seized their guns. Henry Cocks was equally cool. He ordered his possemen to dismount, hobble the horses, and remove their spurs. Then, with military precision, he directed them to surround the adobe, assigning each man a position that provided both cover and a good view of the four respective walls. But Claudio plainly believed that he was master of the situation. He and his gang had pulled off numerous raids and killed at least sixteen victims. He had escaped the San Jose jail and then escaped death after being gutshot by Constable Leary's posse. He was determined that no law officer would ever take him again.

As the manhunters took their positions, Claudio and his band carefully leveled their cocked pistols from inside the adobe and squeezed the triggers. The heavy thud of gunfire shattered the night air. Muzzle flashes from their guns burst from the windows and doors, but the night was so black the outlaws could not see their pursuers. The posse returned the fire, and Claudio quickly realized that they were surrounded. Moments later he and his pistoleros boldly burst out the front door, six-shooters blazing in all directions. But the possemen did not flinch, and they were so well concealed that the desperadoes' bullets all went wild. The manhunters kept up a hot fire, sending a fusillade toward the adobe. The shots missed Claudio, who raced on foot a short distance in the dark until he suddenly slammed head-on into Henry Cocks. The former marine grabbed the diminutive bandido with one hand and held him in a viselike grip.

For a moment, Claudio was stunned.

"*Estoy dado, senor. No tengo armas,*" he exclaimed. "I surrender, sir. I have no arms."

The bandit leader let his empty six-shooter drop from his fist to the ground. Cocks, always a fair-minded man, and believing that Claudio had surrendered, released his grip on the bandido. As Claudio stood facing Cocks, two of the possemen spotted the outlaw surreptitiously reaching down toward his goatskin leggings. They saw the glint of metal as he began pulling out a long-bladed dagger. Claudio Feliz had made his last move. The two manhunters instantly pulled their triggers. One slug slammed into Claudio's face under the left eye and ripped through his skull. A second bullet tore into his left leg and severed the femoral artery. Both shots were fatal, and Claudio dropped to the ground, dead.

The brush-choked Salinas River in the area where the adobe of Manuel Espinosa was located. There, on the night of September 12, 1852, Claudio Feliz met his bloody fate. *Photograph by the author.*

At almost the same instant, his compadres Pablo Valdez, Esteban Silva, and the one-eyed Mateo Andrade fled from the front of the adobe. The posse fired another volley, and Valdez sprawled lifeless with two bullets in his neck and shoulder. Another ball tore into Andrade's leg, but he kept running. Cocks and his possemen raced after Andrade and Silva, but the pistoleros vanished in the darkness. Cocks then returned to the adobe, where he found the terrified wife and child of Pablo Valdez cowering inside. The owner, Manuel Espinosa, and his compadres, Antonio Valenzuela and Juan Alvitre, were also hiding in the adobe, but they had taken no part in the shooting.

As the heavy black powder gunsmoke drifted away, the posse lit lamps, and Espinosa gazed wide-eyed at the two bullet-riddled bodies in his yard. Henry Cocks and his manhunters, after questioning the adobe's occupants and learning the names of the outlaws, prepared to leave. Cocks said later that he ordered Espinosa and his two compadres, "that if they saw the two escaped men, Silva and Mateo, to take them dead or alive." Espinosa, despite his petty criminal record, was eager to obey Cocks and avoid a return to jail. The justice of the peace and his men rounded up the bandidos' horses, some of which turned out to have been stolen from neighboring ranchos. Then they rode back to their homes and sent a messenger to notify the county coroner in Monterey of the deadly shootout. Cocks, before he left, told Espinosa to leave the bodies where they were, and explained that he would return the next day with the coroner's jury from Monterey.

In the morning, the desperado Esteban Silva slipped through the heavy brush and returned to the adobe, hoping to find a horse. He was wearing a red serape and carried a single-shot pistol and a long bowie knife. Manuel Espinosa spotted Silva outside his house. Espinosa proved true to his word to Henry Cocks. He grabbed a rifle and ordered the outlaw to throw down his weapons. Silva obeyed, and Espinosa and his compadres, Alvitre and Valenzuela, tied him up with their rawhide reatas. Then they waited for several hours for Cocks to return with the coroner's jury. At about two o'clock that afternoon, when his captors were not watching, Silva managed to free himself from his bindings. Seizing his pistol and knife, he burst out of the adobe and ran toward the thicket of willows. Espinosa, Alvitre, and Valenzuela, however, caught a glimpse of him as he fled. They whipped out their knives and raced after him. Silva tried to fight, but he was outnumbered, and his three captors slashed him to death with their razor-like dirks.

The Monterey coroner's jury finally arrived at Espinosa's adobe the following morning, along with Cocks, Agapito, and several of the possemen. The jurors examined the bodies of Claudio, Valdez, and Silva. From Silva's corpse, they removed a small single-shot English percussion pistol made by Hopkins of London. He had also carried a long-bladed bowie knife manufactured by R. Hallam of Sheffield, England. The knife was held in a red leather sheath, ornamented with the figure of a mounted vaquero lassoing cattle. The coroner's jury, by recording those items in their report, provided one of the few detailed descriptions of weapons carried by a gold rush bandido. The jurors also took testimony from Henry Cocks, Agapito, the posse, and those who lived in Espinosa's adobe. The jury found that there was no doubt that Cocks and his men had killed the notorious bandit leader: "This Claudio is said to be the same man who has been robbing and murdering within the last three years around San Jose and the placers of the Stanislaus and Tuolumne [Rivers]. He is a light complected, small made man, said to be a native of Hermosillo in Sonora, five feet, four inches, about nineteen years old; was very quick and agile, and made a desperate resistance with a revolver and bowie knife, has an old wound under the right ribs and two others about his stomach. Some of the witnesses knew him at the Sonorian Camp three years ago."

Claudio's wounds were those he had suffered in the shootout with Constable Leary's posse five months earlier. And the witnesses who had known him in Sonora were Cocks's brothers-in-law, the Garcias. The coroner turned over the body of Pablo Valdez to his wife. The other men dug graves for Claudio Feliz and Esteban Silva and buried them near the adobe. Then Cocks, accompanied by a constable from Monterey, began searching the willows and chaparral along the Salinas River for the wounded Mateo Andrade. The next day, they finally found the fugitive and jailed him in Monterey. He was tried for grand larceny and robbery, convicted, and sentenced to eleven years in the state prison. Andrade broke out in 1854 and was later reportedly captured and lynched in San Luis Obispo.[20]

The killing of Claudio Feliz received surprisingly little notice in the California press. San Francisco's *Daily Alta California* provided a very brief and garbled report: "We learn that Claud Felix, for a long time known to be at the head of a gang of desperate thieves, was shot dead by a Californian a few days since, at a fandango near the Mission of San Jose." The newspaper added, correctly, that the dead man had escaped jail in San Jose after being arrested for murder. The *San Joaquin Republican* in Stockton published a somewhat longer account of the shootout, but failed to even mention Claudio's name. The *San Francisco Herald* was the only newspaper to detail the story. It reprinted a long letter from a correspondent in Monterey, giving all the particulars as well as the findings of the coroner's jury. There were several reasons for the scant coverage. One was the slow communications of the era, for there were no telegraph lines, and roads were primitive. News was delivered by express riders, and it took several days for a horseman to journey from Salinas to Stockton or San Francisco. Additionally, violent crime had become so commonplace by 1852 that gold rush journalists had trouble keeping up with it. Last, Joaquin Murrieta was not yet a nationally known outlaw, and the fact that Claudio was his brother-in-law would only become publicly known in the months to come. As a result, few recognized the importance of the gun battle on the Salinas River.[21]

Despite the sudden and violent end to Claudio Feliz's career as a bandit chieftain, Joaquin Murrieta proved more than eager to take over the reins.

CHAPTER 10

MURDER IN LOS ANGELES

Mission church bells clanged loudly as Joaquin Murrieta and Reyes Feliz nudged their horses into the crowded streets of Los Angeles. After separating from Claudio Feliz, they had headed for Southern California, oblivious to their leader's bloody fate. It was a balmy fall day in 1852 when the pair rode leisurely through the pueblo. The two pistoleros saw a wealthy and bustling village of flat-roofed adobe houses clustered around the town square called La Plaza. The streets teemed with colorfully attired riders mounted on California mustangs, Mexican packers driving mule trains, and teamsters struggling to control their wagons and yokes of oxen. Los Angeles was home to about 1,600 permanent residents and a transient population of a thousand more. Nine out of ten were Latino, many recent arrivals from Mexico. Its affluent citizens resided in grand haciendas surrounded by adobe walls and lush gardens, and those less well off lived in small jacales. Covered wagons filled with immigrants poured into the pueblo, bringing gold seekers from across the deserts of the Southwest. A stagecoach arrived daily from the port at San Pedro, twenty-five miles south, laden with passengers, mail, and newspapers from the steamships that plied the Pacific Coast. Several *zanjas*, or aqueducts, brought water from the Los Angeles River into the pueblo. On the west side of the plaza was the church of *Nuestra Senora La Reina de Los Angeles*—Our Lady Queen of the Angels. Its bronze bells regularly called the Catholic faithful to worship.

Yet Joaquin was more interested in riches than religion. Los Angeles was the center of vast cattle ranges, where rancheros prospered by driving beef herds north and selling them in the gold country. One Anglo who arrived in Los Angeles at about the same time as Joaquin was impressed by the pueblo's wealth. "The streets were thronged throughout the entire day with splendidly mounted and richly dressed *caballeros*, most of whom wore suits of clothes that cost all the way from $500 to $1,000, with saddle and horse trappings that cost even more," he recalled. "Everybody in Los Angeles seemed rich, everybody *was* rich, and money was more plentiful, at that time, than in any other place of that size, I venture to say, in the world."[1]

At that time, Los Angeles, despite its affluence, was the most violent community in America. Horace Bell, a pioneer soldier and lawyer who later wrote two popular books about the burgeoning adobe town, declared, "I have no hesitation in saying that in the years of 1851, '52, and '53, there were more desperadoes in Los Angeles that in any place on the Pacific Coast, San Francisco with its great population not excepted. It was a fact that all of the bad characters who had been driven from the mines had taken refuge in Los Angeles, for the reason that if forced to move further on, it was only a short ride to Mexican soil, while on the other hand all of the outlaws of the Mexican frontier made for the California gold mines, and the cutthroats of California and Mexico naturally met at Los Angeles, and at Los Angeles they fought. Knives and revolvers settled all differences, either real or imaginary. The slightest misunderstandings were settled on the spot with knife or bullet, the Mexican preferring the former at close quarters and the American the latter."[2]

Although Horace Bell's colorful stories of frontier Los Angeles were sometimes unreliable and often exaggerated, he did not overstate the amount of violent crime in the little pueblo. During the twelve-month period before September 1851, thirty-one killings took place in Los Angeles and its suburbs, which

Calle de los Negros, or Negro Alley, was the most dangerous street in frontier Los Angeles. *John Boessenecker collection.*

was home to only 2,500 people. That resulted in the highest known homicide rate in American history, more than 150 times the modern national rate. The most dangerous place in Los Angeles was Calle de los Negros, or Negro Alley, which ran south from La Plaza. In Spanish, the word *negro* means black or dark. Calle de los Negros got its name from several dark-complected Californios who had lived in the adobes that lined the alley. The name was considered insulting, and in the 1880s, it was renamed and became part of Los Angeles Street. Today Calle de los Negros is gone, but the old plaza is part of the Plaza Historic District in downtown Los Angeles.[3]

Joaquin Murrieta and Reyes Feliz made Calle de los Negros their favorite stomping ground. Horace Bell described it vividly: "There were four or five gambling places, and the crowd from the old Coronel building on the Los Angeles Street corner to the plaza was so dense that we could scarcely squeeze through. Americans, Spaniards, Indians, and foreigners, rushing and crowding along from one gambling house to another, from table to table, all chinking the everlasting eight square $50 pieces up and down in their palms. There were several bands of music of the primitive Mexican-Indian kind that sent forth most discordant sound, by no means in harmony with the eternal jingle of gold—while at the upper end of the street, in the rear of one of the gambling houses, was a Mexican *maroma* [circus] in uproarious confusion. They positively made the night hideous with their howlings. Every few minutes a rush would be made, and maybe a pistol shot would be heard, and when the confusion incident to the rush would have somewhat subsided, and inquiry made, you would learn that it was only a knife fight between two Mexicans, or a gambler had caught somebody cheating and had perforated him with a bullet. Such things were a matter of course, and no complaint or arrests were ever made."[4]

At some point, Joaquin was joined in Los Angeles by a twenty-two-year-old paramour who called herself Ana Benites and claimed that she was born in New Mexico. However, Ana Benites was undoubtedly an alias, because no woman by that name appears in New Mexico birth and population records of the period. Also, as it turned out, she was extremely loyal to Joaquin and plainly was a longtime companion and not someone whom he had just met in Los Angeles. Given those circumstances, coupled with her same first name, her identical age, and the fact that she was known in Los Angeles as Joaquin's woman, it seems evident that she was Maria Ana Andrada, commonly known as Mariana. She and Joaquin lived together for about two months in an adobe house in the little pueblo.[5]

Murrieta and Reyes Feliz soon began riding with Salomon Pico, who by then was the most notorious bandit chieftain in Southern California. They both knew Pico through his connection with Claudio Feliz at San Jose two years earlier. Pico was accused of committing numerous murders and robberies on El Camino Real, the main road between San Jose and Los Angeles. In April 1851, four months after Claudio broke out of the San Jose jail, Pico and four of his gang were captured near Monterey. One of them was the ear-collecting Domingo Hernandez, and another was William Otis Hall, a notorious American horse thief. Hernandez got released without charge, while Pico's wealthy family posted his $6,000 bond. Instead of appearing in court, Pico jumped bail, and his relatives forfeited the bond money. Soon after, his partner Hall broke out of Monterey's crumbling adobe calaboose and joined him. The pair fled south and were suspected of robbing and killing a US mail rider near San Luis Obispo. Then they rode on to Los Angeles, where an alert lawman recognized Hall and captured him. He was sent back to Monterey, convicted of horse theft, and sentenced to four years in the state prison brig. But Hall never served his sentence. In August 1851, a band of vigilantes—most of them Californios who had suffered heavily from livestock theft—broke into the jail and lynched him.[6]

Salomon Pico remained in Southern California, protected and sheltered by the many friends of his distinguished family. One night in November 1851, he rode up to the Los Angeles office of Benjamin Hayes, a prominent lawyer who later became a county judge. Pico was enraged that Hayes had previously prosecuted several members of his gang for murder. He yanked his pistol and fired at Hayes, tearing off the attorney's hat. Hayes was unscathed, and Pico fled with a sheriff's posse in pursuit. In the resulting shootout, Los Angeles County Sheriff James Barton wounded Pico in the arm, but the bandit chieftain managed to escape. Two of his gang, Mariano Hernandez and Domingo Hernandez—who were not related—had no such luck. Eight months later, in July 1852, both were captured and lynched in Santa Cruz. Once again, most of the vigilantes were Californios. These violent deaths should have been a warning, but Murrieta and Reyes Feliz showed little hesitation in joining Pico's band in Los Angeles. Two other desperadoes rode with them. One was Benito Lopez, a murderous bandit. The other was the notorious Pancho Daniel, who had returned to Los Angeles, greatly angered by his brother Bernardo's robbery and murder of the Mexican man in the Livermore Valley a year earlier.[7]

During the first week of November 1852, Joaquin and Ana rode from Los Angeles to San Gabriel to attend the *maroma*, a popular type of traveling Mexican circus that featured acrobats and tightrope walkers. The Mission San Gabriel, located nine miles northeast of Los Angeles in the San Gabriel Valley, was a large adobe church that had been established eighty years earlier by missionary priests. Next to it stood a number of spacious adobe buildings that had once been used as housing and workshops, as well as a convent school for young Indian girls. Many small adobes had sprung up nearby, housing a few hundred people. The spot was more than picturesque. Surrounding the mission, and spread along the banks of the San Gabriel River, were vast orchards and vineyards. A few miles to the north, the eight-thousand-foot-high San Gabriel Mountains towered over the valley. During the 1830s, the Mexican government had secularized the missions. The chapels and padres' homes remained church property, but the adjacent buildings and lands were sold to private buyers. By 1852 the large adobes next to the San Gabriel mission housed a number of businesses, including a popular drinking spot, the Headquarters Saloon.

Joaquin and Ana cantered leisurely into San Gabriel and stopped at the home of a friend, Jesus Rico, situated in the cluster of jacales and adobe houses near the mission. The house was crowded with Rico's friends and family, among them his wife and son, Juanito. Murrieta and his paramour stayed for a day or two at Rico's adobe. Several of the occupants, including Joaquin and Ana, slept outside in the *ramadita*, a brush shelter covered with tree branches. On the evening of November 7, 1852, Joaquin and Ana walked a short distance from the adobe to the *maroma* and took their seats in the throng of spectators.

The most prominent Anglo in the audience was General Joshua H. Bean, thirty-four, a popular civic and military leader. Bean, a native of Kentucky, had served with the US forces in the Mexican War, then arrived in California in 1849. He settled in San Diego and in 1850 became the town's first Anglo mayor. The following year, Bean moved north to San Gabriel, where he opened the Headquarters Saloon, situated in a corner of one of the large mission buildings. Connected to it was Bean's small general store and his living quarters. That same year, Bean was appointed major general of the state militia. Soon after, a group of Native Americans rebelled against American rule, and Bean led his troops in suppressing the uprising. When he lived in San Diego, he was joined by his younger brother, Roy Bean, later famous in Texas, and then nationally, as "the Law West of the Pecos." Roy, unlike his brother, was quarrelsome and disreputable. In February 1852, he engaged in a duel on horseback with a monte dealer and shot him in the leg. Roy Bean was arrested, but he escaped the San Diego jail and joined his elder brother in San Gabriel.[8]

The two Bean brothers were handsome ladies' men who spoke Spanish, rode California mustangs, and enjoyed dressing in ranchero jackets and silver-buttoned *calzoneras*. In Los Angeles County, Joshua Bean became well-known as General Bean, and he and his militia company played an important role in tracking down Native American horse thieves. In the spring of 1851, a heavily armed band of twenty-five horsemen rode into Los Angeles. They were a mixture of American border ruffians and Sydney Ducks from Australia, and their leader was John "Red" Irving, who claimed to have been a Texas Ranger captain in the Mexican War. They told Angelenos that they were on their way to Mexico to fight Apaches, but in fact they were bandits. For several weeks, they terrorized Californios and Anglos, disrupting the courts and threatening local officials, until they were finally confronted and cowed by a troop of US cavalry.

Red Irving then led his men out of town and headed east toward San Bernardino. On their way, they looted three ranchos, stealing horses, butchering cattle, and threatening to rape the Californio women. General Bean and his militia were then camped in Cajon Pass, north of San Bernardino. The rancheros and their families fled to Bean's camp for protection. Bean and his volunteers began hunting for Red Irving, who divided his men, sending half of them to the Colorado River with their stolen booty in wagons. Irving made a fatal error by not going with them. A band of friendly Cahuilla Indians, eager to help the Californios and Anglos, surprised Irving and the rest of his men and trapped them in a box canyon. Greatly outnumbered, Red Irving and ten of his riders died. The Cahuillas riddled them with arrows and crushed their skulls with rocks.

The next day, General Bean and his men found the dead bodies, swarming with buzzards. Many of Bean's volunteers were outraged that Indians had slaughtered white men, and they began preparing to attack the Cahuillas. Bean would not stand for that. As one witness explained, "Parading his men, who were then in a state of open mutiny, he informed them that they would have to pass over his dead body before they left that ground for the purpose of commencing an attack upon the friendly Indians . . . General Bean rode up in front of his men, and ordered them to lay down their arms. This order, after some hesitation, was reluctantly obeyed." Only one of Bean's officers had supported him. The witness concluded, "To Major General Bean then, and to his dauntless courage, is due the credit of averting this danger and sacrifice." A coroner's jury found that the

Cahuillas' actions were lawful. And not surprisingly, Joshua Bean quickly became a hugely popular and respected figure in Southern California.[9]

At the *maroma* exhibition in San Gabriel, General Bean was surely the topic of conversation and would have been pointed out to those who did not know him, including Murrieta. Joaquin was undoubtedly told of Bean's campaigns against outlaws and thieves. Late that night, when the performance concluded, the crowd dispersed and headed for their homes. Joshua Bean, armed with a pistol on his belt, walked alone toward his lodgings in the old mission building. He was almost there, and very close to the adobe of Joaquin's friend, Jesus Rico, when a shadowy figure stepped out of the darkness. He leveled a pistol and fired once at point-blank range. The bullet slammed into Bean's right breast, tore completely through his body, and exited his back. Reeling backward, he managed to jerk his revolver and fire three wild shots. Then Bean staggered a short distance and collapsed in the dirt street. His neighbors, awakened by the gunfire, rushed outside and carried him to his bed. Three doctors, including his close friend Alexander W. Hope, rushed to San Gabriel. Despite their persistent efforts, Bean lingered in agony for twenty-four hours before he finally died.[10]

The killer vanished without a trace, and the assassination of the prominent soldier quickly caused an uproar in Southern California. Los Angeles had experienced dozens of murders, but none of such an important public figure. A large crowd attended Bean's funeral. Reported the *Los Angeles Star*, "He was a general favorite, and could boast of many warm and devoted friends. His death has created a deep sensation in this community, and his remains were followed to their last resting place by a procession of citizens much more numerous than we ever before witnessed in this city. The coroner's inquest, which has been in constant session since the tragic occurrence, but as yet arrived at no conclusion, and the mystery

Mission San Gabriel as it looked at the time of General Joshua Bean's murder. *California State Library*

of the whole affair, from present appearance, is incapable of a satisfactory conclusion."[11]

It turned out that General Bean, while on his deathbed, had some lucid moments and was able to utter a few scattered words. Hours before he died, he gasped that Patricio Ontiveros, the twenty-three-year-old son of a respected ranchero, had been at the scene with at least one other man. Bean said that Ontiveros "handed the pistol to the man who shot him." But General Bean was unable to identify the shooter, probably because he did not know him. Thirty years later, Horace Bell would write that the killer was Felipe Reid, who happened to be the brother-in-law of Ontiveros. Based on Bell's claim, Reid has gone down in history as the man who killed Joshua Bean in the most infamous murder of early Los Angeles.

Felipe Reid, a youthful *mestizo* who was half Native American and half Californio, had been adopted by a wealthy ranchero, Hugo Reid, who immigrated to Los Angeles from Scotland. Hugo Reid married Felipe's widowed mother and became the adoptive father to her three children. One Los Angeles pioneer described Felipe as "an attractive young fellow of splendid physique, Spanish in appearance and so well dressed as to seem a trifle foppish. He looked twenty-four or twenty-five years old and was more interested in horse racing that anything else in life. His horse, wearing a silver studded bridle and elaborate saddle ending in long *tapaderas* [leather stirrup protectors], appeared as showy as himself. Poor Felipe always was overfond of pleasure and never distinguished himself in business or in politics."[12]

The inquest by the coroner's jury had begun right after Bean's funeral. Patricio Ontiveros, on hearing that General Bean's dying statement had implicated him, voluntarily appeared at the inquest and testified before the jury. As the *Los Angeles Star* reported, he "established a perfect alibi, as we are informed by several gentlemen who attended the examination." Because Ontiveros was from a respected Californio family, the jurors accepted his alibi, evidently concluding that Bean's statement was a case of mistaken identity. In the end, the jurors could not unravel the case, and they found that "General J.H. Bean came to his death by a shot received from some person or persons unknown to the jury." But Bean's enraged friends were not willing to give up so easily. One of them was Alexander W. Hope, a physician and Mexican War veteran. A year earlier, Hope had organized a volunteer patrol to assist the Los Angeles sheriff and police in combating the pueblo's rampant violence and theft. Later the group would be organized into a state militia company called the Los Angeles Rangers, and they would take an active role in fighting banditry in Southern California. Another of Bean's infuriated comrades was J.T. Overstreet, a medical doctor from Washington, DC. Just a few months later, Overstreet would himself be shot and killed during a wild brawl at a dance in Los Angeles.[13]

Hope and Overstreet, along with Alexander Bell, the uncle of Horace Bell, and several others, promptly organized a vigilance committee. Californios also participated, for they were no strangers to vigilantism. As early as 1836, during the Mexican era, Californios had lynched a murderer in Los Angeles. One of the most prominent members of the vigilance committee was Antonio Coronel, a military and political leader who was highly respected by both Californios and Anglos. As Coronel recalled, "Bean's friends, Doctor Hope and Doctor Overstreet in particular, took great pains to find out exactly who committed the murder. They and other friends armed themselves to apprehend the suspects, and the matter became so serious that Anglos and Californios alike were alarmed. It was agreed, therefore, to name a committee to investigate and make the results public. The committee was made up of Americans and Californians: Alexander Bell, Doctor Overstreet, another American, Manuel Requena, and I. I didn't want to serve, because I have always been against any measures that depart from legal precedent, but I was given to understand the committee was purely one of inquiry. Testimony would be taken and made public, so as to avoid any imputation of partiality on one side or the other. Finally I agreed to serve. At this point, the pursuit of Murrieta and his band had already begun."[14]

Joaquin Murrieta was then largely unknown in Southern California, so the manhunt initially focused on Salomon Pico and his gang. The murder of General Bean was plainly an assassination and not a drunken quarrel. Salomon Pico's hatred of Anglos, and his attempted assassination of attorney Ben Hayes a year earlier, made him an obvious suspect. The vigilantes, working closely with Los Angeles County Undersheriff William Osburn, conducted a weeks-long investigation. Finally they identified six persons of interest, among them young Juanito Rico, who lived in his parents' adobe, where Joaquin and Ana had spent the night of the murder in the ramadita. Rico was arrested but soon released for lack of evidence. Two other suspects were Reyes Feliz and Cipriano Sandoval, the village shoemaker of San Gabriel, but both had disappeared.[15]

Another of the suspected killers was Benito Lopez, one of the Salomon Pico band. In mid-November, while the investigation was going on, Lopez encountered a pair of riders who were headed north from Los Angeles. One was a Comanche Indian named Sosa, and the other a black woman named Mary who had fled from her slave owner in Northern California. Although California had entered the union in 1850 as a free state, many slave holders ignored the law. Lopez joined Sosa and Mary on the trail north. The pair were riding a roan mare and a black mule. Lopez later said that Sosa boasted to him of robbing and killing two Anglos in the mining camp of Coloma, where gold had been discovered in 1848. According to Lopez, the Comanche admitted that he took from his dead victims the mare and the mule, as well as a rifle and pistol. The three riders stopped to rest in what is now the city of Encino, in the San Fernando Valley twenty miles northwest of Los Angeles. Lopez suddenly struck Sosa over the head with a club and beat him to death. His companion, Mary, pulled a knife and charged at Lopez, but the outlaw swung his club and killed her as well. Taking the two animals and the guns, he rode back to Los Angeles and stopped at the house of Joaquin's paramour, Ana. Lopez left the stolen rifle with Ana and kept the pistol in his waistband.[16]

Soon after this, Undersheriff Osburn arrested Ana as a material witness. Osburn, who spoke Spanish and was married to a Californio woman, kept Ana in his house for a week and interrogated her at length. She gave her name as Ana Benites and claimed that she was from New Mexico. Most importantly, she admitted being the woman of Joaquin Murrieta. Even though at that time few people in Los Angeles outside of Salomon Pico's gang had any idea who Joaquin Murrieta was, Ana did everything she could to cast suspicion away from her lover. "My name is Ana Benites, twenty-two years old, born in Santa Fe, New Mexico," she said. "[I] reside in Los Angeles. Did not know General Bean. Heard him mentioned. Know who killed him.

Know from the mouth of the person the manner in which he was killed. Cipriano (don't know his other name) told me that he had killed him."

But as we will see, the man she identified—the shoemaker Cipriano Sandoval—was innocent. Ana went on to provide intricate and intimate details of the events surrounding Bean's death: "There was a performance of the maromas the night General Bean was killed. I was present with Joaquin Murieta. I left the maromas with him, returned to my house and went immediately to bed. All the people of the house went to sleep. Extinguished the lights. Rico, Rico's wife, and family, also a certain Sancedo and his woman—the name of the latter I do not know—were in the house; some of them slept in the house and others slept outside. Myself, Joaquin Murieta, Juanito Rico, and a young lad whom I do not know, slept in the ramadita. After I laid down and before I went to sleep, heard no noise nor voices that attracted attention. At a later part of the night, I heard some shots, and during the three shots heard voices; could not, however, distinguish whether they were Americans or Mexicans. A short moment afterwards I heard some more shots, the voice of General Bean, who arrived, crying, 'Rico! Rico! Rico!' I then sat up and saw Bean, who came dragging a cloak. Senora Jesus [Rico] opened the door, and Juanito Rico was already holding him in his arms, and said, 'Mother, it is General Bean.' The shots were fired in the direction between the house of Rico and Pena. First, three were fired; then a single shot, which was fired when the General came crying out towards the house."

Ana's last statement should have been a clue to Undersheriff Osburn that she was at best unreliable, and at worst was not telling the truth. The initial witnesses who arrived on the scene reported that one shot had been fired into Bean's chest, and then he had fired three wild shots in return. That was confirmed by the fact that Bean had one bullet in his body and three empty chambers in his pistol. Ana instead had described a conflicting scenario in which Bean fired the first three shots before he was struck by the fatal bullet. She then went on, saying, "I told Joaquin Murieta to go in search of a doctor, but in the first place an alcalde, in order that they might see what had taken place. The moment Joaquin left, a man by the name Cipriano approached, and ran back. I asked Bean who had killed him, whether it was an American? He answered, 'No.' Sonorian? 'No.' Californian? 'Yes, sir,' in English, in an affirmative manner. I again asked, 'A Californian?' To which he gave a negative nod with his head. Then Dona Jesus [Rico] came, took me by the shoulders, and said to me, 'You meddle in things that you have not to care about. There is also Christoval wounded, asking for a confessor [priest].'"

But contrary to Ana's statement, no one named Christoval, or Cristobal, was involved, let alone wounded. And in retrospect, the idea that Joaquin Murrieta would seek out an alcalde, a judge, or anyone else to report a murder is beyond incredible. Ana continued, "Then different persons arrived, also the doctor and the alcalde. This took place on the night of a Sunday. The next day Murieta and myself came to Los Angeles, and after having passed the little ditches [aqueducts], close to the Mission, Cipriano overtook us, and spoke to Murieta. He said, 'Hombre, I confide or charge you with the secret of what I have done. There is no danger here, and [I] request and charge your woman to act the same as yourself, in order that among the Americans they may not get anything out of her against us.' Cipriano came very much excited. [He] wore a serape on his shoulders and a six shooter in his waistband. Then I asked Joaquin, 'Is that the one that killed Bean?'

"'Yes,' he said. 'And why?' 'Because the General was very much intoxicated, dragging the Indian woman; and she is with a sister of Christoval. And so I earnestly charge you with the secret. If by chance they should call on you as a witness, say that you do not know. They shall not get anything out of you; neither

An artist's depiction of General Joshua Bean, murdered by Joaquin Murrieta in 1852.
City of San Diego

shall they harm you. Moreover, if I learn that you say the least thing, I shall be your worst *duende* [demon]. If you should even put yourself into the guts of the Yankees, I shall take you out. They shall not take from you what I shall do to you.'"[17]

Ana was plainly protecting Joaquin by naming Cipriano Sandoval as the killer and by providing her lover with an alibi. In an apparent effort to prevent Sandoval from being lynched, she claimed that he had shot Bean to protect an Indian woman. And she also shielded herself by claiming that Joaquin had threatened her if she talked. As a result of Ana's false statements, the lawmen and vigilantes focused on Cipriano Sandoval as the assassin. Though he had disappeared, the manhunters soon captured him. They also continued searching for the other suspects. Undersheriff Osburn's son, years later, recalled Ana's confession and said, "She gave some of the gang away and father one night dressed her up in men's clothes and took her to an acrobatic performance given in Nigger Alley, in the center of the present Chinatown. While there she pointed out one of the Murrieta gang to father and he arrested him." The man Osburn captured in Calle de los Negros was most likely Reyes Feliz. The vigilantes also collared Benito Lopez, whom they found in a hotel in Los Angeles, and relieved him of the pistol he had stolen from the Comanche, Sosa. On November 25 and 26, they brought the suspects into Los Angeles. Because the county jail—a one-story adobe near the plaza—was considered too insecure, the vigilantes guarded the prisoners night and day.[18]

Ana, not long after making her confession, decided to inform on Lopez. As the *Los Angeles Star* reported, "The woman, Ana, subsequently stated that Benito Lopez, one of the prisoners [was] a member of Solomon Pico's band, acting generally as a messenger to bring provisions, etc. She stated Lopez came to her house in Los Angeles on his arrival from above, bringing with him a roan mare, a black mule and a rifle, all of which he told her he had taken from two Americans. She also accused him of having stolen some handkerchiefs in town a week or two ago, for which he was severely flogged, and of telling her he intended to rob some three or four Americans that same night."[19]

The vigilantes subjected Reyes Feliz, Benito Lopez, and the other suspects to brutal third-degree treatment. "Dr. Hope had them in custody, and before we took their declarations he had threatened them and even applied torture," Antonio Coronel later explained. "Dr. Hope was determined on revenge at all costs." Benito Lopez first gave several conflicting accounts about the stolen animals and guns, but finally admitted that he had murdered a Comanche Indian and a black woman in Cahuenga Pass, eight miles northwest of Los Angeles. He also declared, "I knew that Ana belonged to the gang of robbers, because she herself told me that she was the woman of Joaquin. She told me that Joaquin had gone to the Tulares [San Joaquin Valley] to sell about thirty horses that he had stolen, and that he would be back in about twenty days. Another man was with Ana when I went to her house. He was a tall, thin, white complexioned man, had pantaloons, a jacket and a white hat. I went to her house twice, once in the morning, and once early at night."[20]

The man Lopez had seen with Ana was probably the notorious Pancho Daniel. As we have seen, Daniel was tall, light-complected, and nicknamed El Guero, the Blonde. He and Ana became lovers after she was released by Undersheriff Osburn. Antonio Coronel later recalled that "Pancho Daniel . . . seduced her [Ana] away from Murrieta, and left the band with her." He said that Pancho and Ana then disappeared. As Coronel explained, "It appears that Murrieta swore vengeance on Daniel and [Ana]. She turned him in in self-defense, knowing that Murrieta, her former lover, had first sent a man named Vergara to kill her. Vergara deserted, however, and got a job on the ranch of Palos Verdes." Coronel was incorrect about Ana turning in Joaquin, for although she revealed his name for the first time in Los Angeles, she did not claim that Murrieta had killed General Bean. Ana's would-be assassin was Manuel Vergara, who later became a noted bandit. In 1853 he murdered a cattle buyer near Los Angeles, then fled toward Mexico. When attempting to cross the Colorado River at Yuma, Arizona Territory, US soldiers tried to arrest him. Vergara drew a pepperbox revolver, and the troopers shot him dead. Both Ana and Pancho Daniel would feature prominently in the violent events to come.[21]

Benito Lopez insisted to the vigilance committee that he was innocent of Bean's murder. In order to convince the vigilantes that he was telling the truth, he offered to lead them to the spot where he had killed his two victims. He guided them northwest to Encino, where the vigilantes quickly found the skeletons of two bodies that had apparently been devoured by animals, as well as various pieces of clothing and personal articles. After burying the remains, they brought Lopez back into Los Angeles and held him under guard.[22]

The vigilantes also interrogated Reyes Feliz. It did not take very long for him to come clean. On November 29, just a few days following his arrest, and nineteen days after Bean's murder, the youth broke down and made a detailed confession to the vigilance committee: "My name is Reyes Feliz, am fifteen or sixteen years old, was born at the Real de Bayareca [Baroyeca], state of Sonora; did not know General Bean; don't know who killed him. Here, in Los Angeles, I heard some gentlemen, whose names I do not know, say that Murieta's woman had said that Joaquin Murieta had killed him." Feliz admitted that he had planned to rob two American gamblers in San Gabriel, and that he had killed Anselmo Marias in Sonora a year earlier. But most importantly, he said, "I belonged to the company of Joaquin Murieta and the late Pedro [Gonzales], who was killed by Americans in the 'cuesta del conejo' [Conejo Mountain]. I was not then with Pedro. I was then ill in the Tulares of the effects from bites of a bear. We robbed, Joaquin Murieta, the late Pedro, and myself. In Avisimba [Orestimba Creek], 'orilla de la Sierra' (foot of the mountains) in front of the Pueblo of San Jose, we robbed twenty horses, which we brought to the Tejon [Pass]. There the Indians took some of them from us; others, the owner took, who went in pursuit of us. I don't know his name, he was a Mexican. I have not robbed any more. I did not kill anybody else. I know nothing more about the death of General Bean."[23]

Young Reyes Feliz had been terrorized into telling the truth. His admission that he was one of Joaquin Murrieta's gang, and his statements about the killing of Pedro Gonzales by Harry Love and the recovery of stolen horses by Chief Zapatero and his Tejon Indians, were all true. Word of his confession spread quickly, and a large throng gathered for a vigilante trial at the courthouse. At that time, the Los Angeles courthouse was situated in rooms inside the two-story Bella Union Hotel, on North Main Street, two blocks from the plaza. As Horace Bell later wrote of the trial, "The place was packed to suffocation, with a dense crowd outside." According to Bell, after the evidence against Feliz was presented, the chief of the vigilantes announced, "Gentlemen, the court is now ready to hear any motion." At that a "ferocious looking gambler" stepped atop a bench and roared, "I move that Reyes Feliz be taken to the hill and hung by the neck until dead."

"All in favor of the motion will signify the same by saying 'aye,'" the vigilante leader called out.

"Aye! Aye! Aye!" yelled the crowd.

Reyes Feliz was kept under heavy guard that night, and a Catholic priest visited him, took his confession, and administered the last rites. At noon the next day, November 30, 1852, the vigilantes marched him to the top of Fort Moore Hill, also called Gallows Hill, three hundred yards north. It was the location of a small fort that had been occupied by American troops in the Mexican War. Today the site is the Fort Moore Pioneer Memorial, and the views from the hill are largely obstructed by tall buildings. Young Feliz climbed onto the temporary gallows that had been set up and gazed out at the mission church, the plaza, and the adobes of Calle de los Negros, all spread out below him. It was the last he saw of the old pueblo. A reporter for the *Los Angeles Star* was present and wrote, "Just before he was launched into eternity, he addressed a few words to the assembly, saying that his punishment was justly merited, and advising them to never put faith in woman." Feliz's latter comment was no doubt directed at Ana. Continued the *Star*, "He persisted to the last in knowing nothing of the death of General Bean." The vigilantes then pulled a black hood over his head and affixed a rope around his neck, and a moment later, Reyes Feliz plunged through the scaffold's trap door.[24]

A vigilante jury of twelve men, Anglos and Latinos, spent the next few days poring over the evidence and debating the fate of Benito Lopez and the shoemaker, Cipriano Sandoval. Finally they announced that they would render their verdict on Sunday, December 5. That morning, as a crowd gathered at the Bella Union Hotel, word arrived of yet another murder. Two Mexicans

The Los Angeles Plaza with the old Plaza Church, about 1870. Behind it is Fort Moore Hill, also called Gallows Hill, where Reyes Feliz and others were lynched in 1852. *Huntington Library, San Marino, CA*

from Sonora got into a quarrel, and one, Yginio Barumas, whipped out a knife and stabbed the other in his heart, killing him. Local Native Americans, motivated by a $50 reward, quickly tracked down Barumas and marched him to the Bella Union. The vigilantes gave Barumas a short trial in which two witnesses testified that they had seen him do the killing.

By this time, the only evidence the vigilantes had of Cipriano Sandoval's guilt was double hearsay: Ana's statement that Joaquin had said that Sandoval had killed Bean. Nonetheless, Dr. Hope, the vigilante leader, was determined that someone should pay the penalty. As Antonio Coronel said, "He insisted that if we couldn't clarify exactly which one of them was the assassin,

Sandoval should be hanged. When the committee had finished its investigation, the results were turned over to the vigilantes. Although we didn't think they justified the death penalty even for Sandoval, the people resolved to hang all three of them for the murders they had confessed."[25]

At three o'clock that afternoon, Undersheriff Osburn, the vigilantes, and a huge crowd of Anglos and Latinos escorted Lopez, Sandoval, and Barumas to the rude gallows atop Fort Moore Hill. They were accompanied by the Catholic padre. Each of the condemned men was allowed to address the throng, and Sandoval did so, insisting that he was innocent of Bean's murder. A journalist who was present wrote, "Lopez appeared to be most affected at the situation in which he found himself. He acknowledged the justice of his punishment, and, like Reyes, cautioned the spectators to avoid bad women." Finally Yginio Barumas gave a long speech and condemned the vigilantes and their summary trial. "We made a mistake in coming to this country, amigos," he said to the Mexicans in the crowd. "They are too active for us. Go back, every one of you, to Sonora, and obey the laws, or you will soon be traveling this same road." Then, turning to Undersheriff Osburn, he barked, "And now, sons of bitches, do your worst!"

Osburn fastened a hemp rope around each man's neck. Horace Bell later wrote that he had attended the hanging and watched the final moments. "They all kissed the crucifix, the rope was cut, the trap fell, and the five men were launched into eternity. A peal of thunder announced the end of the tragedy. Slowly and silently the crowd dispersed. The rain commenced to fall in torrents, and the grim bartender at the Bella Union reaped a golden harvest on that gloomy Sabbath afternoon." Whether Bell was actually there, or simply repeated stories he had heard, is unclear. However, it is unlikely that if he really witnessed a triple hanging he would forget that crucial detail and change the number to five. Either way, Bell concluded his account by criticizing the vigilantes. "The author retired early on that evening, pondering sadly and solemnly over the events of the day, and could not refrain from thinking that humanity would have been greatly benefitted, if about four-fifths of that mob had been disposed of in the same way as had been the hapless Mexicans who were hung."[26]

Horace Bell also said that Joaquin Murrieta had remained unsuspected in Los Angeles until Reyes Feliz talked: "At the time this confession was made, Joaquin was walking around, as unconcerned as any other gentleman; but when the minions of the mob went to lay heavy hand upon him he was gone." Murrieta then fled north, leaving behind one of the longest standing and most perplexing questions in the history of frontier Los Angeles: Who killed General Joshua Bean? According to Bell, "One of the prisoners, Cipriano Sandoval, the village cobbler of San Gabriel, also, after having for several days maintained his innocence, and denied any and all knowledge of the murder, came out and made a full confession. He said he was on his way home from the maromas at about 11 o'clock one night, it being quite dark. He heard a shot, and then the footsteps of a man running toward him; that a moment after he came in violent contact with a man whom he at once recognized as Felipe Read [Reid]. They mutually recognized each other, when Felipe said, 'Cipriano, I have just shot Bean. Here is five dollars; take it, say nothing about it, and when you want money come to me and get it.'" Bell's account has been followed by most writers and historians ever since, and today the murder is generally attributed to Felipe Reid.[27]

However, contrary to Bell's claim, Cipriano Sandoval never confessed to having any knowledge of or complicity in Bean's killing. Even standing on the gallows, he insisted on his innocence. And not a single contemporary source, other than Bell, names Felipe Reid as a suspect in the murder. The *Los Angeles Star*, which provided detailed accounts of the case and published the confessions of Ana Benites, Reyes Feliz, and Benito Lopez, printed not a word of Sandoval's purported admission. In fact, a year later, the *Star* published an editorial decrying vigilantism, saying, "We cannot forget the inhuman execution of Cipriano Sandoval, who affirmed his innocence, and whose character as a peaceable, estimable and industrious man, was certified by many persons well known." But the *Star* said nothing about Felipe Reid being the guilty man, nor of Sandoval taking money to protect him. In 1857, *El Clamor Público*, the Spanish language newspaper of Los Angeles, also asserted Sandoval's innocence and likewise made no mention of Felipe Reid.[28]

In 1852 the Los Angeles vigilantes not only had never heard of Joaquin Murrieta but also had no idea that Reyes Feliz was his brother-in-law. Had they known who Murrieta and Feliz were, they surely would have given more credence to the youth's confession. Feliz's statement, in which he implicated Joaquin in the Bean murder and also admitted to stealing horses and killing a man in Sonora, was, in legal terms, an admission against his own penal interest. In other words, few, if any, would falsely admit to committing such serious crimes, especially in the gold rush when horse thieves and killers were frequently lynched. Reyes Feliz's disclosure that Joaquin had slain General Bean is clear evidence of Murrieta's guilt. And the unavoidable fact is that one of the most murderous outlaws in American history was just paces away from the scene of Bean's murder. In the end, there can be no serious question that Joaquin Murrieta killed General Joshua Bean.[29]

The young bandido, after escaping from Los Angeles, returned to the Mother Lode. Within a few months, everyone in California—and then throughout North America—would know the name Joaquin Murrieta.

CHAPTER 11

JOAQUIN, THE MOUNTAIN ROBBER

Nothing had gone right for Joaquin Murrieta. Since his arrival in California, he had been abused by Anglos and driven from his mining claim. With gold everywhere, he could not get his hands on it without stealing. A proud young man and a natural leader of men, he had stooped to dealing monte for a living. Now his woman had left him for Pancho Daniel, and his brothers-in-law, Claudio and Reyes Feliz, had both been slain. He had surely heard of their demise by word of mouth, for reports of their deaths, especially that of Reyes and his confession that implicated Murrieta in General Bean's murder, had been published in both English and Spanish in California newspapers. Although Californios had been prominent in the killings of both men, Joaquin blamed Anglos. He seethed with anger and thirsted for revenge, as well as for riches.

Murrieta rode back to the mining region, where he began gathering together a gang of dangerous bandidos. His leadership abilities, coupled with his charismatic personality, made it easy for him to find recruits. Those qualities were best recounted by his paramour, Ana, also known as Mariana. As a journalist who later interviewed her wrote, "She describes him as possessing such powers of fascination over the Mexicans with whom he associated that there was a constant rivalry among them for admission to his band."[1]

Joaquin Murrieta and Three Fingered Jack, in an illustration by artist Charles Christian Nahl. *John Boessenecker collection.*

Chief among Joaquin's men was the violent Bernardino Garcia—Three Fingered Jack. He harbored many of the same resentments as Joaquin: his homeland had been conquered by Yankees, his marriage to Hilaria had failed, and any chance of achieving prosperity through her ranch and sawmill was gone. The gang included Joaquin's half-brother, Jesus Murrieta, and his sole surviving brother-in-law, Jesus Feliz, then about nineteen years old. The bullet-scarred Jose Barrillo, who had shot and killed William W. Janes at the fandango in Stockton eight months earlier, also rode with them. Another, Pedro Sanchez, was known as "a bold, daring, and blood-thirsty scoundrel" whom Joaquin made one of his trusted lieutenants following the death of Claudio Feliz. Also prominent among the recruits was the notorious Joaquin Valenzuela, alias Joaquin Nacomoreno, who most likely was accompanied by his brother, Jesus, alias Chiquito. Antonio Valencia, a young Mexican, rode with the gang, as did an anonymous Englishman who had reportedly come to California with the Regiment of New York Volunteers in 1847. Yet another was a burly Mexican desperado, known to Anglos as Big Bill. Several other outlaws, never identified, also joined Joaquin's band.[2]

Murrieta and his men made camp at an isolated spot high in the Bear Mountains of Calaveras County. The tallest point in the range, at 2,800 feet, is still called Joaquin Peak, and today it looms above Highway 49 a few miles south of San Andreas. One Calaveras pioneer later described their hideout: "A beautiful stream, originating in a large spring in the mountain, after flowing through a dark, deep canyon, emerges into a plateau two or three miles in length, descends one side of the mountain abruptly, forming several cascades or waterfalls, of surpassing beauty, then wanders away through deep canyons and undulating meadows to the Calaveras River . . . It was a wild, weird place, reached by a bridle path that wound around the mountains, by giant rocks, by tremendous trees, sometimes scaling steep ascents, sometimes on the verge of deep precipices, and over steep inclines."[3]

That winter was one of the most severe on record. In December 1852, the Sierra foothills saw heavy snow and rain that flooded creeks and rivers. Several bridges across the Cosumnes, Mokelumne, and Calaveras Rivers were washed away. Wagon roads and trails became muddy swamps, and streams were almost impassable. Despite the harsh weather, Joaquin and his men began planning a series of daring bandit raids. One night in mid-January 1853, the outlaws saddled their mounts and headed north to San Andreas, where they split up into smaller groups. Riding to the surrounding ranches and mines, they stole seventy horses and returned to their mountain hideout at daybreak. The stolen animals would prove essential in carrying out a spree of bloody forays that would be remembered for more than 170 years in legend, history, and lore.

A few days later, on January 20, 1853, Murrieta and two of his men swung into their saddles and rode down from Joaquin Peak. They continued a few miles northeast and reined up at a small mining town on the banks of Willow Creek, three miles south of San Andreas. It was called Yaqui Camp because it had been first settled by Yaqui Indians from northern Mexico. Surrounded by oaks, pines, and manzanita brush, it consisted of fifty or sixty rude cabins and tents clustered above the flooded creek bed. Yaqui Camp was a thriving settlement, home to about four hundred settlers, some Anglo and Chinese but most Latino, who shoveled gravel into sluice boxes along Willow Creek.

At first the bandidos attracted little attention as they casually dismounted. But they suddenly burst into a tent occupied by several Chinese miners. Brandishing revolvers, Joaquin and his riders robbed the stunned Chinese men of two leather gold pokes filled with $160 in dust. Murrieta and the rest then leaped back onto their horses and galloped out of Yaqui Camp before any of the townsfolk could react. Determined to get more gold, the gang rode a mile north to a small Chinese mining claim. Here they came across another tent with a number of Chinese prospectors inside. According to a local journalist, the three robbers began "assaulting its inhabitants, holding loaded pistols at their heads to keep them quiet, and robbed them of two bags of gold dust, $90 and $60." One miner named Ah Kop refused to turn over his gold, and he tried to put up a fight. It was a deadly decision. One of the bandidos yanked out a razor-sharp knife and slashed him to the ground. Ah Kop died almost instantly.

Murrieta and his pistoleros sprang into their saddles and made the short ride back to their hideout on Joaquin Peak. By that time, news of the murder had quickly spread to the surrounding mining camps. Outraged Anglo miners started a manhunt around Yaqui Camp and soon picked up a Mexican from Chihuahua named Reyes Juarez. But instead of summarily hanging him, they put their prisoner on a horse and rode with him to Mokelumne Hill. It was then the Calaveras County seat, located nine miles north of San Andreas, and popularly known as "Moke Hill." The town was perched atop a mountain near the Mokelumne River and boasted a population of almost ten thousand. It was one of the busiest and most important settlements in the mining region. Today Mokelumne Hill has less than seven hundred residents, but many of the old buildings are still standing. The posse brought Juarez into Moke Hill and through the crowds of miners, pack trains, and rumbling wagons on the main street. The townsmen at first were oblivious to the prisoner, and no lynch mob gathered. The manhunters turned Juarez over to the county sheriff, who locked him in jail. Juarez was then promptly charged in court with the murder of Ah Kop. The evidence against Reyes Juarez is unknown, but he was either released for lack of evidence or broke out of jail, because he never ended up at the end of a rope, or in the state's prison brig.[4]

On January 21, the day after Ah Kop's murder, Murrieta and his band rode out again from Joaquin Peak on a reckless foray of robbery and murder. The bandidos had little fear of manhunters. They stormed back into Yaqui Camp, six-guns flaming, and shot and killed an Anglo miner. Then they galloped through the hilly terrain to the Bay State Ranch, a small mining settlement two miles northwest of San Andreas. Nearby they robbed and murdered a Chinese prospector. Next the bandidos raced a few miles south to Foreman's Ranch, situated just a mile east of their Joaquin Peak hideout. It was named after David Foreman, who had built a hotel and ferry across San Antonio Creek, and is known today as Fourth Crossing. Joaquin and his men charged in, shot another American miner to death, and then fled. There were no eyewitnesses to the three killings. The victims' bodies were not discovered for at least a day, and their names were not recorded in the newspapers.[5]

Two days later, on the morning of January 23, a Mexican riding an expensive horse stopped at the Bay State Ranch. The ranch, owned by John Hall, was situated on the North Fork of the Calaveras River. Nearby, on the main wagon road from Stockton to Mokelumne Hill, was a ferry operated by David Davis. The rancher, Hall, was on the alert due to the recent murders. He spotted the suspicious rider and thought that his horse was stolen. Apparently, however, he did not connect the horseman with the killings. Hall arrested the Mexican and guarded him inside the ranch house. Soon afterward his ferryman neighbor, Davis, walked up. As Hall stepped outside and described the arrest to Davis, the Mexican removed his boots and spurs and slipped quietly from the house. Hall and Davis spotted his movement, and the man broke into a dead run. The rancher and ferryman, both unarmed, mounted horses and pursued the fugitive down the road. They had not gone far when three mounted Mexicans, pistols in hand, appeared in front of them and blocked their path. They were members of Joaquin's band. As the desperadoes covered Hall and Davis with six-shooters, their compadre climbed behind one of the horsemen. Flourishing their revolvers, all three riders galloped off in different directions.

John Hall and David Davis raced back to the ranch, where they sent a horseback messenger into San Andreas for help. Then the pair grabbed their guns and started in pursuit of the outlaws. They trailed them south to Yaqui Camp and then a few miles east to the mining town of Calaveritas, situated on a creek of the same name. There Hall and Davis were joined by three possemen who had responded from San Andreas. One was Charles H. Ellis, a twenty-three-year-old constable and Mexican War veteran. Ellis was a courageous officer who enforced the law without fear or favor. Two months earlier, a pair of Anglo ruffians had robbed two Chinese miners and beat one of them to death. Ellis investigated the murder and captured both of the culprits. Another member of the little posse was William Jefferson "Jeff" Gatewood, a young

Jeff Gatewood, one of the posse who shot it out with Joaquin Murrieta's gang near Calaveritas. *John Boessenecker collection.*

lawyer who had also served in the Mexican War. Gatewood later became a newspaperman, and following a political dispute, he shot and killed a man in a formal duel in San Andreas. He then settled in San Diego, where in 1868 he founded the *San Diego Union*, which is still published today.[6]

Charles Ellis, Jeff Gatewood, and the other three manhunters tracked the outlaws up a gulch near Calaveritas, then followed them east for several miles across the foothills. As the possemen reached the base of a hill, they suddenly spotted a dozen riders resting their mounts on its chaparral-covered peak. The horsemen were Joaquin and his gang. One of the posse swung up his rifle, took dead aim, and squeezed the trigger. His heavy slug slammed into a mounted bandido, who slumped over his saddle, then dropped from sight behind the hill. Murrieta and his men were enraged, for until then, no one in Calaveras had dared resist them. The pistoleros leaped onto their mounts and raced pell-mell down the hill, charging directly at the manhunters. But instead of fleeing, Constable Ellis and his little posse dove for cover behind a pile of rocks. Joaquin and his compadres swept forward, their terrified horses foaming with sweat as smoke and muzzle flashes exploded from the outlaws' pistol barrels.

The bullets whined by the manhunters and tore harmlessly into the ground behind them. Ellis and his comrades immediately opened a blistering fusillade with their rifles and six-guns. The dull thud of gunfire echoed through the hills, and clouds of gunsmoke enshrouded the combatants. They traded numerous shots at close range, and three more of the Mexicans reeled in their saddles, wounded by bullets. Finally Joaquin and his bloodied bandidos wheeled their horses about and fled. The possemen were more than relieved, because they had run out of ammunition. Ellis, Gatewood, and their comrade galloped into San Andreas for help, while John Hall and David Davis rode back to the Bay State Ranch.

Murrieta was both unfazed and infuriated by his close call with the posse. Instead of vanishing into the oak-covered foothills, he and his bandidos rode back south to Yaqui Camp to seek revenge. They thundered in on their mustangs, six-shooters blazing. The outlaws fired at every Anglo they saw. One of their bullets struck a young miner named John Carter, killing him. The gang then rode five miles east through the Sierra Nevada foothills and along Calaveritas Creek until they reached the Phoenix Quartz Mill, arriving that night. The mill, owned by the Phoenix Quartz Mining Company, was situated on Calaveritas Creek, in a deep canyon downstream from a spot that ever after was called Joaquin Gulch.[7]

Despite its remote location, the Phoenix Quartz Mining Company employed the most advanced technology available, including a stamp mill, powered by a steam engine. The stamp mill crushed quartz ore so that pure gold could be extracted. The Phoenix Mill was a major operation and employed numerous mechanics and laborers. Seven months earlier, a visitor to the site described it: "They have erected the most solid and substantial quartz mill that we have seen anywhere in our travels. There are fifteen stampers, each weighing nine hundred pounds. The crushed rock passes from these between two iron rollers, weighing together six thousand pounds, which are intended to pulverize it to the last degree. It is then carried into an iron amalgamator, twelve feet in diameter, where by a circular motion imparted to its contents, the gold and quicksilver are made to unite. The foundation and every part of the mill have been constructed under the supervision of an old quartz miner, in connection with an experienced architect, and no pains or expense have been spared to render them most solid and durable. A steam engine of seventy-five [horsepower] is attached to the mill, and sets the whole in motion."[8]

The millhouse, a rude log cabin with a canvas roof, was occupied by Peter Woodbeck and another miner. Both men were asleep when the sound of gunfire jarred them awake. As Joaquin's gang poured a volley into the millhouse, Woodbeck and his comrade seized their guns and opened fire on the bandidos. At first, behind cover, the pair seemed to have the best of the fight, and they wounded two of the desperadoes. Then another robber scrambled up the millhouse wall, lifted the canvas roof, and fired down on them. Woodbeck and his companion shot back, one with a pistol and the other with a shotgun, and wounded their assailant twice in his shoulder. But the bandido kept firing, and the two miners died, riddled with bullets. Joaquin and the rest then fled, taking two of their wounded *compadres* with them and leaving the third one to fend for himself.[9]

The gang had murdered seven men in four days, two of them Chinese. Though surely spurred on by a hatred for Anglos, their targeting of unarmed Chinese gold hunters showed that their principal motivation was pure greed. Word of the slaughter spread like wildfire, and the next morning, January 24, three hundred armed miners held a mass meeting in Calaveras County. Instead of focusing their rage on the bandit gang, they directed it at Latinos in general. A local journalist reported that they passed resolutions "making it the duty of every American citizen at all events to exterminate the Mexican race from the county. The foreigners should first receive notice to leave, and if they refused they were to be shot down and their property confiscated." The mob quickly put words into action. Two days later a Calaveras pioneer wrote in his diary, "They then started the Mexicans out, and ordered them away from the mines and set fire to all their houses. The Mexicans all left and today I saw several of them on the road to Stockton with their women, children, and what they could pack on their backs. I also understood that two hundred men had started this morning for San Andreas to rout the greasers from there, as they had all flocked in there."[10]

Because Joaquin was well known in Calaveras County, witnesses recognized the young gambler and identified him as chief of the rampaging band. As early as January 29, 1853, just nine days after the raids began, the editor of the *Calaveras Chronicle* reported, "The leader of the gang is a desperate fellow named Joaquin." The Anglo miners now began focusing their efforts on the bandidos rather than innocent Mexicans. They organized a huge manhunt, with groups of men divided into numerous smaller posses. Some rode to the ferries on the Calaveras and Stanislaus Rivers in an effort to block the outlaws' flight. Another posse galloped to the Phoenix Quartz Mill, where they discovered the bullet-riddled bodies of Peter Woodbeck and his fellow miner inside the millhouse. The manhunters located a blood trail and followed it down Calaveritas Creek, where they found a wounded Mexican hiding in a tent. He was the same robber who had been shot at the mill and then abandoned by Joaquin and his band. The possemen quickly produced a rope, strung it over a tree limb, and lynched the anonymous bandit.

At the same time, a large posse raided Yaqui Camp, where they discovered the Mexican desperado whom Anglos called Big Bill. According to the editor of the *Calaveras Chronicle*, Big Bill had "boasted of having killed Americans last year, and . . . was supposed to have been concerned in the present murders." The manhunters captured Big Bill, dragged him to a nearby tree, and put a rope around his neck. As the *Calaveras Chronicle* said, "He was hanged forthwith." The possemen buried his body near the base of the lynching tree, then spurred their horses eight miles south to the mining town of Cherokee Flat, situated just north of Angels Camp. Angels Camp would become famous twelve years later in Mark Twain's popular short story, "The Celebrated Jumping Frog of Calaveras County." As the manhunters rode into Cherokee Flat, they spotted two Mexicans leaping onto their horses to flee. The posse opened fire, killing one Mexican instantly. They captured his companion and discovered that he had fresh wounds inflicted by pistol and shotgun. The *Calaveras Chronicle* reported that "a bullet hole and a charge of shot was found in his shoulder." He turned out to be the bandido who had been shot on the roof of the Phoenix Quartz Mill. The posse marched their wounded and nameless prisoner to the town's hotel, the Cherokee House. There they stood him under a tree, tossed up a rope, and hanged him on the spot. Needless to say, Mark Twain omitted that gory incident from his humorous anecdotes of the frontier.[11]

The manhunters, after killing the three desperadoes, rode back to Yaqui Camp to begin a search of the Bear Mountains. Joaquin Peak was plainly visible from the camp, and atop it was a tall, half-dead tree with a single bough at the top, resembling a flag. It was widely known as the "flag tree." The possemen believed that the site of the tree served as a lookout for Joaquin's band. They scaled the mountain but found no trace of the outlaws. Then, while several posses were busy hunting the gang, a mob of enraged Anglos descended on Yaqui Camp. Convinced that it was Joaquin's headquarters, they drove out all the Latino miners and destroyed almost every house and tent in the camp. Four years later, a journalist visited Yaqui Camp and found nothing left of the once prosperous settlement. He wrote that "there remains not a single house, all having been destroyed during the Joaquin excitement . . . so effectually were they destroyed that not a single post or other mark remains." The newspaperman added that "the stump of a tree still stands, upon which the exasperated citizens, hung one of the great robber's compeers, known as Big Bill. He was buried near the tree, and his body remained there until last fall, when some Mexican relatives or friends removed it."[12]

By this time, the mining camps of Calaveras County were gripped with terror and rage. "The band is led by a robber, named Joaquin, a very desperate man," a local journalist reported a few days later. "He levied his 'black mail' generally upon the Chinese population, a very peaceable and industrious class. With his band, he would frequently enter their tents, and compel them to furnish him with money and cook for him and his accomplices whatever food they required. This has been done in many instances." The newspaperman added that a large mob of angry miners "resolved to burn the habitations of the Mexicans indiscriminately, deprive them of the arms they might have in possession, and give them all notice to quit . . . The entire Mexican population has been driven from San Andreas and the forks of the Calaveras. The greatest excitement prevails in every direction. If an American meets a Mexican he takes his horse, his arms, and bids him leave."[13]

Not all Anglos agreed with such vigilantism. One who ran a general store in Murphys wrote in his diary that he was jolted by the "shocking news . . . of the murder of six persons by a party of Mexicans, or greasers, as they are termed." However, he added, "The pursuers are reported to have destroyed all the Mexican tents or dwellings that came in their way, which [I] believe to be cruel and unjust, the innocent must suffer in that case. But many persons who are prejudiced say they are all alike, 'a set of cut throats and should be exterminated or drove out of the country.'"[14]

On January 26, a miner named David C. Cady, who claimed to be a US Army captain, recruited a band of vigilantes, thirty strong, in San Andreas. Cady was, in fact, a colorful former soldier who had fought in the Texas Revolution in 1836 and then served as a Texas Ranger captain in the Mexican War. Cady had received word that Joaquin was holed up in the mining settlement of Jesus Maria, eleven miles north. Jesus Maria was a booming camp, settled mainly by Mexicans and Chilenos. Cady and his men mounted their horses and headed out of San Andreas, determined to capture Joaquin's gang. They approached Jesus Maria that evening, quickly surrounded the camp, and declared martial law. When Cady spotted two Latino miners winking at each other while working their placer claim, he arrested them both as "suspicious characters." One was named Ygnacio Moretto—a common misspelling of Murrieta—but whether he was related to the bandit chieftain is unknown. Cady and his men placed a guard over the two prisoners. Then they forced the town baker to provide them with food and liquor and made camp for the night.

In the morning, they brought Moretto and his fellow miner into San Andreas and turned them over to Theophilus W. Taliaferro, the town's justice of the peace. Taliaferro was a fair man, a Mexican War veteran who, three years later, would marry a Latina woman in San Francisco. An angry lynch mob quickly gathered around Judge Taliaferro and the prisoners, but he warned them off. After listening to the testimony, Taliaferro found that there was no evidence to hold Moretto and his compadre, and he ordered their release. That decision infuriated Captain Cady, and he threatened to report Taliaferro to the War Department in Washington, DC. Soon afterward, however, the editor of the *Calaveras Chronicle* announced that Cady was not an active US Army captain and declared him to be *non compos mentis*, or insane.[15]

A few days later, on the night of January 31, miners in Angels Camp captured a young Mexican whom several witnesses identified as a brother of Joaquin. Upon questioning, he admitted that he was Joaquin's brother, but refused to say anything else. The miners grabbed a rope, strung him to a tree, and hoisted him into the air. Then the vigilantes dropped the youth to the ground and ordered him to confess. As a local journalist reported, "This he refused to do, saying that he knew nothing of the doings of his brother, and that he never engaged in any of the outrages. He was again dragged up and on being let down, he confessed that he was associated with the gang, and that it had been his business to spy out the course of the Americans, when it was possible to mislead them as to the course taken by his brother. He had also reported to the band the movements of other men whom they designed to rob, and as a general thing, had been engaged in a most desperate game. The citizens instantly hung him up."[16]

Within minutes the youth was dead. He was likely Jesus Murrieta, Joaquin's half brother. Joaquin and the rest of the gang were nearby, unaware of his fate. The same night, they rode up to the Hawkeye House, a hotel four miles east of Angels Camp, on the wagon road to Murphys. There they robbed and murdered two Chinese miners and vanished into the darkness. Another manhunt was quickly organized. "About twenty citizens are out after Joaquin," said a local reporter, who added that it was "hardly possible that he will escape. Guards and watchmen are stationed in every direction, and the county is being secured all over. If he is taken, there will be an end to his career."[17]

One of the men on the lookout for the gang was Noble B. Hubbell, an Ohio medical doctor turned gold seeker. He was near the gold camp of Vallecito, not far from the Hawkeye House, when he spotted Joaquin Murrieta, Three Fingered

Angels Camp, where gold miners captured and lynched Jesus Murrieta, Joaquin's half brother, in 1853. *John Boessenecker collection.*

Jack, and two other bandidos. Hubbell was close enough to get a good look at Murrieta and his men. He recalled that his "first impulse was to shoot him, and the reason he did not shoot was that there were three with Joaquin." Hubbell had only a single-shot rifle and knew he was outnumbered. He later explained that he "felt the chances were against him and therefore he did not shoot." Once again Joaquin and his riders escaped.[18]

By this time, several possemen returned from their manhunt convinced that Murrieta was bulletproof. Declared the editor of the *Calaveras Chronicle*, "He has been seen on several occasions and fired at. When shot at, he receives the balls in the breast with a complacent smile. It has been a matter of surprise to his pursuers that the balls fired at him have no effect. We learn from a gentleman who shot at him from a short distance that he wears a coat of mail beneath his clothes." The newspaper's story of Joaquin and his bulletproof coat would be repeated for generations. Because chain mail and bullet proof vests did not exist on the California frontier, it is far more likely that the posse riders were simply poor marksmen.[19]

Elwood T. Beatty, the justice of the peace who led a posse after Joaquin and his band. *Idaho State Historical Society*

Despite the fact that he had been identified, and five members of his band slain, Murrieta was unfazed. Calaveras County was swarming with posses and vigilantes, so Joaquin and his men rode toward Campo Seco, a mining town thirteen miles west of San Andreas. Confusingly, it had the same name as the Campo Seco located near Sonora. Two miners who were hunting stolen horses spotted the bandidos and rushed into Campo Seco, where they notified the justice of the peace, Ellwood T. Beatty. The latter was a thirty-seven-year-old carpenter from Pennsylvania who had joined the gold rush in 1849. Beatty first settled in San Francisco, where he built houses in the booming city. Following the great fire of 1850, in which much of the downtown was destroyed, he headed for Calaveras County and became a miner. In 1852 Beatty was elected justice of the peace, and he took his duties seriously.[20]

The job of a justice of the peace was to preside over minor criminal cases in court; it was the justice's constables who made arrests. But gold rush law enforcement was so primitive that such distinctions were often ignored, as in Henry Cocks's killing of Claudio Feliz. On February 4, 1853, Beatty raised a posse and rode out of Campo Seco in search of the gang. He quickly learned that the bandidos had robbed several local Chinese miners. The Chinese victims told him that the robbers were Mexicans, five in number, well-dressed, heavily armed, and mounted on fine horseflesh. That evening Beatty rode to Winter's Bar, a small gold camp five miles west of Campo Seco, where a ferry crossed the Mokelumne River. Winter's Bar is now covered by the Camanche Reservoir. There Beatty ordered the ferrymen, "Let no one pass during the night."

Beatty hoped to trap the outlaws on the south side of the Mokelumne River. However, instead of guarding the ferry landing themselves, he and his posse returned to their homes and beds in Campo Seco. Beatty's warning to the ferrymen was to no avail. At midnight Joaquin and his men galloped up to Winter's Bar and forced the ferrymen at gunpoint to take them across the surging Mokelumne. In the morning, word was sent to Beatty in Campo Seco, and he reorganized his posse and started in pursuit. They crossed the Mokelumne River and headed north, spending the next week hunting the bandits in the rugged hill country that is now Amador County. Beatty heard rumors that Joaquin and his riders had murdered some Chinese miners at Big Bar, on the Cosumnes River, and had stopped and looted a stagecoach on the wagon road to Sacramento. Those reports, which spread quickly through the terrorized mining camps, turned out to be totally false, and caused Beatty and his posse to waste precious time. Finally they got a real tip: the outlaws were at Camp Opera, a mining settlement near the Mokelumne River. However, by the time Beatty and his men galloped through a driving rain into Camp Opera, Joaquin and his bandidos were gone. The posse began a search, and in the nearby hills, Beatty found two horses that had been stolen by the gang. "They are in bad order, having been left by Joaquin," Beatty later reported. He and his exhausted possemen rode back to Campo Seco empty-handed, save the stolen animals.[21]

The isolated foothills, covered with chaparral and scrub oak and scored with countless flooded creeks and ravines, proved ideal for Murrieta's band to evade capture. It turned out that Joaquin and his men, after crossing the ferry at Winter's Bar, had made camp north of the Mokelumne River that night. Then they continued twenty-five miles farther north through the foothills to the deep canyon of the Cosumnes River. At noon on February 8, Murrieta and three of his gang rode up to Big Bar, a small mining camp on the north bank of the Cosumnes. William McMullen, a twenty-six-year-old gold hunter, was inside the general store. He spotted the four riders approaching. Then they plunged their horses into the roiling stream and swam them across to Big Bar. He was immediately suspicious of the well-dressed, heavily armed strangers.[22]

McMullen was a born leader, and he had a strong instinct for dealing with danger. A native of New York, he had served in the Mexican War, then caught gold fever and arrived in California in 1849. Two years later, he settled at Big Bar, where he operated a placer mining claim. Later, after a decade of gold hunting, McMullen bought the local newspaper, the *Amador Dispatch*, in 1860. McMullen was a fervent Unionist, and when the Civil War broke out, he recruited a company of volunteers in Amador County. He was then appointed a captain in the First Infantry, California Volunteers, popularly known as the California Column. They marched nine hundred miles to the Southwest and skirmished with Confederate forces in Arizona and New Mexico. McMullen, due to his skill, was promoted to lieutenant colonel in 1864, and spent the rest of his life in New Mexico.[23]

William McMullen's military campaigns, however, were far in the future. On that wintry day in 1853, he closely watched the four riders ford the Cosumnes and head up the river toward Possum Bar, a mile distant, situated south of modern-day

Latrobe. At that time, Possum Bar was home to a group of Chinese miners. Joaquin and his men disappeared from McMullen's sight and continued up the trail. Reaching Possum Bar, they galloped into the camp, forced the unarmed Chinese out of several tents, and helped themselves to their food. Two of the Chinese miners slipped away and dashed down the riverbank to Big Bar for help. McMullen was still in the store a half hour later when the pair came running up, yelling, "The Mexicans are no good!"

McMullen accompanied the two Chinese prospectors back to Possum Bar, and the trio crept unnoticed into the camp. The Mexicans' horses were hitched in front of a miners' tent, and Murrieta and his compadres were lounging inside another tent nearby. McMullen suspected immediately that they were Joaquin's band. He crawled away quietly and rushed back to Big Bar. At the same time, Joaquin and his three compadres finished their meal. Then they began robbing the Chinese, ripping money belts from their waists and looting their tents. When two Chinese tried to resist, Murrieta and his men opened fire, wounding one in the hand and another in the neck. Then the four bandidos mounted up and rode casually out of Possum Bar.

Meanwhile McMullen reached Big Bar and spread the alarm. In less than an hour, he managed to raise an armed group of eleven miners, mounted on fast horses. McMullen and his posse charged up the Cosumnes riverbank to Possum Bar. According to a journalist who later interviewed McMullen, "Before reaching the camp, several Chinamen ran out to meet them, beckoning at the same time for them to increase their pace. One of these had been shot through the hand, and another through the neck, without receiving any serious injury. The camp had been plundered by the robbers of its most valuable effects, and when the Chinamen refused to give up their money, their belts containing it were stripped from their bodies in a brutal and determined manner."

McMullen and the possemen started up the river in pursuit. They had not gone far when they met two Anglo miners who said they had encountered the four bandits on the trail. The desperadoes had approached them on horseback, but one of the Anglos pulled his six-gun and warned them off. At that, one of the Mexican outlaws declared, "We intended no harm to Americans. We are only attempting to frighten Chinamen."

The two prospectors said that the bandidos made no trouble and then galloped away. McMullen's posse continued to track the robbers, but the manhunters lagged far behind them. Joaquin's band rode south for ten miles through the brush-choked hills and stopped at a Chinese mining claim north of Dry Creek, which flows into the Mokelumne River. They held up the miners and escaped with $200 in gold. Then they continued south, raided a second Chinese camp, and finally looted a third Chinese settlement on the banks of Dry Creek. The bandidos then forded the creek and struck the main wagon road, now Highway 88, that led east into the important mining town of Jackson. Jackson was a busy settlement of several hundred people, situated on one of the main routes from Sacramento to the mines. The location was a picturesque one, in a valley watered by Jackson Creek and surrounded by forested hills.

Jackson was also the site of the famous hanging tree where Jose Cheverino and three other men had been lynched. A large, twisted oak, it towered over Main Street in the center of town. But that prospect hardly fazed Joaquin. Skirting the hamlet, he and his compadres continued north two miles to Jackson Gate, arriving that evening, February 9. Jackson Gate was a small gold camp named after a gap in a nearby high rock wall. Joaquin was so brazen that he made no effort to hide from the townsfolk. William McMullen, who later learned of Murrieta's visit, recalled that the outlaw had once been a gambler in Jackson Gate. "Joaquin himself, who is well known in the neighborhood, was one of the number," McMullen said. "He had presided over a monte table, at one of the Spanish houses in the village." The townsfolk remembered Joaquin well from his sojourn there more than a

The gold camp of Jackson, showing the hanging tree on Main Street in the center of town. *John Boessenecker collection.*

year earlier, when he had drifted through the gold camps, dealing cards. Murrieta and his men spent a restful night camped just outside Jackson Gate.[24]

The next day, Joaquin and the gang saddled up and cantered south out of Jackson Gate. They soon spotted Dr. Volney Smith, a dentist from Jackson, coming up the road on horseback. As Smith approached, the bandidos drew their guns. But the alert dentist was too quick for them. He wheeled his horse and dug spurs into its flanks. Bent low over the saddle, Smith raced two miles back into Jackson. The doctor had "escaped by being well mounted," according to a local newspaperman. Soon after the encounter with Dr. Smith, Murrieta and his band came across two more riders on the same wagon road. One was John Horsley, a miner from Calaveras County, the other a mail rider carrying letters into Jackson. The desperadoes tried to rob them, but they had no better luck. Horsley and the pony rider were, like Smith, better mounted, and they managed to flee to safety. That night Joaquin and his compadres rode into Jackson, where they stole three valuable riding horses and left their worn-out animals behind.[25]

Meanwhile William McMullen and his posse laboriously followed the outlaws' trail and tracked them from Possum Bar southeast to Dry Creek. The manhunters passed through the first of the two Chinese mining camps that Joaquin and his men had raided. By then it was dark, and the posse spent the night at the ranch of Jack Sutherland on Dry Creek. Sutherland's ranch was near the present-day town of Ione, which at that time was variously known as Bedbug, Freezeout, and Hardscrabble—names bestowed upon it by luckless forty-niners. In the morning, four of the possemen—out of either fear or fatigue—quit and returned to their homes at Big Bar. But McMullen was determined to press on. He and his remaining six men cut the bandits' sign and found where they had crossed Dry Creek, headed south. The posse passed through the third Chinese camp that Joaquin's gang had robbed, then followed the bandidos' trail to the main wagon road that led east into Jackson. There were so many horse and wagon tracks in the road that the possemen lost the trail. Then they continued on into Jackson, where three more of the posse gave up the hunt.

McMullen and his last three men spread word of the raids, and they soon learned that four mounted Mexicans, matching the description of the robbers, had been spotted riding toward Butte City, three miles south of Jackson. They rushed to Butte City, where they found that two of the desperadoes had been in town earlier that day, asking for directions to Secreto, a mining camp occupied by Chilenos. The manhunters rode six miles east to Secreto but found no sign of Joaquin and his gang. Finally McMullen and his posse, worn out after a long day of hard riding, returned to Jackson and spent the night.[26]

It was the next morning that McMullen heard about Joaquin's brazen visit to Jackson Gate. He and his possemen swung into their saddles, headed north, and soon found where the desperadoes had made camp outside the town. They also recovered the three run-down horses that the outlaws had abandoned. When McMullen heard a rumor that two of the gang were still at Jackson Gate, he and his men searched the little mining camp but came up dry. The posse, undaunted, returned to Jackson and started out again the next morning, February 11, 1853, accompanied by two new volunteers. Once again they found the bandidos' tracks and followed them to Lower Rancheria, a Mexican mining camp about six miles north of Jackson. As McMullen's posse approached the camp, they spotted their quarry ahead, resting on the ground with their horses next to them. Joaquin and his riders immediately spotted the manhunters. The robbers swung into their saddles, galloped into the dense brush, and vanished from sight. That close encounter with the bandidos may finally have been too much for some of the posse, for three of them quit on the spot.

McMullen, despite that setback, continued on the following day with only two men left. They tracked the pistoleros ten miles northeast through the foothills to Fiddletown, so-called because the Missourians who founded the camp in 1849 were "always fiddling." While the three manhunters approached the town about noon, they spotted a pair of Mexicans hiding in the roadside brush. McMullen ordered his possemen to watch the two suspects, and he continued on toward Fiddletown, two hundred yards distant. He had not gone far when one of his men yelled to him that there were three horses picketed in a field about four hundred yards away. At the same time, the other posseman shouted that a third Mexican was hiding behind a tree. The Mexican, hearing the shout, burst out from the tree and raced on foot into Fiddletown. At least one of the posse recognized the fleeing man as Joaquin.

McMullen ordered one of his men to watch the two Mexicans in the brush while he and the other manhunter rode toward the field to seize the grazing horses. But Murrieta was too quick

Fiddletown, where Murrieta and his men escaped from William McMullen's posse. *Nelson Atkins Museum of Art, Kansas City, MO*

for them. He ran into Fiddletown, where he had left his horse. Leaping into the saddle, he galloped toward the brush thicket to rescue his two compadres. The possemen opened fire with their guns, and Joaquin and the other two pistoleros returned it, shot for shot. The bandits quickly threw away their blankets and other gear. As Joaquin grasped the reins of his mustang, one of his compadres swung up behind him. The third desperado seized the animal's tail, and in a scene out of a comic film, all three tried to escape on a single horse. By this time, the miners in Fiddletown had grabbed rifles and revolvers and rushed out of the camp to join the fray. Several townsmen began shooting. A bullet struck the face of the horsetail outlaw, knocking him to the ground.

Joaquin and his rider jumped down and hoisted the wounded man onto the saddle. Then they started to run on foot, leading the animal by its reins. The pursuers kept up a hot fire, and suddenly the horse dropped with a bullet in one leg. Murrieta and his compadre, supporting the wounded man, dashed off into the chaparral and disappeared. McMullen, his two possemen, and their horses were too worn out for any further pursuit, but now another band of armed miners from Fiddletown took up the chase. But their efforts were in vain, for once again, Joaquin and his men managed to evade their pursuers. McMullen returned to the field near Fiddletown, where he recovered the three abandoned horses. A few days later, he rode fifty miles to Sacramento, leading the recovered mounts. As soon as he arrived, he gave a journalist for the *Sacramento Union* a detailed account of his six-day manhunt for "the notorious mountain robber Joaquin."[27]

Murrieta was more than encouraged by his narrow escape from McMullen's posse. He also had learned that Chinese miners made easy victims. As Joaquin and his men headed back south from Fiddletown, the Chinese prospectors of the Mother Lode could little anticipate what was about to happen in their once tranquil mining camps.

CHAPTER 12

MARAUDERS OF THE MINES

They called it *Gum Shan*, or Gold Mountain. For the twenty thousand Chinese miners who had flocked into California, the gold rush represented an opportunity for wealth and independence. Most of them came from Guangdong, or Canton, the coastal province of southeast China. Their voyage to California was a long one, two months by sailing ship across the Pacific Ocean. Once in the Mother Lode, Chinese miners frequently worked together in small companies of five to ten men. Often they took over "played out" claims abandoned by Anglos who had left in search of easier diggings. Chinese miners then arduously worked the old claims and the leftover tailings, and with patience and persistence, they found their share of the glittering treasure. But just like the early success of miners from Mexico, their labors incited jealousy from Anglos, and the Foreign Miners' Tax Act was vigorously enforced against them.

Most Yankees had never laid eyes on an Asian person before coming to California. To them the Chinese stood out because their features, customs, clothing, and speech were exotically different. Anglos called them Celestials, because the "Celestial Kingdom" was then a common name for China. Many others referred to them by the racist terms "Coolies" and "John Chinaman." In 1851 a Stockton newspaperman, seeing arriving riverboats crammed with fifteen hundred gold seekers, remarked, "Amongst these are large numbers of Chinese, whose strange costumes and uncouth language have excited the curiosity of the natives." The Chinese faced extreme prejudice, and Anglos often believed that they were indentured servants—almost slave-like—who were forced to dig for gold to pay off family debts. In fact, most Chinese were independent gold hunters, just like forty-niners from the East Coast, Europe, and Latin America. Such nativist thinking was exemplified by California's Governor John Bigler, who in 1852 called for "the passage of an Act prohibiting 'Coolies' shipped to California under contracts, from laboring in the mines of this State." The Chinese soon faced a much deadlier threat in the Mother Lode.[1]

In the early years of the gold rush, most Chinese miners were unarmed and unmounted. Although the Chinese had pioneered gunpowder and firearms, at the time of the gold rush, modern Western rifles and revolvers were largely unknown to China's civilians. At the same time, most of the Chinese who journeyed to California had no experience in owning, raising, and riding horses. Without guns for protection and horses for flight, Chinese prospectors were ready victims for robber gangs. That vulnerability led to increasing gun ownership, and by the late 1850s, Chinese miners increasingly armed themselves with rifles and revolvers for self-defense. But that was in the future, and in 1853 Joaquin and his raiders chose Chinese victims because they almost always had gold and frequently were defenseless. As the editor of the *Calaveras Chronicle* remarked, "It is well known that the Celestials are prompt in their payment of taxes, and it is equally notorious that they receive no protection whatever, but present to the ruffian of every nation an easy prey and rich booty."[2]

Because of the language barrier, firsthand accounts by Chinese miners in the gold rush and their experiences with crime and racism are exceedingly rare. In 1853, a bilingual Chinese man in Sacramento wrote, "We cannot pass along the streets without being subject to insult many times of the vilest kind." An educated Chinese merchant complained that "robbers of foreign nations commit the greatest excesses. It is a small thing

Chinese and Anglo miners working a sluice box during the gold rush.
California State Library

with them to drive us away and seize our property. They proceed to do violence and kill us; they go on in a career of bloodshed without limit, since they find there are none to bear testimony against them . . . If a Chinese earns a dollar and a half in gold per day, his first desire is to go to an American and buy a mining claim. But should this yield a considerable result, the seller, it is possible, compels him to relinquish it. Perhaps robbers come and strip him of the gold. He dare not resist, since he cannot speak the language, and has not the power to withstand them. On the other hand, those who have no means to buy a claim seek some ground which other miners have dug over and left, and thus obtain a few dimes. From the proceeds of a hard day's toil, after the pay for food and clothes very little remains. It is hard for them to be prepared to meet the [Foreign Miners' Tax Act] collector when he comes for the license money."[3]

On the bitterly cold morning of February 13, 1853, a group of Chinese miners were shoveling sand into their sluice boxes at Cook's Gulch, a remote spot on Sutter Creek, about four miles north of Jackson. Suddenly Joaquin Murrieta, accompanied by two pistoleros, galloped into the camp, taking the Chinese men by surprise. One of Joaquin's riders was the young Mexican, Antonio Valencia, and the other may have been Three Fingered Jack. Murrieta, after escaping from McMullen's posse at Fiddletown, had ridden fifteen miles south to the bustling mining town of Sutter Creek, arriving that morning. It was named for John Sutter and was located on the creek of the same name. From Sutter Creek, Joaquin's band rode along the stream a short distance west to Cook's Gulch, where they found the Chinese men laboring with picks and shovels. Joaquin and his bandidos were ruthless. They opened fire with their pistols, killing one Chinese gold hunter in cold blood. Then they looted the camp, stealing all the gold dust they could find.

Murrieta led his men as they galloped away and headed south. The outlaws warily skirted the village of Jackson, then rode west for two miles to a Chinese mining camp on Jackson Creek. They charged in on horseback and held the miners at gunpoint. This time they spared the prospectors' lives. The robbers searched the Chinese, as well as their tents, and rode off with sacks of golden booty. They continued on to a nearby Chinese camp, and those prospectors were not so lucky. As Joaquin and his riders thundered in, the terrified gold seekers raced for cover. Two of the Chinese didn't make it. The desperadoes ruthlessly shot the pair down in their tracks, killing them both. Leaping from their horses, Murrieta and his men pillaged the camp, remounted, and galloped off as quickly as they had arrived. Then, as if killing three Chinese in a few hours was not enough, they rode toward a fourth camp. On the way, the bandidos encountered yet another Chinese miner. They gunned him down and left him to die. Then they charged into the camp, a larger settlement with about fifty Chinese gold seekers working the placers. Flourishing their six-guns, Murrieta's little band drove all the Chinese out of the camp and, according to a local journalist, "carried away or destroyed their tents."

Joaquin and his pistoleros then rode back toward Jackson. On the trail just outside town, they encountered Joseph Lake, a twenty-seven-year-old butcher who had joined the gold rush from Philadelphia, Pennsylvania. Without hesitation the outlaws pulled their guns and shot him twice in the chest and once in the side, knocking him out of the saddle. Then one bandit yanked out his knife and rammed the blade through Lake's neck. After stealing his mule, they galloped off, leaving the butcher bleeding in the dirt.

Soon after, several terrified Chinese men, refugees from the plundered mining camps on Sutter and Jackson Creeks, raced on foot into the town of Jackson. They pleaded for help, and the Anglo miners complied. That evening a correspondent in Jackson wrote, "All of our citizens who could procure horses immediately started out in pursuit, and had hardly left town when news arrived from a third Chinese encampment that they had also been robbed by the same party, and two of their number killed." The posse from Jackson first rode north to Cook's Gulch, where they found the dead Chinese victim. From there they trailed the outlaws south to Jackson Creek, where they discovered the body of one of the other three Chinese miners who had been murdered by Joaquin's gang. Nearby on the trail they found Joseph Lake, weltering in his own blood. He was still alive but unable to talk. A few minutes later, Lake, with the posse gathered around him, breathed his last.

By this time it was evening, and the manhunters remounted and urged their horses on. As they approached a dense thicket of chaparral two miles north of Jackson, they spotted Joaquin Murrieta,

Antonio Valencia, and two others casually seated on the ground, eating their supper. Behind them was a steep mountainside, also covered with chaparral. The desperadoes had removed the saddles and blankets from their horses, which were picketed next to them. Joaquin and his compadres looked up from their meals and caught sight of the manhunters, who were closing fast. Knowing that there was no time to saddle their mounts, all four outlaws fled on foot up the steep slope. The possemen opened fire. One bullet grazed Antonio Valencia, inflicting a minor but bloody wound, but they saw him stagger and thought they had killed him. Joaquin's band disappeared into the brush, which was so dense that the manhunters could not follow on their horses. That was fortunate, for Murrieta and his men could easily have ambushed them from their high ground.[4]

The brutal murders of five men in one day created a frenzy of fear and alarm. A correspondent from Jackson declared, "This town is under the greatest excitement. A large meeting of the citizens was held this evening, at which measures were taken that must lead to the eventual capture of the murderers. Nearly our whole population has volunteered to turn out in pursuit tomorrow. Woe to the Mexicans, if they are caught." Then a group of Jackson townsmen rode eight miles south to Mokelumne Hill, arriving after midnight. They galloped down the main street, raising the alarm. As a local journalist wrote, "The quiet of our village was broken at a very early hour this morning by the ringing of bells and gongs, and the beating of drums, calling men to arms, to go in pursuit of Joaquin and his party. The report of the murder of three Chinamen yesterday, near Jackson, was fully confirmed and another came in, that a fourth Chinaman was so badly injured as to be past recovery; still a fifth arrived—an American [Joseph Lake], while in the pursuit of his business of selling meat, at the place of the murders, shared a like fate."[5]

At daybreak, February 14, a large posse headed out of Mokelumne Hill, accompanied by members of the Calaveras Guards, the local militia company. The Calaveras Guards had been organized a year before, with Charles A. Clarke, a Mexican War veteran, as lieutenant. Twelve of the manhunters were mounted, and due to the scarcity of horses in the diggings, another twenty were on foot. According to a local journalist, they "started in different directions, disarming every Mexican they found, and arresting every suspicious person." That night the posse bedded down at a ranch near Camp Opera, also called Camp Ophir, about twelve miles west of Mokelumne Hill. The next morning, the wounded Antonio Valencia showed up in Camp Opera, which was home to several hundred Mexicans. He knew that his bloodstained jacket and trousers were sure to cause suspicion. Valencia spotted several Mexican women washing clothes in a gully. He approached one and showed her his bloody clothing and handkerchief. According to a local man, Valencia offered one of the women "a pretty good price if she would wash them immediately for him."

She was immediately suspicious, and quietly told the other washerwomen to get help. One of them ran to the posse's nearby campsite and warned them. They promptly mounted up, surrounded Camp Opera, and searched it. Before long they captured Valencia. The manhunters brought their prisoner into Jackson, where an angry crowd quickly gathered. Several of the Chinese miners who had been robbed at their camp on Jackson Creek recognized Valencia as one of the bandidos. The outlaw was lodged in the town jail, constructed of heavy logs, but within five minutes the mob broke in and dragged Valencia outside. As one townsman said, "He was tried and found guilty and immediately escorted to that fatal oak tree, fronting the Astor House, which was now destined for the fifth time to bear a peculiar kind of fruit. Before being strung up he was asked to confess, but he stubbornly refused to make any statement whatever." A Catholic priest was summoned to administer the last rites, but Valencia refused to talk with him. Then, according to one spectator, "He confessed he was one of the party, but killed no one. He only took the money."

A wood engraving, made after a daguerreotype, showing an 1855 lynching on Jackson's hanging tree, the same tree upon which Antonio Valencia was hanged in 1853. *William B. Secrest collection*

Today Jackson's notorious hanging tree is gone, but the spot is marked by a plaque. In 1853 it was a large oak on the east side of Main Street, with heavy branches that hung across the road. In the previous two years, four murderers had been lynched from its limbs, including Claudio's compadre, Jose Cheverino. At 5:30 that evening, Antonio Valencia made his final statement. The mob then seized the hanging rope and hoisted him into the air. "He now swings on a tree, two doors from where I write, as a warning to all evildoers," wrote one townsman. "The evidence against him was of such a character as to satisfy everyone of his guilt. A number of Chinamen swore positively to several articles of clothing worn by the Mexican, as well as to the individual himself." Added another local writer, "Not a person witnessed the execution who did not consider that he richly merited his fate." In the end, a total of ten men would meet their fates on the limbs of Jackson's hanging tree.[6]

By this time, exaggerated rumors of the bandit raids had spread like wildfire. A San Francisco newspaper reported, "At the Big Bar of the Cosumnes, on Tuesday, in the day time, a party of five Mexicans attacked a Chinese camp and killed six Chinamen, and robbed them of over $6,000. The Mexicans were supposed to be a portion of Joaquin's party headed by Joaquin himself, and were pursued by a party of Mexicans through Jackson to the Butte [City], where, at last accounts, all traces of them were lost. They were well mounted and did not follow the road at all. It is understood that the citizens of the Cosumnes in the vicinity have offered $1,000 reward for Joaquin, dead or alive." But as we have seen, no Chinese were killed in the raid near Big Bar.[7]

According to a breathless report in a Sacramento newspaper, on February 10, "Joaquin rode through the village of San Andreas at a quick gallop, and shot three Americans as he passed through the streets. Joaquin is a young man, of about nineteen years of age, and must be one of the best shots with a revolver in this or any other country, as nearly all these men were shot through the neck. The whole band, it is supposed, consists of about sixty men, all of whom are thought to be Mexicans." But the fact is that on February 10, Joaquin was robbing men near Jackson, sixteen miles from San Andreas; no other reports confirmed the alleged shooting in San Andreas. And the gang consisted of about a dozen men, not sixty.[8]

Next a Stockton newspaper announced, "Last evening, at about eight o'clock, the stage running from Sacramento to Mokelumne Hill was set upon by Joaquin's band of desperadoes. The driver, and two American women, were killed." If true, that would have been California's first stagecoach holdup. But the editor of the *Calaveras Chronicle* quickly reported that the story was false. And if the facts were not bad enough, on February 14 a correspondent from Mokelumne Hill wrote, "It has been rumored here this evening, but not generally believed, that a large number—some dozen or more—have been murdered at Campo Seco today." Once again the *Calaveras Chronicle* promptly announced that "there is no truth in the communication." Nonetheless, many of the murderous raids were all too real. As a Stockton journalist declared, "No man dare travel a step unless armed to the teeth, or sleep without having firearms already in his grasp. Life is not safe for a day and the utmost excitement prevails at every camp."[9]

The Mother Lode was gripped by terror, and soon baseless rumors about Joaquin himself became rife. A San Francisco newspaper, the *Daily Whig*, printed what it claimed was an accurate biography of the bandit. The *Whig* reported that its source was "an intelligent Mexican who resided in the city of Mexico." According to the *Whig*, "Joaquin was born in the Villa de Catorce, in the department of Jalisco. He is aged about thirty-five years and has ranked among the most crafty and daring guerillas of Mexico. He is chief of a notorious band of robbers now infesting the vicinity of the city of Mexico, and though living in California, has a regular chain of communication with his associates in his native country. He has been known to enter the capital cities disguised as a friar, has been arrested several times, but through the expertness and influence he wielded among the soldiery, he has been discharged. He is about six feet in height, and of immense muscular strength; is well versed in the use of arms and in disposition cruel and sanguinary. He has a dark sallow complexion, and during the Mexican war was known to wear a coat of armor. He has committed numberless murders, has burned many ranches, and has resided in San Francisco. He has frequently obtained information of Mexicans leaving California with money, who have been dogged and robbed by detached portions of his band. In some instances they have been robbed on their arrival at Mexico—the news of their departure, and the sums of money they had about them, having been forwarded by means of the associates living along the road. Joaquin belonged to the band of guerillas commanded by the famous Padre Jurata, who was captured and shot during the Mexican war. The Mexicans look upon him as a brave man and he is considered as a person of some education."[10]

Of course, there was not a word of truth in the *Whig*'s account. Though Padre Celedonio Dómeco de Jarauta (1814–1848) was indeed a guerrilla leader in the Mexican War, he had no connection with Joaquin Murrieta. Nonetheless the *Whig*'s yarn was widely reprinted and just as widely believed. A correspondent in Jackson, however, later provided a more accurate description of Joaquin, though he misstated Claudio's name. "A friend of mine, who has seen *the* Joaquin, says that he is a very ordinary looking man, about five feet six inches in height, twenty-two years of age, and has a scar on his right cheek, but which is commonly covered by the ribbons of his hat, which he keeps tied under his chin. He was a member of McCloud's band, in which he received his first lessons."[11]

Alarmed miners began clamoring for protection from the state government. A Mokelumne Hill correspondent declared, "A petition is in circulation praying the governor to offer a reward for the capture of Joaquin or any of his party. How long must the present deplorable state of things continue? How long must it be that we have to record the robbery and murder of men at their own doors and by the wayside, or while in the pursuit of their honest employment? Although the arena of their dark deeds is at present in this county, yet is it not a matter that interests and affects the whole community? How long before the cruel and wanton band may raise their murderous hands against other sections of our State? May we not reasonably expect that prompt and effective measures will be taken on the part of the State in this serious and important matter?"[12]

Despite the hue and cry, Murrieta and his men were undeterred from their reckless campaign of banditry. On February

16, the day after Antonio Valencia died on Jackson's hanging tree, they boldly returned to the same chaparral thicket where they had fled the posse's gunfire just three days earlier. The spot was near the wagon road, modern-day Highway 49, two miles north of Jackson. The bandidos spotted a lone German miner headed north on the road. Joaquin and his riders stepped into the roadway and covered the German with their guns. Instead of killing him, the bandits relieved their victim of $600 and sent him on his way. The German raced back into Jackson and raised the alarm. A posse of more than twenty men quickly mounted up and galloped out of town, reaching the chaparral at four that afternoon. The manhunters spotted several bandidos and recognized one as Joaquin. "They fired at the Mexicans," reported a writer in Jackson, "killing one and hitting Joaquin in the cheek with a ball. The remaining Mexicans then rushed into the chaparral, which is so thick, except in a single place, that even a dog cannot get through it. They were reinforced by other Americans, and Indians during the evening, and kept watch all night." If the posse was correct about wounding Murrieta, his injury was a minor one.

The citizens of Jackson offered local Native Americans a thousand dollars "for the head of Joaquin." In that era, Native Americans were often the most skillful trackers, and a price offered for a man's head frequently meant that he was wanted dead or alive. By the next morning, the mountainous thicket was surrounded by fifty Anglos and a hundred Indians. The manhunters were certain that they had Joaquin and his band surrounded, but they disagreed on how to proceed. "Some proposed to set fire to the chaparral and thus force them from their hiding place, while others proposed to cut a road through the chaparral until they could see the Mexicans and then open their fire on them." In the end the argument proved moot, for Murrieta and his men managed to slip out of the brush and vanish on their stolen horses.[13]

Meanwhile Joaquin's compadre, the third man who had been wounded in the Phoenix Quartz Mill gunfight, was recovering in Campo de los Muertos. Also known as Los Muertos and Camp of the Dead, it was a small mining settlement situated a mile south of Angels Camp. A few days after Joaquin's escape from the posse near Jackson, Constable Charles Ellis of San Andreas got a tip that a badly wounded Mexican youth was hiding out in Los Muertos. A local gold seeker, nineteen-year-old John Daggett, later recalled that the outlaw "was in the care of a Spanish woman in the camp." On February 20, Constable Ellis searched Los Muertos and soon found the man. "His body had been pierced in four places by musket balls," the *Calaveras Chronicle* reported. The constable brought his wounded prisoner into San Andreas. On the way, Ellis passed through Yaqui Camp, where the teenaged Mexican was recognized as one of the bandidos who had raided and killed there a month earlier. He was also identified as one of the robbers who had attacked the Phoenix Quartz Mill.

In San Andreas, a crowd gathered and held a summary trial. The youth, whose name was not recorded in the contemporary accounts, soon confessed and admitted that he was a member of Joaquin's band. The editor of the *Calaveras Chronicle* reported that he heard the bandit's statement: "He was of Joaquin's party, but not a conspicuous or leading member. His obligations confined him to a certain district, out of which he dare not travel. He was compelled to be in readiness at all times, and to turn out immediately on receiving an order from any of his superiors. He was also required to notice passing events, and to apprise the company of anything that transpired affecting their welfare. He was bound to shelter, and protect any of the brethren who were in danger, to procure horses, and assist them in their escape at all hazards, rendering all the aid and comfort to the band which lay in his power . . . The leaders of the band were Joaquin, Claudio, and Reiz [Reyes]. These were the party who killed the Sheriff of Yuba, Claudio having fired the first shot."

Like Claudio, the young pistolero mistakenly believed that the gang had killed Sheriff Buchanan. He also declared that there were thirteen men in the band. According to another witness, the youth boasted "that the gang were connected clear through to Shasta" in the northern end of the state. Although there were scattered reports that Joaquin and his raiders had appeared as far north as Shasta County in early 1853, that seems most improbable, given that Murrieta was more than two hundred miles distant at the time. The witness also said, "He implicated several Mexicans, and some persons who speak English." The wounded bandido also claimed that Claudio had taken a band of cattle to Monterey and that "Reiz" was still riding with Joaquin. In true outlaw fashion, the teenaged desperado had insisted that he was not a leader of the gang and that he had only been following orders. And to cover for his compadres, he blamed the raids on Claudio and Reyes Feliz, who were both dead.[14]

The vigilantes were enraged by his admissions. Young John Daggett was then mining in San Andreas, and he attended the vigilance committee trial. Thirty years later, Daggett, who hailed from upstate New York, served as lieutenant governor of California. He never forgot the scene that day: "After giving him a trial by jury he was condemned to be hung and was placed on a dray and was carted to the butcher's corral in the lower part of town. A rope noose was placed around his neck, the other end thrown over the limb of an oak tree and tied to the trunk, after which the dray was driven away from under him. And—but oh—what a spectacle was presented to a youth not yet out of his teens!"[15]

By this time a determined posse was hunting Joaquin's band. Five citizens of Mokelumne Hill donated a purse of $400 to pay their expenses. The leader was Charlie Clarke, the lieutenant of the Calaveras Guards and the county's undersheriff. Clarke, a thirty-four-year-old Canadian, was tough as nails. He had fought in the Texas Revolution and saw combat at the Battle of San Jacinto in 1836, where Texans attacked Mexican forces with the famous battle cry, "Remember the Alamo!" Six years later, Clarke took part in the ill-fated Mier Expedition, when Texas militiamen invaded Mexico. He was captured and escaped death in the infamous Black Bean Episode, in which those who drew a black bean from a pot filled with white beans (about one of every ten) was executed by firing squad. Clarke's Canadian-British citizenship eventually won him his release from a Mexican prison. During the Mexican War, he served as a lieutenant in the Texas Rangers, and he was one of the first Anglo miners to settle in Calaveras County. In 1851 he became a deputy sheriff in Mokelumne Hill. One of Clarke's comrades later described him: "A perfect gentleman; soft hearted as a child, but with courage that never flinched. He was the pride of all the gals on the Hill, and the terror of horse thieves."[16]

Undersheriff Clarke handpicked a posse of five well-mounted and well-armed horsemen. On February 18, two days before the lynching in San Andreas, Clarke and his posse rode out of Mokelumne Hill. Clarke wisely decided to retrace the gang's steps. The manhunters first headed north to Big Bar on the Cosumnes, swam their horses across the river, and continued on through Jackson, finally reaching the mining camp of Sutter Creek that evening. They carefully searched the village, but found no trace of Joaquin and his riders. After making camp that night, at daybreak they rode north through a driving rain to Dry Creek. They scoured the brush-choked foothills, checking the various places where Joaquin and his gang had raided. Clarke and his posse also visited several Chinese mining camps but still discovered no sign of the elusive bandits. It was dark when they made camp at Willow Springs, on the stage road three miles west of Drytown. This was the same spot where, ten months earlier, Murrieta and his men had murdered the hotelkeeper, James Clark.

The next day, as Undersheriff Clarke later reported, "[We] left Willow springs, taking a trail for Ione Valley, passing through several camps on the way. From Ione Valley we rode to a small camp called the Saw Mill, thence to Stone & Baker's ranch, and on to Camp Opera. Here we learned that four Mexicans on foot had stolen a boat, and crossed the [Mokelumne] river. The [posse] was increased here by seven Americans from Jackson, and the whole, numbering thirteen, rode on to Winter's Bar. Here we divided into three squads, and bent our course towards Campo Seco, searching several Mexican camps on the way. [We] arrived at Campo Seco, stopped for the night, and learned that a party of Mexicans had stolen some saddles the previous night."[17]

Undersheriff Clarke was certain that Joaquin and his men were returning to the scenes of their prior raids south of the Mokelumne River. In the morning, February 21, he and his five possemen headed to San Andreas and then continued a few miles south to Foreman's Ranch. It was the hotel and ferry near Joaquin Peak, today called Fourth Crossing, where exactly a month earlier Murrieta and his band had murdered an Anglo miner. As Clarke later reported, "Here we learned that Joaquin's party had been to Rich Gulch the night before, killed three Chinamen and wounded five, robbing them of $10,000."

The prior evening, February 20, Joaquin and four of his gang had entered Rich Gulch, a Chinese mining camp on the North Fork of the Calaveras River, five miles northeast of Mokelumne Hill. As indicated by its name, Rich Gulch was a wealthy settlement with canvas tents lining the gully, which had been extensively excavated for several miles. The five bandidos, six-shooters in hand, rounded up some fifty Chinese miners, held them at gunpoint, and then searched the entire camp for their gold dust and nuggets. When some tried to resist, the outlaws opened up with a barrage of fire, killing three and wounding four or five more. Then the killers looted the camp's general store, mounted up, and galloped off into the blackness. One Yankee in Rich Gulch reported that the gang had stolen upwards of $30,000 in gold. Whether the amount taken was $10,000 or $30,000, it was

Joaquin's biggest and bloodiest raid yet. Another Anglo dashed off an urgent message, "calling on the people of San Andreas for assistance, and for surgeons to attend the wounded Chinamen."[18]

By the time Charlie Clarke and his men got word of the raid at Rich Gulch, it was too late in the day to ride north in pursuit. He and his posse bedded down for the night near Foreman's Ranch. Meanwhile Murrieta's band rode nineteen miles south from Rich Gulch to Foreman's Ranch. It was after midnight that Joaquin and his men approached Foreman's, unaware that Clarke's posse was camped nearby. Because of the rampant robbery and horse theft, the ranch owner, David Foreman, had hired several Chinese men to guard his hotel, store, and barns. The bandits slipped into Foreman's stable to steal his horses, but the Chinese watchmen spotted them and shouted a warning. Then they ran to warn the manhunters. As Clarke later explained, "At one o'clock in the morning, Chinamen gave information to our party that there were five Mexicans in camp." The possemen mounted up and followed Joaquin's band in the dark, finally spotting them after daybreak. "[We] went in pursuit, one of our party fired, but unfortunately struck one of the Mexicans in the hand only," reported Clarke. "They took to their horses and went out of sight in an instant. We followed over a mountain, and on reaching the summit heard the report of several pistol shots in a Chinese camp at the foot of the hill. We rode down as quick as possible, and on arriving at the camp, we found three Chinamen dead and weltering in their blood, and five others mortally wounded. The Mexicans had gone about ten minutes, carrying with them $3,000. We pursued them about three miles, when we lost the trail."

Joaquin and his gang were so audacious that they had robbed and murdered with a pursuing posse in hot pursuit. By this time, darkness was falling, and Clarke knew better than to expose his men to an ambush. He and his possemen were exhausted, having been in the saddle all day. The manhunters rode back to

Reynolds Ferry on the Stanislaus River. Nearby, on February 21, 1853, Joaquin and his band murdered eight Chinese miners. *Don Gordon collection.*

Foreman's Ranch, where they again camped for the night. "At daylight [we] took the trail and followed them, passing through several China camps and finding that each had been plundered," Clarke later recounted. "Kept on their trail the whole day until about five in the evening. As we arrived on the summit of a hill, we saw them about three quarters of a mile distant, robbing some Chinamen. They turned and saw us advancing, but they stirred not an inch until we were within half a mile of them, when they mounted their horses and rode off at the speed of the wind. There were five well dressed Mexicans, well armed, and mounted on beautiful animals. We attempted pursuit, but our horses were worn out, and we found it impossible to continue the chase. We went to Reynolds Ferry and remained for the night, and the next day were compelled to return, almost worn out."[19]

Reynolds Ferry, the spot where Clarke and his men lost the pursuit, was on the Stanislaus River, now covered by the New Melones reservoir. Once again, Murrieta and his riders had robbed with a posse close on their heels, this time in full view of the manhunters.

And their slaughter of eight Chinese miners near Reynolds Ferry was by far the gang's bloodiest raid. After Clarke's men got back to Mokelumne Hill, one of the posse reported, "I have been engaged a week in hunting Mr. Joaquin and his party, and we had a right lively time of it after the greasers. We followed them all over the country, and, while we were on their trail, they killed and wounded fifteen Chinamen and stole seven or eight thousand dollars. We got one or two chances at them, but they were so well mounted that they beat us running all to hell."[20]

A journalist who interviewed the manhunters on their return to Mokelumne Hill added, "Great credit is due the band of volunteers from this place, and others who joined them on the route, for their vigilance and perseverance in the difficult task they undertook. Although unable to capture any of the villains, yet no efforts were spared, and no privations avoided, to accomplish the desired end. More, probably, would have been accomplished, had fresh horses been at their service at different stations. Strong evidence has been obtained, that some bearing the name of Americans, are connected with Joaquin's band."[21]

Charlie Clarke did not know the names of the Anglos who rode with the gang. But no matter their backgrounds or their ethnicity, Murrieta and his fellow marauders were bound together by the thrill of danger, gunsmoke, and gold.

CHAPTER 13

NO MAN TAKES ME ALIVE

William Burgess, shotgun in hand, trudged through the heavy snow in the mountains above Jackson. Like so many Argonauts in a region where food and supplies were scarce, he hunted regularly for wild game to fill his cookpot. Burgess, a twenty-seven-year-old miner from England, little suspected that Joaquin and his gang, between raids, hid out in a remote camp in the same mountainous country. He later penned a detailed account of that day in his journal.

> The weather had been unusually severe, wet, and cold, finishing up the week with quite a severe snow storm. While the snow remained on the ground, I thought it likely I might get a deer, so early in the morning, taking my shotgun loaded with buckshot, I started for the hunting ground. Hills covered with low brush extended for miles. The snow was about six inches deep. Following up one of the ravines, I struck the fresh trail of a California lion. Yielding to the temptation, I followed it, knowing as well as anyone that it was useless to do so with a shotgun, the probability being that if I got sight of the game, it would be out of reach of the buckshot. Nevertheless, I pushed on.
>
> The trail was so fresh there was no difficulty in following it. It led up a steep hill, toward a dense growth of pine trees. Suddenly the direction changed, [going] along a steep side hill. I was about to follow when my attention was attracted by a

slight sound, not a few paces from me. Looking up, I was not a little startled to find myself face to face with a powerful looking, swarthy Mexican, dressed as though he had that moment leapt from the back of a horse. He had on well worn buckskin pants, open at the sides, with silver buttons, close together, sewn to them. Leather leggings, with a bowie knife handle projecting from the top, huge Mexican spurs, and a red sash round his waist. I could just see the handle of a revolver on one hip, while the empty sheath of another was attached to a strap on the opposite side, as though the weapon had just been withdrawn from it. This man's hands were both behind him, and doubtless he held the pistol in one. His face was almost hidden in black hair, its expression and his general appearance was that of a fierce ruffian. I had been carrying my gun ready for instant use, with hammers up, and my fingers on the triggers. When I saw he was approaching I instantly turned both barrels towards him without, however, altering the level of the gun. He looked so threatening my mind was made up to fire both barrels if he molested me. He signed for me to come no nearer, and then in Spanish asked, "Why do you come this way? There is no road here." Nodding toward my gun, I replied that I was hunting. "There is no game here. Who told you?"

Pointing to the tracks in the snow, I said, "No one told me. I followed the trail." He looked suspiciously at me, but when he saw the lion's tracks, he seemed satisfied. Pointing down the hill with his left hand, keeping the right in the same position behind him, he said, "It is bad for you to come up here, you might get killed. Vamos, pronto." This I was perfectly willing to do, but I dared not turn round, so keeping my face toward him and both barrels pointing straight in front, I commenced to back down the hill until I reached some brush, when, without delay, I made good time toward Jackson.

Joaquin Murietta had been committing depredations in Calaveras County, near San Andreas, and in Amador County.

The pencil sketch by William Burgess, depicting his encounter with one of Murrieta's gang. *California Historical Society*

> All to whom I related the above markedly concluded that I must have accidentally come upon the camp of the gang, and that the Mexican whom I saw would surely have shot me had he not felt satisfied that I had no motive in going up the hill but to hunt. Being able to point to the tracks was proof that I spoke the truth, and probably saved my life.[1]

Burgess, at the same time he recorded his encounter with one of Joaquin's band, made a pencil sketch of the event. He later became an illustrator in San Francisco, well-known for his artistic scenes of California pioneer life.

In a month's time, Joaquin and his gang had murdered twenty-six men, twenty of them unarmed Chinese miners. Because of the language barrier, the names of the dead Chinese, except for the miner Ah Kop who was slain in Yaqui

Camp, were not recorded in the newspapers. According to an old tradition that began with John Rollin Ridge, Three Fingered Jack had slaughtered all the Chinese miners. Ridge claimed that Joaquin tried to stop Garcia, but the desperado reveled in bloodletting and stabbed each of the Chinese men to death. On one occasion, Three Fingered Jack supposedly tied together the queues of six Chinese and killed them all by slashing their throats. However, no evidence supports this yarn. Most of the murdered Chinese were shot to death, not stabbed. And as we have seen, Joaquin had taken part in numerous cold-blooded murders, especially the six men robbed and killed in the mountains north of Marysville, well before Three Fingered Jack joined the gang.

As violent as the gold rush was, the mining region had never seen an organized gang of outlaws commit so many robberies and murders so quickly, nor with such impunity. During the previous few years, most of the violence involved men who were shot or stabbed in personal quarrels. At the same time, there were scattered highway robberies, but a majority of the thefts were burglaries in which cabins or tents were looted while their occupants were digging for gold. Murrieta and his gang presented an entirely new threat. The editor of the San Francisco *Alta California* observed, "Joaquin is the first chief of banditti having under his command a regular confederation of cutthroats, and carrying on his operations in the broad acknowledgment of his calling that we have yet had in the State since the gold was discovered." A correspondent in Calaveras County explained how the gang so often evaded capture. "The secret of Joaquin's successful escapes seems to be in his always being well mounted. As soon as his party ride down one set of horses, they immediately procure others. The horses deserted by them are generally used up, and of no value. Probably a hundred horses have been stolen in this county the past month by this band, and at least thirty persons have been murdered."[2]

[BY AUTHORITY.]

PROCLAMATION!

One Thousand Dollars Reward.

WHEREAS, it appears to me, that one *Joaquin Carillo* is the leader of a band of robbers and murderers in Calaveras and the adjoining counties, and has perpetrated a number of heinous offences against the lives and property of the people of that portion of the State, and that the said Joaquin Carillo is now at large:

Now, therefore, I, JOHN BIGLER, Governor of the State of California, by virtue of the power in me vested by the laws and constitution of said State, do hereby offer a reward of one thousand dollars for the apprehension and safe delivery of the said Joaquin Carillo into the custody of the sheriff of Calaveras county, to be dealt with according to law.

WITNESS my hand and the seal of State, at the city of Benicia, this twenty-first day of February, A. D., 1853.

Attest— JOHN BIGLER,
J. W. DENVER, Governor.
Secretary of State.

Description:—Said Joaquin Carillo is a Mexican by birth, 5 feet 10 inches in height, black hair, black eyes, and of good address.

The $1,000 reward notice for Joaquin Murrieta that was printed in California newspapers. It misspelled his birth name as Joaquin Carillo instead of Carrillo.
John Boessenecker collection

As the band carried out its bloody raids, public outrage continued to grow. The citizens' petition that demanded a reward for Joaquin reached the desk of Governor John Bigler at the state capital in Benicia, at the northern end of San Francisco Bay. One year later the capital would be moved from Benicia to Sacramento. After receiving the petition, Governor Bigler promptly ordered that a supply of ammunition be sent to the Calaveras Guards. On February 21, 1853, while Charlie Clarke's posse was in the field, Bigler issued a state reward for the daring bandit leader, and it was quickly published in California newspapers: "PROCLAMATION! ONE THOUSAND DOLLARS REWARD. Whereas, it appears to me that one Joaquin Carillo is the leader of a band of robbers and murderers in Calaveras and the adjoining counties, and has perpetrated a number of heinous offences against the lives and property of the people of that portion of the State, and that the said Joaquin Carillo is now at large: Now, therefore, I, John Bigler, Governor of the State of California, by virtue of the power in me vested by the laws and constitution of said State, do hereby offer a reward of one thousand dollars for the apprehension and safe delivery of the said Joaquin Carillo into the custody of the sheriff of Calaveras county, to be dealt with according to law." The reward notice also included a description of the outlaw: "Said Joaquin Carillo is a Mexican by birth, 5 feet 10 inches in height, black hair, black eyes, and of good address." Although such state rewards would become common in the years to come, this was one of the first rewards offered by a California governor.[3]

Because Joaquin was known by his birth name of Carrillo in Calaveras County, as well as in other camps of the Southern Mines, the citizens who signed the petition had identified him by that name, albeit slightly misspelled. And Murrieta had light brown hair, not black. The inability to obtain and dispatch an accurate description of Joaquin hampered efforts to capture him. A few days later, a journalist in Stockton vividly described the public terror and frustration, and used the correct spelling of Joaquin's surname. "Neither in the pages of romance nor in the authentic annals of history have we found a robber whose career has been marked with atrocities half so dreadful as that of Joaquin Carrillo, who now ranges the mountains, within sixty miles of this city. It has been the fashion of the historian and the novelist to trace in the characters of their bandit heroes some redeeming traits, but in the conscience of this blood-thirsty villain there appear to be no qualms, no mercy or reproach. He rides through the settlements slaughtering the weak and unprotected, as if a mania for murder possessed his soul. So daring and reckless is he, that he marches in the day time through thickly peopled settlements and actually corrals the Chinese by the score, and yet so fertile is he in expedients, and so accurate in his knowledge of that wild region, that he baffles his pursuers and defeats the plans of the many thousands who are lying in wait for him. So complete is the organization of the band under his control that (we are told) relays of the fleetest horses in the country await him at almost every step."[4]

The newspaperman's claim of a high level of organization was colored by fear and anxiety from the bloody raids. Joaquin and his gang were clearly skilled horsemen who knew the mining region very well. But their forays were reckless and opportunistic and, though planned, were certainly not carried out with any kind of sophisticated organization or military precision. But that fact was of no comfort to the victims. Murrieta's attacks were so remorseless that many Chinese gold seekers packed up and fled for their lives. As one San Francisco newspaper reported, "The Chinese population of Calaveras County are leaving the remote camps and betaking themselves either to cities, or more thickly populated sections, on account of the depredations of Joaquin's band."[5]

The governor's reward had no effect on Joaquin Murrieta. Instead, it was the outraged miners who concerned him most. Seven of his gang had been killed by manhunters or lynched by vigilantes. Every gold washer in Calaveras County was on the lookout for him. It was the right time to get out of Calaveras, so Joaquin and his men mounted their horses and rode south. Their absence from the Calaveras foothills was quickly noted. As a correspondent in Mokelumne Hill wrote, "Our county is again quiet. The excitement which existed here a short time since, occasioned by a series of murders and other crimes, has subsided. At present, life and property remain unharmed. It is a matter of speculation where the enemies have gone, and when they may return to commence again their desperate career."[6]

Murrieta and his band headed south into Tuolumne County. Soon a newspaperman in Sonora reported that the bandit chieftain had been "lurking about" the area, adding, "People who say they know Joaquin well positively declare that they have seen him." Then Murrieta made a leisurely ride fifty miles south to the mining camp of Hornitos ("Little Ovens"). Hornitos was a busy village that had been settled by Mexicans a year earlier, named for its numerous small outdoor ovens used for baking food. Today, its old stone and brick buildings, many in ruins, are popular with visitors and curiosity seekers. But in 1853, Hornitos consisted of adobes and canvas tents that housed raucous cantinas, bordellos, fandango houses, and gambling halls. Joaquin knew the area well, for he had mined there several years earlier when he frequented Billy Henderson's general store and hotel in nearby Quartzburg. The bandit chieftain rode into Hornitos in late February, accompanied by about a dozen desperadoes. They were strangers, and at first no one recognized Murrieta. Joaquin caused no trouble and spent his time in a gambling house playing monte with an Anglo dealer. But as a local correspondent later explained, "He got to drinking and betting very high, and would in all probability have exposed himself to the dealer but for the timely entering of three of his band who carried him off by force."

The gang disappeared for a few days. Then on March 4, they slipped onto the ranch of William Prescott, situated four miles from Hornitos. Prescott ran a nearby mine known as the Prescott Lode, and he was absent from his ranch when Joaquin and his men ran off with all of his horses. Then they brazenly returned to Hornitos to celebrate. Meanwhile Prescott returned to his ranch and discovered the theft of his animals. He managed to track his herd to Hornitos, where he arrived after dark. Prescott found the thieves inside a large tent that was used as a fandango hall. He stepped away quietly, then quickly organized a seven-man posse. They included a young man named Henry Crowell and a well-known miner, Leroy "Lee" Vining. The town of Lee Vining, situated on Mono Lake in the eastern Sierra Nevada, was later named after him. The manhunters, carrying lanterns and guns, entered the fandango tent. One of them instantly recognized the outlaw leader, and yelled out, "Joaquin!"

Hornitos, where Joaquin and his band shot and wounded two possemen who tried to capture him. *Hornitos Historical Society*

Murrieta, instead of trying to escape, immediately charged at the possemen. Several of them seized him, and a desperate brawl ensued. Some of Joaquin's gang heard the commotion from a distance and ran to the tent with drawn guns. Bursting through the entrance flap, they opened fire, wounding Prescott in the side and Crowell in one hip. Lee Vining, armed with a double-barrel shotgun, leveled it at one of the bandits and fired both barrels at point-blank range. The outlaw was lucky. Each of Vining's percussion caps snapped and failed to ignite the gunpowder. Joaquin and his men fled the tent, leaped into their saddles, and raced out of Hornitos.

Miners in Hornitos and nearby Quartzburg formed posses and began hunting the outlaws. Soon afterward a journalist reported, "The people in the vicinity of Quartzburg are in arms, and riding over the mountains and plains every day in search of Joaquin. It is to be hoped that their labors will be crowned with success, for citizens are in danger of their lives going from one house to another . . . If this is allowed to go on much longer it will be impossible to pass the roads in any direction safely.

Will not Governor Bigler offer a reward, a sufficient sum to pay a party of men to seek him out, and take him dead or alive?" Like many in California, he believed that the $1,000 state reward was too paltry.[7]

But once again, Joaquin and his gang evaded the manhunters. It was probably at this point that Murrieta and several of his men rode up to the cattle camp of John Cocanour in the hills west of Hornitos. Cocanour, later a prominent rancher and civic leader, had arrived in California in 1850 but failed to find gold in the Southern Mines. He turned to raising beef in the grassy Sierra foothills and driving them for sale to hungry miners in Mariposa and Hornitos. One evening Cocanour and a few of his vaqueros were at their campfire, about to eat supper, when Murrieta and several horsemen galloped up. Cocanour immediately recognized Joaquin, whom he had seen frequently in the mines. The bandit leader, speaking English, said they were hungry. Cocanour, realizing that he and his cowhands were outgunned, and without letting on that he knew who Joaquin was, invited them to dismount and eat. After the meal, both cowmen and outlaws settled in for an uneventful night. At daybreak, as they ate breakfast, Murrieta turned to Cocanour and asked if he knew him.

"Certainly," Cocanour replied. "You are Joaquin. I know you well."

"Why, then, did you receive me?" the bandit asked.

"There were too few of us to resist you," said Cocanour. "You said you were in need of something to eat, and as you have never injured me, I could not refuse you."

Joaquin responded that Cocanour would "never fear harm from any of the band." Then he and his men swung onto their horses and rode off. Cocanour later described the encounter to a journalist in Sonora, saying, "And the robber chief kept his word." He added, "There may be honor among thieves, after all."[8]

Murrieta's repeated, audacious bandit raids created a type of mass hysteria that even extended to San Francisco, where wild rumors circulated that Joaquin was in town. On the morning of April 9, San Francisco's *Alta California* breathlessly announced, "We have received a communication from a writer, who wishes his name concealed, stating that the renowned Joaquin Carillo is now in this city. The writer says he knows him well, and describes his dress and person. He assures us that he is under strict surveillance and cannot escape." Later that day, San Francisco police arrested a man on a sailing ship on the waterfront. They loaded him onto a handcart and began pulling it toward the city prison on Portsmouth Square. Word quickly spread that the arrested man was Joaquin Murrieta, and that he had been caught trying to flee California by clipper ship. A large crowd excitedly followed the handcart to the jail, then a dungeon in the basement of city hall at the corner of Kearny and Washington Streets. Hundreds of gawkers crammed elbow to elbow into city hall, demanding to see the notorious bandit chieftain. But they were sorely disappointed. As the *Alta* reported, "This prisoner was a poor, mad Italian, who was taken from the ship *Julia Ann*."[9]

Joaquin, however, was indeed in the San Francisco Bay Area. He and several of his men had ridden across the San Joaquin Valley and over the Coast Range to San Francisco Bay. On April 5, 1853, two of the gang—one of whom was, by tradition, Three Fingered Jack—were riding down the wagon road that followed the east side of the bay and led south to San Jose. The road skirted the marshland and passed through tall thickets of wild fennel. The pistoleros fell in with a horseman named James Walsh, who was carrying a leather pouch bursting with $350 in coin, as well as a gold watch and a Colt revolver. As they neared Mission San Jose, located in modern-day Fremont, Walsh either boasted foolishly of his money or the bandits caught a glimpse of his purse. One of the desperadoes suddenly reined back his horse and swung his reata over Walsh's neck. Jerking him from the saddle, the outlaws charged forward and dragged Walsh down the road for almost a mile. The dirt and gravel ripped the flesh from his face as he wailed in agony. Finally the robbers dismounted, drew their knives, and slashed him to death. Then they rode off with his horse, saddle, and everything of value found on his body. Walsh had died in the same manner as the gang's six victims murdered in the mountains above Marysville more than a year before, among them George Mather, John Gardner, Andrew Jinkerson, and Isaac Pray.[10]

A large manhunt, conducted by Anglos and Californios, promptly swung into action. The possemen searched Mission San Jose and heard rumors that "the notorious robber Joaquin and his band were lurking in that vicinity." Then they hunted through the hills above Mission San Jose and discovered what they believed was the outlaws' camp. According to a San Francisco reporter, "Some deserted tents were found, but the occupants had fled." The manhunters arrested several suspects, but they were all released due to lack of evidence. Then, on April 21, two weeks after the Walsh murder, a pair of Californios rode into the pueblo of San Jose and told Sheriff Joseph W. Johnson that they could identify Walsh's killers. They also pointed out the adobe house in San Jose that the desperadoes were hiding in. Sheriff Johnson promptly raised a posse that included the two Californios, a man named Wilson, and several others. Johnson and his men surrounded the house, boldly burst inside, and seized the two murder suspects. As they dragged the pair out the front door, the pistoleros broke loose and took to their heels. The sheriff instantly whipped out his revolver, thumbed back the hammer, and squeezed the trigger. But as was so common with percussion firearms, the cap was defective. The hammer snapped, and the pistol failed to fire. At that, posseman Wilson leaped onto his horse and raced after one of the outlaws, yelling for him to surrender. The fleeing desperado paid no need, and Wilson's revolver did not misfire. Drawing a bead on the fleeing badman, Wilson shot him dead. The other outlaw escaped, and the dead man was found to have a fresh gunshot wound from a prior encounter. No one could identify them, and their names were never learned.[11]

Joaquin Murrieta wisely left the San Jose area. He and two of his pistoleros made a leisurely, sixty-mile ride south to the Salinas Valley. It was a dangerous venture, for his journey brought him into the same neighborhood where Henry Cocks and his posse had slain Claudio Feliz six months earlier. On about April 12, a week after the murder of James Walsh, Joaquin and his men rode up to the adobe ranch house of a Californio family on the Salinas River. It was late at night when they knocked loudly on the front door. The occupants opened the door and were startled to find three heavily armed strangers outside. Murrieta had two six-guns in a pair of pommel holsters, one on each side of his saddle, plus two more revolvers and a bowie knife around his waist. Despite his ferocious appearance, Joaquin's demeanor was more than polite. Speaking in Spanish, he explained that they had "lost the road" and "were on their way to the south to purchase cattle."

Murrieta asked for food, and the ranchero complied. The ranchman later said that the trio's horses were the best he had ever seen and described their leader as "a tall, handsome man, about twenty-one years old, with a long beard, and apparently false moustache." That disguise, coupled with the heavy armament, made the ranchero suspect that his guest might be the notorious Joaquin Murrieta. A Monterey journalist reported that the Californio asked "if he had just come from the placers and if any news had been heard of Joaquin, as he was told a great many parties were sent in search of him, with the expectation of receiving a large reward."

In response, Murrieta placed his hand over his heart and declared, "Sir, I am that Joaquin, and no man takes me alive, or comes within one hundred yards of me with these good weapons."

Then, with little emotion, he began telling his story, as the ranchero recalled: "He had been oppressed, robbed, and persecuted by the Americans in the placers—had lost $40,000—been driven from a piece of land which he was working with an American companion—had been insulted and grossly maltreated without justice—had been flogged—and he was determined to be revenged for his wrongs fourfold. He had robbed many—killed many, and more should suffer in the same way. He appeared then to grow very serious, and became excited."

Joaquin drew a long breath and proclaimed, "I was once a great admirer of the Americans and thought them the most generous, noble, and liberal people in the world, from having seen so many of them in my own country and here, who were men of the most generous and honorable principles, to whom tyranny and injustice were as hateful as the rule of Gachupins [Spaniards] to the Mexicans. I hated the insecurity and revolutions of Mexico and came here, thinking to end my days in California in peace as a citizen of the United States. With an American friend I took up a piece of land not far from Stockton, and was getting a fine little farm under way, when I was annoyed, insulted, and injured to such a degree by my neighbors that I could not live in peace. I then went in the placers, and was getting on very well, when I was driven from my hole by some of my lawless neighbors. I was in trade and business there, and was wronged and cheated by every one I trusted. At every turn I took, I lost or was swindled and robbed, and that, too, by the very men for whom I had the greatest friendship and admiration. I saw them daily commit acts of the most outrageous and lawless injustice, or of cunning and mean duplicity, hateful to every honorable mind. I then said to myself, I will avenge my wrongs and take the law in my own hands. Those who have injured me I'll slay, and those who have not I'll rob—my track shall leave a trail of blood, and he that seeks me shall bite the dust, or I will die in the struggle. I will get my money back some way or other, and I at least will not submit unrevenging to outrage."

According to the ranchero, "Joaquin said that hearing a large reward was offered for his head or his living body, he rode into Stockton disguised, walked leisurely around with his serape thrown over his shoulders, reading the different hand bills posted up about town. Coming to one of these, in a public thoroughfare, where $5,000 was offered for his capture, he wrote in pencil underneath, 'I will give $10,000 myself—Joaquin,' and leisurely rode out of the town."[12]

After finishing their meal at 1:00 a.m., Murrieta and his riders galloped off into the darkness. No sooner had the dust from their mustangs' hooves settled than rumors of the encounter began to spread. A journalist in Monterey got wind of the story, and before long it was featured prominently in newspapers, first in the *San Francisco Herald* and then throughout the country. Apparently some readers were skeptical, which prompted another Monterey newspaperman to investigate the account. "There is no doubt that Joaquin passed south, through Monterey County," he reported. "The real name of the bandit is Joaquin Muliati. He speaks English fluently, and in his foraging expeditions has always a fresh horse at hand. He was heard to say that he would never kill a Spaniard." The correspondent concluded, "The conversation reported in the *Herald* between Joaquin and the ranchero is confirmed."[13]

There can be little doubt that the heavily armed and disguised young man was indeed Joaquin Murrieta. Given that if the bandit chieftain was captured he would face certain death, no imposter would risk his life by making such a false claim. Joaquin's assertion that he had started a farm near Stockton was most likely untrue, for when he was arrested for theft in Stockton in 1850, he testified that he was a miner, not a farmer. And his claim that he was in trade and business in the placers also rings false, for other than digging for gold, the only other trade he engaged in was dealing monte. Yet Joaquin's account of being cheated and mistreated by Americans was undoubtedly truthful, and helps explain the brutality and ferocity of his bandit raids.[14]

One of the stories Murrieta told the ranchero would soon be widely believed in California. It was the colorful yarn in which he claimed that he had come upon a $5,000 reward poster in Stockton, and had written on the notice, "I will give $10,000 myself—Joaquin." The story would be repeated over and again in the years to come, supposedly having occurred in towns all over California. But the fact is that by April 1853, no $5,000 bounty had been offered for Joaquin. And as a Stockton newspaper reported the same month, "Now, no handbills offering any reward were ever posted in Stockton, so this portion of the story at least is a fiction."[15]

By this time, the editors of the *Sacramento Union* had engaged a local artist, Thomas Armstrong, to prepare a portrait of Joaquin Murrieta. They published it on the front page of their "Steamer Edition," which was a special pictorial issue sent by steamship to readers on the East Coast. The first purported image of the bandit chieftain, it was an engraving, showing him from the shoulders up, with long, curly, dark hair falling from under the brim of a straw hat. A serape was draped around his neck, and he gripped the barrel of a pepperbox revolver in his left hand. The portrait, titled "Joaquin, the Mountain Robber," was accompanied by a reprint of the story in the San Francisco *Daily Whig* that claimed Joaquin was thirty-five years old and had fought under Padre Jarauta during the Mexican War. As a result, the image shows a man in his mid-thirties, not his early twenties. And because Armstrong had never laid eyes on the fugitive bandido, even the most casual reader would have understood that the portrait was a fantasy. Nonetheless, it has been republished ever since as an authentic image of Joaquin Murrieta.[16]

Joaquin, the Mountain Robber, the imaginary depiction by Sacramento artist Thomas Armstrong. *John Boessenecker collection*

Meanwhile law officers continued their lookout for Jose Barrillo, who, a year earlier, accompanied by Joaquin, had killed William Janes at the fandango in Stockton. They finally captured him at a ranch near Stockton on April 15, 1853. The grand jury indicted Barrillo on two counts of grand larceny, as well as for the murder of Janes. A month later, he was legally tried by a jury, convicted, and sentenced to death. On the day of his hanging, June 3, 1853, a crowd of more than 1,200 people gathered. Barrillo made a full confession and admitted to numerous crimes, including three murders. A newspaperman who was present wrote, "He confessed that he belonged to Joaquin's band, and said that the deed for which he was executed was prompted by his leader—although Janes was not the intended victim. The body of the felon was scarred with wounds, and there is no doubt of his having been a desperate criminal."[17]

George Tinkham of Stockton, later a writer and historian, was then a young boy. Decades later he recalled, "On the day of the hanging, I was playing with companions on Main street near Colburn's barn, where the Gnekow block now is, when looking down the street, I saw a procession of about fifty horsemen approaching, chatting, laughing, and smoking cigarettes. Each man was armed with a revolver and their little mustangs were prancing and champing on their bits, the foam from their mouths flecking their breasts. The horsemen surrounded a wagon drawn by two horses, and in the wagon the condemned man sat, handcuffed and fastened with a riata to his chair. By his side stood a good padre, reciting the prayers for the dying, at the same time holding before the criminal's gaze a small cross. On arrival at the gallows, which in this instance was a large oak tree then standing on the southeast corner of Main and Stanislaus or Grant street, the wagon was driven beneath an overhanging limb, and the rope, already dangling, was placed around the prisoner's neck. He was then loosened from the chair and the wagon was driven out from under him. The Mexican was strangled to death, and the body was left hanging until the coroner came and cut it down."

Tinkham, in old age, decried Barrillo's hanging and the uneven application of the death penalty in the gold rush. "He was quickly tried, convicted and sentenced to be hanged, for at that time a bitter hatred existed between the whites and all foreigners, especially the natives of Mexico. So intense was this hatred that only two months previous to the execution, two Mexican muleteers, lying asleep by the side of their pack mules on the banks of the Mormon slough, in the early dawn were brutally shot and killed by two white men passing by. The white brutes saw the Mexicans quietly lying asleep, and drawing their revolvers they 'blazed away,' and then ran off. No efforts were made to find these murderers. But Jose Barrillo's case was different. He, a Mexican, had killed a white man, and, regardless of the law or evidence, he must hang."[18]

CHAPTER 14

CAPTAIN LOVE AND THE RANGERS

Phil Herbert was drunk but determined. He rested against the bar in the cavernous saloon in the basement of the new state capital building. After gulping down his final shot of whiskey, he made his way upstairs to the first floor. Herbert was a member of the state assembly, the lower branch of California's legislature, and in 1853 heavy drinking was part and parcel of a politician's job. He stood at his desk on the assembly floor and prepared to address his fellow legislators. Joaquin Murrieta was the subject of his speech. Herbert was convinced that something had to be done to stop the murderous raids by Joaquin's gang.

For weeks, gold miners, businessmen, politicians, and newspapers had clamored for the state government to take action against the bloody robbers. The public fear of the bandidos was more than justified. Between December 1850 and April 1853, members of the Feliz-Murrieta gang had murdered at least forty-five men. That number did not include several murders of which Joaquin was suspected, including those of Buckskin Smith, Allen Ruddle, and Captain Wilson. They were by far the bloodiest outlaw gang of the Old West. By comparison, the West's most infamous robber, Jesse James, did not come close. Between 1866 and 1875, the James-Younger gang killed "only" ten men.[1]

A journalist in Sonora declared, "It is a source of great complaint about here that the authorities do not take more active measures to break up this gang of banditti. It is said that the Governor has already gone to the limit of his power in offering $1,000 for the capture of the leader. Suppose he cannot offer more than $1,000 for any one criminal, is it not well-known that there is a large gang of desperadoes, many of them as bad as Joaquin, and if that amount were offered for each of them severally then it would be an object for a strong company to turn out and hunt them down, but to offer barely a thousand dollars for the ringleader is mere folly. It will take a numerous force to exterminate the gang, nor can it be done without a long hunt."[2]

Up to then, manhunts for the bandidos had been made primarily by volunteers, equipped and supplied by local merchants and miners. But posses in the field needed fresh horses, guns, lodging, feed for their mounts, and cash to bribe informants. It became evident that the state government had to take action by funding a mounted police force to track down Joaquin Murrieta's gang. In late March 1853, Philemon T. "Phil" Herbert, the assemblyman from Mariposa County, decided to proceed. Herbert, twenty-seven, was a typical gold rush politician—hard drinking and quarrelsome. He came from Alabama, and while attending college he had stabbed a fellow student and fled to Texas. In 1847 Herbert enlisted in the Texas Mounted Volunteers, and after the Mexican War, he joined the gold rush. After failing as a miner, he earned his living as a professional gambler before turning to politics. At the state capital in Benicia, Herbert introduced legislation in the assembly that would pay a $5,000 reward "for the capture of Joaquin, dead or alive, and $500 for each of his accomplices."

Despite broad support for the bill, it was opposed by another legislator, Jose M. Covarrubias. Unlike Herbert, Covarrubias was a decidedly atypical gold rush politician. An influential Californio leader from Santa Barbara, he had been one of the signers of the California state constitution in 1849. Covarrubias saw problems with the proposed legislation. He complained that "the principle involved in offering such reward is not justifiable in equity, nor would it be a safe and effectual mode of remedying the evil which we suffer. To set a price upon the head of any individual who has not been examined and convicted by due process of law, is to proceed upon an assumption of his guilt." After pointing out that the newspapers had published some false reports about Joaquin and his gang, he continued, "The magnitude of the reward might tempt unscrupulous and unprincipled men to palm off by purchased evidence the head of another for that of Joaquin, and thus defraud the state treasury." Finally, as Covarrubias concluded, "There are citizens of this state, descendants of ancient and honorable families, who bear the name of Joaquin Carrillo . . . One is a very respectable citizen of the County of Sonoma, and the other is the district judge of the Second Judicial District, who enjoys a distinguished reputation."[3]

Due to Covarrubias's objections, Herbert's bill failed. As a result, two petitions were circulated in Mariposa County, seeking state action against Joaquin's band. One of the petitions came from Harry Love, who had tracked down and killed Pedro Gonzales after the murder of Allen Ruddle. Among those who signed it were William Prescott, Henry Crowell, and Lee Vining, the trio who had shot it out with the gang in Hornitos a few weeks earlier. Despite the fact that Prescott and Crowell were still recovering from their gunshot wounds, they took pains to include their signatures. The petitioners demanded that the state do more than simply offer a reward for Joaquin—they wanted a state police force to break up the gang for good. The signers asked that Harry Love be appointed to head the force. Love was then mining in Quartzburg, near Hornitos, and his reputation as a Texas Ranger and express rider on the Rio Grande was widely known. More than two hundred miners and ranchers of Mariposa County signed the two petitions. One was sent to the state legislature, and Harry Love personally presented the other to the office of Governor John Bigler in Benicia.[4]

The signers who petitioned Governor Bigler complained that "our county is now being ravaged by a band of robbers, under the command of the daring bandit, Joaquin" and that "the civil authorities are totally incapable of protecting us from the maraudings." They asked the governor "to call out a company of rangers of at least twenty men, to be armed, equipped, and paid by the State . . . Your petitioners would most respectfully recommend Captain Harry Love as a person eminently qualified to command such a force, from his experience in border warfare, and a long residence on the frontiers of Texas, and more particularly by reason of his intimate acquaintance with the topography of this county, and his undoubted bravery, indomitable energy, and wise prudence and caution." The other petition, addressed to the legislature, demanded that the state "organize a company of twenty or twenty-five good horsemen, well armed and equipped and be so organized to be called 'the California Rangers.'"[5]

In response, Phil Herbert introduced a new bill in the state assembly, eliminating the $5,000 dead-or-alive reward and calling for the establishment of a company of rangers to track down "the robber Joaquin." It quickly passed and went up to the California senate for a vote. Once again a prominent Californio took exception. This time it was state senator Pablo de la Guerra, son of a distinguished ranchero family in Santa Barbara County. He moved that the vague description "the robber Joaquin" be stricken from the bill, because Joaquin was a common name. The senate agreed and approved the bill, and three days later, on May 17, 1853, Governor Bigler signed it into law. It was entitled "An Act to Authorize the Raising of a Company of Rangers" and read, "Captain Harry S. Love is hereby authorized and empowered to raise a company of mounted Rangers not to exceed twenty men, and muster them into the service of the State for the period of three months, unless sooner disbanded by order of the Governor, for the purpose of capture the party or gang

An engraving of Captain Harry Love, leader of the California Rangers.
John Boessenecker collection

of robbers commanded by the five Joaquins, whose names are Joaquin Muriati, Joaquin Ocomorenia, Joaquin Valenzuela, Joaquin Botellier, and Joaquin Carillo, and their banded associates." Each ranger was to provide his own horse, guns, and food, and would be paid $150 a month.[6]

The "five Joaquins" identified in the act were in fact only two men: Joaquin Murrieta and Joaquin Valenzuela. The legislators used the five names by which Murrieta and Valenzuela were known. Joaquin "Muriati" was an Anglo misspelling of Murrieta, and Joaquin Carrillo was his birth name. "Bottelier" was a corruption of the name Botero, for Harry Love believed that Jose Botero, the killer of Captain William Wilson in Los Angeles, was Joaquin Murrieta. Joaquin Valenzuela's nickname was Nacomoreno, misspelled as "Ocomorenia." The use of the five names for the two bandidos would soon cause no end of confusion and controversy. As the editor of the *Los Angeles Star*, in detailing passage of the new "Five Joaquins" bill, remarked sarcastically, "It is barely possible that *the* Joaquin is included in the above enumeration, but if so, his identity is destroyed, and with it all the notoriety he has acquired. A dangerous name is 'Joaquin,' and all who bear it must needs keep a sharp lookout, especially during the period of service of the twenty mounted rangers." But the *Star*'s editor forgot that just six months earlier, he had published the confession of Reyes Feliz, which included Feliz's identification of Joaquin Murrieta as the assassin of General Joshua Bean.[7]

Harry Love left Benicia and headed south to Mariposa County to raise his company of California Rangers. On the way, he stopped in Stockton on May 20, where he was interviewed by one of the town's newspapermen. "Harry Love, who has been authorized by the legislature to raise a company for the capture of Joaquin and his gang, passed through this city yesterday," the journalist wrote. "An important power has been delegated to this gentleman and we hope that he will exercise it with vigor, yet with discretion."[8]

The new captain of the California Rangers was more than qualified for the position. He was born Henry S. Love in Vermont in 1810. As a youth, he quarreled with his stepmother, left home, and became a cabin boy on a ship captained by his uncle. Love grew into an able seaman, and for years he sailed the Atlantic, the Caribbean, and the Pacific. A friend described him as "a Hercules in strength, standing six feet in his socks, a magnificent man, with curly black hair falling over his broad shoulders, moustachios of the same somber hue half covering his determined and aggressive chin." Love first saw California in 1839 when his ship docked at a West Coast port. By 1842 he was in Texas when the Mexican army tried to recapture the future state. Love enlisted as a private in the Army of the Republic of Texas for a three-month enlistment. He then received his first military training and soon became an expert rider and rifleman. From Texas he drifted east into Louisiana, where he labored as a crewman on keelboats and barges on the Mississippi River. Love next got work as a stevedore in Mobile, Alabama, and there he became enamored with a young woman. But then the Mexican War broke out, and soon after, in May 1846, he enlisted in the Alabama Volunteers. Love and his fellow soldiers boarded a Gulf steamer and a week later disembarked at the mouth of the Rio Grande. They marched upriver and joined the forces of General Zachary Taylor in the lower Rio Grande Valley.[9]

Harry Love and the other recruits spent their time marching and patrolling the border, but they saw no combat against the Mexican army. At thirty-six, Love was substantially older than many of his fellow volunteers, and he soon received a promotion to sergeant. The greatest danger the soldiers faced was not Mexican rifles and artillery, but death from dysentery and measles. Disease killed scores of the Alabama Volunteers before the unit was disbanded that summer. Love and the rest returned to Mobile, where he learned that his paramour had turned her attentions to another man. Heartbroken, he promptly went back to the Rio Grande. There he served as a Texas Ranger and gained valuable experience as a scout, tracker, and manhunter. By the end of the Mexican War, in February 1848, Love was a civilian express rider for the US Army. He carried military dispatches, letters, and newspapers from one army post to another along the Rio Grande, and became extremely well-known on the border.[10]

Several of the army officers' wives were much taken with the rugged frontiersman. One called him "a brave, manly fellow, with a mind full of native talent, learned from no other code but the instincts of his own uneducated and generous nature." She added, "His physique was that of a real 'Green Mountain

Boy,' six feet three, and stalwart and robust in proportion, as bold and intrepid as a lion, and a mild blue eye, which softened the otherwise fierce aspect of his rough, sun-burnt face, which was half concealed by a flowing beard and heavy moustache." Another described Love in a letter to her mother: "I wish I could picture him to your vision, as he came dashing down the street, well mounted as he always is, sitting his horse as if he were a part of the noble animal he rides, his long black curls flowing in the wind, his chest thrown out, his expression cool, frank, and resolute, his saber and spurs clashing, his clothes torn by the chaparral and covered with dust, one of Colt's revolvers, a six-shooter, fastened to his side and an additional brace of pistols in his [pommel] holsters."[11]

Harry Love frequently brought dispatches deep into Mexico, where US forces were still stationed in a number of cities and villages. In early September 1848, he rode out of the city of Chihuahua and headed for Brownsville, Texas, a seven-hundred-mile journey that took almost a month. Although the war hostilities were over, bands of marauding Comanches and Apaches posed an equal danger. Love stopped to rest at a rancho near the Mexican village of Parras, about three hundred miles due west of Brownsville, when it was suddenly surrounded by a Comanche war party. The warriors wounded several vaqueros and rode off with a herd of horses and mules. Harry waited a full day to be sure the Indians were gone before he and a companion, William Sherman, trotted their horses out of the rancho. Their two-day ride took them a hundred miles through desolate desert mountains, when at dusk they approached the mountain village of San Antonio. Love spotted several riders approaching, and thinking they were Mexicans, he called out a greeting. In response Love and Sherman received a volley of arrows from a charging band of thirty Apaches. One arrow struck Sherman's mustang. Harry and his comrade wheeled their horses and fled into the nearby mountains.

They hid out for a day, then returned to the road and resumed their journey. But the Apaches were waiting for them and quickly picked up their trail. Love spotted the warriors, and the pair tried to flee, but their escape was blocked by a rain-flooded arroyo. Leaping from their saddles, Love and Sherman shouldered their rifles and waited for the Apaches to come into range. As the warriors charged up with their chief in the lead, Love and his companion opened fire. Their bullets tore the Apache chief from his saddle, killing him, and the rest of the band scattered for cover. Then, to escape the Apaches, Love and Sherman leaped onto their mounts and plunged them into the swollen creek. Harry made it to the opposite bank, but Sherman's horse, weakened by its arrow wound, lost its footing. The animal was swept downstream and over a seventy-foot waterfall. But for Love's quick thinking, Sherman would have met the same fate. Love grabbed a lariat from the pommel of his saddle, swung it over his floundering comrade, and dragged him to shore. They lost not only the horse but also a carbine, a rifle, and two pistols.[12]

Harry Love and William Sherman escaped the Apaches and made it back to Brownsville alive. Love's next assignment proved equally dangerous. He was ordered to ride twelve hundred miles north to Santa Fe, New Mexico, deliver his dispatches, and then return south another seven hundred miles to San Antonio, Texas. Given that the longest trip ever made by a Pony Express rider from 1860 to 1861 was less than four hundred miles, it was a herculean task. Harry, leading an extra saddle horse, rode out of Brownsville on the same road through Mexico where he had encountered the Apaches and Comanches. After an exhausting seven-hundred-mile ride to Chihuahua, he rested in the pueblo for almost a week. A Texas journalist who later interviewed him wrote, "The whole way from Parras to Chihuahua the country was devastated by the Indians, and at the latter place he was advised by the American residents to take an escort, as several Mexicans had been slain within a few miles of the town by the Apaches." Love ignored their advice, and headed north to El Paso. Twice he outrode pursuing Indians and finally passed through El Paso and arrived in Santa Fe in late March 1849, after six weeks in the saddle.[13]

Two months later, Love, covered with trail dust, arrived in San Antonio to complete his journey. By that time, newspapers reported that he had been murdered by Indians in Mexico. After delivering his dispatches to the military commander, he took a much-needed rest and then rode back south to the army post in Brownsville. One of the army wives gushingly recorded his arrival in a letter to her family: "Harry Love came dashing up to the office last week, his horse covered with foam, bearing dispatches from Colonel Washington. He is a perfect specimen of the Border Dandy, browned by exposure to wind and weather, of magnificent physical proportions, and altogether bearing himself with a dashing, easy kind of grace that would astonish you. We had heard he had been murdered and the joy of his safe return was unbounded."[14]

News reports of Love's extraordinary ride were published in major newspapers from New Orleans to New York, and he became a nationally known figure. By this time reports of the California gold strike had swept through Texas, and Harry began making plans to join the rush for riches. His army commander worked hard to dissuade him. Aware of Love's long experience as a sailor and riverman, he engaged him to captain a keelboat to explore the Rio Grande. They christened it the *Harry Love*, and with a small crew, its namesake spent the next year making trips up the river and exploring its shallow, uncharted canyons, all in an effort to make the Rio Grande a navigable waterway. Once again newspapers across the country reported his expeditions and dubbed him Captain Love. But Harry wanted fortune as well as fame, and in the late fall of 1850, he rode across Mexico to the Pacific port of Mazatlan. There Love boarded a California-bound steamship and arrived in San Francisco on December 11, 1850.[15]

Harry Love headed for the Northern Mines, but like so many, he had little luck in hunting for gold. After supervising the building of a mining dam in Placer County, he rode to the Southern Mines. Always gregarious, he made many friends in Tuolumne and Mariposa Counties. In February 1852, some of them announced that Harry would accompany a group of prospectors to the Gila River in Arizona. But Love thought better of it and stayed in the gold country, his days spent laboriously shoveling gravel into streamside sluice boxes. Two months later, he heard of the reward that had been offered for the killers of Allen Ruddle. His successful manhunt, resulting in the killing of gang member Pedro Gonzales near Los Angeles, brought him acclaim in Mariposa County.[16]

Harry Love, following his appointment as captain of the California Rangers, returned to Mariposa County to recruit his company. He wanted men who could ride, shoot, and fight, but politics was also part of the equation. Throughout the nineteenth century, and until the establishment of civil service reforms beginning in the 1880s, the spoils system was in effect in most American communities. After an election, the prevailing political party would fire all of the government employees and replace them with members of their own party. Because Governor John Bigler was a Democrat, most of the men Love appointed were Democrats. He first rode to the Buena Vista ranch, four miles southwest of Hornitos, owned by twenty-six-year-old William J. Howard and his older brother, Thomas. Bill Howard was a friend of Assemblyman Phil Herbert; the pair had come to California in the same wagon train. Another of Howard's comrades was Captain Patrick Edward Connor, a Mexican War hero who later became a Union Army general in the Civil War. Howard and Connor had first met in Galveston, Texas, during the Mexican War. Harry Love, after explaining to Bill Howard the purpose of his visit, said, "Howard, you are more familiar with the fighting men of this part of the country. I wish you would pick the men you consider best suited for this undertaking."[17]

Bill Howard recommended his friend Patrick Edward Connor as a man with leadership and military skills, and Love wasted no time in appointing Connor first lieutenant of the rangers. As Howard recalled, "Captain Love, while as brave as a lion, was not a good organizer, and General Connor and I selected most of the men and made many of the preliminary arrangements. The men were picked very carefully, and every one of them was known to be an experienced marksman and courageous [and] was well mounted and fully armed." They quickly recruited a company of fighting men, "all of whom have smelt powder either in Mexico or Texas," as one ranger later remarked.[18]

Patrick Edward Connor was well suited to be a leader of the California Rangers. Born in Ireland with the surname O'Connor, he emigrated to New York City with his parents in 1832, at age twelve. Seven years later, to escape a life of poverty, the youth enlisted as a private in the US Army. Connor was also motivated by a yearning for excitement. Years later he said that he had been "inspired by the wild tales of trappers and hunters" and was "in search of novelty and adventure." Connor was assigned to a cavalry regiment, the First Dragoons, and sent to the remote frontier post at Fort Leavenworth, Kansas. He served five years on the prairies of Kansas and Iowa, guarding the settlements from attack by Plains Indians. Discharged in 1844, Connor returned to New York City and found work in a grocery store. There, in an apparent effort to escape anti-Irish bigotry, he changed his last name to Connor and eliminated his first name, ever after calling himself P. Edward Connor. But he found life as a grocery clerk more than boring, and a year later, Connor left for the Texas frontier.[19]

With the Mexican War brewing, Edward Connor enlisted in the Texas Volunteers. His previous army experience led the men in his company to elect him first lieutenant. He and his

Patrick Edward Connor, lieutenant of the California Rangers. *John Boessenecker collection*

fellow volunteers took part in the invasion of Mexico and saw heavy combat. Connor was promoted to captain and in February 1847 he took part in the Battle of Buena Vista, which pitted 4,500 American troops under General Zachary Taylor against an overwhelming force of 20,000 Mexican soldiers commanded by General Antonio López de Santa Anna. Connor's company came under heavy fire, and several of his men, including two lieutenants, died. Connor was lucky and suffered only a bullet wound in one hand. Many of the outnumbered volunteers fled in panic, but Connor ordered his men to take cover behind the adobe walls of the Buena Vista hacienda. He was determined to protect the army's left flank. As Connor and his men prepared to make a desperate last stand, the fleeing soldiers took heart and joined them. Then the Mexican cavalry attacked in numbers. Despite his wound, Connor led his men in firing volley after volley into the charging horsemen. At one point in the battle, General John E. Wool called out to him, "Captain Connor, where are your men?"

"General, there," shouted Connor, pointing to the bodies of dead soldiers all around him. He and his volunteers killed or wounded many of the charging cavalrymen, and finally the Mexicans withdrew. Connor had lost fifteen men, including the two lieutenants. Two months later, due to his wound, he resigned his commission and received a disability pension. But Connor soon recovered, and after the discovery of gold, he rode horseback across Mexico to the Pacific Coast. There he boarded a steamship to San Francisco and arrived in January 1850. A few weeks later, Connor heard rumors of a large gold strike on the Trinity River, south of the Oregon border. He and several companions, determined to be among the first to the new El Dorado, chartered a vessel and sailed north. When they reached modern-day Crescent City, Connor and nine others clambered into a whaleboat and headed for shore. But the boat overturned in heavy surf, and five of the men drowned.[20]

Once again Connor escaped with his life. He returned with the survivors to San Francisco, undeterred. Two months later, he led a second expedition to the Trinity River, this time overland. The group was forty strong, each man mounted on a mule, with their provisions carried in six wagons. But Connor never struck gold on the Trinity, and during the next few years, he engaged in business and led several expeditions to remote parts of California, always seeking his fortune. By his own admission, he was "flat broke" when Harry Love offered him the commission as first lieutenant in the California Rangers. Connor jumped at the chance.[21]

One of the most valuable recruits was Bill Byrnes, who had settled in Mariposa. Because he had known Joaquin at the monte tables in the Southern Mines and could readily identify him, his participation was crucial. The twenty-nine-year-old Byrnes was a colorful, yet hard-drinking and murderous, frontiersman. A native of Maine, as a boy he moved west with his parents to Missouri. Byrnes worked as a boatman on the Mississippi River and grew into a large, powerful man, standing six-feet-two, with

Bill Byrnes, Joaquin Murrieta's monte partner who became a leading member of the California Rangers. *William B. Secrest collection*

dark brown hair and flashing gray eyes. When the Mexican War broke out in 1846, Byrnes enlisted in the Second Regiment, Missouri Mounted Volunteers, led by General Sterling Price. The regiment rode south through Texas to New Mexico, where Byrnes and his comrades saw combat in several engagements against Mexican forces.

Byrnes was mustered out the following year and later claimed that he became a scalp hunter with Jim Beckwourth, the famed African American mountain man, and Robert Carson, one of Kit Carson's brothers. At that time, the Mexican government offered a bounty for Apache scalps. Byrnes once told a San Francisco journalist that he and his fellow scalp hunters killed several hundred Apaches in northern Mexico, for which they received $50 a head. The newspaperman described how his scalp hunting career came to a sudden end. "Byrnes, as he relates, had just settled up with his party the results of a successful hunt after the Apaches, and had started out again from the headquarters at Chihuahua for fresh operations, when a singular circumstance terminated his engagement in the business. He experienced a strange dream that foreboded evil if he continued on the trail, and the impression even awakened in his mind a sense of the inhumanity of the pursuit. The following morning his resolution was fixed, and calling his companions around him, he addressed them in a short speech, declaring his determination to withdraw."[22]

Bill Byrnes returned to Missouri, but soon after he got home, news arrived of the gold strike in California. He wasted no time in traveling overland to the Mother Lode, first settling in Placerville, known as Hangtown because several men had been lynched there. One pioneer recalled that Byrnes was a "desperado . . . and could be seen visiting and lounging around the various bar-rooms, carrying a miniature U.S. arsenal around his waist." On one occasion, Byrnes quarreled in a Placerville saloon with another miner, then reached for his six-gun. The gold hunter instantly thrust his clenched fist into Byrnes's face.

"Yes, draw your weapon," the miner exclaimed, "and I'll bet drinks for the crowd that I knock you down before you can cock it."

As the witness recalled, "Byrnes eyed the huge fist, concluded that he would like its appearance better at a distance, put up his weapon, and treated the crowd [to drinks]." Bill Byrnes drifted south to Murphys Camp, where he became a well-known gambler and Murrieta's monte partner. The following year, he returned to Placerville, where the El Dorado Indian War had erupted. The conflict began after a number of Native Americans were murdered by gold seekers. Indian warriors retaliated by making raids on the Overland Trail between Placerville and the Carson Valley in the territory that is now Nevada. Byrnes was elected captain of a militia company that engaged in one fight with Indians, and then spent months guarding the Carson Valley against attack. He became very popular and in November 1851 was elected Nevada's first sheriff.[23]

One day in the spring of 1852, a hardcase named N.R. Haskill, who owned a trading post in the Carson Valley, challenged Sheriff Byrnes to a shooting match. Byrnes agreed, despite the fact that Haskill held a grudge against him. The sheriff drew his revolver and fired all six shots at a target. As soon as his pistol was empty, Haskill pulled his own gun and shot Byrnes repeatedly. Bystanders seized Haskill, and because there was no court system, they held a vigilante trial. Haskill was lucky. Instead of being hanged, he was ordered by the vigilantes to leave the territory. Bill Byrnes slowly recovered from his wounds. When he was able to ride, he began searching for his assailant in California. Apparently Byrnes found him and exacted vengeance, for he later told a friend that he "was even now, and should hunt no more for Haskill." Early in 1853 he returned to the Southern Mines, and did not hesitate when asked to join the California Rangers.[24]

Billy Henderson, who had also known Murrieta in the gold fields, was another valuable recruit. As one of his comrades later explained, "Henderson was urged to join the company for the purpose of identifying the bandit." He was born William Tilford Henderson in Tennessee in 1826, and grew into a handsome, square-jawed young man with bushy, reddish-brown hair. After service in the Mexican War, Henderson settled in Missouri, but when gold was discovered, he traveled overland by wagon train and arrived in California in 1849. With two partners, he opened a hotel and general store near Quartzburg, and all three prospered. Henderson became a popular figure in the Southern Mines, with a peaceable reputation. Nonetheless, he carried a Colt Dragoon revolver and bowie knife on his belt. "No braver man ever lived," a friend once said. "He was absolutely without fear. He was a man of temperate habits, quiet and unobtrusive in manner, but he was a man of fixed determination."[25]

Bill Howard offered his Buena Vista ranch as headquarters of the California Rangers. Howard and his brother Thomas were

Billy Henderson, California Ranger, is armed with a Colt Dragoon revolver in an 1853 daguerreotype. *Madera County Historical Society*

natives of Virginia and expert horse breeders. Bill Howard, though only twenty-three, was a Mexican War veteran who had struck pay dirt in the Mother Lode. With dashing good looks, he boasted a shock of dense brown hair, a fashionable drooping mustache, and a long goatee. He used his newfound riches to acquire a pack train and general store near Hornitos. Then he and brother Thomas bought the nine-hundred-acre Buena Vista ranch. They hired fifty local Native Americans to grow crops and raise hogs, cattle, and horses. The Indian laborers built a roomy adobe hacienda and a huge corral surrounded by a rock wall. Bill Howard's passion was horse racing, and the Buena Vista ranch became noted for producing some of the finest saddle animals in the Southern Mines. In addition to helping recruit the rangers and providing the company's headquarters, Bill and Tom Howard supplied them with the best of horseflesh.[26]

Many of the other ranger recruits were also veterans of the Mexican War. George Evans had been badly wounded by a saber gash in hand-to-hand combat in the Battle of Buena Vista. He wore a large scar across his forehead as a badge of honor. Charley Bludworth, twenty-three, was both politically ambitious and no stranger to violence; in 1851 he had shot and wounded a Mexican during a fracas in Stockton. Another, Major Walter Harvey, had quarreled with Jim Savage, a noted mountain man and "white Indian chief" who was the first non–Native American to explore Yosemite Valley. Harvey shot Savage dead in 1852 and escaped punishment on grounds of self defense. John Sylvester, a miner and rancher, bore a much more peaceful reputation. He had held several minor political offices and had made an unsuccessful run for sheriff of Mariposa County. Nicholas L. Ashmore, twenty-one, came from a respectable family. Just three years earlier, he had been a schoolboy, living on his family's Kentucky farm, before joining the rush for gold. Ashmore was strikingly handsome, standing six-foot-three and always dressed in the height of fashion. Lafayette Black, twenty-nine, hailed from Tennessee. He first moved to Texas, then came to California by wagon train in 1849. A comrade on the journey called him "one of the most noble minded gentlemanly young men that I ever met with." Black made his home in Mariposa, where he worked as a trader before joining the rangers. William Prescott also signed up, no doubt to seek revenge against Murrieta's gang for wounding him in Hornitos two months earlier. Even the assemblyman, Phil Herbert, joined the rangers briefly, but the tough days in the saddle proved too much for him, and he soon resigned. A number of other recruits also quit and were promptly replaced by new men, including the Howard brothers and James A. "Coho" Young, a gold miner and US mail express rider.[27]

This, then, was the roughhewn bunch that was about to ride out on one of the most famous manhunts of the Wild West.

CHAPTER 15

I AM THE LEADER OF THIS BAND

Fields of wild oats swayed in the April breeze as Joaquin Murrieta and two of his pistoleros rode south along El Camino Real. The spring grass grows tall in the Salinas Valley, and it provided plenty of feed for their mustangs. Above the riders, left and right, spectacular mountain ridges loomed tall in the distance, their slopes dotted with grazing cattle and an occasional deer. Flocks of quail passed overhead as the horsemen followed the old mission trail that skirted the Salinas River and meandered through the center of the valley. But Joaquin and his riders were not there to enjoy the breathtaking scenery.

The night before, Murrieta had visited the adobe ranch house on the Salinas River, leaving its Californio occupants gape-mouthed at his story of mistreatment at the hands of Yankees. Joaquin and his men were now on their way to Southern California to embark on yet another series of bandit raids. For the next few days, they rode more than a hundred miles, passing through the mission towns of Soledad and San Miguel before reaching San Luis Obispo. The little pueblo, popularly called San Luis, had grown up around the Mission San Luis Obispo de Tolosa, built in 1772. Its population in 1853 was no more than two hundred, mostly Latino, with fewer than a dozen Anglo residents.

Despite its small size, San Luis Obispo was the stomping grounds for numerous outlaws and highway robbers. Chief among them were Joaquin Valenzuela and his brother, Jesus, alias Chiquito. Joaquin Valenzuela was one of the so-called "five Joaquins"—which were actually only he and Murrieta—and his nickname of Nacomoreno was misspelled as "Ocomorenia" in the legislative bill. Also prominent in San Luis were Salomon Pico, Pancho Daniel and his brother, Bernardo, and Pio Linares, the violent son of a local Californio family. The pueblo was remote and its law enforcement lax—a perfect place for Joaquin to recruit men into his gang. Murrieta made his headquarters at a rancho near San Luis, and within a few weeks, some fifteen desperadoes had joined him, among them Three Fingered Jack. As rumors of his presence swirled, Joaquin had one of his men write a letter to a neighboring ranchero. According to a local journalist, Murrieta stated that "he was in their midst, but would do them no harm, commit no outrage, provided he were let alone. It was his purpose to leave as soon as he was ready for Mexico." The correspondent added, "The citizens did not consider themselves strong enough to attack him, and he remained quietly recruiting."[1]

Finally Murrieta decided to pay a visit to the little pueblo—no doubt because of its many attractions: cantinas, fandango houses, and attractive senoritas. He first sent one of the gang in to advise the residents that he and his men were peaceful and intended to stay a few days before heading to the Mexican border. But, according to one pioneer, the bandit warned "that should any attempt be made to molest himself or any of his party, the town would be sacked." The next day, Murrieta and the rest rode boldly into the pueblo and made camp in the spacious garden behind the Mission San Luis Obispo—to this day a popular tourist attraction. The ruffians presented a jarring contrast with the beautiful mission flowers and greenery. "They were a desperate looking, swarthy set, dressed in buckskin suits, some having coats or jackets died [sic] green," recalled the pioneer. "All were well armed. The leader was symmetrically formed, with regular features, an open countenance, but a gloomy expression." They stayed for several days, and Joaquin paid an eleven-year-old local girl, Susan Banta, to wash his clothes. She would later remember the bandit chieftain well. The outlaws did not disturb anyone except a gambler whom they robbed before galloping out of San Luis Obispo.[2]

Murrieta and his fifteen-man gang continued two hundred miles south toward Los Angeles. Their route took them to the colorful mission town of Santa Barbara and then along the coast, with heavy Pacific waves crashing onto the beaches. They rode through Ventura and directly past Conejo Mountain, where Harry Love had shot and killed Pedro Gonzales a year before. Joaquin, undeterred by the specter of his compadre's violent death, rode on to bustling Los Angeles. His large band—heavily armed, well mounted, and colorfully dressed—attracted much attention as they trotted their horses down the pueblo's dusty streets. Because Joaquin had frequented the pueblo just six months earlier, a number of Latinos quickly recognized him. But by the time word of his presence spread, he and his riders were gone.

The gang continued sixteen miles east to the settlement of El Monte, where Murrieta was recognized by more Californios and Mexicans. The sightings created a panic. By June 5, rumors of raids by Joaquin's gang began to sweep through the Southland. A Californio youth, out hunting for stray horses, was shot in the leg by a Mexican desperado, and the crime was blamed on Joaquin and his band. Then came a report that Dr. J.W. Gaylord, the first dentist in Los Angeles, "had been shot, stabbed, hung, drawn, quartered and decapitated and the fragments of his form buried forty fathoms deep" in an arroyo five miles east of town. But the story, as the *Los Angeles Star* quickly reported, "turns out to be a pure fabrication. Consequently, that ubiquitous scoundrel, Joaquin, has one less crime to answer for. Dr. Gaylord is not only alive and well, but bids fair to live and practice his profession for many years to come."[3]

The hacienda of Andres Ybarra as it looked around 1875. The adobe was attacked and robbed by Joaquin Murrieta and his gang.
California Historical Society

Joaquin and his compadres did not linger about Los Angeles or El Monte. They rode on another hundred miles south to the Las Encinitas Rancho in San Diego County, owned by Andres Ybarra. Its hacienda was situated in what is now Stagecoach Park in the coastal town of Carlsbad. On the evening of June 9, 1853, Murrieta and three other desperadoes galloped up to the adobe and recklessly opened fire. After wounding one man in the leg, the outlaws burst into the hacienda, overpowered three others, and bound them with rope. Then they plundered the house, taking money and clothes, and fled back north with a *remuda* of stolen horses. The next day, a posse led by another ranchero, Lorenzo Soto, started in pursuit. The manhunters pressed Joaquin and his riders so closely that the outlaws abandoned four of their jaded animals, but at nightfall, the pursuers lost the trail. Soto and his possemen gave up the chase, but they sent messages to several local Indian tribes asking them to hunt the bandidos. Joaquin and his riders then stole eight fresh horses and vanished into the rugged hills. The bandit leader was recognized by local Mexicans who knew him by his birth name, Joaquin Carrillo.[4]

Six days later, on June 15, Murrieta's gang reappeared in Los Angeles County. He and eight of his pistoleros rode onto a large rancho near the stage road that connected the pueblo of Los Angeles and the port town of San Pedro. The desperadoes made camp in the hills, and when a local vaquero rode too close, they captured him. The vaquero knew two of the outlaws, Juanito Ramirez and Rafael Mazuca. The bandidos, probably because they had been recognized, threatened to kill him. Murrieta, however, interfered, and declared that the vaquero "was of no account." Joaquin ordered his release, and the vaquero quickly rode away and reported the incident to the authorities in San Pedro. The town's alarmed mayor promptly alerted the San Pedro Blues, its local militia company. A correspondent in San Pedro who wrote about the gang's movements to the *Los Angeles Star* said, "The supposition is that they are waiting an opportunity to rob the stages. Our vigilant mayor has been practising rifle shooting this afternoon, and this evening he is engaged in loading revolvers. He would have ordered out the San Pedro Blues, but, in time, he ascertained that the corporal was the only fragment that remained in town, and so he ordered that every citizen should barricade his door and keep a candle burning." The correspondent added, "If Joaquin does attack this city, he will be welcomed—to a bloody time."[5]

A week later, the *Los Angeles Star,* which was then published in English and Spanish, printed a long editorial about Joaquin in its Spanish language columns. "Who is Joaquin?" its Mexican-born editor began. "Here is the question that everyone asks and although it seems like an easy solution, not many can answer it categorically." He reported that some Latinos thought "that Joaquin cannot be anything other than one of the cursed spirits of the

Lord, who delight in practicing evil . . . Others believed they saw in Joaquin a man-eater who feeds on the flesh of his victims and tries to quench his inexhaustible thirst with the blood drawn from their hearts. Many think that Joaquin does not exist, neither in body nor in spirit, but rather it is an imaginary name that some groups of robbers use to attribute the crimes they commit, and in this way they ensure that all the crimes are directed at a non-existent being, allowing them to commit their crimes with greater impunity."

The Latino editor then addressed the issue of Joaquin as a folk hero seeking revenge against the Anglos. "There are others (and these are the stupidest) who represent him as a hero, an avenger of some personal grievances that we may have received from the Americans . . . Poor people! They do not see that the man accustomed to crime, whose conscience is dulled, makes no distinction between nations. The only thing he wants is money to maintain fame [and] horses for his quick escapes." The journalist closed by saying, "Joaquin, in our opinion, is nothing more than a cunning and daring robber; cunning because he has known how to create prestige by telling stories to the gullible, and daring because he has undertaken extremely dangerous actions, and into which his own desperate situation has led him. He knows well that there is no alternative for him other than hanging, and this same situation makes him ignore any danger, as long as it offers him the slightest hope of being able to prolong his existence."[6]

The newspaperman's obvious point was that most of Joaquin's victims in Southern California were Californios or other Latinos. However, it was often the ricos—the rancheros and merchants—who saw Joaquin as a common criminal. Many working-class Latinos—*peones*, *mineros*, and vaqueros—began to view him as a rebel and avenger. To disenfranchised Mexicans and Californios, Murrieta would eventually become a full-fledged folk hero.

As more reports of Murrieta sightings poured into Los Angeles, the *Star*'s Anglo editor remarked, "The news circulating regarding Joaquin is so varied and contradictory that we do not dare to affirm anything other than what everyone agrees on and that is, that this notorious bandit is in the vicinity of this town." But the bandit chieftain was too wily to stay in one place for long, and he and his men headed back south toward San Diego. Reported the *Star*, "Many men of veracity assert positively that Joaquin Murieta and his band are now somewhere between San Juan Capistrano and San Diego, bound down to Lower [Baja] California. That Joaquin passed through this city is just as certain as anything else; and it is equally certain that no one was frightened."[7]

However, the gang did not ride to Baja California. On the Fourth of July, they raided the Rancho Buena Vista in northern San Diego County and stole a remuda of horses. Whether Murrieta himself led the raid is unclear. However, a journalist in San Diego reported that the thieves were "part of the famous Joaquin band, and that enterprising individual himself is said to have been recognized in Los Angeles, on his way down the country." He added, "This report is strenuously doubted by many incredulous and obstinate persons, who openly question the fact of the existence of that popular gentleman; but it is sufficiently ascertained that there are parties of armed banditti continually on the move between the different ranches and towns of Southern California, and that the outrages committed are traceable to the same gang."[8]

The brazen raids created terror in Southern California. Wild and exaggerated accounts of the attack on Andres Ybarra's adobe at Las Encinitas Rancho quickly spread. Several newspapers reported that Joaquin Carrillo and no less than seventy men had attacked a group of ranchers who were carrying $70,000 from the sale of a large flock of sheep. The battle lasted three days, and several men were slain on both sides. Then a posse of thirty-five heavily armed Mormon settlers supposedly rode to the rescue, but when they arrived, they found no trace of any battle. The reason, of course, was that no such fight had taken place. The *Los Angeles Star* proclaimed, "This county is in a state of insurrection, clearly and plainly. A large gang of outlaws, many of them expelled for crime from the mines, are in open rebellion against the laws, and are daily committing the most daring murders and robberies. Good citizens should devise plans to defend themselves."[9]

But Murrieta's band rarely numbered more than a dozen men at a time, and he certainly did not attempt to lead an insurrection in California. Joaquin, Three Fingered Jack, and the rest of the gang rode north through Los Angeles County unmolested. They were accompanied by a hardened thirty-year-old desperado named Antonio Lopez, as well as Jose Maria Ochovo, aged about twenty-three, who had met the gang in San Diego County. Ochovo later said that their plan was to continue north through the Coast Range and then proceed to plunder the mining country. They would unleash a final series of raids against the Chinese and Anglo mining camps and then return to Mexico for good. On their way, the band stopped at the ranch of General Andres Pico in San Fernando, twenty miles north of Los Angeles and situated in the center of the San Fernando Valley. Today the San Fernando Valley is home to vast suburbs of Los Angeles, but then it was wide-open grazing land. Andres Pico, its most prominent resident, was the famed Californio military hero and first cousin of Salomon Pico. According to General Pico, Joaquin rode at the head of "twenty-five men, all armed with revolvers, double-barreled guns, swords, and lances. The robbers have visited several ranches in that vicinity." If Joaquin indeed had twenty-five men with him, it was the largest his gang had ever been.

The desperadoes stole fifty of Pico's horses and continued north fifteen miles to the Rancho San Francisco, in the modern-day city of Santa Clarita. There they were confronted by a vaquero who recognized the stolen horses. When Murrieta learned that the animals belonged to General Pico, he promptly turned over forty-three head to the vaquero. He told the herder to return them to Pico, but insisted that he "had need of the other seven." Either Joaquin feared the former soldier or, more likely, he did not want to steal from the cousin of his compadre, Salomon Pico. By this time, the gang was much smaller than twenty-five. Murrieta and his men rode north through the Tehachapi Mountains and passed by the Native American camp of Chief Jose Zapatero. A year earlier, he and his warriors had captured Joaquin, Reyes Feliz, and Pedro Gonzales and relieved them of their herd of stolen mustangs. Zapatero immediately recognized Murrieta, and he later reported that the bandido was accompanied by only six riders. But the chief was either unaware that Joaquin was wanted, or he was outgunned, for this time Zapatero made no effort to stop the gang. Murrieta and his men turned their horses west and headed toward the coast. They rode eighty miles to Santa Barbara County and then cantered leisurely along the west side of the Coast Range. From there they intended to cross the mountains and return to pillage the Mother Lode country.[10]

While Joaquin was raiding in Southern California, other members of the gang had stayed behind in the gold region. Among them were the belligerent Pedro Sanchez as well as Jesus Feliz, Joaquin's brother-in-law, and an Anglo horse thief named McLean. Several other Anglos were associated with the gang, including Robert Scott, the murderous bandit and partner of Joaquin Valenzuela, and a desperado known only as Dawson. That winter Robert Scott had been raiding near the Oregon border, and as a result, he had taken no part in the gang's murderous rampage in the Mother Lode. But Scott still maintained ties with Murrieta's band. By late April 1853, he was riding with the outlaw Dawson and two others, Frank Freeman and a man called Dublin Jack. They were accompanied by several of Joaquin's bandidos whose names are unknown. One of the Mexican pistoleros was a suspect in the murder of James Walsh, stabbed to death by the gang at Mission San Jose earlier that month.

Robert Scott later said that he separated from the band, and the rest of the robbers rode to the prosperous mining camp of Mormon Island. It was located on the South Fork of the American River, northeast of Sacramento, and is now covered by Folsom Lake. There, late on the night of April 29, the gang, led by Dawson, with Freeman, Dublin Jack, another Anglo, and three Mexicans, rode up to the Adams & Company Express office. Dawson, with two of the bandits, stepped inside, pulled out six-guns and bowie knives, and covered a pair of clerks.

"Joaquin is not dead!" one of them exclaimed. "Say not a word, or you die. We want your money. We know you've got it, and we're bound to have it!"

They quickly tied up the clerks with buckskin straps and gagged them with neckerchiefs. The gang demanded the key to the office safe, but the clerks gasped that they didn't have it. While several of the outlaws kept watch outside, the others ransacked the office, searching for the key. They were so rash that they spent a casual two hours inside. While one desperado relaxed in a chair reading a newspaper, the others conversed in English and Spanish. Some of the outlaws lit up cigars that they found in the office and cursed their poor quality. At the same time, the robbers interrogated the clerks, then pricked them with knives and threatened to kill them unless they gave up the key. Finally one clerk admitted that the express agent, who was in charge of the office and was asleep in his house nearby, had the key to the safe. The robbers marched the clerk to the agent's door, removed his gag, and had him call out to the expressman. The ruse worked, and the instant the agent opened the door, he was bound, gagged, and dragged into the office.

Within moments the bandits opened the safe and poured $7,000 in gold dust and coins into a large sack.

The robbers then began arguing over whether they should kill their three captives. Finally their leader, Dawson, convinced them otherwise. Leaving the expressmen tied up inside the office, the freebooters warned that if the captives raised any alarm, they would return and kill them all. Then Dawson and the rest rode off on the wagon road toward Sacramento. But no sooner had they left than the express agent managed to free himself. He rushed into the street and began banging on a gong that served as the town fire alarm. The camp was immediately aroused, and a posse of citizens started in pursuit. They tracked the outlaws to within ten miles of Sacramento before they lost the trail. Adams & Company Express promptly offered a reward of $2,000 plus 25 percent of any of the loot recovered, but it seemed that the bandits had vanished into thin air. Dawson, however, would come to dread the California Rangers.[11]

Meanwhile the quarrelsome Pedro Sanchez, unconcerned that he might be recognized after the gang's bloody raids, boldly returned to his old stomping grounds in Columbia and nearby Martinez. According to a journalist's letter written from Columbia, Sanchez was "a sort of terror to his countrymen, but seldom interfered with Americans. The past week he has been very troublesome, and has threatened to kill a number of Mexicans." On May 30, 1853, Sanchez fought with an Irishman near Sonora and stabbed him, inflicting a serious but not fatal wound. A few days later, on June 3, Sanchez got into a quarrel with a Mexican, Albino Leyba, and made more death threats. The following night, Sanchez and Leyba were playing blackjack in a gambling hall in Martinez. They fought again, and when Sanchez pulled a bowie knife, Leyba fled outside. The bandido followed, flourishing his poniard. Leyba drew his six-shooter, faced Sanchez, and warned him to stop.

The desperado was not used to anyone standing up to him. He ignored Leyba's warning and advanced with his knife raised. Leyba didn't hesitate, unleashing four shots as fast as he could cock and fire. Three balls missed, but the last one ripped into Sanchez's chest, killing him instantly. The next day, Leyba turned himself in to Constable John Leary, Columbia's capable lawman. Leary took Leyba into Sonora and locked him in jail. A day later, the Tuolumne County grand jury, which happened to be in session, heard testimony from witnesses and indicted Leyba for manslaughter. But the case was obviously one of self-defense, and the charges were apparently dropped, for Albino Leyba never served time in the state prison.[12]

A week later, on June 12, Joaquin's brother-in-law, Jesus Feliz, with three Latino desperadoes and the American horse thief, McLean, were spotted with a band of stolen mustangs near Mariposa. A posse of citizens started in pursuit. In an effort to get rid of the evidence and make it appear that the animals had been stolen by Indians, the outlaws killed four horses by riddling them full of arrows. The possemen captured one of the suspects, but Feliz, McLean, and the others managed to escape. Two weeks later, on June 29, Feliz and McLean rode into the mining camp of Vallecito. It was situated on the stage road midway between Angels Camp and Murphys in Calaveras County and was home to numerous Mexican and Chileno miners. The outlaws were mounted on two mules, and they planned on rustling a herd of cattle from the camp butcher in Vallecito. However, two alert local men, A.H. Forsyth and R. Warren, recognized their mules as having been stolen. Before Forsyth and Warren could arm themselves and take action, McLean left town and rode a few miles north to French Camp to play cards in a monte parlor. Jesus Feliz, on the other hand, made the mistake of lingering in Vallecito. Forsyth and Warren quickly captured young Feliz without a fight. Probably in exchange for leniency, Feliz admitted the cattle stealing scheme and revealed

Joaquin Murrieta, as illustrated by Charles Christian Nahl in 1854.
John Boessenecker collection

that McLean had gone to the gambling hall in French Camp. Forsyth and Warren galloped to French Camp, arriving that night, and found McLean dealing monte. As the manhunters stepped up to the table, McLean went for his six-shooter. But Forsyth beat him to the draw. According to a local journalist, Forsyth "swore if he did not take his hand off his weapon, he would blow his brains out." McLean wisely surrendered. Jesus Feliz was quickly identified as the brother of Claudio. He and McLean were jailed on suspicion of being "confederates of the Joaquin party." The capture of Jesus Feliz would prove to be a crucial development in the manhunt for the Murrieta gang.[13]

By this time, Harry Love and his rangers had begun hunting Joaquin's band, unaware that Murrieta and part of the gang had ridden to Southern California. The California Rangers began their work in early June by scouring the foothills of Mariposa County, searching for any trace of the outlaws. Each ranger was armed with one or more Colt revolvers and a shotgun or rifle. Pack mules carried their food, provisions, and cooking gear. After a few days of hard riding, the rangers achieved some initial success. As Lieutenant Edward Connor reported from Quartzburg on June 3, "Tomorrow we start for the mountains. We have taken the horse that Mr. James Welsh [Walsh] rode when he was shot, between San Jose and Santa Clara, about two months since, and we are now in pursuit of the Mexican who sold the animal in this place." Captain Love, at the same time, sent a letter to Stockton advising that they had also recovered thirty-one stolen horses. The rangers quickly tracked down the Mexican who had sold Walsh's horse and arrested him. Apparently a local judge released the unnamed suspect without charge, much to the frustration of the rangers.

A few days later, newspapers published sensational stories proclaiming that two of the rangers had been ambushed and killed: "A member of Captain Love's company who are in search of Joaquin's gang sends us the report of the death of Major Harvey and Mr. [Coho] Young. Their bodies were found on the trail yesterday between the San Joaquin and the Fresno [Rivers]. It is supposed that the murders were committed by Indians." But the report turned out to be false. What actually happened was that Coho Young had been riding near the San Joaquin River when he fell from his mount and suffered serious injuries.[14]

Due to the winter's heavy snowfall, the 1853 spring runoff flooded the rivers that drained the Sierra Nevada and turned large sections of the San Joaquin Valley into shallow lakes. Love and his rangers found that those conditions made manhunting more than difficult. On June 8, one of the rangers, most likely Lieutenant Connor, wrote to a Stockton newspaper from the Howard brothers' Buena Vista ranch. "The Head Quarters of the Company for the present is at the above ranch, from which scouting parties are sent dispatched to various parts of the county to capture such of the numerous bands of horse thieves infesting this county as we may be able to find. Robberies of stock are matters of daily occurrence and all are laid to the hands of one or more of the five Joaquins . . . The haunts of some of these robbers are known to us, but we are prevented from visiting them at present, on account of the high waters in some of the rivers we would have to cross. Our object is to first run them out of this country and then capture them in their mountain lairs. They will probably give us a good fight of it, but I am confident that the Rangers are able to meet any number of them." He added that the Howard brothers "are whole souled gentlemen and great favorites of the Rangers, whose stomachs they fill with the best of elk and antelope meat, when not away on duty."[15]

Captain Love and his men, despite making daily scouting trips through the Mariposa foothills, had trouble locating any members of Joaquin's band. On June 15, Love and a group of rangers scouted along the Fresno River, fifty miles south of their Buena Vista ranch headquarters. They believed that Murrieta and his men were hiding out in the camps of mesteneros in the San Joaquin Valley, but the flooded streams prevented them from searching the valley. The same day, one of the frustrated rangers, probably Connor, scribbled a letter to a Stockton newspaper: "I have been most of the time since my last [report] roaming over the prairies and visiting the old haunts of the mustang catchers, whose camps are the rendezvous of horse thieves and murderers. We have only encountered one or two of these hombres, most of them, for some reason, having moved to the other side of the San Joaquin, where we will soon be upon them. We have made some arrests and captured some stolen animals. The men we have turned over to the civil authorities, but not in one case has there been a conviction, although stolen property has invariably been found in their possession. The only way to do the State service would be to take the law into our own hands."[16]

While the California Rangers were in the saddle, they came under political attack from the *Alta California*. The *Alta* was not only San Francisco's oldest and most widely read newspaper, it bitterly opposed Governor John Bigler. A year earlier, the *Alta*'s founder and editor, Edward Gilbert, had quarreled with a prominent politician, James W. Denver. He was a state senator and Bigler supporter for whom the city of Denver, Colorado, was later named. In one of the West's most famous formal duels, the two fought with single-shot rifles at forty paces, and Denver put a bullet into Gilbert's abdomen, killing him. Gilbert's close friend, Edward C. Kemble, took over as chief editor. The killing of Gilbert triggered Kemble's and the *Alta*'s deep enmity against anyone or anything connected with John Bigler. Because the rangers had been appointed by Bigler's administration, they were fair game for the *Alta*'s potshots. On June 20, the newspaper reported that the rangers had just returned to their headquarters with two captured horse thieves. According to the *Alta*, "These were at once started, under guard, to Quartzburg for trial. Subsequently to the return of the guard, they [the thieves] were found dead on the wayside, perforated with half a dozen balls each." Then, a few days later, the *Alta* referred to Lieutenant Connor's pro-vigilante report and declared, "Love's Rangers have determined to take the law into their own hands, on the singular ground that juries are disinclined to convict Mexican horse thieves! The two prisoners, who were shot on the way to Quartzburg, were not, until after the discovery of their corpses, reported to have attempted to escape from their escort. Astonishing accuracy to have emptied a six-shooter into the body of a man in flight!"[17]

But the *Alta*'s story was false. Two Mexican horse thieves had indeed been shot, but the incident took place weeks before the rangers were organized. On April 26, 1853, several horses had been stolen near Sonora. The owners formed a posse and caught two of the thieves. They ordered the prisoners to ride with them to the justice of the peace in Quartzburg. When the two Mexicans tried to escape, the possemen shot and killed them both. The *Alta*'s spurious account infuriated the rangers, and one of them—apparently Connor—responded in a letter written from the Buena Vista ranch. He said that the killing of the two men "happened before the State Rangers were in existence and a short time previous to Captain Love leaving the county with his petition to the Legislature for the act to organise a company. I have been informed by respectable citizens of this place that those who shot the Mexicans were justifiable in so doing. The Mexicans were taken with two animals in their possession which they had stolen from Sonora a day or two previous, and were endeavoring to escape from the officers when they were shot. I am also informed that the act was reported to a magistrate in less than ten minutes after the occurrence."[18]

It was not long before the *Alta* took another crack at the rangers, and even questioned whether "the fabulous robber chieftain Joaquin" had ever existed. "We think their present occupation [is] scouting for a man whom nobody ever saw, and who, perhaps, has no existence except in the imaginative brains of legislators, and who, if he does exist, is most likely out of the State or in a place of safety," the *Alta* declared. "The politicians are shouting loud hosannas to the Joaquin Rangers for their brilliant services—where or when rendered is not stated by the panegyrists." The newspaper's editors had conveniently forgotten that just months earlier, they had published numerous accounts of Joaquin and his bloody raids. This would not be the *Alta*'s last attack on the California Rangers, and its casting doubt on the very existence of Murrieta would later become a huge issue in the bandit's saga.[19]

By early July, the heavy spring runoff had receded, and the rivers, as well as the swamp-like San Joaquin Valley, became passable. In the blistering summer heat, which often exceeded one hundred degrees, Harry Love, with a detachment of rangers, rode out to search the great valley. They knew that they were looking for a needle in a haystack. The vast San Joaquin Valley stretched three hundred miles from Sacramento south to Tejon Pass and the Tehachapi Mountains, and fifty miles wide, from the Sierra foothills to the base of the Coast Range. Today the valley is dotted with cities and towns, and everything in between is farms, crops, orchards, and grazing lands for livestock. But then the valley was more than isolated, and many of its major cities, like Fresno and Bakersfield, did not yet exist. Other than a few villages like Stockton and Visalia, the great valley was populated mainly by herds of antelope, tule elk, and wild mustangs. Huge flocks of ducks and geese flew overhead as Love and his rangers cautiously made their way across the valley. As Ranger Bill Howard later explained, "In the days of 1853, there was scarcely a settler in the whole San Joaquin Valley, south of Stockton." Among its few human occupants were the mesteneros, some of whom harbored outlaws in their remote camps.[20]

The rangers spent more than a week searching the west side of the San Joaquin Valley, without success. Then they returned to their headquarters in the Mariposa foothills for supplies and a much-needed rest. While at the Buena Vista ranch, they finally caught two big breaks in the manhunt. First, news reports of Joaquin's opening raids in Southern California were brought north by steamship and reprinted in the newspapers of San Francisco, Sacramento, and Stockton. That explained why the rangers had been unable to find any trace of Joaquin in Mariposa County or in the valley. Second, and most significantly, the prisoner Jesus Feliz was turned over to Harry Love, probably by law officers from Calaveras County, where he had been jailed. Love immediately recognized the importance of Feliz's arrest and offered him a deal: if he would help locate Joaquin, they would set him free. The youth may well have blamed the deaths of his brothers Claudio and Reyes on Joaquin, for he admitted to the rangers that he was Murrieta's brother-in-law and he agreed to cooperate. Love, based on information he got from Feliz, concluded that Murrieta and his men would return north from Los Angeles to the camps of mesteneros and horse thieves in the Coast Range. And it was undoubtedly from Jesus Feliz that they learned an unnamed gang member, a suspect in the murder of James Walsh, was hiding out in Stockton.[21]

While Love and the rangers made preparations for another long manhunt, Lieutenant Connor and Bill Howard mounted their horses and rode ninety miles north to Stockton. The pair arrived on July 15 and began searching for the Walsh murder suspect. The town was small, and it did not take them long to find a criminal informant. He revealed that the Anglo bandit leader, Dawson, had been in Stockton and had asked him to join the gang. Dawson boasted that he was part of a large band of robbers, and that they had held up the Adams express office at Mormon Island. The informant said that Dawson was riding a fast mustang that he had stolen in Coloma, the spot where gold had first been discovered. He explained that Dawson and his partner, Frank Freeman of the Mormon Island robbers, had gone to the horse races at the ranch of David F. Douglass, situated on the Calaveras River twenty miles east of Stockton. Douglass was a prominent soldier and politician, and his large ranch boasted a popular racetrack.

On the morning of July 18, Rangers Connor and Howard, accompanied by Deputy Sheriff Edward Canavan, rode out of Stockton and headed for the Douglass ranch. There they found several hundred spectators gathered around the track, laying down bets on the horse races. Connor and Howard soon found the stolen animal, a small black mustang with a diamond-shaped brand on one shoulder. At about the same time, Deputy Sheriff Canavan spotted Dawson and Freeman in the crowd. He pulled his six-shooter and covered them, but Dawson started to run. Canavan charged after Dawson, "begging him to surrender," as a local journalist said.

"Shoot and be God damned!" yelled Dawson, at the same turning and drawing his pistol from its holster. But the outlaw's gun never cleared leather. Canavan fired just once. The heavy slug tore through Dawson's stomach and lodged in his spine. He dropped like a stone, desperately wounded. Freeman, not wishing to meet the same fate, threw up his hands and surrendered. Deputy Canavan and Lieutenant Connor brought Freeman to jail in Stockton. They learned from Freeman that he and Dawson had planned to ride in one of the races and swindle the gamblers by "fixing" their match. The officers left Dawson behind at the Douglass ranch, under the care of a local physician. The robber lingered for ten days in excruciating pain and even begged the doctor to give him a fatal dose of laudanum. Dawson refused to provide any information about the gang, other than to admit that he and Freeman had been two of the Mormon Island robbers. Before Dawson died, he boasted that he "was the greatest rascal the world ever saw." Law officers took Frank Freeman to Sacramento, where he was jailed for the Adams express robbery. Despite the fact that Dawson, in his deathbed statement, had implicated Freeman, a judge released Freeman after his lawyer produced an alibi. The editor of the *Sacramento Union* criticized this result, pointing out that the alibi witness was disreputable, and proclaimed, "There is but little doubt of his guilt."[22]

By this time, during the first week of July, Harry Love and thirteen of his rangers had left the Buena Vista ranch, accompanied by young Jesus Feliz. They made a long, hard ride in the sweltering heat, first across the plains of the San Joaquin Valley, then over the Coast Range to San Jose. There Love announced that he had received word that Joaquin was in Los Angeles, and he and his rangers then rode south out of town. But it was merely a ruse to disguise their plans. They continued forty-five miles to the little village of San Juan Bautista, then and now one of the most picturesque mission towns in California. The Mission San Juan Bautista was established in 1797 in the Pajaro

River Valley, east of the Gabilan Mountains and thirty miles north of Monterey. The pueblo that grew up around the mission, known as San Juan, was the hometown of both Salomon Pico and Domingo Hernandez, the bandit leader who been lynched in Santa Cruz in 1852. Next to the mission plaza was a large adobe—still standing—with a tavern and hotel run by Patrick Breen and his wife, both of whom had survived the Donner Party tragedy in 1847. The rangers no doubt first stopped for drinks and food at Breen's hotel.

San Juan had a post office, and on July 12, the day after their arrival, Love mailed a letter to Governor Bigler: "I leave this place this night for the mountains. I have arrested a Mexican Jesus a brother in law of Joaquin's. He says he will take and show us to Joaquin if we will release him. I will try him a while to see what it will end in. There appears to be quite a number of horse thieves hid in the mountains back of this place and between here and the Tulare [San Joaquin] Valley. I hope I may make him useful to me in hunting them out. We get a few stray stock every few days but nothing of importance has occurred."[23]

In San Juan Bautista, Harry Love learned that neighboring ranchers had been plagued by a gang of horse thieves. Guided by Jesus Feliz, the rangers rode out of the pueblo and began hunting the band. On July 15, they captured five of the outlaws and brought them back into San Juan. Love sent a messenger to Lieutenant Connor in Stockton with the news. "The prisoners have confessed and pointed out the headquarters of the horse thieves," he wrote. "They state that there are some fifty in the band, who live in the coast range mountains, on the border of Tulare Valley. They have a band of some three hundred stolen horses with them. They described their comrades as being ill clothed and ill fed, some having nothing but shirts on their bodies, others with no coats, and so on." Jesus Feliz believed that Joaquin and his men were likely to hide out with this gang of horse thieves on their way back from Southern California.[24]

From San Juan's merchants, Love and his men bought enough provisions to last them for eighteen days. Then the rangers again spread the word that they were going to ride southward along the coast. That afternoon, their pack mules laden with food and supplies, they headed down the wagon road into the Salinas Valley. In the evening, the rangers stopped and made camp on the Salinas plains, but when darkness fell, they packed up, mounted their horses, and backtracked toward San Juan. Skirting the pueblo, they struck camp and spent the night in an isolated canyon nearby. The rangers guarded Jesus Feliz closely to make sure he could not escape. The posse rested in the canyon all day, out of sight, and at dusk they again started out along the rugged trail that followed the San Benito River into the secluded heights of the Coast Range. A forty-mile ride south brought them to the Las Aguilas Mountains, about five miles west of modern-day Mercey Hot Springs. Once again the rangers stayed all day in camp and kept out of sight. Feliz had undoubtedly warned them that they might be spotted by mesteneros, who in turn could warn Joaquin's gang.

That night the rangers rode eighteen miles south to Panoche Pass, where they set up a base camp. Through the confessions of Feliz and the five captured outlaws, Love and his men believed that Murrieta's band would most likely hide out in the horse thieves' camp, located somewhere in the vast foothills between Panoche Pass and the San Joaquin Valley, 2,200 feet below. This region, then and now, is one of the most remote and isolated in California. For the next few days, the rangers split up into small posses and rode out from their camp, scouring the rugged hills and gorges for any trace of the outlaws. Finally, on July 20, Captain Love and a group of his men stumbled upon a large group of vaqueros camped near the headwaters of Cantua Creek, about thirty miles southwest of Panoche Pass. Cantua Creek, named after a prominent Californio family, runs through a deep canyon on the east side of the Coast Range for about seven miles before flowing into the San Joaquin Valley north of modern-day Coalinga.

Love and his men watched the vaqueros from a distance and saw that they numbered about seventy, with a huge herd of horses watering along the banks of Cantua Creek. The rangers could not tell if the men were horse thieves or honest mustang catchers, so they quietly retreated into the mountains and spent the night. The next day, they boldly rode into the vaqueros' camp, nudging their mounts through the dense herds of neighing animals. The rangers asked nothing about Joaquin Murrieta, but announced that they were searching for stolen horses. They scoured the camp, closely examining the remuda, which they estimated at more than seven hundred horses. At the same time, Bill Byrnes and Billy Henderson looked over all the Mexicans, but Joaquin was not there.

The rangers questioned the vaqueros, and some claimed that they were hunting mustangs while others said they were gathering wild cattle. But Love and his men found that none of the animals were wild mustangs, which indicated that many of the horses had probably been stolen from ranchos on the coast. Therefore most of the vaqueros in the camp were horse thieves, not mesteneros. Love had brought with him a document containing sketches of the brands of various stolen horses. The rangers confiscated about ten mounts with brands that matched his list. The thieves declared those horses were strays that had somehow drifted into their herd. Although the outlaws and mustang catchers greatly outnumbered the rangers, they made no resistance. Love and his men were heavily armed, but they made it clear that they did not intend to arrest any of the vaqueros.

Before they rode off, Love announced that he and his men were headed back to San Juan Bautista. This was another ruse. The rangers retreated ten miles into the Coast Range and again made camp. For the next few days, the posse watched the horse thieves from a distance, hoping to make them think that they had left the mountains. Then on July 24, the rangers rode back to the camp on Cantua Creek, but found it totally deserted. Love and his men proceeded slowly down the creek, cautiously peering around ledges and boulders to make sure no desperadoes were lying in ambush. After riding about three miles, they stopped at nightfall to rest and water their horses. At two the next morning, July 25, 1853, they saddled their mounts. In the moonlight, the rangers continued carefully down Cantua Creek another three miles. Just at daybreak, they reached a ridge overlooking the spot where the creek bends around a tall hill before entering the San Joaquin Valley. There Cantua Creek is bordered on its south side by a steep earth embankment, about fifteen feet high. On the opposite bank, a sloping ridge rises from the streambed. This spot is two miles southwest of today's intersection of Interstate 5 and Highway 33.

Among the thirteen rangers with Captain Love were Bill Byrnes, Billy Henderson, John White, John Sylvester, and Charley Bludworth. Love peered from the top of the ridge and spotted in the distance the smoke of a campfire wafting above the streambed. He, Billy Henderson, and several others rode closer, while Bill Byrnes and the rest of the men followed well behind them. Love quickly approached the camp, which was situated on a flat above the south bank of the creek bed. To the rangers' right was the steep hill on the south side of Cantua Creek, and to their left was the embankment that dropped down to the creek bottom. The lower section of Cantua Creek was then dry, but a seasonal spring in the streambed provided water for man and horse. Love spotted eight Mexicans, several of whom were cooking their morning meal. Others lay sleeping in blanket rolls, their horses picketed nearby. The manhunters saw that the animals were badly jaded, showing that their riders had just made a long journey.

As the rangers closed in on the camp, its occupants saw them approaching. The Mexicans quickly scattered, with three run-

The dry bed of Cantua Creek, looking west toward the Coast Range. The California Rangers found Joaquin Murrieta and his band camped on the left, between the base of the hill and the embankment above the creek. *Photograph by the author.*

ning toward their horses while others raced for their saddle blankets to grab their guns. The rangers galloped up, and Billy Henderson spotted a dozing Mexican spring up from his blanket roll. The man pulled on his sombrero and raced toward his horse. Henderson spurred his mount forward, covered him with his double-barrel shotgun, and yelled at him to halt. The Mexican, his hat pulled down over his face, obeyed.

At the same time, Love and the other rangers, guns drawn, approached the other men and stopped them from mounting their horses. As Henderson later recalled, "Captain Love began interrogating the Mexicans as to their business. They uniformly replied that they were catching mustangs." Henderson said that the man he was guarding "made several attempts to go to the place where he had slept, to secure his saddle and pistols." But Henderson's cocked shotgun stopped him in his tracks. The

Mexican was young, about twenty-three years old and handsome, with long, light brown hair and a fair complexion. He stepped forward and addressed Love.

"Talk to me," he said. "I am the leader of this band."

The speaker was Joaquin Murrieta. The seven men with him included Three Fingered Jack Garcia, Jose Maria Ochovo, Antonio Lopez, and four anonymous desperadoes. They had arrived at Cantua Creek the night before, after their long ride across the Coast Range from Santa Barbara.

Just as Murrieta spoke, Bill Byrnes thundered into the camp with the rest of the rangers. He took one look at the young Mexican and cried out, "This is Joaquin, boys! We have got him at last!"

Three Fingered Jack and several of the other outlaws, on hearing the word "Joaquin," instantly threw off their cloaks and serapes, whipped out their pistols, and opened fire. In a wild, close-quarters shootout, the rangers stood their ground and shot back, killing one outlaw and wounding two others. Amidst the hail of bullets and clouds of gunsmoke, the rangers were unscathed. Three Fingered Jack and the other pistoleros, seeing that they were outnumbered and outgunned, fled toward their horses. Bill Byrnes and several rangers raced after Three Fingered Jack and engaged him in a running gunfight. The desperado, firing his six-shooter, unleashed five bullets at his pursuers, but his marksmanship was poor. The manhunters fired nine times in return. The last shot came from Byrnes's gun. He took dead aim and sent a slug into Garcia's face, tearing though his skull and killing him instantly. Three Fingered Jack crumpled to the ground, his cocked revolver clutched in one hand and his thumb still on the hammer. Seeing that, Jose Ochovo and Antonio Lopez promptly dropped their pistols and surrendered. The other three outlaws—two of them wounded—leaped onto their horses and galloped off into the brush-covered hills.

While the bullets flew, Joaquin Murrieta yanked loose the

lariat that picketed his horse and leaped onto the animal bareback. As the bandit chieftain dug his heels into the horse's flanks, Billy Henderson, still on horseback, swung up his shotgun and fired. But the ranger's mount, spooked by the raging gunfire, reared back and spoiled his aim. Henderson's blast of buckshot tore harmlessly past Murrieta. Henderson and John White, who wielded a Model 1841 Mississippi rifle, known as a Mississippi yager, galloped after the fleeing outlaw. Joaquin, riding like a Comanche, swung down and clung to one side of his horse to avoid the gunfire. Suddenly he burst upright and, desperate to escape, leaped his mustang down the fifteen-foot embankment and onto the dry creek bed. His horse landed hard, and without a saddle, Murrieta slipped from the animal's back. He slammed into the gravel and landed on his back, while his terrified mustang froze in its tracks. Of its rider, Henderson later said, "The fall had knocked his hat off, which had been fastened on his head by a broad, black ribbon, and his face was left uncovered, and the broad scar on his cheek was plainly visible." At that point, Henderson finally recognized Joaquin.

The athletic Murrieta was uninjured, and he quickly sprang to his feet and jumped back onto his mustang. As Joaquin raced along the creek, Henderson threw away his shotgun, seized both reins, and plunged his horse down the vertical bank. Henderson then charged along the creek bed, at the same time drawing his heavy Colt Dragoon six-gun. He fired, and the .44 caliber bullet nicked one leg of Joaquin's horse, a flesh wound that only made the animal run faster. Ranger John White, seeing that Murrieta was escaping, put spurs to his mount. He galloped after the bandido from atop the high creek bank, hoping to cut him off. Joaquin, clinging to his mustang, reached a low spot on the creek-side bluff and then veered his horse in an effort to ride up and out of the streambed. Henderson fired again, striking the bandit's mustang in the same leg and causing heavy bleeding.

The death of Joaquin Murrieta, in an illustration from 1905.
William B. Secrest collection

Joaquin's animal kept running. Henderson took dead aim with his revolver and unloosed a third round. This one struck Murrieta in the small of the back and ripped completely through his body. But the bandit clung to his horse's mane and urged the animal on. At that, John White, from the bluff above the creek, squinted down the barrel of his single-shot Mississippi yager. The heavy rifle boomed, and its lead ball struck the fleeing outlaw in the back, ranging upwards toward his chest. This bullet tore Joaquin out of the saddle and knocked him to the ground, but still he would not give up. The outlaw staggered to his feet and began running down the streambed. Murrieta made it thirty yards when Henderson fired again, and his pistol ball slammed into the bandido's heart. He dropped like a stone.

"*No tire mas. Yo soy muerte,*" Joaquin gasped, as the rangers galloped up. "Don't shoot any more. I am dead."[25]

CHAPTER 16

BRING ME THE HEAD OF JOAQUIN MURRIETA

Bill Byrnes had a bloody job on his hands. Clutching a bowie knife in one fist, he kneeled in the creek-side gravel and gazed down on the corpse of his erstwhile gambling partner. Byrnes and Love understood that they needed proof that the rangers had killed Joaquin Murrieta. They also wanted to ensure that they would collect the standing reward. A photograph of the dead bodies of Joaquin and Three Fingered Jack was impossible. The only type of photography in existence in 1853 was the daguerreotype, taken inside a studio by a large, unwieldy camera. The image was exposed onto a mirror-like metal plate, then cased inside a glass enclosed frame. There were only a handful of photographers, known as daguerrean artists, in all of California. And the closest photography studios were in Stockton and Sonora, more than 130 miles distant. By the time the rangers could pack the bodies on mules and carry them through the San Joaquin Valley heat, the two corpses would have decayed beyond recognition.

There was only one thing to do. Byrnes seized Joaquin's flowing brown hair and lifted up his head. Then he lowered his long-bladed bowie knife and set to work. Slicing, hacking, and sawing, Byrnes cut through the bandido's throat, then severed the neck vertebrae. After slashing the tendons and muscles, the ranger ripped the head free from its torso. Once he had

Cantua Creek, looking east toward the San Joaquin Valley. This is the approximate spot where the fleeing Joaquin Murrieta was slain by the California Rangers. *Photograph by the author.*

decapitated Murrieta, Byrnes turned his attentions to Three Fingered Jack. He sliced off Garcia's head, and for a bit of extra proof, removed the bandit's deformed hand. Byrnes and the other rangers wrapped up the grisly trophies in an old cloth, then threw in a bunch of willow leaves in an effort to preserve them. They also closely examined Joaquin's corpse. In addition to the scar on his right cheek, he had a healed bullet wound in his right breast, two more in one leg, and another long scar where a bullet had coursed its way across his back.

Meanwhile the other rangers began interrogating their two prisoners. The younger one, plainly terrified, gave his name as Jose Maria Ochovo. He readily admitted that the man whom Billy Henderson and John White had killed was Joaquin Murrieta. He said that he had accompanied Joaquin from Southern California but insisted that he had not taken part in the gang's robberies. Ochovo explained that Joaquin had been "on his road from San Diego to the mines, with the intention of making one more foray upon the Chinese and Americans, and then returning to Sonora." The other prisoner identified himself as Antonio Lopez. Muscular, athletic, and unafraid, Lopez refused to admit anything but his name. Bill Byrnes held up the severed head of Murrieta in one hand, with his bowie knife, dripping with blood, in the other.

"Tell all you know, or say your prayers," Byrnes ordered.

"Cut away," Lopez retorted. "I'll not tell."

Byrnes's efforts at interrogation failed, so Love ordered him and John Sylvester to rush the severed heads and hand to the nearest army post, Fort Miller. There Love hoped that the army surgeon could preserve them in alcohol, something that was commonly done with animal and biological specimens in that era. Fort Miller, now covered by Millerton Lake, was a seventy-mile ride northeast, across the San Joaquin Valley. Byrnes and Sylvester put the prisoner, Lopez, onto his horse and tied him to the saddle. Then they galloped out of Cantua Creek with their prisoner and the severed heads and hand. At the same time, the other rangers searched the bandidos' camp, looking for stolen loot. They found no gold, only seven revolvers and seven horses, all of them California mustangs, as well as five saddles and bridles. Then Love and a detachment of rangers tracked the three escaped outlaws for thirty miles into the Coast Range. They took Jesus Feliz and the cooperative Jose Ochovo with them as guides, hoping that they could lead them to the band's hideouts. The rangers finally gave up the hunt when their horses played out.[1]

By then Byrnes and Sylvester had made a hard ride across the San Joaquin Valley. They left the morning of the shootout, July 25, 1853, and after crossing the sweltering plains, the rangers reached the Tulare Slough, which was then part of Tulare Lake. At that time, Tulare Lake was the largest inland body of water in California and covered much of the lower San Joaquin Valley.

Today, however, it is a fraction of its former size, and Tulare Slough no longer exists. But in the 1850s, Tulare Slough was a long, shallow marsh that spread north from Tulare Lake and had to be crossed by any rider trying to reach the east side of the great valley. The rangers found Tulare Slough not only deep from the spring runoff, but muddy and choked with tule brush. The three riders started across, but suddenly Antonio Lopez raised one hand above his head, let out a wild yell, and dug his spurs into his horse's flanks. The animal charged forward and then plunged down, instantly disappearing under the water. Because he was tied to his animal, Lopez became trapped in the mud, and he and his horse quickly drowned. The rangers believed that he committed suicide, but Lopez may simply have been trying to escape.

Byrnes and Sylvester rode on to dry ground and made camp for the night. Starting again early the next day, they arrived at the ferry across the San Joaquin River that afternoon. It was situated on the Fresno Indian reservation, about ten miles north of the modern-day city of Fresno, and the ferry was operated by Sam Bishop, a burly twenty-seven-year-old Virginian. The mountain town of Bishop in the eastern Sierra Nevada was later named after him. As he recalled, "While I was attending to my duties around the reservation, I saw two men ride up hurriedly to the opposite bank of the river. They seemed very much excited, and yelled across to me that they had killed Joaquin Murietta and Three Fingered Jack, who was also noted as being the bandit's most desperate and able lieutenant. The horsemen asked me to ferry them over the stream, and I took a whaleboat that I had and went over after them. The men had quite a large bundle wrapped in an old cloth which they laid carefully in the bottom of the boat. Their horses swam alongside and we soon reached the buildings of the reservation.

"I then asked the men what proof they had that they had killed Murietta and his confederate. They smiled grimly as they

Sam Bishop in 1870. He ran the ferry across the San Joaquin River and supplied the keg and whiskey used by the Rangers to preserve the severed head of Joaquin Murrieta.
San Jose Public Library

pointed to the bundle which they had laid on a table. One of them removed the cloth, and a number of green willow boughs were disclosed. These were spread out, when three ghastly objects met my gaze. They were two human heads and a human hand with only three fingers upon it. I quickly recognized the repulsive features of Three Fingered Jack, and the testimony of the mutilated hand was undeniable. The features of the other face were very light in complexion for a Mexican and I recognized it as the head of a dashing and handsome young man whom I had often seen riding around in the vicinity of the reservation. I never suspected that he was the famous desperado. His features were very regular and somewhat pleasing. He had a very small mustache and did not appear to be more than twenty-one years old . . .

"Burns [Byrnes] and Sylvester were anxious to push on to Fort Miller with their trophies, and as the weather was quite warm they feared that they might have trouble in preserving them. At my suggestion they took a ten gallon keg and, after opening it, placed the heads and hand in it. We then filled the keg with whisky from a forty gallon barrel that I had on hand. The keg was then securely sealed and strapped on the back of a mule that I hired to the officers for the purpose. They then continued on their way to Fort Miller."[2]

The two rangers hurried eastward along the San Joaquin River toward Fort Miller, twenty miles distant. The heat was insufferable—115 degrees in the shade—and Byrnes and Sylvester were worried about the heads decomposing, despite the whiskey. They arrived at the fort that afternoon, having covered the seventy miles from Cantua Creek in two days of hard riding. At Fort Miller, wide-eyed soldiers gathered around to gawk at the severed heads, while the two rangers met with the post surgeon. The doctor provided more alcohol to preserve the heads, but that of Three Fingered Jack was beyond saving. Although Sam Bishop had recognized Three Fingered Jack, by the time the rangers arrived in Fort Miller, Garcia's head had become badly decayed. The bullet through the skull, coupled with decomposition, made it impossible for anyone to recognize his features. Byrnes and Sylvester buried Garcia's head at Fort Miller, then rode to their headquarters near Quartzburg. At the same time, an express rider raced north out of Fort Miller to spread the sensational news that Joaquin Murrieta was dead.[3]

Harry Love kept his promise to Jesus Feliz and released him. A few days later, Love and the rest of the rangers rode back into Quartzburg with the captured Jose Ochovo. Love could not have been happy to learn of Antonio Lopez's death. Even though the bandido had refused to talk, he might have proved an important witness. Love gathered up the head of Joaquin and the hand of Three Fingered Jack. On July 30, accompanied by several of his men and Ochovo, he rode twenty miles to the county seat at Mariposa. On the way, they met a Mexican who immediately recognized Ochovo and said that his real name was Salvador Mendez.

The rangers made quite a stir when they trotted their horses into the rowdy mining camp, and news of their exploit spread like wildfire. One Mariposan reported, "Captain Love and a portion of his company arrived in town, having in charge a Mexican, one of the band who have infested the country so long, and also the head of the veritable Joaquin himself, preserved in a keg of whiskey." Another wrote, "The greatest excitement prevails at Mariposa and Quartzburg, no doubts being entertained there that it is the real Joaquin, who has at last met with a well deserved fate." Love turned Ochovo over to the Mariposa County sheriff who locked him in jail, a primitive log cabin on the bank of Mariposa Creek.[4]

The rangers then returned to Quartzburg, where on August 4, Love wrote out a detailed report to Governor Bigler: "I have the honor to report that on the 25th of July I encountered the notorious robber Joaquin Muriatta and his gang on the Arroyo Cantugo [Cantua] near the Coast Range of mountains on the Tulare plains. When we discovered Joaquin he was encamped on the above river and appeared to have made some hard days marches previous, by the jaded looks of their horses. On being perceived by some of the Company, Joaquin was immediately recognized and on his being aware of that fact immediately sprang to his horse and endeavored to escape. He was closely pursued by some of the Company and his horse shot from under him, when he took to flight on foot, and he being wounded, some of the men shot him dead before going far. In the meantime, others of the Company were pursuing the remaining part of the band who fought bravely while retreating, each of them being armed with two six-shooters, some badly wounded. And three of their number killed, while the remainder escaped."

Love continued, "The head of Joaquin I have now in my possession at this place. I will bring it with me to Benicia at the expiration of my term of service . . . There is not the least doubt that the head now in my possession is that of the noted Joaquin Muriatta, the chief and leader of the murderers and robbers of the Calaveras, Mariposa, and other parts of the state. The prisoner now in jail in Mariposa acknowledged such to be the fact to the authorities of Mariposa County and there are numerous persons in this county who will also testify to the head being Joaquin's. Captain Burns [Byrnes] who was formerly intimately acquainted with the celebrated robber recognized him immediately. I will take the testimony of the persons acquainted with him in this county as soon as I can procure a glass jar to put the head into. I cannot too highly recommend to your excellency the conduct of the different members of the Company. They have been constantly in the saddle since being mustered into service and have performed their arduous duties cheerfully. Their conduct throughout was that of gentlemen and good soldiers." Love closed his report by saying that the rangers would spend the remainder of their term of service in hunting other members of the gang.[5]

The next day, Jose Ochovo appeared in the crowded courthouse in Mariposa for his preliminary hearing before a justice of the peace. Per the rangers' request, the court clerk dutifully recorded the proceedings and then had eighteen men sign as witnesses. "We the undersigned citizens," he wrote, "were present at the trial before Justice [Abraham] Powell of the prisoner Jose Maria Ochovo who was taken by Capt. Harry Love and his company of Rangers while in the company of Joaquin Morietta. The prisoner stated then as he still states now that he knew Joaquin Morietta well and that the head taken by Capt. Love and his company and now in their possession at Quartzburg to be the head of the great murderer and robber Joaquin Morietta. The prisoner was further identified at trial as one of Joaquin's band." Among those who signed it were Mariposa County's sheriff, district attorney, and a former state assemblyman. A copy of

An engraving of the severed head of Joaquin Murrieta, drawn by an artist for the San Francisco *Overland Monthly* magazine in 1895. *John Boessenecker collection*

the document was given to the rangers as proof that they had slain the right man.[6]

Electrifying reports of Joaquin's death quickly appeared in California newspapers. Within days, some journalists began to question the accounts, eventually causing no end of controversy. The *Stockton Journal*, which opposed Governor Bigler, was the first to raise doubts about the killing, and even claimed that Dawson, the Mormon Island robber, was the real Joaquin: "It is remotely intimated that the reported capture and decapitation of the bandit Joaquin may be a humbug. Without endorsing the rumor, we may be allowed to say that the trophy is slow in making its appearance. Perhaps some hombre who had the misfortune to be born a Mexican, has lost his head; but strange doubts have arisen as to the identity of the one now on the way to the capital. As an item of interest, we may notice a suspicion that is gradually obtaining converts, to the effect that the man Dawson, who was shot near this place, was no less a person than the far famed outlaw, whose deeds at one time filled the country with alarm. Many believe that Joaquin was a myth, and that the monstrous crimes charged upon him were the work of a confederation of rascals. If Dawson's story was true, that he was associated with a large band of men equally desperate as himself, we can credit the suspicion very easily."[7]

Not surprisingly, San Francisco's *Alta California*, eager to discredit anyone or anything associated with Governor Bigler, quickly jumped on the bandwagon. "The renowned robber chief Joaquin, who has been made a great hero of romance by newspaper writers and legislators, has at length been captured by the State troops raised for the purpose—at least a man supposed to be him has been taken. The Joaquin war has cost the State a good round sum of money, and has resulted in nothing more than is accomplished by the taking of a thief or robber by a constable or any other private citizen. The Joaquin that there has been so much talk about is purely a fabulous character, whose exploits of villainy have been announced as occurring on the same day in half a dozen different places and at the extremes of the State." The *Alta* ignored the fact that few people had yet to even see the severed head. A few days later, the newspaper doubled down on its claims. Its editor declared that the dead man "is not the Joaquin after all that Love's Rangers were organized to make such tall walking after. He is not the roving, daring, formidable, murderous, ubiquitous, sharpshooting and notorious Mr. Joaquin of whose exploits we have heard so much. Is he?"[8]

The editor of the *Placer Times and Transcript* in San Francisco was on the fence. "That all the murders and robberies attributed to Joaquin and his party were committed by them, we are scarcely prepared to admit. On the other hand, that Joaquin is an entirely fabulous character—a supposed being to whom for convenience sake or to gratify the love of the marvelous, the outrages have been attributed, as many have claimed—seems to us from all accounts hardly to be credited either. Doubtless he was instrumental in many if not most of [the] deeds of villainy, while others have been attributed to him for the want of a better. That such a scoundrel and assassin named Joaquin is in existence, can be vouched for by competent witnesses, who have seen him, and who knew him as a monte dealer at Stockton." He added that "the head preserved in spirits for identification" would "satisfy those who knew him, and the public generally, that it is the villain himself who is dead."[9]

At first Harry Love was unaware of the controversy. On his return to Quartzburg, he publicly displayed the head and severed hand. Onlookers flooded in to gape dumbstruck at the grisly relics while Love collected notarized affidavits from people who had known Joaquin Murrieta. One was Bill Byrnes, who declared, "I do hereby certify that the Mexican head now in the possession of Capt. Harry Love is Joaquin Muriati, I having known him ever since the spring of 1850." Another was the eleven-year-old girl, Susan Banta. She had lived with her mother and two sisters in San Luis Obispo, and the family had recently settled in Quartzburg. Young Susan recognized Murrieta from his sojourn in the mission town a few months earlier. Her affidavit similarly read, "I do hereby certify that the head now in possession of Capt. Harry Love is the head of Joaquin Muriati, I having known him at San Luis Obispo and done some washing for him at various times." A second girl from San Luis Obispo also recognized the head. Twelve-year-old Juliet G. Thorp, who was apparently related to Susan Banta, swore that she too had known Joaquin in San Luis Obispo. Love obtained five more affidavits authenticating the head, including signed statements from two Mexicans. One, Pedro Manta, declared that he known Joaquin for eighteen years, since Murrieta's boyhood. Another, Jose Maria Vega, swore that "the head Capt. Harry Love has is the head of Joaquin Muriati, I having known him some two years."[10]

Meanwhile Love sent Lieutenant Connor north to Stockton to obtain two glass jars large enough to hold the severed head and hand. Then he boarded a Stockton-bound stage, bringing with him the wooden keg with the relics inside, as well as the signed affidavits. By that time he had learned that several newspapers had accused him of killing the wrong man. Love promptly wrote a letter to a friend in Stockton. "We have got the real Joaquin, and no mistake. The papers may say what they please, but I know what I say is true." He recognized that the only way to rebut those claims was to put the head on public display. Love and Connor immediately began making arrangements to show the relics for two days at the Stockton House, the town's main hotel. The exhibit created a sensation. Gold miners, gamblers, businessmen, and vaqueros rushed to see the gruesome trophies in their glass jars.[11]

The editor of Stockton's *San Joaquin Republican* gazed wide-eyed at the head and listened to Love's recounting of his manhunt. He gave his readers a detailed description of the outlaw: "Joaquin Muriatta was a young man between twenty-two and twenty-three years of age, of light complexion, rather well made, and gentlemanly in his manner. He was as sprightly as a cat. He had a keen, penetrating blue eye, very heavy eyebrows, light brown hair which is inclined to be curly. He had a small scar on the right cheek, a scar on the right breast, another scar describing the course of a bullet, across his back just below the shoulders. There were two scars on his leg, the records of two bullet holes. He had a high forehead, prominent cheek bones, and his face tapered off towards his chin. His beard was very light, as if he had never shaved." At least some of Joaquin's bullet wounds were probably received during his gun battles with posses earlier in the year, most notably the fight on February 16 near Jackson when a bullet had grazed him.[12]

The Stockton display was so successful that Connor had broadsides printed up that, in bold, black print, announced the exhibit for the following day, August 12. Love and Connor used that occasion to obtain more affidavits from onlookers who

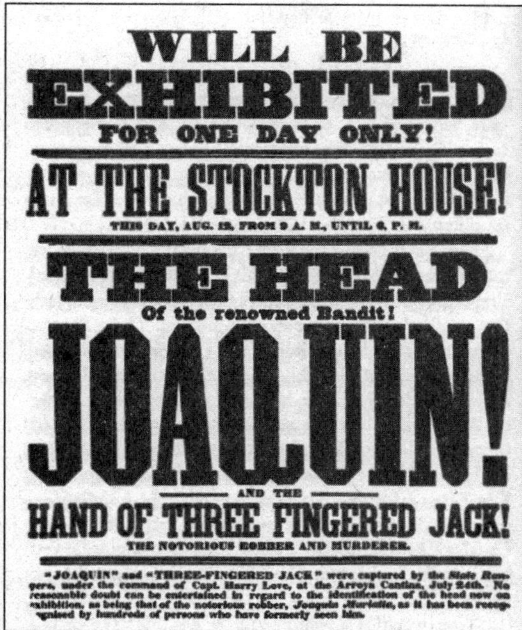

Broadside advertising the display of the head of Joaquin and the hand of Three Fingered Jack in Stockton.
John Boessenecker collection

had known Joaquin. Most prominent among them was Father Dominique Blaive, the Catholic priest who had met Murrieta in Stockton in 1851. Father Blaive swore "that he was acquainted with the notorious robber Joaquin; that he had known him two years ago, and knew him at the Hotel de Minas in the city of Stockton; and that he has just examined the captive's head, now in the possession of Capt. Connor of Harry Love's Rangers, and that he verily believes the said head to be that of the individual Joaquin Muriatta." Henry V. McCargar, the young gambler who drank with Joaquin in the Southern Mines, swore "that he is well acquainted with Joaquin, the celebrated and notorious Mexican robber" and that the head belonged to "Joaquin Muriatta, the same man whose depredations on the Calaveras are so famous." Dr. Noble B. Hubbell, who had encountered Murrieta and Three Fingered Jack near Vallecito in January, also identified the head and signed an affidavit.[13]

Even more significantly, four Mexicans—Clemente Morales, Jose Maria Rivera, Francisco Rivera, and Bernardo Reyna—recognized the bandido. They swore that they "are all well acquainted with Joaquin Muriatta, the famous Mexican robber, whose depredations were lately so notorious on the Calaveras. They severally say that they have known said Joaquin from his boyhood, and one of them, Francisco Rivera, says that he reared him; and each and all knew him in Mexico and also in this State of California." Rivera had evidently helped Joaquin's mother, Eduviges Hipolito, care for her young children after her first husband, Juan Carrillo, died. Finally George W. Havens, a gold miner and ship carpenter, declared that "he has known said Joaquin three or four years in the mines in this state, and knew and knows his sister and brother in law" and recognized "the head of the veritable and notorious robber, Joaquin Muriatta." Havens did not name Joaquin's two family members, but they were probably Vicenta Murrieta and Jesus Feliz, as both Claudio and Reyes Feliz were long dead.[14]

The editor of the *Stockton Journal* viewed the head and the signed affidavits and then recanted his newspaper's prior account. "The head does not appear natural, being discolored by the blood that has settled in the face and about the mouth. It is readily recognized, however, by those who knew the bandit, by the deep scar that marks the right cheek. There can be no doubt that this is the Joaquin whose depredations occasioned such terror in Calaveras county last winter, but to satisfy all surmises on this score, we publish below two affidavits from gentlemen who knew Joaquin, testifying to the identity of the head now in the possession of Capt. Love. Besides these two, the captain has a large number of affidavits from men of respectability in Mariposa and Calaveras county, who personally knew Joaquin, asserting the same thing." The *Journal* then printed in full the affidavits of Father Blaive and Henry McCargar.[15]

In Stockton, Love was joined by two of his rangers, Lafayette Black and John Nuttall. He instructed them to board a San Francisco–bound river steamer with the head, hand, and affidavits. Black and Nuttall arrived in the bay city on August 14 and began displaying the relics and supporting affidavits at King's Saloon on Sansome Street, with a $1 admission charge. They published an ad in the *San Francisco Herald*, announcing that "Joaquin's head is to be seen at King's." At King's Saloon, they obtained at least one more affidavit, signed by Ignacio Lisarraga of Sonora, Mexico. Lisarraga declared that he "was well acquainted with Joaquin Murrieta, and that the head exhibited . . . is and was the veritable head of Joaquin Murrieta, the celebrated bandit."[16]

A reporter for the *Herald* visited the saloon and then provided a detailed word portrait of the grisly exhibit: "The head itself is in a complete state of preservation, and bears the impress of his character in every feature and lineament. It is that of a man about the middle size, apparently between twenty and twenty-five years of age. The forehead is high and well developed, the cheek bones elevated and prominent, and the mouth indicative at once of sensuality, cruelty and firmness. The hair—of a beautiful light brown with a golden tint—is long and flowing; the nose high and straight, and the eyebrows, which meet in the middle, dark and heavy. The eyes, now closed in death, are said to have been dark blue, with a keen restless glance, and when excited a glare of ferocity like that of an infuriated tiger. The face tapers off to the chin—upon which, and on the upper lip, there is a thin beard like that of a young man who had never shaved. Under his right eye there is a small scar—the mark, no doubt, of some desperate conflict."[17]

Crowds flocked to King's Saloon to see the rangers' trophies and affidavits. Black and Nuttall were more than unhappy when the *Alta California* reported that the "head preserved in spirits

JOAQUIN'S HEAD!!
IS TO BE SEEN
AT KING'S,
CORNER OF HALLECK AND SANSOME STS.,
OPPOSITE THE AMERICAN THEATRE.
ADMISSION $1. au18 tf

The following is one of the many affidavits, certificates, Inc., proving the identity of the Head:

STATE OF CALIFORNIA—COUNTY OF SAN FRANCISCO, ss: Ignacio Lisarraga, of Sonora, being duly sworn, says:- That he has seen the alleged head of Joaquin, now in the possession of Messrs. Nuttal and Black, two of Captain Love's Rangers, on exhibition at the Saloon of John King, Sansome street. That deponent was well acquainted with Joaquin Murrieta, and that the head exhibited as above is and was the veritable head of Joaquin Murrieta, the celebrated Bandit. And further says not.

IGNACIO LISARRAGA.

Sworn to before me, this 17th day of August, A. D., 1853.
CHAS. D. CARTER, Notary Public.

The advertisement for display of Joaquin's head, placed in the *San Francisco Herald* by Rangers John Nuttall and Lafayette Black. *California Digital Newspaper Collection*

is now on public exhibition by his decapitators. The public interest will be somewhat modified by the information that this wonderful head was taken from the shoulders of some plebian robber, and that the real hero of so many romances—the veritable Joaquin, is quietly enjoying the fruits of his adventures, at his native home in Mexico." Not surprisingly, the *Alta*'s editor failed to offer any proof that Joaquin was in Mexico. John Nuttall continued displaying the head and hand for two weeks and ignored the criticism. The *Alta* then launched another attack, calling Nuttall "a brutalized wretch who has been exhibiting in this city . . . the horrible spectacle of a human head severed from the body." The paper added that "we hope he will be met by the loathing and disgust that his inhuman and beastly occupation deserves."[18]

A few days after the head went on display, the *San Francisco Herald* published a letter signed "Joaquin Carrillo." It read, "Señor Editor Herald: As my capture, or supposed capture, seems to be the topic of the day, I will, through your kindness, inform the readers of your valuable paper that I still retain my head, although it is proclaimed through the presses of your fine city that I was recently captured and became very suddenly decapitated." The *Herald*'s editor remarked, "We have no idea that the letter is genuine but give it for what it is worth." Of course, the letter was a hoax, for Joaquin was not only dead, he was illiterate. Nonetheless, some newspapermen and citizens, especially those opposed to Governor Bigler and the Democrats, increasingly began to question the bandit's death.[19]

The *Alta California* then published the most detailed attack yet on Love and his rangers. An anonymous correspondent, writing from Los Angeles, announced, "It affords some amusement to our citizens, the reading of the various accounts of the capture and decapitation of the 'notorious Joaquin Murieta.' The humbug is so transparent that it is surprising any sensible person can be imposed upon by the various statements of the affair which have appeared in the prints. The very act of the Legislature authorizing the raising of a company 'to capture the five Joaquins, to wit, Joaquin Carrillo, Joaquin Murieta, Joaquin Valenzuela,' etc., etc., was in itself a farce." The journalist continued, "Joaquin Murieta is undoubtedly a very great scoundrel . . . At the time of the murder of General Bean, at the Mission San Gabriel, Joaquin Murieta was strongly suspected of the crime, and efforts were made to arrest him, but he managed to escape; and since then every murder and robbery in the country has been attributed to Joaquin. Sometimes it is Joaquin Carrillo that has committed all these crimes; then it is Joaquin Murieta, and then Joaquin something else; but always Joaquin."

The writer then provided some specifics: "A few weeks ago a party of native Californians and Sonorians started for the

Tulare Valley, for the express and avowed purpose of running mustangs. Three of the party have since returned, and report that they were attacked by a party of Americans, and that the balance of their party, four in number, had been killed; that Joaquin Valenzuela, one of them, was killed as he was endeavoring to escape, and that his head was cut off by his captors as a trophy. It is too well known that Joaquin Murieta is not the person killed by Capt. Harry Love's company at the [Panoche] pass. The head recently exhibited in Stockton bears no resemblance to that individual and this is positively asserted by those who have seen the real Murieta and the spurious head."[20]

The *Alta*'s story was widely read and reprinted in numerous newspapers, and its false account would be recalled and relied on by journalists and historians for more than a century and a half. Its writer was correct in pointing out that Joaquin was the main suspect in the killing of General Bean, but he got little else right. It was certainly not true that every murder and robbery in the gold country was blamed on Joaquin. The reporter did not know that the Five Joaquins were but two men, Joaquin Murrieta and Joaquin Valenzuela, or that the head had been repeatedly identified as that of Joaquin Murrieta. Nor did he explain how the purported mustang runners, if they had fled to Los Angeles after the attack by Americans, could have known that one of their group was subsequently beheaded. And last, as we will see, Joaquin Valenzuela was alive and well, and his bandit raids would continue for another five years.

John Nuttall was so angered by the *Alta*'s account that he paid for publication of a lengthy response in the *San Francisco Herald*. He pointed out that the rangers had obtained twenty-five to thirty affidavits "furnished gratuitously by gentlemen of the highest respectability in the country, both Americans and Mexicans, who had the most undoubted means of knowing Joaquin, and who have identified him without a single doubt or qualification . . . That the head in question and now opened to inspection in this city is the veritable head of Joaquin Muriata, I consider so palpably proven, that further comment would be entirely out of place." Nuttall closed his remarks by publishing in full the notarized affidavit signed by Father Dominique Blaive.[21]

Harry Love, spurred on by the false reports, was determined to display the head and hand throughout the mining region in order to allay any doubts. But he still had manhunting duties to perform, and he wanted the rangers' three-month term of enlistment to be extended. A Stockton journalist interviewed Love and reported, "As captain of the State Rangers he has obtained a mass of information relative to their organization, their haunts, and their leaders, that may be made of eminent use to our citizens. The various bands of guerrillas extend from Sonora to Shasta, but their principal haunts and strongholds are in the coast range of mountains between Santa Clara and the Los Angeles valleys . . . Harry Love says Joaquin, at a pinch, could have raised two thousand desperadoes; and he believes that such was that bandit's purpose, to scour the entire southern country [and] sack the small settlements." The reporter concluded, "Thus, we think, it would be desirable for the Rangers to be kept in the field. Harry Love knows the men who are leaders of the brigands, is probably one of the only men acquainted with their haunts; his companions know not what fear is, have proved their worth, and merit the praise of all."[22]

Love, in his attempt to extend the rangers' enlistment, had greatly exaggerated the size of the bandit gang. Then, to prove his point, he led a party of his rangers from Stockton across the Coast Range in yet another effort to capture the bandidos who murdered James Walsh near Mission San Jose. On August 23, he and his men arrested a Mexican suspect and delivered him to the sheriff in San Jose. Though the man's name and fate are unknown, he was apparently released, for no murderer from San Jose was sent to the state prison during the ensuing year. Love then proceeded to San Francisco, where he picked up the head, hand, and affidavits and boarded a bay steamer for Benicia. On August 27, he met with Governor Bigler in his offices at the capitol building. According to Bill Howard, who was inclined to exaggerate, Love "threw the ghastly trophy at the feet of the Governor" and demanded the state reward. Given the care with which the rangers preserved the head, it is far more likely that he simply placed the glass jar and affidavits on Bigler's desk. The governor looked over the papers and then wrote out an order that Love be paid the $1,000 bounty. Bigler, concerned about the claims that the rangers had murdered the fugitive, wrote at the bottom of the document, "This certifies that Joaquin could not have been taken alive and delivered to the authorities as he was mounted and endeavoring to make his escape when he was shot on my order." Then he had Love sign the statement.[23]

Because Joaquin Murrieta was dead, Harry Love was unable to convince Bigler or the legislators to renew the rangers' three-month commissions. The next day, the company was officially disbanded. Love collected the reward payment and turned the head and hand over to Rangers Billy Henderson and Jim Norton. Though they were no longer employed by the state, the rangers had decided to tour the mining region with the severed head and hand to prove, once and for all, that they were right. Henderson and Norton proceeded by riverboat to Sacramento, where on September 9 they began displaying the relics in the Whig Headquarters Saloon. As a newspaperman reported, "Yesterday our eyes were interested by beholding this unusual spectacle, now on public exhibition. The head of the noted murderer is preserved in a glass jar, whose convex sides have the effect of magnifying the features into an unnatural expression. To obviate this objection, a string is made fast to the crown of the head, by pulling which it is raised above the surface of the liquid and exhibited more in accordance with what it should be." Henderson and Norton advertised their exhibit in the *Sacramento Union*, proclaiming, "As there has been considerable doubts as to his being the genuine

Joaquin, we have taken considerable pains to procure affidavits from persons who knew him in different parts of the State."[24]

Harry Love joined Henderson and Norton in Sacramento, and the three boarded a stagecoach for Marysville. There they displayed the head and hand for two days. "We took a look at it this morning, in company with a number of our citizens, and we readily recognized the features of an individual whom we had seen frequently in this city," wrote the editor of the *Marysville Herald*. "There can be no doubt that the head on exhibition is that of Joaquin Murieta . . . We saw and conversed with a Mexican this morning who said he knew Joaquin well, and that the head now in possession of Capt. Love was the head of Joaquin. Many of our citizens recognize this head as belonging to one of the men who shot Sheriff Buchanan a couple of years ago, and who made his escape from the officers of justice with two others."[25]

The editor of the *Marysville Express* was equally impressed by the display: "While we were present, a Mexican was brought in who had known Joaquín since he was a boy ten years of age. Previous to examining the head, he stated that there was a certain mark on the cheek and a mark under his chin. These marks were found in the designated places and corresponded with the description given, exactly. The sheriff and his deputy [and] Justices Danby and Filkins, all say that they recognize a striking resemblance in the features to one of the Mexicans arrested in 1851 for shooting Sheriff Buchanan. He also recognizes the head." But although Sheriff Buchanan certainly could have identified Joaquin as one of the men who shot him, the newspaper was mistaken, for Murrieta was never arrested in Marysville.[26]

The three rangers made quite a stir in town. They arrived dressed in the height of fashion, each sporting a dark suit, vest, white dress shirt, and flowing necktie. Their Colt Dragoon revolvers hung from holsters on their belts, while Love and Norton each wore a sheathed, ivory-handled bowie knife. At one

Left to right, California Rangers Jim Norton, Harry Love, and Billy Henderson in the daguerreotype taken in Marysville on September 16, 1853. *Nelson Atkins Museum of Art, Kansas City, MO*

point, they stepped into a photograph gallery and posed for a daguerreotype. The trio sat in wicker chairs, weapons prominently displayed, with Love in the middle, his distinctive black hair falling across his shoulders. After sitting for the image, Billy Henderson posed alone for a second photograph, gazing fiercely into the camera with his hand resting on the butt of his six-gun. Those images were destined to become among the rarest and most iconic of the California gold rush.[27]

The editor of the *Marysville Herald* interviewed Love, who was plainly bitter about the disbanding of the rangers and the small remuneration they had received for risking their lives. Love also complained that rancheros in Southern California had harbored Joaquin and his gang. He said that Murrieta had left a fortune in stolen loot "deposited with a wealthy ranchero in the southern country" and that "Joaquin was upheld by many of the gentlemen of fortune in that vicinity." Love's statement was hardly true, given that Californios took an active role in hunting the band. He also declared that "the head would probably be given by the Rangers to some institution, or gatherer of notable things, where it might be safely preserved. The object in this exhibition is not to represent a bloody trophy, nor yet for the accumulation of money." But Love ignored the fact that the rangers had charged viewers a dollar each at their exhibit in San Francisco. He insisted, "The object of the exhibition is simply to let it become fully known and established that the much dreaded assassin and robber is at last captured and slain."[28]

The next morning, September 17, the three rangers prepared to leave Marysville. For safety, Love had kept their trophies hidden at night under the bed in his hotel room. But when he returned to his room, he found that the hotelkeeper had already rented it out to Tom Lane, a boyish gold seeker, and his much older mining partner. Lane recalled that they were sound asleep when they were wakened by a loud rapping at the door.

"Who is there?" the older miner called out.

"Captain Harry Love. I wish to come into your room a moment."

The man got up and let him in. Love then said to him, "I have been exhibiting here and have some traps under the bed which I wish to get, as I show tonight in another town. I am exhibiting the head of Joaquin, the notorious robber and murderer, and the hand of the almost equally notorious Three Fingered Jack."

Lane said later, "I pretended to be asleep while the 'traps' were being examined by my companion." At that, Love asked, "Who is that boy with you?"

"My partner," he responded.

"Wake him up and let him have a look at my show, as it will probably be his last chance."

But young Lane was having none of it.

"Not much!" he cried out. "I don't want to see your show, and I wouldn't have slept in this bed for $1,000 had I known what was under it." As Lane recalled, "I turned my face to the wall until the 'show' was removed, and that was my first meeting with Captain Harry Love and my first and last opportunity of seeing the head of Joaquin and the hand of Three Fingered Jack."[29]

Fortunately for the rangers, most onlookers were not as squeamish as Tom Lane. Love, Norton, and Henderson traveled south by stagecoach to Auburn, where they displayed their exhibit in the National Hotel. "There is no doubt of the identity of Joaquin," wrote a town reporter. "Many have recognized him." Harry and his men then continued south, first showing the head and hand in Placerville, then in Jackson, and finally, in mid-October, in Mokelumne Hill. By that time, they had with them two more trophies: Joaquin's six-shooter and his serape. One newspaper correspondent who viewed the head wrote that it was seen by people "who knew him well, and seen him frequently in the county of Calaveras. There is at present residing on Mokelumne Hill at least twenty-five persons who have examined the head and recognized it as the head of the veritable Joaquin Carillo or Morieta, and amongst that number there are three who recognized his pistol and cloak." Another local pioneer recorded in his journal, "I was well acquainted with many Mexicans who knew Joaquín well, and they all testified to the identity of the head and agreed that this renowned bandit chief was now *muerto* [dead]. A Mexican woman at Mokelumne Hill, who had known Joaquín intimately from childhood up, was much affected on seeing his head and shed tears over it."[30]

Captain Love and his men proceeded ten miles down the road to San Andreas for yet another exhibit. But not everyone there was happy to see the severed head and hand. Some of the spectators were either friends of Joaquin or associated with his gang. Word spread that Love intended to ship the head by stagecoach to Columbia, and that several Mexicans "swore to capture [it] before it reached Columbia." That night, October 15, the coach from San Andreas was rattling down the stage road near Jackass Gulch on the Stanislaus River, about six miles from Columbia. Its oil lantern headlights suddenly illuminated three armed Mexicans blocking the road. The highwaymen ordered the driver to hand over Joaquin's head, but when he insisted that the *cabeza* was not on board, they allowed him to drive on. The following night, at the same spot, several Mexicans opened fire on another stage from San Andreas. Surprisingly, none of the passengers were armed, and the driver whipped up his team and raced into Columbia. There he removed his lanterns to inspect the coach and found several bullet holes in the top of the stage and in the window curtains.[31]

Despite the two attacks, the rangers managed to bring their trophies into Columbia safely. There were many people who knew Murrieta in his old stomping grounds. As the editor of the *Columbia Gazette* reported, "Joaquin was probably better known here than any other section of California, having long resided in this vicinity. A number of Mexicans and Americans recognized the head upon first sight. Among the number of those who recognized the head as that of Joaquin Muriata was a Mexican who had known him in the state of Sonora, Mexico, from boyhood and had been his partner in this vicinity. A number of the Chinese, who had seen him in his forays against their countrymen in Calaveras, recognized the head instantly, and gave certificates to that effect."

Another journalist reported from Columbia, "Captain Harry Love has been exhibiting Joaquin's head in this town for several days past. Here the bandit was well known and all concur that it is the apex of the veritable robber. His old partner recognized his features at a glance; and in fact, all those hereabouts who had the *honor* of Joaquin's acquaintance testify in the affirmative." The *Columbia Gazette* concluded, "Many may have had their doubts of the capture of this notorious robber chieftain before Capt. Love's visit to Columbia, but the concurrent testimony of all who had known Joaquin, and saw his head, was so conclusive that there are now no doubts in the minds of the people up here, that Harry Love and his gallant Rangers have performed to the letter all they promised to do when they started in pursuit of this notorious set of bandits."[32]

Love and the rangers then took the head and hand a few miles to Sonora for yet another exhibit. By this time, they had covered almost the entire mining region, from Marysville in the north to Mariposa in the south. On October 21, they returned to Stockton, bringing with them many affidavits that they had collected on their trip. The next day, they met with a group of rangers, including Edward Connor, who had just been appointed undersheriff of San Joaquin County. The rangers decided to turn the relics and affidavits over to Connor for safekeeping. A town journalist reported on the meeting and described the "numerous certificates, which they have brought with them, signed and sworn to by a large number of respectable Americans, besides Mexicans and Chinese." He added, "Among the certificates alluded to are some from Chinese whose camps on the Calaveras, Joaquin robbed. They recognised the head instantly, and were exceedingly rejoiced at his capture."[33]

In San Francisco, several Chinese business organizations decided to pay a reward to the California Rangers. The *San Francisco Herald* reported that they raised a purse of $1,000, and reminded its readers, "The Chinese, it will be remembered, were the especial objects of Joaquin's ferocity, and suffered severely by his outrages." The *Herald* declared, "The Chinese here, although in no manner bound, have with commendable liberality come forward with this contribution of $1,000, in token of their appreciation of the rangers' services. They have proved themselves in this city, on many occasions, a liberal and public spirited people."[34]

A few months later, in April 1854, a bill was introduced in the state legislature to pay Love $5,000 for his successful manhunt. The editor of the San Francisco *Alta California* declared, "A proposition for the relief of Capt. Harry Love is before the Legislature. Of what Captain Love wishes to be relieved is not stated in the Legislative report, but probably it is of an empty pocket, and his claims are probably founded on having, during the last spring, headed a lot of rangers in the southern mines. These rangers shot down men said to be robbers, took them prisoners and took stock from them without legal warrant, and contrary to the constitution and laws, but not, that we know positively, contrary to justice. To pay Mr. Love for such acts would be a dangerous precedent." But contrary to the *Alta*'s claims, Joaquin Murrieta and his two gang members were lawfully killed while resisting arrest, and no peace officer, then or now, needs a warrant to seize stolen property. The *Alta*'s editor, in a surprising conclusion, retracted its numerous false claims that the rangers had slain the wrong man. "It is generally conceded that his company killed Joaquin, and Capt. Love has been much praised for his public services, and we do not know that he or his men ever did an unjust act, but we ask that the Legislature shall not approve his acts until they are proved to have been good."[35]

By this time no serious question remained—Joaquin Murrieta was dead. But his legend, as well as his gang, rode on.

CHAPTER 17

END OF THE TRAIL

Jose Maria Ochovo gazed anxiously through the barred window of the Mariposa jail. He was terrified, though not quite as terrified as when he watched Bill Byrnes decapitate Joaquin Murrieta and Three Fingered Jack. Ochovo knew that the calaboose, made of roughhewn logs, was not secure, and that if he stayed there, he was liable to be dragged out and lynched by vigilantes. He also understood that he was a target for the remaining members of Joaquin's band, because newspapers had reported his cooperation with the California Rangers. Ochovo must have been elated when he learned that the rangers intended to move him far from the Southern Mines. Harry Love had decided that because he was a material witness, Ochovo, like the severed head and hand, belonged in the state capital at Benicia. Bill Howard later said that he was detailed to guard the bandit and transport him to Martinez, which had the jail closest to Benicia. He first took Ochovo to his Buena Vista Ranch near Hornitos, then brought him on horseback one hundred thirty miles north to Martinez, just across the Carquinez Strait from Benicia. Howard guarded his prisoner well. According to his account, he "was with him constantly for two weeks, sleeping at night with the prisoner's arm handcuffed to his own."

The Contra Costa County jail in Martinez was a secure one by gold rush standards. Instead of adobe or wood, its walls were made of stone. The jail, built three years earlier, was small, with just a few cells. Bill Howard rode into Martinez with Ochovo in tow and locked him in the little calaboose on the west bank of Alhambra Creek, not far from the village wharf. Howard, apparently unaware that no one guarded the lockup at night, left his prisoner in charge of the local jailer. Ochovo was held safely in his cell for several days. Then, on the morning of September 2, 1853, the jailer walked from his home to the stone building and found it broken open and his prisoner gone. He made a brief search and discovered Ochovo's dead body dangling from a nearby tree.

A San Francisco newspaperman reported, "This act is supposed to have been committed by Mexicans, who were fearful that he was about to make important disclosures in relation to the various bands of horse thieves who are now committing depredations in various parts of the State." But another journal remarked, "This is a silly story; if the man's 'friends' had rescued him from prison, is it more probable that they would have left him hanging on the tree? Or that they would have taken him along with them?" The journalist believed that Ochovo had instead been hanged by vigilantes. However, as Bill Howard later explained, "The Mexicans regarded Murieta as a patriot, and executed the prisoner under the belief that he had or was about to become a traitor and turn state's evidence." The mystery of who hanged him was never solved.[1]

Jose Maria Ochovo was but the first man connected with Joaquin's band to meet a violent end following the climactic gun battle at Cantua Creek. Two weeks after Ochovo's lynching, Bernardo Daniel, brother of the notorious Pancho Daniel, was riding with a gang of robbers south of San Jose. At least one woman accompanied the bandidos. Near San Juan Bautista, they came across Ignacio Maldonado, a merchant from San Jose, and his hired man, both on horseback. The pair carried on their pack mules about $2,000 in dry goods, including two trunks filled with expensive silk clothing. Bernardo Daniel, just as he had done in the Livermore Valley two years earlier, showed that he had no compunction about attacking a Latino victim. He and the other bandidos murdered Maldonado and his hired man, took their goods, money, and horses, and headed south. On September 26, the gang rode into San Luis Obispo. There, according to a witness, "They uttered fierce threatenings against the Americans. After committing various outrages, they stole ten horses and left in the night."[2]

A sheriff's posse pursued Bernardo Daniel and the rest southward from San Luis Obispo. They captured one of the outlaws riding a stolen horse and jailed him in Santa Barbara. The possemen then caught up with another of the band on the Santa Clara River, just south of Ventura. The bandido whipped out his six-shooter and emptied it at his pursuers, but they returned the fire and killed him with a bullet in the head. The sheriff and his men left his body with a local ranchero and tracked the rest of the gang into Los Angeles, where they arrived on October 1, 1853. They found that Bernardo Daniel and the band were already in the pueblo, creating a rowdy spectacle. According to the *Los Angeles Star*, the outlaws "rode several times through the streets, attracting considerable attention by their wild, reckless extravagancies." The manhunters from San Luis promptly sought the assistance of the newly formed militia company, the Los Angeles Rangers. The next day, the two groups trapped the gang in a house on the outskirts of the pueblo. They captured three desperadoes named Anastacio Higuera, Manuel Olivas, and Ramon Espinosa, as well as a woman, Cayetana Espinosa. A fourth man, who probably was Bernardo Daniel, managed to escape. The possemen also seized ten horses and more than $1,000 worth of new silk dresses and other items that the robbers had stolen from their murdered victim, Ignacio Maldonado.[3]

The manhunters, in a repeat of the vigilante trials of Reyes Feliz and Cipriano Sandoval almost one year earlier, brought the bandits before a "people's court" in the Los Angeles courthouse. Their vigilante trial was attended by numerous Anglos and some

Californios. There the female prisoner, Cayetana Espinosa, admitted that she had been with the gang when they murdered three Anglos in Northern California, but she refused to testify any further against her compadres. One witness swore that the outlaw who had escaped from the house "was the right hand man of the notorious Joaquin"—most likely Bernardo Daniel. After a six-man jury found the men guilty, a vote was held to determine their punishment. A majority of those present agreed that the three bandits, Higuera, Olivas, and Espinosa, should be hanged. Two days later, the vigilance committee held a second meeting, which included many Californios, among them General Andres Pico. This time there was a bitter argument between the Anglos, most of whom were armed with pistols, and the Californios, who carried knives. But no violence took place, and Californio leaders managed to convince the Anglos that since the prisoners had committed no crimes in Los Angeles, they should be sent to San Luis Obispo for trial. The vigilantes finally agreed, and while the woman, Cayetana Espinosa, was held in jail, arrangements were made to ship the three desperadoes by steamer to San Luis Obispo.

On October 7, members of the sheriff's posse from San Luis Obispo put Higuera, Olivas, and Espinosa aboard a steamship at the port of San Pedro. They sailed north and the next day arrived at Avila Beach, the steamboat landing for San Luis Obispo. The spot was isolated, about ten miles south of San Luis, with just one small cabin on the beach. A group of ten Anglo vigilantes from San Luis met the steamer, and after the prisoners were brought ashore, they began debating what to do with them. According to a witness, the Anglos feared that the bandits "would be rescued if taken up to the town by the Mexican population residing there, and be again let loose with their appetite for plunder and murder whetted by revenge." They loaded the bound prisoners onto a wagon, drove them underneath a tree on a nearby hill, and looped hanging ropes over a limb. The vigilantes tried to get their prisoners to confess, as the witness explained: "They were told they could have the attendance of the padre from the Mission, if they wished it, but they all refused to see him. They made no confession, but persisted in declaring their innocence."

Anastacio Higuera, when asked if he had any last words to say, declared "that he would die happy if he could be freed long enough to flog one Yankee." The observer described what happened next. "As the three stood up, side by side, with the ropes around their necks and their hands tied behind them, the wagon was driven from beneath them, and they struggled in the agonies of death. Their weight bent the bough somewhat, but not sufficiently to allow their feet to touch the earth. After hanging for some time, they were cut down and interred in the neighborhood." News of the lynching outraged many Californios in San Luis Obispo.[4]

The triple hanging should have been a warning to Bernardo Daniel. Instead, the bandido rashly returned to San Luis Obispo, where, sheltered by friends, he believed that he was safe. On October 13, five days after the lynching, the sheriff of San Luis Obispo County got a tip that Daniel was in town. He quickly arrested the outlaw and seized from him one of the silk-filled trunks that had been stolen from the merchant, Maldonado. The sheriff took Daniel before the local justice of the peace for his preliminary hearing. At that time, both the San Luis Obispo court and the jail were located in rooms in the long, colonnaded wing of the mission building, which today houses a museum crowded with tourists.

A visitor from San Jose who had just arrived in the pueblo heard about Daniel's arrest and offered to testify in the hearing. He took the witness stand and swore that he had seen some of the distinctive silk clothing in the possession of Maldonado and his hired man before they had left San Jose. The justice of the peace ordered that Daniel be held for trial. The sheriff, afraid that either a mob of Anglo vigilantes or a band of Daniel's compadres would try to free him from jail, became increasingly nervous. To build up his courage, the lawman first got drunk, and then, accompanied by numerous armed spectators, took Daniel to a jail cell. The sheriff's judgment was dulled by alcohol. For some reason, he decided to put two of the Anglo bystanders into the cell with Daniel, apparently to keep an eye on the prisoner. The pair refused to enter the jail cell, and a scuffle broke out. During the confusion, Daniel bolted out of the mission building and ran fifty yards before anyone realized that he had escaped.

The crowd started in pursuit as the bandido raced toward Cerro San Luis Obispo, a tall hill that overlooks the town. The pursuers, firing their pistols wildly, chased Daniel up the hillside and finally captured him unharmed. They dragged the desperado back to the jail and locked him up. That night a band of vigilantes appeared and demanded that the jailer turn over the cell key. He promptly complied. The mob interrogated Daniel, but he refused to talk. Finally the vigilantes allowed the mission padre to meet with Daniel in his cell, and the desperado made a long, but private, confession to the priest. That done, the vigilantes draped a noose around Bernardo Daniel's neck, looped the other end around a ceiling joist, and hoisted him up. The young bandido slowly strangled to death.[5]

Once again, local Californios were infuriated by the lynching. However, it turned out that the murdered merchant, Ignacio Maldonado, had left a widow and infant son in San Jose. Maldonado's brother-in-law made the long trip from San Jose to San Luis Obispo, where he looked over the trunk and silks that were recovered from Bernardo Daniel, as well as from the bandits in Los Angeles. He identified all the items as having belonged to Maldonado. When that became well-known, along with the fact that the murdered victim was Latino, any Californio sympathy for Daniel and the other lynched bandits quickly evaporated. As one townsman explained, "There is but one voice among the Americans and Californians of San Luis Obispo in

Mission San Luis Obispo. Bernardo Daniel was lynched inside the county jail, then located in the long, colonnaded section of the mission building. *Bancroft Library*

regard to the hanging of the men who committed the murder, and that is that they deserved and well merited their fate."[6]

A week after the hanging of Bernardo Daniel, on October 20, 1853, the bloodthirsty Robert Scott was playing cards in a fandango house in the gold town of Auburn, far to the north. When he ran out of money, he asked another gambler, Andrew King, for a $3 loan. King refused, and Scott stormed out of the dance hall in a rage. The next day, armed with two Colt Model 1849 five-shot revolvers, Scott strode up to King's cabin and called him outside. "We walked away from the cabin about fifteen paces, when he stopped and asked me what I wanted," Scott said later. "I told him that I had heard of some remarks which he had made derogatory to my character and he must fight me, at the same time cocking the pistols, and reached him one of them, which he refused to take. I then threw it at his feet and told him three times to take it and defend himself. I then told him I would shoot him anyhow. He made no attempt to pick up the pistol. I then cocked my pistol and shot him through the heart."

Scott fled on foot thirty miles south to the Cosumnes River. There he came across a Mexican miner, whom he shot and killed. He took $15 from the body. A pair of lawmen from Auburn hunted Scott for two days and finally captured him on the Cosumnes. They returned him to Auburn, and in February 1854, he was tried for murder. As a journalist who attended Scott's trial observed, "The prisoner, throughout, maintained the greatest firmness. Though I watched him closely, I could not detect the quiver of a single muscle, until [his] counsel, Mr. Hall, made an allusion, in the course of his eloquent appeal to the jury, to the mother and sisters of the prisoner in the Atlantic States. Then the spirit of the strong man yielded, and he wept, showing that callous and hardened as he appeared, there was one tender spot in his heart that yielded beneath the soft and hallowed touch of a mother's love."

But the jury was having none of it. They promptly found Scott guilty, and he was sentenced to death. While awaiting execution, Scott wrote out a detailed narrative of his bloody career in California and gave it to his jailer. A San Francisco publisher later released it as an eight-page pamphlet, titled *Confession, History, and Life of Robert Scott.* It was one of the very few firsthand accounts provided by a gold rush outlaw. On March 31, 1854, a crowd of two thousand gathered in Auburn to watch the killer die. While Scott calmly smoked a cigar, the sheriff loaded him into a wagon in front of the jail and drove him a short distance to the scaffold. Scott bounded up the gallows steps and took his position on the trap door. The sheriff then asked, "Do you have anything to say?"

Scott stepped to the edge of the scaffold and addressed the throng below him: "I have but few words to say. I have had a fair and impartial trial, and am willing to abide by the law. I have done no more than I would do again to any man who would not give me satisfaction for what he had said." He thanked the sheriff and jailer for the kindness to him and concluded with a parting shot at the county prosecutors: "As for the paltry mob who have urged on my trial before I was ready, they are too mean for my curses. I have done."

The sheriff tied Scott's hands and feet with rope, then fastened a white robe across his shoulders and dropped a black hood over his head. Affixing the hangman's knot under one ear, the sheriff stepped back and pulled the gallows lever. Scott plunged through the trap, his neck broken by the fall. "He gave but a shudder or two and all was over," said one witness. "It was an awful sight, and one which no man could look upon without feelings of regret." Only later, after his confession was published, did the public learn that Robert Scott had admitted eighteen murders, making him one of the bloodiest outlaws of the Old West.[7]

By this time, Jesus Sanate, the Mexican gambler and robber who had raided with Claudio Feliz in 1851, was achieving notoriety in Los Angeles. Early in 1853, he quarreled with a man in the old plaza and killed him. Sanate escaped and a warrant was issued for him, but he managed to evade arrest for many months. Finally, on the evening of December 7, 1853, Constable Jack Whalen spotted Sanate in what was called Sonora Camp, north of the plaza. Whalen, an Irishman, was a veteran of the New York Volunteers and had come to California with that regiment during the Mexican War. He had only recently been elected constable. Whalen approached Sanate, who was sitting on the ground playing cards, surrounded by a group of twenty gamblers. He seized Sanate, but the desperado broke loose. As Whalen grabbed him again, Sanate whipped out a long-bladed knife and stabbed the officer twice in the chest. One of Sanate's thrusts plunged completely through Whalen's body, piercing his heart and exiting his back.

Within moments Constable Whalen was dead. Jesus Sanate fled the scene, running toward the Los Angeles River and vanishing in the darkness. None of his fellow gamblers made any effort to stop him. And due to fear or indifference, none of them would provide the killer's name or description. However, Sheriff James Barton and a group of Los Angeles Rangers learned that the culprit was Sanate. They immediately began a manhunt, but Sanate managed to elude them. Jack Whalen's death, and the failure of bystanders to act, created even more racial friction between Anglos and Latinos in the violent little pueblo. He was the first lawman killed in the line of duty in Los Angeles County. The *Los Angeles Star* had both praise and criticism for Whalen, saying that he "had proved himself an efficient police officer. He was brave and reckless, and has lost his life through a careless indifference to the desperate character of the man he arrested." Sheriff Barton offered a $500 reward—dead or alive—for Jesus Sanate.[8]

The desperado continued to loiter about Los Angeles. He was accompanied by Luis Burgos, who boasted of being a member of Murrieta's gang and even declared that he was "the veritable and terrible Joaquin." Another member of the band was a handsome young man named Atanacio Moreno. An old tradition claimed that he had ridden with Murrieta on his raids in Calaveras County. A number of Los Angeles pioneers asserted that Moreno came from a respectable family in Mexico and had operated a store in the old pueblo until he went bankrupt. Although those accounts are within the realm of possibility, the fact is that Moreno's first documented offense took place in May 1851 when he pulled an armed robbery in Stockton. He escaped and managed to avoid public attention for three years. Then, early in 1854, he first achieved notoriety.[9]

At three in the morning of January 20, a month after Constable Whalen's murder, Atanacio Moreno, with Jesus Sanate, Luis Burgos, and four other bandidos, rode up to the house of Martin Lelong. The latter was a Frenchman who had immigrated to the US and, like Whalen, had journeyed to California with the New York Volunteers. After the Mexican War, Lelong settled on a farm on the Los Angeles River, half a mile east of the plaza, and married a Californio woman, Josefa Alanis. Lelong was a prosperous fruit grower, and he and Josefa were newlyweds with an eight-month-old son.

The couple was sound asleep. Lelong, suffering from illness and weakened by fever, was aroused by his dogs barking in the yard. Then he heard a loud knocking at the door and opened it, only to find six armed desperadoes facing him. Atanacio Moreno brandished a sword, while Jesus Sanate, Luis Burgos, and three others covered Lelong with their pistols. The seventh desperado stood outside, holding the gang's horses. Moreno shoved his sword into Lelong's face and ordered him to fork over his money or face instant death. The fragile Lelong did not protest and immediately produced the keys to two locked trunks. The outlaws ransacked them and removed $50 in coin, some clothing, four gold rings, and his wife's earrings. Moreno pocketed Lelong's ornate gold watch, while another of the gang stepped into Lelong's stable and took his horse and saddle. But that was not enough for the bandidos inside the house. Several of them seized Josefa Lelong, threw her down, and gang-raped her. Then Sanate, Burgos, Moreno, and the rest mounted up and galloped away into the night.

Martin Lelong staggered half a mile into the pueblo and raised the alarm. Sheriff James Barton and the entire company of Los Angeles Rangers quickly mounted up and made an intensive manhunt, but they returned empty-handed. A few days later, Atanacio Moreno and Jesus Sanate were hiding out in the bandidos' camp outside Los Angeles while the rest of the gang were out stealing. Moreno had learned of the dead-or-alive reward for Sanate for the murder of Constable Whalen. While Sanate was cleaning his saddle, Moreno suddenly pulled his six-gun and shot him in the head, blowing his brains out. As he wrapped a blanket around Sanate's body, Luis Burgos rode into the camp and asked who had fired the shot.

"Sanate's gun accidentally went off," Moreno replied.

Burgos asked where Sanate was.

"He's sleeping, there," Moreno said, pointing to the blanket.

Burgos dismounted, bent down, and pulled the blanket off Sanate's body. Just as he glimpsed the corpse, Moreno drew his sword and rammed the blade into Burgos's heart. Then Moreno, with the help of a local Mexican, loaded the bodies into an ox cart and drove into Los Angeles. It was dark when the pair arrived at the jail. Moreno told the jailer that he had been abducted by the gang and was forced to participate in the raid at Lelong's house. A message was sent to Sheriff Barton, who rushed to the jail, took possession of the two bodies, and paid Moreno the $500 reward. These events created a sensation in Los Angeles, and Moreno became an instant hero. As one pioneer recalled, "For a few days he was the lion of the town, and lived royally upon his blood money." At one point Moreno even "borrowed" a horse that belonged to the Los Angeles Rangers and failed to return it.

Moreno's bounty did not last long, for in true outlaw fashion, he gambled and drank the money away. Two weeks later, on February 8, 1854, he entered a jewelry shop in Los Angeles and offered a gold watch for sale. The jeweler was stunned, because he recognized the watch as one that he had sold to Martin Lelong. He told Moreno that he had to step out of his shop to get the money, then rushed down the street to alert the Los Angeles Rangers. They quickly arrested Moreno and took him to the courthouse. There Martin Lelong identified the gold watch and swore that Moreno was one of the leaders in the raid. He also declared that Moreno was wearing a shirt the gang had stolen from his house. Apparently Moreno did not take part in the rape of Josefa Lelong, because he was charged only with robbing the Lelongs, as well as grand larceny for stealing the rangers' horse.

Moreno's lawyer sought a change of venue to Santa Barbara County. The attorney claimed that Moreno could not get a fair trial because Martin Lelong was inflaming potential jurors.

The lawyer also argued that "throughout the county [Moreno] is believed to have been connected with a band of robbers and murderers under the command of two desperadoes called Sanate and Luis Burgos, alias Joaquin Murieta, who have committed various depredations in the said county of Los Angeles, but which [Moreno] says is not true." The judge denied the attorney's request, and Atanacio Moreno was tried twice. One jury found him guilty of robbing Lelong and sentenced him to ten years behind bars. A second jury convicted him of horse theft and gave him another five years. Moreno was taken by steamship to the new state prison at San Quentin, across the bay from San Francisco. Incredibly, he served only four years before the state governor issued him a pardon and ordered him deported to Mexico. Moreno, however, later returned to Los Angeles, where he was arrested for grand larceny in 1863 and received a ten-year prison sentence. He served his time, earned credits for good behavior, and was released in 1872. Atanacio Moreno then disappeared, and most likely returned to his family in Mexico.[10]

Three Fingered Jack's partner in the Mexican War, Blas Angelino, was the next of these notorious bandidos to be heard from. In 1846, Angelino and Three Fingered Jack had tortured and murdered the two Bear Flaggers, Thomas Cowie and George Fowler, near Sonoma. After the war, Blas Angelino lived in and around San Francisco with his wife. They had several children before she died in 1850. He then embarked on a career of banditry. According to one early account, Angelino and his partners, Francisco "Negro" Garcia and Sebastian Flores, had been part of the gang led by Claudio Feliz. By 1854 they had formed their own band of robbers and horse thieves. "Negro" Garcia earned that nickname due to his long, distinctive black beard. He and Angelino, both Californios and aged about forty, were much older than most of the Mexican bandidos in California. Their compadre Sebastian Flores was a twenty-five-year-old Californio, and a fourth member of the gang was a Native American desperado known only as Indian Juan.[11]

Negro Garcia had a wife, Manuela, and several children who lived in a house in San Jose, but he also owned a small ranch and cabin about forty miles south, on Llagas Creek, an isolated, wooded spot near the modern-day city of Gilroy. His Llagas Creek cabin served as the gang's hideout. On the night of October 19, 1854, Francisco Garcia and Blas Angelino, with their band that included several Anglos, rode up to an inn and tavern on the Salinas River. It was the very same that was run by James Anthony, the African American pioneer for whom the Calaveras gold camp of San Antonio was named. Two years earlier, Anthony had been one of the posse that killed Claudio Feliz in the bloody gun battle at the remote adobe on the Salinas River. He was a well-liked figure by both Anglos and Californios, who variously called him "Antone" and "Antonio." His business, which included a ferry across the Salinas River, was a successful one. Anthony resided in the hotel with his wife, Mary, a free black woman, their five-year-old son, John, and their hired man. A year earlier, he had sent $500 to his elderly father, John Anthony, to pay for his passage to California. His father made the long ocean voyage from his home in Massachusetts and lived with them in their pastoral home on the Salinas River.

It was nine o'clock when Angelino, Garcia, and six other desperadoes dismounted in front of the tavern and stepped inside. They ordered supper, which was served by James and Mary Anthony and their hired man, a Frenchman named Joseph. All of the visitors were heavily armed, which caused Anthony no alarm because travelers routinely carried guns and knives for self-protection. After eating their meal, the strangers ordered cigars. As Anthony was handing them out, a bandit suddenly grabbed him from behind. At the same time, the other brigands seized Mary, the elder Anthony, and Joseph. Then one of the gang announced in English, "We are robbers, but if your money is given up, no harm will befall you."

A terrified Mary Anthony agreed to cooperate, and she stepped into another room and returned with $2,000 in cash. The outlaws took the money and began ransacking the house. One of them, a Mexican, declared, "I am Joaquin's brother. I want the world to know that if Joaquin is dead, his brother lives!"

Then he struck the elder Anthony over the head with his revolver, knocking him senseless. Others of the gang, wielding six-guns and bowie knives, began to beat and stab Mary Anthony and her little boy. One of them ordered Joseph, the Frenchman, "You must go to camp with us!"

Before James Anthony could react to protect his family, another outlaw hammered his head with the butt of a pistol. He fell to the floor, unconscious, but regained his senses a few minutes later. During the tumult, the lamps were accidentally extinguished, and in the darkness, Anthony crawled out the door and staggered into the brush. As he stumbled through the streamside thickets toward a neighbor's home in the distance, Anthony looked behind and saw his tavern in flames. By the time he could get help and return to the scene, it was daybreak. The house had been burned to the ground. Inside the ruins were the charred corpses of his wife, his son, his father, and his hired man. Nothing was left but two stolen horses the killers had left behind. Blas Angelino, Negro Garcia, and the rest had committed one of the most horrific murders of the California gold rush. Although it is possible that they had randomly targeted the black pioneer and his family, it seems just as likely that the attack was made in revenge for Anthony's part in the killing of Claudio Feliz. And whether one of the gang was actually a brother of Joaquin, or merely a braggart, will likely never be known.[12]

Anglos and Californios were outraged by the murders. A correspondent from Monterey wrote, "If they be caught, it is very probable they will not have a trial by jury, but be hung on the nearest tree."The county sheriff led a large posse from Monterey after the gang, but the outlaws fled across the Coast Range and vanished into the vastness of the San Joaquin Valley. Negro Garcia's gang continued its raids the following year, and were suspected of robbing and killing a Frenchman south of San Jose. Finally Indian Juan told Angelino and Garcia that he wanted to quit the band, and he demanded his share of the loot. Garcia refused, so Indian Juan threatened to ride into San Jose and "peach" on the gang. That was a deadly mistake. On December 15, 1855, the desperadoes were near Garcia's cabin on Llagas Creek when Blas Angelino, concealed in the chaparral, fired his rifle at Indian Juan, wounding him. Negro Garcia and Sebastian Flores then rode up on horseback, and Garcia pulled his pistol and put three slugs into the Indian. Garcia ordered Flores to do the same, but his compadre refused. At that, the cold-blooded Angelino stepped out of the brush, aimed his rifle at Indian Juan, and finished him off with a death shot to the head. Then they buried the body in an isolated spot in the woods.

By this time, Sebastian Flores was having second thoughts about his bandit career. Two months later, he appeared in the San Jose courthouse and swore out a complaint against Blas Angelino and Francisco Garcia, accusing them of the murder of Indian Juan. Law officers quickly arrested Angelino and jailed him in San Jose, but Garcia escaped and fled to Mexico. A jury found Angelino guilty, and on September 12, 1856, the sheriff escorted him to the gallows. Before he died, he admitted his guilt in front of a large throng of Anglos and Latinos that filled the jail yard. As a San Jose journalist reported, "On the scaffold he addressed his countrymen, confessed his sentence to be just, and warned them earnestly to avoid all evil." Another newspaperman who was there remarked, "Quite a crowd collected—men were swearing, children crying, and the women (Lord save them) were standing agape with wonder, as if the sight had a strange fascination!"[13]

For the next sixteen years, Negro Garcia was a fugitive from justice. He hid out in Mexico, and managed to return to San Jose several times, undetected, to visit his wife and children. He was finally captured in Los Angeles in 1872 and taken to San Jose to stand trial. Sebastian Flores, who during those years had lived an honest life as a vaquero, was the principal witness against him. Garcia's family hired an Anglo lawyer who was skilled in criminal defense work. Garcia's wife, Manuela, testified at length and swore that her husband was with her in San Jose the day Indian Juan died. Of his flight to Mexico, she declared, "My husband said he was going away because he knew Flores had come to town and made complaint that he had killed the Indian, and because he was afraid the vigilantes would get hold of [him] and kill him." Several defense witnesses swore that during the 1850s, there had been great prejudice against Latinos, and vigilantism had been common. Another problem for the prosecution was that the case rested entirely on the word of Flores against that of Garcia. The jury deliberated only fifteen minutes before finding Garcia not guilty. But it was a Pyrrhic victory. Three months later, in August 1873, Garcia met Flores by chance in a saloon near the Mission San Jose. The pair exchanged heated words, and Garcia slapped Flores in the face. It was a deadly error by the erstwhile bandit leader. Flores instantly yanked his knife and stabbed Negro Garcia to death. Sebastian Flores was arrested, convicted of manslaughter, and sentenced to a lenient five years in San Quentin. And in the end, no one was ever arrested or punished for the butchering of James Anthony's family on the Salinas River.[14]

Meanwhile Joaquin Murrieta's former partner, Pancho Daniel, was well on his way to achieving infamy. He was thoroughly reckless and also unswayed by the lynching of his brother, Bernardo, in San Luis Obispo. Pancho Daniel even boasted that he had killed forty men during his bloody bandit career. He had many friends in San Jose, and made the little pueblo his stomping grounds. As early as 1852, Claudio Feliz's cellmate, Teodor Vasquez, before he died on the gallows in San Jose, had confessed and described many of the crimes committed by Pancho and Bernardo Daniel. Yet many of the town's Anglos and Latinos either forgot about Vasquez's confession or chose to disregard it. One Anglo resident described Pancho Daniel in the late 1850s, saying he was "about twenty-eight years of age, above medium height, not heavy, but active and muscular—his features are good—his hair of a dark sandy color, and of fairer complexion than usual with his countrymen. He once was considered a very respectable resident of San Jose, and on his testimony alone a Mexican was convicted of grand larceny."[15]

But his honest reputation in San Jose was wholly undeserved. The "Mexican" whom Daniel got convicted was actually a young Californio, Juan Antonio Valenzuela. In 1855 Daniel accused Valenzuela of stealing horses. With Pancho Daniel as the sole witness, Valenzuela was convicted of grand larceny and sentenced to ten years in San Quentin. Several years later, however, evidence surfaced that Daniel had been a bitter enemy of Valenzuela and had fabricated the charges. The horses had not even been stolen. General Andres Pico then circulated a petition seeking a pardon from the governor, which was granted, and Valenzuela was released in 1861.[16]

A year after Pancho Daniel's false testimony, he publicly revealed his true colors. On the night of July 8, 1856, the city marshal of San Jose, with the help of several citizens, captured a Mexican mounted on a stolen horse. Suddenly Daniel and a compadre rode up to free the prisoner, yelling at him in Spanish to flee. The marshal ordered Daniel to halt, but he and the other rider put spurs to their mustangs. The two desperadoes galloped to safety through a hail of gunfire unleashed by the marshal and his men. A month later, the city marshal heard a rumor that Pancho Daniel was back in San Jose. He and a posse began hunting the outlaw, and at dusk they spotted him near the Guadalupe River, just north of the village. Daniel spurred his horse. As he tried to escape across a bridge over the river, the possemen opened fire. One bullet from the marshal's pistol struck Daniel in the right arm, fracturing the bone, and another killed his mount. Daniel drew his six-shooter with his left hand, emptied it at the posse, then leaped over a fence and vanished into the blackness. At daybreak the marshal and his manhunters discovered a blood trail and followed it for more than a mile, but they could find no sign of the bandido. According to a San Jose journalist, Daniel "succeeded in reaching the house of some of his friends, where he remained concealed until the search after him was abandoned."[17]

Two months later, Pancho Daniel emerged as the leading figure in one of the most violent events in the history of frontier California. It began on October 8, 1856, when several convicts escaped from San Quentin. The prison then consisted of a single stone cellblock with no surrounding wall. One of the escapees was Juan Flores, a twenty-year-old Californio, serving a three-year term for stealing horses in Los Angeles. Flores fled south to San Jose, where he soon met Pancho Daniel, who was recovering from his gunshot wound. When Daniel was well enough to ride, the pair headed for Los Angeles, collecting fellow pistoleros along their way. By the time they reached the Southland, they had thirteen followers, all Californios and Mexicans. In mid-January 1857, the gang committed a number of robberies and thefts around Los Angeles. Then, on the morning of January 22, they rode into the idyllic mission town of San Juan Capistrano, sixty miles south of Los Angeles. The bandidos first opened fire on a shopkeeper, forcing him to flee, and then looted his store. Pancho Daniel, Juan Flores, and the rest rode out of town with their booty, but in the evening, they brazenly returned. They stole eight horses from a Californio and several more from other Latino residents. Then the desperadoes robbed three more stores, one of them owned by a Latino, and shot down a German shopkeeper in cold blood. With the German's bloody corpse at their feet, Daniel and his men calmly sat down at a table and ordered the dead man's clerk to feed them supper. Then, while the terrified townsfolk hid inside the old mission, the outlaws loaded their spoils onto the stolen horses and rode off into the night.[18]

By this time, a seven-man posse led by Los Angeles County Sheriff James Barton was hunting the bandits. The sheriff was accompanied by Constables William H. Little and Charles K. Baker and four other men. The morning after the bloody raid on San Juan Capistrano, Sheriff Barton and his possemen rode up to a rancho in what is now the city of Santa Ana. Its vaqueros told the posse that they had seen the outlaws in the hills to the south. They warned Barton that the bandits were "at least fifty in number" and "would kill the whole party should they meet them." Sheriff Barton was skeptical, for gold rush California had never seen an outlaw gang that large. The posse rode on for several miles south across the broad cattle range that later became the sprawling city of Irvine, about thirteen miles north of San Juan Capistrano. Suddenly they spotted a lone rider approaching in the distance. Behind him was a long, low hill stretching from north to south.

Constables Baker and Little galloped forward to intercept the horseman. They were about four hundred yards in front of the rest of the posse, approaching the base of the low hill, when their hearts almost stopped. The entire fifteen-man gang, led by Pancho Daniel and Juan Flores, suddenly appeared at the crest of the hill, horses foaming and the riders brandishing rifles and revolvers. One posseman, far to the rear, shrieked a warning to Baker and Little: "These are the robbers! Shoot them! Shoot them!"

The two constables, well in front of the rest of the posse, didn't stand a chance. They opened fire at the desperadoes but missed. The outlaws charged forward, sending a barrage of shots at Baker and Little. Juan Flores, in the forefront, spurred his horse up to Constable Baker and shot him dead. At the same time, another of the gang killed Constable Little with a bullet to the head. By then Sheriff Barton and his men had galloped up. Ignoring the fact that they were outmanned and outgunned, they charged toward the hill, pistols blazing. The possemen shot three of the outlaws out of their saddles, wounding each of them. Barton, clenching a six-shooter in one fist, rode directly toward Pancho Daniel. The bandido yelled at him, "God damn you, I have got you now!"

The sheriff took aim with his six-gun and roared back, "I reckon I have got you, too!"

Barton was wrong. Daniel got off the first shot, which slammed into the sheriff's heart. He fell dead from his horse. At close quarters, the other possemen fired back and wounded Daniel. Soon the posse's guns were empty, and they used them to club the mounted bandits, then finally turned their horses to flee. Three of the manhunters were riding fast mustangs, and they managed to outrun the killers, but one posseman rode a much slower mule. After a three-mile pursuit, the outlaws overtook the mule rider and shot him to death. Several of the gang pursued the fleeing manhunters for twelve miles before giving up. Pancho Daniel and the other desperadoes stayed at the scene of the gunfight, where they fired bullet after bullet into the lifeless bodies of Barton and the two constables. Then they rifled the dead men's pockets, taking everything of value, including their watches, money, and guns. The murders of Sheriff Barton and his three possemen would not be equaled in California until the Newhall Incident of 1970, in which four highway patrolmen were shot to death during a traffic stop near Los Angeles. The low hill in Irvine where the sheriff's posse died later became known as Barton Mound, located just southeast of the intersection of Interstate 405 and the Laguna Freeway. Just like Conejo Mountain, where Harry Love killed Pedro Gonzales, countless motorists daily pass the spot, situated just yards off one of the busiest interstates in America.[19]

News of the deadly ambush quickly reached Los Angeles and created an uproar. Crowds gathered as the bodies were brought into town in wagons. The *Los Angeles Star* reported that "all business was suspended, gloom pervaded the entire community—stores were closed, and the emblems of mourning were generally displayed by our citizens. The flags were lowered to half-mast—the houses were draped with crepe—and every evidence exhibited respect for the dead, and every honor paid to their memory." The Spanish language newspaper, *El Clamor Público*, declared that "some of the best men in this city lost their lives . . . A company of cavalry was immediately formed to go out in pursuit of the murderers. Many Californios gave, with their accustomed liberality, horses and weapons, and around 8:00 p.m. more than thirty well armed and equipped men left; and if they meet, the thieves will receive a terrible and exemplary retribution for their crimes and evils that they have been committing for so long."[20]

Thus began the biggest and best organized manhunt of the California gold rush. Among its leaders were General Andres Pico and Tomas Sanchez, who was later elected sheriff of Los Angeles County. Local lawmen, US soldiers, and citizen posses of Anglos and Californios, hundreds strong, quickly blocked off the mountain passes, trails, and roads leading out of the county. General Pico, who had close relations with local Native Americans, obtained their help. On January 29, 1857, six days after the murders, Indian trackers cut the outlaws' sign in Santiago Canyon in the Santa Ana Mountains, thirteen miles northeast of Barton Mound. Two posses, one of Californios led by Pico and Sanchez and another of Anglos, entered the rugged canyon from both ends, north and south. They trapped Juan Flores and part of the gang at a promontory, ever after known as Flores

General Andres Pico, the prominent Californio who led the manhunt for Juan Flores. He was also the first cousin of bandit chieftain Salomon Pico. *John Boessenecker collection*

Peak. After a pitched gunfight, the posse captured three of the bandidos, but Flores and two others abandoned their horses and fled on foot into the mountains.

Two days later, manhunters located Flores and his men hiding in a mountain cave. The outlaws shot and wounded one posseman, but after the manhunters poured a volley of fire into the cave, the three bandits surrendered. They were searched and disarmed; Flores had Sheriff Barton's gold watch in his pocket. But that night, after the posse made camp with their bound prisoners, Flores and his men managed to slip loose from their bindings. Amidst a shower of lead fired by the possemen, they fled into the blackness. The manhunters sent word of the escape to General Pico in Santiago Canyon. Pico was so enraged that he and his men promptly hanged two of their prisoners. Meanwhile Juan Flores rode north for seventy-five miles, stealing horses as he went. On February 3, he cantered through the spectacular jagged rocks of Santa Susana Pass, west of the San

Fernando Valley. Suddenly two US soldiers stepped out from behind a boulder and captured him at rifle point. Flores was jailed in Los Angeles, and on February 14, a huge public meeting was held to determine his fate. Both Anglos and Californios voted that he should be hanged. Anglo militia companies, accompanied by General Pico and his Californios, marched Flores to Fort Moore Hill, where Reyes Feliz had been lynched four years earlier. Before a crowd of three thousand wide-eyed spectators, Juan Flores mounted the scaffold and died at the end of a rope that belonged to one of Barton's murdered deputies.[21]

Other vigilantes, in a frenzy of lynching, tracked down and hanged nine other suspects. Only four of them were definitely members of the Pancho Daniel–Juan Flores gang. Daniel, despite his bullet wound, managed to evade the dragnet. The governor offered a $1,000 reward for him, but he fled back to the San Jose area and stayed out of sight for almost a year. At some point he married, and was protected by his wife and his friends. His wife's name is unknown, but as we will see, she was not Maria Ana Andrada, whom he had seduced away from Joaquin Murrieta in Los Angeles in 1852. A local journalist reported that Daniel was "living in the vicinity of San Jose, which place he would frequently enter at night, and boldly pass persons who, as he knew, would have shot him down at once, had they recognized him." On December 28, 1857, Santa Clara County Sheriff John Murphy got a tip that Daniel would visit a house at the southern end of San Jose that night. He and his posse hid nearby, and at eight o'clock, they spotted Daniel and another Mexican enter the house, then quickly leave. Murphy, carrying a double-barrel shotgun, ordered them to halt, but the pair broke into a run. The sheriff fired one barrel of his shotgun at Daniel and the other at his compadre. Three buckshot struck Daniel in the back, but the wounds did not stop him. Amidst a hot fire from the posse, he kept running and vanished into the willow trees along the Guadalupe River.

Sheriff Murphy kept up his manhunt through the Christmas season. Four days later, on New Year's Day, 1858, he got word that a man was hiding in the fields near Coyote Creek, three miles south of San Jose. The sheriff and his posse mounted their horses and raced to the scene. Pancho Daniel was nowhere to be found, and the only man near the hay field was a Californio who claimed that he knew nothing about the fugitive. Then Murphy and his men put a rope around the man's neck and hoisted him to a tree limb. The Californio suddenly reconsidered. He pointed to a nearby haystack and declared that Daniel was hiding inside.

The possemen surrounded the pile of straw, and Sheriff Murphy shouted, "Come out!"

Pancho Daniel characteristically refused to comply.

"Come out, throw away your pistols, and walk backward to us, or we burn the haystack," Murphy ordered.

The wounded outlaw now knew he had no choice, and he climbed out from the stack and surrendered. The sheriff relieved him of three revolvers and bundled him into a wagon. On the posse's return to San Jose, large crowds gathered around the wagon as it passed along the streets to the county lockup. A newspaperman who was there wrote, "Daniel is now in the San Jose jail, loaded with twenty pounds of chains, and watched by a guard every night. He is of Spanish blood, probably a Mexican, and is a large, strong, active, fine looking man. His surname is pronounced with an accent on the last syllable." Daniel told everyone that he was innocent of the killing of Sheriff Barton. But when a further search of the haystack was made, Barton's silver embellished pistol belt was found hidden under the straw.[22]

Law officers loaded the bandit chieftain onto a coastal steamship and took him south to Los Angeles. By this time, the lynching frenzy in Los Angeles had subsided, and Pancho Daniel was locked safely in jail. Like Negro Garcia, he engaged an experienced Anglo attorney to represent him in his trial for murder of the sheriff's posse. A newspaperman who saw Daniel in the courthouse reported, "The appearance of the prisoner, as he was brought into the courtroom by Sheriff Thompson, was quiet and gentlemanly. He was very pale, was well dressed, and had a cross hanging about his neck. As he came out of court to go back to jail, his wife at the door threw her arms about him and wept passionately." Pancho Daniel's wife could not have been Maria Ana Andrada. Daniel's connection with Joaquin Murrieta was by then well-known in Los Angeles, as was the fact that Maria Ana Andrada had been the lover of both men. His wife attended his murder trial, and either the lawmen or vigilantes would surely have recognized and identified her if she was indeed Ana.[23]

During the ensuing months, Daniel's trial began three times. In each instance, his lawyer successfully challenged all the jurors on grounds that they had prejudged Daniel and believed him guilty. Several hundred jurors were disqualified. When it became clear to the judge that a fair trial could not be held in Los Angeles, he ordered a change of venue to Santa Barbara County. To local vigilantes, as well as friends of the murdered possemen, that was the last straw. At daybreak on November 30, 1858, an armed mob of two hundred surrounded the Los Angeles lockup and forced the jailer to hand over the keys. They marched Pancho Daniel out of his cell, tied his hands, and led him outside to the jail yard gate. The vigilantes tossed a rope over the crossbeam and ordered him to stand on a stool.

Later that day, a witness provided a firsthand account: "The prisoner was brought out and was asked if he had anything to say. He rather broke down at first, and said, 'No,' and then recovered and told them to bid his wife good-bye. [He] said he was ready, and stood up to his fate like a hero—or bravado, as he was. A black handkerchief was tied over his head, covering his face—the fatal knot was adjusted, and he was soon hanging between heaven and earth, a lifeless corpse. Justice was served.

An 1870 lynching near the Los Angeles jail, similar to the hanging of Pancho Daniel. *John Boessenecker collection*

Thus ended the life of Pancho Daniel, the notorious outlaw and bandit!" A week later, in what may have been a first for California, the state's governor offered a $1,000 reward for the arrest and conviction of anyone involved in the lynching. Needless to say, no members of the mob were arrested, and the reward was never paid. No serious effort to prosecute vigilantes in California would be made until the infamous Lookout Lynching case of 1901, when five men accused of a series of minor thefts were hanged by a mob in Modoc County.[24]

Unlike Pancho Daniel, the notorious Salomon Pico managed to evade lawmen in Southern California. Pico must have been pleased by the killing of James Barton, for the sheriff had shot and wounded him in a gunfight in 1851. During the early 1850s, Pico and his gang, which included American and Australian bandits, were the main suspects in numerous robberies and murders between Monterey and Los Angeles. Whenever things got too hot for him, the bandido would slip across the border to Baja California. Despite his fearsome reputation, Pico's outlawry was winked at in Mexico due to his prominent family connections. In January 1854, Pico was in Todos Santos, near the southern tip of Baja, when four Anglo sailors deserted a whaling ship and sought safety with the town's alcalde. Pico, enraged that a Mexican official would protect Anglos, strode into the alcalde's adobe and stabbed one of the seamen to death. The alcalde shouted at the other sailors to flee, and they managed to escape with their lives.[25]

Remarkably, Jose Castro, the governor of Baja California and former Mexican governor of Alta California, appointed Salomon Pico captain of his bodyguards in 1857. Castro also rewarded Pico with a large land grant on the Baja frontier. Two of Pico's compadres, who had been in Pancho Daniel's gang when they killed Sheriff Barton, also became bodyguards for Castro. In August of that year, Pico stepped into a restaurant in the coastal village of La Paz and spotted an Anglo eating at one of the tables. Stepping close, he whipped out a knife and slashed him to death. Then he barked in Spanish, "You son of a bitch of an American! There goes thirty and nine that I have killed with my own hand, thank God!"

A journalist in San Diego reported, "Pico seems to be driving a high horse below there, having very deliberately cut the throat of an American, a few days ago, for the heinous crime of asking him for something at the table! It is said that the authorities are so much afraid of this Pico that he does about as he pleases, and swears that he will spend his leisure time in cutting the throats of the damned Yankees." In fact, Pico's victim turned out to be an Englishman, not a Yankee. That same month, three Anglos tracked down and killed two Baja California horse thieves, one an American and the other a Mexican. The trio were jailed in Santo Tomas and guarded by Salomon Pico and his men. When one of the prisoners admitting the killings, Pico insisted on shooting him dead, but a bystander dissuaded him. Soon after, on September 4, 1857, a band of Mexican vigilantes surrounded the jail and tried to lynch the three Anglos. This time Pico had a change of heart. He and his fellow soldiers stood off the mob and protected the prisoners. As a San Diego newspaperman remarked, "Salomon Pico—outlaw that he is—deserves praise for preventing the mob from massacring those in custody."[26]

On April 5, 1860, one of Pico's men got into a drunken quarrel with Governor Jose Castro. The pair drew knives, and Castro gave his bodyguard a slight wound in one hand. That night the two encountered each other on horseback, and the bodyguard shot Castro dead. The audacious killing created a sensation in Baja California, and the new governor decided to crack down on lawlessness. He ordered a general roundup of desperadoes, and during the next few weeks, twelve pistoleros were captured and summarily shot. Salomon Pico was one of them, executed by firing squad on May 1, 1860. It was an ignominious end for a man who had once been considered by some a Californio hero and patriot.[27]

And what of Joaquin Valenzuela, the last of the so-called Five Joaquins? As we have seen, those five names actually represented only two men—Murrieta and Valenzuela. After Murrieta's death, Valenzuela, alias Nacomoreno, hid out in Santa Barbara County, where he rode with Jack Powers, a notorious desperado. Powers, born in Ireland in 1827, had grown up in New York City. During the Mexican War, he and an older brother came to California as members of the New York Volunteers. They were stationed in Santa Barbara, where Jack Powers made his home after the war. An expert horseman and gambler, he learned Spanish, acquired a rancho, and became greatly admired by the Californios. As Horace Bell recalled, "Jack was a great gambler and when he walked through a crowd of gamblers it was with the air of a lion walking among rats." In the spring of 1853, Powers lost a lawsuit over the legal title to his rancho. When the county sheriff and his posse tried to evict him, violence erupted. During the ensuing melee, the sheriff was stabbed, and his possemen shot and killed two of Powers' friends.[28]

Jack Powers, deeply embittered, soon turned to cattle theft. Joaquin Valenzuela, along with Pio Linares, the twenty-two-year-old son of a prominent Californio family in San Luis Obispo, joined his gang. Valenzuela and Linares were unlike most young bandidos in that each was married. During the next year, they stole cattle in the coastal region and drove herds to the mining country for sale. Valenzuela, Powers, and Linares were also suspected of robbing and killing travelers on the road between San Luis Obispo and Santa Barbara. On the evening of June 7, 1856, Joaquin Valenzuela led a gang of six desperadoes to the Las Cruces Rancho on the Santa Barbara coast. His band included a man named Jesus—most likely his brother, Jesus "Chiquito" Valenzuela—and Juan Salazar, who had reportedly ridden with Joaquin Murrieta. They dismounted and looted two adobe houses, stealing $200 and shooting and badly wounding a Latino man. Then Salazar, inside one adobe, seized and choked a sixty-year-old Latina widow, tied her hands with rope, and ruthlessly raped her.

The outlaws fled into the darkness, and the sheriff of Santa Barbara raised a posse and hunted the gang for four days. Finally they captured Joaquin Valenzuela and Juan Salazar and lodged them in the county jail. Salazar's trial came up first, in August, and he was convicted of grand larceny and rape and sentenced to ten years in prison. But two days later, a dozen of his compadres cut a hole in the jail wall and released him. Salazar fled two hundred fifty miles north to Santa Cruz County, but he lived only two months. A posse arrested him for horse theft, and as they brought him to jail, Juan Salazar tried to escape into a thicket of wild mustard. The manhunters shot him dead.

Joaquin Valenzuela also managed to escape from the leaky Santa Barbara jail. After his close call, he decided to turn over a new leaf. He hired on as a vaquero for David W. Alexander, one of the owners of Rancho San Emigdio, west of Tejon Pass. Alexander was a prominent merchant, rancher, and politician. Though he had served one term as sheriff of Los Angeles County, it is not clear how much, if anything, he knew about the background of his new vaquero. Joaquin Valenzuela and his wife settled on Alexander's rancho. Valenzuela, when not riding for Alexander, made occasional visits to San Luis Obispo. On November 30, 1857, he attended a horse race and fandango at Santa Margarita, ten miles north of San Luis Obispo. Amidst the crowd of gamblers and colorfully attired senoritas, he encountered his old compadres Jack Powers, Pio Linares, and several of the gang. Powers told Valenzuela that they were on their way to rob a pair of Basque cattle buyers and invited him to join them.

"I have formerly been in such things, as you know," Valenzuela replied. "But I have given it up."

Early the next morning, Powers and his men mounted their mustangs and rode north on El Camino Real thirty miles to San Miguel. The desperadoes continued on a few miles toward the Basques' camp, but on the way, they suddenly encountered the two cattlemen on horseback. The bandidos opened fire, and after a brief gunfight, they killed both Basques, then looted their bodies. A manhunt swung into action, and several weeks later, Francisco Castro, the Californio sheriff of San Luis Obispo County, managed to arrest one of the gang. But because the victims were both dead, there was no eyewitness to the murders, and a jury found the outlaw not guilty. Two months after the trial, on May 10, 1858, Pio Linares, with eight other robbers—one of them Joaquin's brother, Chiquito Valenzuela—rode toward a remote rancho in northern San Luis Obispo County. They intended to rob its two French owners, but temporarily abandoned their plan when Linares was thrown from his horse and injured. He returned to San Luis to recover, and two days later, the rest of the band rode to the ranch, killed both Frenchmen, and plundered their house. Then the gang continued on to the cabin of a young Anglo hunter and murdered him as well.

The audacious slayings quickly ignited yet another large vigilante movement. Anglos and Californios were fed up with the banditry that had long plagued San Luis Obispo County. Almost one hundred fifty men joined the vigilantes and signed their muster roll; more than 40 percent were Latino. A reward of $3,000, dead or alive, was offered for Jack Powers, Pio Linares, and the rest of the gang. The vigilantes and Sheriff Castro methodically tracked down the outlaws. They shot and killed Pio Linares in a pitched gun battle and captured and lynched six of the gang in front of the Mission San Luis Obispo. Several of the band, including Powers and Jesus Valenzuela, managed to escape. During the manhunt, a posse led by Sheriff Castro rode across the Coast Range and came upon Joaquin Valenzuela at David Alexander's Rancho San Emigdio. Some of the possemen recognized him as the brother of Jesus Valenzuela, a friend of Jack Powers, and the former partner of Joaquin Murrieta. When questioned, Valenzuela admitted that Powers was his *patron*, or boss, but insisted that he was no longer a bandit.[29]

"I think you should not bother me now, as I have been accommodating for a year past," Valenzuela declared. But Sheriff Castro and his posse brought the bandido back to San Luis and lodged him in jail. On May 21, 1858, he was allowed out of the jail by Sheriff Castro and then publicly tried by the vigilantes, who issued a written decision. "The San Luis Obispo Executive Committee of Vigilance, after hearing the evidence in the case of Joaquin Valenzuela, alias Joaquin Ocomorenia, do find him to be the same person for whose apprehension a reward was offered by the governor of this state in the year 1852, and who was one of the objects of the search made by Harry Love's company of rangers, under authority from the Legislature, in the following year. We do also find him guilty of kidnaping and illegal detention of one Anita, an American child, from its parents, previous to the above date. We have reason to believe that he murdered the father of said child about that time. We find him guilty of connection with a band of robbers two years ago, at or near Purissima in Santa Barbara County, and of complicity in the rape of a woman of advanced years at Las Cruces, for which a companion of his was sentenced to the State's Prison. We find him guilty of having broken jail to avoid the punishment due to the last mentioned offense. For these and other offenses we do hereby adjudge him to suffer the penalty of *Death*, to be inflicted by hanging by the neck until he be dead. Said punishment to be put into execution within four hours from the time of the reading and notification of this sentence."[30]

Notably, the vigilantes found no evidence to connect Valenzuela with the last five murders in San Luis Obispo County. His death warrant was signed by the twelve-man executive committee—eight Anglos and four Latinos. Then Valenzuela dictated three letters to his compadres, including one to former sheriff David Alexander: "I send you my last farewell. In a few hours I will not be any more of this world. Give my last love to my dear wife and I hope I shall see her again in the other world. For what I owe you, you can take what I have got at your place and the balance give to my wife." He asked Alexander to give his "best respects" to numerous friends he named in the letter, and concluded, "I think I shall confess before I suffer death and I hope you will forgive me everything I have done to you." The illiterate bandido signed the letter with an X. Then the vigilantes marched Valenzuela to their makeshift gallows in front of the mission. A crowd of hundreds—almost everyone in town—watched the notorious desperado take his place under the fatal noose. Before he died, Valenzuela warned his erstwhile compadres not to tell their secrets.

"*Porque así se pierde*," he declared. "Because that's how you lose."[31]

David Alexander, the former Los Angeles County sheriff who befriended Joaquin Valenzuela.
Los Angeles Public Library

David Alexander was not happy when he learned about the lynching of his vaquero. A week later, while on a visit to Los Angeles, he complained to the editor of its Spanish-language newspaper, *El Clamor Público.* The ex-sheriff insisted that Valenzuela was "an innocent man . . . torn from his job and from the bosom of his family" and he had never left his ranch "for a single moment." But one of the vigilante leaders quickly responded, insisting that although Valenzuela had never been charged with the final five killings, he was "a comrade of the murderers, brother to one, chum to another, and was proven before the Committee to be as full of crime as an egg is full of meat. In 1853 he was a partner of Joaquin Muriata—the veritable Joaquin. It is notorious that he was one of the five Joaquins upon whose heads Governor Bigler set a price." Rejecting Alexander's claim that Valenzuela had never left his ranch, the vigilante declared, "This gentleman, forgot, perhaps, to tell the editor of the *Clamor Publico* that in November last, he loaned this man $100 to bring up his wife from Los Angeles; that he, Alexander, was informed at the time of the arrest that at the very time when he was supposed to be in Los Angeles, he was here in San Luis, in company with Jack Powers, at the races in and near this place; that he stayed here several weeks, and that during that time instead of living with his wife, whoever the lady may be, he kept with an abandoned Mexican prostitute for whose sake two men had been stabbed and two shot within the last six months."[32]

Needless to say, David Alexander made no more claims about the innocence of Joaquin Valenzuela. The bandido was buried in an unmarked grave, but his bloody deeds, like those of Pancho Daniel, Salomon Pico, and the other men who rode with Joaquin Murrieta, are marked indelibly in the history of the Wild West.

CHAPTER 18

LAST OF THE CALIFORNIA RANGERS

Phil Herbert and a comrade stepped through the lobby of Willard's Hotel in Washington, DC, and settled comfortably into their chairs in the breakfast room. The lush surroundings were a world away from the log cabins, canvas tents, and open campfires of the gold rush. And Herbert had come a long way from his days sponsoring, and then riding with, the California Rangers. After serving in the California state assembly, in 1853 he had been elected to the US Congress by voters in the Southern Mines. Herbert, always a heavy drinker, knew that he held an important political position in the nation's capital, and he acted like it. It was eleven in the morning of May 8, 1856, and he called to a boyish waiter and demanded breakfast.

"Let us have it damned quick," Herbert ordered.

The youth responded that although it was late, he would try to scare up a morning meal. He returned with some scraps of food, and told Herbert, "You can't get any more breakfast. It is too late."

"Clear out, you Irish son of a bitch," Herbert ordered. He then turned to another waiter, Thomas Keating, and again demanded breakfast.

"Go and get us some breakfast or go away from here, you damned scoundrel!" he barked.

Keating responded with a muttered insult. At that, Herbert leaped from his chair and charged at the waiter, punching him in the neck. Herbert then returned to his table, and just as he was sitting down, Keating picked up two plates and shouted, "You are a damned son of a bitch!"

He flung the plates at Herbert's head, and simultaneously the congressman snatched up his chair and threw it at Keating. Now a regular donnybrook broke out between Herbert and his dining companion on one side, and Keating and several other waiters on the other. As Herbert's friend swung another chair at the servers, Keating's brother, Patrick, rushed into the room and seized the congressman. Phil Herbert yanked a derringer from his pocket, but Patrick Keating grabbed the barrel and tried to wrestle the gun away. Herbert broke loose, turned the derringer on Thomas Keating, and shot him in the chest. The waiter collapsed to the floor, desperately wounded. Five minutes later, he was dead.

Phil Herbert stood trial for murder, claiming self-defense. The jurors could not agree, and in a second trial, he was acquitted. But Herbert's political career was over. Even in rough-and-tumble California, many voters frowned on such behavior from a US Congressman. Herbert returned west to campaign for a second term, but he was unsuccessful. He then went to Texas and opened a law office. During the Civil War, he became a lieutenant colonel in the Confederate Army. Phil Herbert was killed in action in Louisiana in 1864.[1]

The California Rangers, like so many men who joined the gold rush, were a tough bunch. And none of them was tougher than Bill Byrnes, Joaquin's old gambling partner. Byrnes's friends later said that during his violent career, he took part in numerous shooting scrapes and was wounded thirty-one times. After the killing of Murrieta, he settled in Sacramento. There, in October 1853, just two months after the shootout at Cantua Creek, a blacksmith seized his wagon, claiming that the former ranger owned him money. The two went for their pistols and exchanged gunfire at close range. Neither was hurt, and because the incident was considered mutual combat, neither was prosecuted. Byrnes next obtained appointment as a guard at the new state prison. San Quentin was then being constructed by convict labor, with the prisoners confined at night in a brig docked on the bayshore. By then Byrnes had become an alcoholic; his friends said that he imbibed for relief from his painful bullet wounds. The state prison, like every place in California, had a saloon, which he patronized regularly while on duty. A San Quentin official later said that "a good many of the guard were in the habit of getting drunk. William Byrnes frequently got on a spree."[2]

A year later, Byrnes resigned and moved south to Monterey. There he became a bodyguard and hired gunfighter for Lewis F. Belcher, known as the "Big Eagle of Monterey." One of Byrnes's fellow bodyguards was Anastacio Garcia, the former constable for Henry Cocks, who in 1852 had taken part in the killing of Claudio Feliz. Lew Belcher was embroiled in a vendetta with William F. Roach, the political boss of Monterey County, over a beautiful Californio widow and her late husband's fortune. It became known as the Roach-Belcher feud and claimed the lives of ten men. When a judge ordered Roach to return money that he had embezzled from the widow, he mounted a horse and fled for Mexico. Lew Belcher sent Byrnes to track him down. Byrnes used relays of fresh horses to pursue Roach to Southern California and captured him in Ventura. But despite his tough reputation, Bill Byrnes took no part in the violent frays of the Roach-Belcher feud. Belcher was assassinated in a Monterey hotel in 1856, and Byrnes found himself out of a job.[3]

In Monterey, Byrnes married and fathered a daughter, but he seems to have abandoned his family a few years later, resulting in divorce. In 1859 he became a captain of volunteer militia organized by William C. Kibbe, California's adjutant general.

Their assignment was to force Native Americans in Northern California onto Indian reservations. General Kibbe was greatly impressed with Byrnes, saying, "Captain Byrnes was an experienced and accomplished Indian fighter, with courage and discretion equal to every emergency. I was particularly fortunate in having his support at the head of one of the detachments throughout the entire campaign." However, one of the militiamen disagreed: "I had been in an Indian war with Byrnes in El Dorado County in 1851 and knew he was not cautious enough to be a good Indian fighter."[4]

During the 1850s, volunteer militias in California's northernmost counties were guilty of numerous massacres of Native Americans. Bill Byrnes, however, seems to have pursued a different course. On August 24, 1859, he led his men on an expedition in which they captured an entire Indian village without firing a shot, and then marched them to a reservation in Mendocino County. Two weeks later, Byrnes and his men seized three Indian chiefs, one of whom spoke fluent English. Byrnes convinced the chiefs, and one hundred of their people, to go peacefully with his company to the reservation. A month after that, Byrnes's command encountered five armed Indians who fled into the brush. Byrnes tried repeatedly to get them to surrender, then cautiously approached them with four of his men. The Native Americans opened fire, and Byrnes and his soldiers responded with a volley of shots, killing all five warriors. In December, Byrnes's command was mustered out of service, and a local journalist offered high praise for its captain: "The feeling of interest manifested by all of his command, forces us to the conclusion that he is the most popular captain that has ever commanded an expedition on the Pacific Coast."[5]

The following year, Bill Byrnes led a prospecting expedition into the Nevada desert, but when he failed to strike pay dirt, he returned to Sacramento. There he continued his descent into alcoholism. His heavy drinking, coupled with the pain from his old wounds, caused psychiatric problems, which were no doubt compounded by the nightmares about his former occupation as a scalp hunter. In February 1868, a policeman spotted Byrnes in downtown Sacramento, "acting as though not in his right mind." The officer talked to Byrnes and found him incoherent, and a judge sent him to the county hospital for treatment. He was soon released and then made his way to San Francisco, where in November 1869 he was jailed as a "common drunkard." Byrnes then went back to Sacramento, where his mental decline continued, and in 1872 he was readmitted to the county hospital. A reporter who visited him wrote, "Racked with the wounds of unnumbered conflicts and the infirmities produced by many years of continuous peril and hardship, the old hero still keeps the wreck afloat. His step is steady and firm, his form erect as the mountain pine, and fire still glistens in the eye that often guided the unerring bullet."[6]

Bill Byrnes was released from the Sacramento County hospital in February 1873 and went to San Jose. But just a month later, he was jailed there as an insane person, and a San Jose journalist tried to interview him: "His mind is terribly shattered, and he is seldom able to recall a single circumstance that has occurred in his life. Singular as it may seem, on meeting Joseph Patton, assistant jailer, he recognized him as an old acquaintance, and remembered to have met him twenty years ago. A few minutes afterwards the circumstance passed from his memory, and he said he had no recollection of having ever seen him. We saw the unfortunate man in his cell on Monday. He stands about six feet high and has been a man of rather prepossessing appearance, but scarcely a vestige of his former self remains now." A judge sent Byrnes to the state insane asylum in Stockton. The following year, newspapers announced that he had died in the facility, but the reports were wrong. He remained in the asylum for ten years, finally succumbing to cirrhosis of the liver on June 16, 1883, aged fifty-nine. His life on the frontier—from scalping Apaches to decapitating Joaquin Murrieta—had been a long and bloody one.[7]

John Sylvester, who with Bill Byrnes had brought the severed head and hand from Cantua Creek, was cut from another cloth. He became a popular figure in the San Joaquin Valley, where he operated a cattle ranch. Sylvester was peaceable, and—surprisingly for that era—he rarely carried a gun. In early July 1859, he left his ranch and headed for Los Angeles, driving a small herd of colts. On July 10, he rode into modern-day Tejon Pass, stopping for a meal at a stage station. While he was eating, a Californio named Jose Olivas rode up and dismounted. Olivas joined Sylvester in the dining room, and the two ate together. Sylvester told Olivas that he was on his way to Los Angeles to buy cattle, and he asked about the quickest route. Olivas replied that when he finished his meal, he would meet Sylvester at a grove of cottonwood trees five miles down the road and point out the trail. An hour later, Sylvester rode out to meet Olivas. The station keeper thought little of the former ranger's visit until later that day when his riderless horse and several of his colts trotted up. The horse's saddle blankets were covered with blood.

The station keeper galloped to Fort Tejon and raised the alarm. A posse of settlers and US soldiers quickly began a manhunt. Because Olivas had ridden an unshod horse, they found it simple to track, for most riding animals wore horseshoes. The possemen followed Olivas east to San Francisquito Canyon but lost the trail when it was wiped out by a herd of cattle. Then two lawmen from Los Angeles took up the hunt and captured Olivas, who readily admitted sharing a meal with Sylvester. However, he claimed that he had waited for Sylvester at the cottonwood grove, but he had never showed up. The officers released Olivas and began searching Tejon Pass for the missing man. As they rode along the trail, they noticed a huge flock of buzzards circling a spot a hundred yards from the road. There the lawmen discovered the body of John Sylvester, partially devoured by wild animals. He had died from two stab wounds, indicating that someone had killed him up close. Nearby the officers found two of his shirts and a Panama hat.[8]

The manhunters rode back to Los Angeles, where they arrested Olivas for murder and then searched his sister's house. Inside the house they found a trunk, and inside that was Sylvester's coat. While Olivas awaited trial in the city jail, vigilantes threatened to lynch him, but they never followed through. After several delays, his trial began in late March 1860 and lasted twenty days, with many onlookers present. One day in the middle of the trial, a quarrel broke out between the prosecutor and the defense attorney. The prosecutor threw a newspaper at the defense lawyer, who responded by hurling a glass of water at his opponent. More glasses were thrown by the two men, and finally the prosecuting attorney reached into his pocket and drew his derringer. Just as he pulled the trigger, a bystander grabbed his arm. The shot went wild, striking a Californio in the leg and inflicting a minor wound.

At that, all hell broke loose in the packed courtroom.

"For God's sake, don't shoot!" spectators screamed. "Don't shoot this way! Run, run, or you'll be all killed!"

The *Los Angeles Star* reported that it was "a scene of indescribable confusion. The court was thronged, and all hands, the jury included, panic-struck, rushed in terror from the room, over benches, through windows and doors, the less expert tripping up, bringing dozens on the top of them, some crawling out on all fours." The judge, who happened to be Ben Hayes—the same whom Salomon Pico had tried to assassinate in 1851—kept his cool and grabbed hold of Jose Olivas to keep him from escaping. Neither of the lawyers was charged with a crime, and the trial continued a few days later. Surprisingly, despite the strong circumstantial evidence against the prisoner, the jury was not satisfied, and they found him not guilty of John Sylvester's murder.[9]

Jose Olivas learned nothing from his narrow escape. He became a horse thief, and three years later, on the night of November 20, 1863, Los Angeles officers jailed him for stealing mustangs. The jail held a number of desperadoes, including Boston "Boss" Daimwood, a notorious highway robber who was suspected of murdering two miners in Baja California and robbing them of $4,000 in gold. Tomas Sanchez, the capable Californio sheriff of Los Angeles County, guarded the jail with his undersheriff. Many Anglos in town had been deeply angered by the acquittal of Olivas, and word of his new arrest spread quickly. By daylight a group of three hundred heavily armed vigilantes surrounded the jail. Sheriff Sanchez tried to reason with them, to no avail. At 10:00 a.m., the mob forced their way inside and overpowered Sanchez and his undersheriff. The vigilantes, wielding sledgehammers and chisels, spent two hours hacking and pounding open the jail cells. The main prisoner they wanted was Jose Olivas, and he was taken out first. But the mob was not satisfied with only one man. They also removed Boston Daimwood and three other robbers, two Anglo and one Latino. The vigilantes dragged the five men outside to the open corridor of the old adobe courthouse. They fastened ropes around the roof beams and, in front of a huge crowd, hanged them all. Although local journalists debated the justification for the lynching, one declared, "Olivas was, without doubt, the murderer of John Sylvester."[10]

Like Sylvester, Billy Henderson followed a respectable and peaceful life after the gun battle at Cantua Creek. He moved to Santa Cruz, where he was elected county assessor in 1857. Decades later a newspaper report falsely claimed that in 1858, Henderson absconded with county funds, along with another man's wife, and was then indicted for the theft. In fact he served out his full two-year term without controversy and then moved south to Tulare County, where he worked as an official recorder of mining claims. During the early 1860s, he helped lead a party of gold

The lynching of Jose Olivas and four other desperadoes at the old adobe courthouse in Los Angeles in 1863. *Los Angeles Public Library*

prospectors that explored the Panamint Range near Death Valley. In the 1870s Henderson acquired a number of gold mines, including one just south of modern-day Yosemite National Park. Over the years, he often provided newspapers with updates on his mining pursuits, but only once did he give an interview about his experiences with the California Rangers and the killing of Joaquin Murrieta. On Christmas Day 1882, the fifty-six-year-old Henderson was dressing to attend a holiday festival when he suffered a sudden stroke and died. A local newspaper remarked, "Deceased was a man of invincible grit, and generally esteemed by the community in which he resided. His funeral was largely attended by the people of that vicinity."[11]

Quite the opposite of Billy Henderson was young Nick Ashmore, the tall and well-dressed ranger from Kentucky. Ashmore's experiences in the gold rush, and in riding with Harry Love's men, seem to have brought out the worst in him. He became a card sharp, and in 1858 rode east to Utah Territory. There one Mormon pioneer later recalled him as "a notorious gambler," and said, "He was a handsome scoundrel and princely in his attire." The Mormon explained that Ashmore wore "a magnificent suit of buckskin, elaborately ornamented with flowers and figures worked in colored silk. The buttons of his vest were $2.50 gold coins." Nick Ashmore concealed his true name and used the alias of Richard Keith Johnson. In a facetious nod to Murrieta, he told everyone that his nickname was Joaquin. As a result, he became well-known in Utah as Joaquin Johnson.[12]

At first Ashmore ran a saloon that catered to some of the 2,500 US soldiers stationed at Camp Floyd, about forty miles south of Salt Lake City. However, he soon began riding with a gang of thieves that preyed on US Army horses. In 1859 he had a run-in with Orrin Porter Rockwell, notorious as the Avenging Angel of the Mormons. Rockwell, who at times served as a law officer, was suspected of committing numerous murders in the 1850s in an effort to keep gentiles, or non-Mormons, out of Utah. He accused Ashmore, whom he knew as Joaquin Johnson, of stealing a herd of government mules. Rockwell tracked down the stolen herd and recovered the mules, but apparently he could not prove that Ashmore had stolen them.[13]

In January 1860, a friend of Ashmore's named Robert Wilburn drove a band of cattle from Southern California across the Mojave Desert, headed toward Utah. About forty miles outside of San Bernardino, he was attacked by Paiute Indians, who killed him with three arrows and drove off his herd. Searchers soon found Wilburn's body in the desert, but the Indians had disappeared. Nothing was heard of the Paiutes for three months. Finally a Mormon, who had been exploring a wagon road between California and Utah, returned to his ranch in southern Utah. He brought with him an eighteen-year-old Paiute known as Indian John, whom he had met in the small Mormon settlement that is now Las Vegas, Nevada. Soon after, rumors spread that Indian John was one of Wilburn's killers. Nick Ashmore heard the rumors and insisted that Indian John "was known to all persons familiar with the southern route to California as a very bad Indian, vicious, treacherous, and murderous." Ashmore also claimed that Indian John had once tried to kill him.

On April 3, 1860, Ashmore rode up to the Mormon's ranch, accompanied by a deputy US Marshal named Kirk who carried an arrest warrant for Indian John. When the young Paiute returned to the ranch driving a wagon loaded with wood, Ashmore whipped out his revolver and barked, "You are my prisoner!"

Indian John did not resist and insisted that he had not killed anyone. Ashmore loudly threatened to shoot the youth, but the rancher stepped forward to protect him. Deputy Marshal Kirk produced the warrant and promised that no harm would come to Indian John. Then he and Ashmore rode off with their prisoner, headed for Camp Floyd, two hundred miles to the north. They only made it halfway. As the trio trotted their horses up to a bridge across the Sevier River, Ashmore drew his six-gun and shot Indian John twice, once in the back and once in the right arm. He fell from the saddle, and Ashmore put two more bullets into him, firing so close his pistol muzzle left powder burns on the youth. Then Ashmore drew his bowie knife and scalped the dead Paiute. He and Kirk carried Indian John's body to the riverbank and threw it into the stream.

The pair then rode thirty miles north to the settlement of Nephi, were they reported that they had shot and killed Indian John when he jumped into the Sevier River and tried to escape. A group of Mormons, rightly suspicious, rode to the bridge. There, after a search, they found the scalped, bullet-riddled corpse a short distance downstream. The killing received prominent attention from newspapers in Salt Lake City. One of the men who discovered the body wrote a letter to a Salt Lake paper, calling Ashmore and Kirk "the perpetrators of this cowardly and cold-blooded murder" and said that they had tried to cover up "the fate of this unfortunate son of the forest." The writer added that Indian John had previously identified Ashmore as one of a gang of horse thieves. Ashmore was enraged when he read the accounts and threatened to kill the editors of the Salt Lake newspapers. At the same time, he boasted of killing the boy and declared that he had taken his scalp so he could send it to Wilburn's children in California as proof that their father's death had been avenged. Despite his admission, neither Ashmore nor Kirk was ever punished for the murder of Indian John.[14]

A few weeks later, on the evening of May 16, 1860, the vindictive Nick Ashmore rode into Salt Lake City and swaggered about the streets, threatening to shoot a Mormon newspaper editor. He bragged that he was going to steal mules from a party of overland immigrants, that he "intended to take a couple of scalps" before he left town, and that his pistols "were in first rate order." But Ashmore carried out none of his threats. The following evening, he was still in Salt Lake City, accompanied by a saloonkeeper friend, Myron Brewer, who had numerous Mormon enemies. At eleven o'clock that night, the pair stepped into a livery stable and asked that their horses be brought out from the stalls. As they waited outside on the sidewalk, the roar of gunfire broke the stillness. Several assassins, armed with shotguns, fired blasts of buckshot into the two men. Ashmore and Brewer died instantly. Police officers heard the shots and ran to the scene, but the killers had fled. The main suspect turned out to be none other than the infamous Avenging Angel, Orrin Porter Rockwell. But Rockwell, frequently protected by Mormon officials, was never charged with the double murder. Late that year, Nick Ashmore's family and friends in Kentucky finally learned of his death. They wrote to Salt Lake City and revealed for the first time the true name of the Utah desperado known as Joaquin Johnson.[15]

Of all the California Rangers, none had a life as prominent or as controversial as its lieutenant, Patrick Edward Connor. After the rangers were disbanded, Connor became undersheriff of San Joaquin County, with headquarters in Stockton. In Febru-

Orrin Porter Rockwell, infamous as the Avenging Angel of the Mormons. He was the prime suspect in the murder of Nick Ashmore, the California Ranger who became a Utah desperado.
Brigham Young University

ary 1854, Harry Love petitioned the state legislature for a further reward of $5,000 and promised to share it with the other rangers. In May, Connor wrote to his friend, former ranger Bill Howard: "Harry Love's bill passed the Senate today, by a large majority; he will not draw his money until Tuesday morning. I expect I will have some trouble to make him stick to his word; maybe not, altho I dread it. There will be hell in the camp sure if he don't stick to his word." He signed it, "Connor, Flat Broke." Given that most of the former rangers were an armed and dangerous bunch, it seems more than probable that Love shared the reward with his fellow manhunters.[16]

A few months later, Connor married, and he and his wife set out to raise a large family. He worked as a general contractor, became a leader in civic and political affairs, and served as captain of the Stockton Blues, a local militia company. After the outbreak of the Civil War in 1861, Connor was commissioned colonel of the 3rd California Volunteer Infantry. He and his eight hundred men marched across the Sierra Nevada and through the high desert to Salt Lake City, where they were assigned to protect the overland mail routes from Indian attacks. In the summer and fall of 1862, near the Idaho-Utah border, starving Shoshone Indians raided Mormon farms and attacked emigrants, taking food and livestock. That December an attachment of Connor's cavalry captured four Shoshone warriors, bound them with rope, and riddled them with fifty-one bullets. Other Indians retaliated, killing ten miners and two expressmen.

A month later, a party of miners arrived in Salt Lake City and reported that they had been attacked by Indians who killed one of their number. Colonel Connor led several hundred troops north to Bear River, Idaho, ostensibly to arrest the Shoshone chiefs. But Connor saw this as an opportunity to achieve glory, and perhaps also as a chance to obtain an army command on the Civil War battlefields of the east. He later admitted that "it was not my intention to take any prisoners." At daybreak on January 29, 1863, Connor and his troops surrounded the Shoshone village on Bear River. Some of the warriors spoke English, and they taunted the volunteers by mocking a common cavalry command known as the Movement by Fours, in which four riders turned their horses in tandem.

"Fours right, fours left," they yelled. "Come on, you California sons of bitches!"

Connor's infantry promptly attacked, but the Indians opened a blistering fire from the cover of a ravine. During two hours of fighting, the Shoshone warriors killed twenty-three soldiers and wounded forty-six. Connor said later, "My men fell thick and fast around me, but after flanking them we had the advantage and made good use of it. I ordered a flanking party to advance down the ravine on either side, which gave us the advantage of gunfire directed from either flank and caused some of the Indians to give way and run toward the mouth of the ravine. I had a company stationed who shot them as they ran out."

Patrick Edward Connor and his son in 1860. He is wearing the uniform of the Stockton Blues. *Haggin Museum, Stockton, CA*

When the Shoshones ran out of bullets, Connor's troops attacked the village. The soldiers slaughtered some 250 Indians, including about ninety women and children. One eyewitness said, "They killed the wounded by knocking them in the head with an axe and then commenced to ravish the squaws which was done to the very height of brutality." Some of Connor's volunteers even raped females who were in the throes of death. The Bear River Massacre, occurring as it did in the middle of the Civil War, was soon forgotten, but today it is remembered as one of the worst slaughters of Native Americans in the history of the frontier.[17]

Edward Connor was promoted to brigadier general, and in 1865 he led the Powder River Expedition against the Cheyenne, Arapaho, and Sioux Indians in the territory that later became Wyoming. The expedition, however, was largely unsuccessful. In Utah, Connor strongly opposed the Mormons, including their leader, Brigham Young, and the practice of polygamy. He also accused Mormons of disloyalty to the Union. After the Civil War, Connor returned to civilian life, successfully developed mines, and, despite his unpopularity with Mormons, became known as the "father of Utah mining." He took an active role in politics, started Utah's first daily newspaper, and operated the first steamboat on the Great Salt Lake. Connor accumulated significant wealth, but lost most of it in the 1880s due to business reverses. When he died in Salt Lake City in 1891, aged seventy-one, his estate was worth only $5,000. And although Connor was a prominent and outspoken Utah booster, politician, newspaperman, and business leader, he never spoke publicly about his three months with the California Rangers and the manhunt for Joaquin Murrieta. That was a strange omission, given that his principled service as a ranger was a far cry from his massacre of Native Americans.[18]

Unlike General Connor, Harry Love spent the rest of his days in California. He used his share of the reward money to purchase a sawmill located at the confluence of the San Lorenzo River and modern-day Love Creek, now in the town of Ben Lomond, situated in the mountains ten miles north of Santa Cruz. His three-hundred-plus acres, heavily forested with redwoods, bordered on the large property of a widow, Mary Bennett. She was an imposing figure, six feet tall, weighing more than three hundred pounds, and fiercely independent. Five years before the discovery of gold, she had arrived in California with her husband and eight children. They settled in San Francisco, where a pioneer merchant later described her: "She was unmistakably the head of the family—a large, powerful woman, uncultivated, but well meaning and very industrious. Her word was law, and her husband stood in becoming awe of her."[19]

Mary was extremely quarrelsome, and the Bennetts squabbled constantly and finally separated. She moved with their younger children to a farm with an adobe house on the outskirts of the little pueblo of Santa Clara, just north of San Jose. During the Mexican War, a skirmish took place between Anglos and Californios near the Mission Santa Clara. Mary's actions—and character—were witnessed by another American woman, who recalled, "She waltzed back and forth in front of the Mission, yelling orders to the men at the top of her voice. Growing more excited, she ran forward and grabbing up a large bone lying in the yard, rushed up to a man who had refused to fight, saying that he had no gun. Stopping squarely in front of the startled fellow, she thrust the bone into his hands and shouted 'Take that, you puppy, and go out there and bat the brains out of some Mexican or I'll use it on you.'"[20]

Mary's husband died in 1849, having first obtained several Mexican land grants that passed down to his wife and children. She relished taking part in property disputes, lawsuits, and squatter problems. Mary met Harry Love at the time he acquired his sawmill on the San Lorenzo River, and the two became romantically involved. Despite the fact that they had known each other only a few months, and at fifty-one Mary was seven years older than Harry, the two wed in May 1854. The marriage was probably one of convenience. He saw her as a wealthy widow, and she viewed him as a noted fighting man who could help with her many disputes. A journalist who knew Love, on hearing of his marriage, jokingly cautioned him—using the words of Charles Dickens—to "beware of the widders." His remark would prove prophetic.[21]

Just two days after the wedding, and in lieu of embarking on a honeymoon, Love left his bride behind, boarded a steamship in San Francisco, and sailed for the East Coast. His plan was to meet President Franklin Pierce in Washington, DC, and seek a commission as a US Army commander. However, within a month of his departure, reports arrived in San Francisco that Love had taken part in an atrocity while en route to Central America. Aboard the ship, an actor named Ned Bingham had

Harry Love, wearing his Colt Dragoon revolver, in 1867.
Bancroft Library

engaged in an affair with a married actress who was traveling with her husband. According to the sensational story, Harry Love and six other passengers collared Bingham and executed him by firing squad. But the truth later came out, and the opposite was true. A group of furious passengers did try to mob Bingham, but Love and the ship's captain protected him from violence. Then, while crossing the Isthmus of Panama, the jilted husband shot and badly wounded Bingham, but the actor survived.[22]

Following the drama in Panama, Love boarded another steamer for New York City, and finally made his way by railroad to the nation's capital. He managed to meet with President Pierce, who scribbled a brief note to his Secretary of War, Jefferson Davis: "Will you send me the recommendations on file for Capt. Love of California?" Love then boarded a return steamship for California, arriving in San Francisco three months after his trip began. It was a lightning-fast journey in that pre-transcontinental railroad era. The following spring, Harry finally received his commission—as a lieutenant in the First US Cavalry, for "service against Indians." This must have been a huge disappointment, for Love had made the long trip to the East Coast hoping for a much more senior command. He apparently never saw active cavalry duty, and two years later, he resigned his commission.[23]

Harry Love instead spent most of his time running his sawmill, assisting Mary with her never-ending lawsuits, and helping with her farm in Santa Clara. He also grew corn and hay on his property along the San Lorenzo River. In the Santa Cruz Mountains, Love was a popular figure, noted for his hospitality to those who visited his house, mill, and farm. The area had once been a Mexican land grant, the Rancho Zayante. Harry occasionally wore a long sword that had been presented to him by a Mexican friend during the war. Because of his flowing black hair, his imposing physique, and his flashy sword, he became known as "the Black Knight of the Zayante." But Love had many problems. In January 1861, a flash flood washed away his sawmill. Several years later, an arsonist—never identified—burned his house to the ground. Then another incendiary torched his hayfield.

At the same time, the Loves' marriage began to fail. Mary disliked the isolated Santa Cruz Mountains and refused to live at Harry's cabin. Instead she stayed at her old adobe house in Santa Clara. The two quarreled frequently over finances, and in 1866, Mary sued him for divorce. She claimed that he had deserted her and failed to provide support. After a trial, the judge ruled that she had failed to prove her case, and he denied her request for a divorce. Harry, in an effort to reconcile with Mary, sold his mountain property late in 1867 and moved to her farm in Santa Clara. She magnanimously allowed him to sleep in the barn and work the fields like a common laborer. In the spring, Mary employed a hired man, a thirty-three-year-old

Dane named Christian Iverson. She told friends and neighbors—falsely, as it turned out—that Harry had beaten her and that she had hired Iverson for protection.

Love became enraged at the young interloper, who seemed to have won Mary's affections. He confronted Iverson and ordered him to leave the farm.

"I was hired and am paid by Mrs. Love," Iverson retorted. "And I'm not leaving until she says so."[24]

By this time, Harry was drinking heavily and spending much of his time in a local saloon. He had failed at business and had no home, no land, and no future. To make things worse, Mary was prospering and had even hired a crew of carpenters to build a new two-story farmhouse. On the morning of June 29, 1868, Harry was on a visit to San Jose when he spotted Mary and Iverson together, running errands. Love exploded in rage, as a local journalist reported: "He left the city making threats; he declared that he would go home and guard his premises, and that if Iverson entered there he should do it over his dead body." But Love was wrong about ownership of the farm. Mary had acquired it before she married him, and under California law, inherited from Mexican law, the farm was her separate property, not his. It was an extraordinary irony that Harry Love found himself in exactly the same position as Three Fingered Jack after his marriage to Hilaria Sanchez failed.[25]

Love climbed into his wagon and drove four miles north to Mary's farmhouse. Pulling up at the front gate, he jumped out, wielding a double-barrel shotgun, a six-shooter, and a bowie knife. Harry told one of the carpenters that if Iverson tried to enter the gate, "He would have to walk over my dead body."

Love then took up a position behind the gate, which was in the middle of a long rail fence. He was prepared for a lengthy wait, for he settled down with a bag of crackers and a pot of hot tea. To one of the workers, he explained, "That's the way Texas Rangers lived when they camped."

Another laborer stepped into the farmhouse to warn Mary's twenty-seven-year-old daughter, Samantha, who was visiting her mother's home.

"That old fool Love has come to take possession of the place," he warned her.

Meanwhile Harry walked back and forth from the gate to his wagon, each time fetching a bottle of liquor and taking a long pull from it. It was late morning when Samantha spotted her mother's buggy approaching, fifty yards down the road, with Iverson at the reins. She ran to the gate, which Harry politely opened for her, then raced toward the buggy, waving her arms. Samantha grabbed the horse's bit and yelled that Love was armed and waiting for them. At the same time, Mary caught sight of Harry near the gate. He was crouching down behind the rail fence, his shotgun pointed at them.

"There he comes!" she shouted. "There he comes!"

Iverson leaped down from the buggy with a pistol in his hand.

"He will shoot you!" Mary screamed.

Iverson paid no heed and walked toward Love, his revolver raised. Love unleashed a blast from his shotgun. Foolishly—or drunkenly—he had loaded it with birdshot instead of much heavier—and deadlier—buckshot. Two birdshot glanced off Iverson's face, while a third grazed Samantha in the hand. Iverson, unfazed, kept advancing. He leveled his pistol and shot twice at Love, but missed. Harry then fired a second blast, which went wild. Dropping the shotgun, he whipped out his six-shooter and unloosed five rounds, striking Iverson in the right arm. Iverson ignored the wound, charged up to the fence, and fired several times at point-blank range. One pistol ball slammed into Harry's right arm and shattered the bone. Love howled in pain and raced toward the house, yelling for help, with Iverson in pursuit.

"Come in and I'll protect you!" one of the carpenters called to Harry. But Iverson caught up with Love and struck him over

The killing of Harry Love, by an artist for Frank Leslie's Illustrated Newspaper in 1868. *William B. Secrest collection*

the head with a terrific blow from his now-empty pistol. The old manhunter collapsed, and Iverson clubbed him again in the head. As the pair grappled on the ground, two of the workers ran from the house and separated them. They carried Love inside, where he gasped, "The two women are murderers."

Bleeding heavily, he muttered that they had hired Iverson to kill him. The workmen sent for help, and three doctors arrived a few hours later. They amputated Love's right arm, but the physicians could not save his life. As one doctor reported, "While dressing the arm, he was very much excited and talked incoherently, and just as we were putting in the last suture he attempted to raise up, and fell back and expired." A coroner's jury quickly ruled that Christian Iverson had acted in self-defense. But Mary Love did not have long to enjoy her triumph. Six months later, in December 1868, she was relaxing in a chair, crocheting. Mary suddenly exclaimed, "There now, you see, I never did get to weigh four hundred pounds."

She then fell backward in the chair and died instantly from a heart attack. By that time, Harry Love lay buried in an unmarked grave in what is now Mission City Memorial Park in Santa Clara. His entire estate, which included his shotgun, his wagon, and a wolf skin, was worth less than $400. Harry Love's death was a sad and sordid end for a colorful frontiersman who had led the final manhunt for Joaquin Murrieta.[26]

Other rangers lived more conventional lives. Lafayette Black, who had toured with the severed head and hand, left California for Texas, where he served in the Confederate cavalry during the Civil War. He then ran a general store, married, raised seven children, and died peacefully in 1885 at the age of fifty-nine. The facially scarred George Evans moved to Santa Cruz a year after Joaquin's death, where he ran a small farm. He failed to prosper, and in about 1880, he settled in Chinese Camp in Tuolumne County. Evans suffered from cancer and died there in poverty in 1884, buried in a pauper's grave. A much more noted figure was Charles Bludworth. From 1855 to 1857, he served as the first sheriff of newly created Merced County in the San Joaquin Valley. Bludworth married into the family of William Snelling, for whom the town of Snelling is named. In December 1857, Snelling was shot and killed by a ruffian who then escaped. Bludworth swore vengeance and exchanged threats with three of the killer's friends. A few weeks later, on January 23, 1858, Bludworth, accompanied by two comrades, encountered the trio in Snelling. A terrific gun battle broke out as all six opened fire at close range. Bludworth put three pistol balls into one of his enemies, killing him. When the smoke cleared, forty shots had been fired and two more men were slain, one from each faction. A jury later found that Bludworth had acted in self-defense, but ever after he was known as Bloodthirsty Charley. In 1868, newspapers reported that he had been killed in a shootout in Snelling. But that was premature, for Charles Bludworth died of natural causes a year later, aged just thirty-nine.[27]

Of all the California Rangers, none lived as long as Bill Howard. After the killing of Murrieta, he and his brother Tom continued to run their Buena Vista Ranch in Mariposa County. In April 1855, three miners led by a man named Champlain stopped at their ranch and asked if they could stay for a few days in an unoccupied cabin on the property. The brothers, ever hospitable, agreed. Several days later, Bill Howard returned to the cabin, only to find the prospectors tearing out the floorboards and using them to make sluice boxes for gold mining. Howard told them that they had five days to clear out. Champlain refused and announced that he and his comrades now owned the property. Howard calmly offered him a horse, and suggested that he ride into Mariposa and ask the county mining recorder to show him the brothers' proof of ownership.

Howard then mounted up and left on a trip to Hornitos, while his brother went to Mariposa. A few evenings later, the brothers returned to their ranch, and at daybreak they approached the cabin. Champlain was in the front yard, loading his revolver. He put his gun away and invited Bill Howard inside, while Tom Howard waited in the doorway. A fire was roaring in the hearth, and Champlain sat down on a bench, looked at Bill Howard, and again declared that the land belonged to him.

"You're a coward!" an exasperated Howard snapped.

Champlain leaped to his feet and went for his six-gun. He wasn't quick enough. Howard whipped out a single-barrel derringer from his coat pocket and pulled the trigger. The ball slammed into Champlain's forehead, killing him instantly. He tumbled backward into the fireplace, and Howard yelled to his brother, "Pull that man out of the fire!"

He then stepped to the bedroom door and covered the other two miners, who had been cowering inside. One of them peered down the barrel of Howard's derringer and gasped, "Oh, don't shoot!"

Howard lowered the gun and ordered one of the prospectors, "Ride to Hornitos and fetch the sheriff."

The miner complied, and the sheriff later arrived at the Buena Vista ranch with a group of thirty men. They formed a coroner's jury, and Bill Howard turned to the two prospectors and said, "You heard it all. You tell the officer."

The miners, as well as Tom Howard, testified that Bill Howard had killed Champlain in self-defense, and the jurors so ruled. Howard later recalled that many years afterward, he happened to meet Champlain's brother at a San Francisco racetrack. The pair, both fans of horse racing, became friends. One day Champlain told Howard that his brother had been killed while mining in Mariposa County, and said he did not know who had committed the deed. Needless to state, Bill Howard did not educate him.[28]

Howard was very popular in the Southern Mines, and in 1856 he won election to the state legislature. California's capital had been moved from Benicia to Sacramento, and there Howard attended many political and social gatherings. At one ball, he met sixteen-year-old Belle Horton, the stunningly attractive daughter of a prominent judge. She was much taken with the handsome and adventurous thirty-year-old miner, horseman, and ranger. Because of California's huge gender imbalance, it was still common for older men to wed teenage girls. Despite their fourteen-year age difference, the couple married in 1857. They had seven children who lived to adulthood, and during the ensuing years, Howard supported his family by raising horses and cattle and working as a deputy sheriff. He even served as district attorney of Mariposa County in 1876.

One day in the spring of 1882, several of Howard's horses wandered away and began feeding in the hayfield of a neighbor, William "Pink" Dodson. The latter became enraged and

Bill Howard and his bride, Belle Horton, on their wedding day in 1857.
John Boessenecker collection

shot the animals, which marked the beginning of bad blood between the two men. Perhaps to avoid Dodson, Howard took his family to Yosemite Valley, where he had built a summer cabin. Although Yosemite could only be reached by horseback or stagecoach, it was already a popular tourist destination. On July 22, 1882, Howard and his twelve-year-old daughter, Dela, were on their way home from Yosemite. Dela enjoyed riding as much as her father, and each of them was mounted on a fine horse. They passed through Mariposa that evening and continued another four miles down the wagon road. Suddenly Howard, who was armed with a Colt Navy revolver, spotted Pink Dodson riding toward them. Dodson saw Howard at the same time. Ignoring the fact that a young girl was riding next to his enemy, he jerked out his six-gun and fired twice. Both shots went wild, and Dodson did not have a chance to shoot again. Bill Howard raised his Colt and squeezed the trigger. The .36-caliber ball ripped into Dodson's face just above his mouth, tearing out several teeth and part of his jawbone, and knocked him out of the saddle.

Howard calmed his terrified daughter, then dismounted and ran forward to check on Dodson, who was sprawled on the road. He bandaged Dodson's mouth and helped him back on his horse, and the three rode back to Mariposa. Howard delivered Dodson to a doctor and then turned himself in to the sheriff. Despite the fact that Howard and his daughter both reported that he had acted in self-defense, he was charged with assault with intent to commit murder. Not surprisingly, when his trial came up three months later, the jury found him not guilty. This was Howard's last gunfight, and the criminal prosecution did not dissuade the sheriff of Mariposa County from appointing him his undersheriff. He held the post from 1884 to 1887, and despite the fact that he was fifty-eight—an elderly man in that era—he was an active and successful officer.[29]

Over the years, Bill Howard enjoyed retelling the story of the manhunt for Joaquin Murrieta. Beginning in 1883, he gave his account of the rangers to numerous newspapers. A popular biography was even written about Howard and published many years later, after his death. Because his main role had been to provide the rangers with food, provisions, horses, and lodging at his ranch, much of Howard's knowledge of Harry Love's manhunt came from the other men in the company. In Howard's earliest interviews, he never claimed to have been present at the climactic gun battle at Cantua Creek. Instead, he merely recounted what the other rangers told him had happened, and for the most part, he got his facts right. But by 1907 he began telling colorful yarns of the final manhunt, describing in detail how he was present at the showdown with the gang and the killing of Joaquin Murrieta and Three Fingered Jack. Howard even claimed that just before the gun battle erupted, he had a premonition of danger, and said to Harry Love, "I feel that something unusually exciting is going to happen."[30]

Howard's story, repeated and reprinted over the years, was widely believed. But the fact is that he was nowhere near Cantua Creek on that fateful day of July 25, 1853. At the very time Harry Love and his men were shooting it out with Joaquin's band, Howard was on his way to a racetrack near Stockton with his prize horse, Winfield Scott, named after the famed US Army general. As Stockton's *San Joaquin Republican* reported the following day, "The great race of the season was run on the 25th, on the new track near this city, between Mr. Howard's Winfield Scott and Mr. Ireland's P. P. [pole position] horse. Both animals were in tip-top condition. They started at five o'clock, Scott winning easily. Some $3,000 changed hands." Howard, in old age, simply could not resist putting himself at the forefront of the Cantua Creek gunfight.[31]

As the years rolled by, Howard remained active and mentally alert. He lived until 1924, his life having encompassed everything from the Mexican War to World War I, from the Pony Express to long-distance telephones, and from covered wagons to airplanes. Bill Howard died at the home of one of his daughters in Portland, Oregon, at the age of ninety-six. He was the last of the California Rangers.

CHAPTER 19

THE WIDOW OF JOAQUIN

Joaquin's paramour, Maria Ana Andrada, was popularly known as Mariana Murrieta. In 1852 Los Angeles, she had famously used the alias Ana Benites, and in the mining country was sometimes called Joaquina or Mariana Joaquina. Mariana was a colorful, articulate, and unscrupulous woman. A journalist who interviewed her in 1874 wrote, "All her life she has been associated with cattle thieves, highway robbers, and murderers." She was extremely proud of her status as Murrieta's former lover and became well-known in the Latino community as the widow of Joaquin. At the same time, she was emotionally unstable and bore the nickname Mariana la Loca, or Crazy Mariana. To those she met, Mariana did not hesitate to describe how Murrieta gave her the long scar across her face. For more than a decade after Joaquin's death, she managed to stay out of the limelight. Mariana seems to have spent most of that time in the San Joaquin Valley and the Coast Range. There, as one Anglo settler recorded in his diary, "She has followed prostitution as a trade." Mariana lived off and on with various vaqueros and shepherds, and she was never far from the haunts of fugitives and desperadoes.[1]

In 1867 Mariana visited the New Idria quicksilver mine. Situated high in the Coast Range, a hundred miles southeast of San Jose, it was well-known as a hideout for outlaws. Several months later, a correspondent in New Idria sent a long letter to the San Francisco *Alta California*, detailing the activities at the mine. As an afterthought, he added that "last year, Joaquin's widow, with the big scar he gashed upon her face in a fit of jealousy, spent some months here." Mariana did not publicly surface again until the manhunt began for Tiburcio Vasquez, a Californio who had taken Joaquin Murrieta's place as the state's most notorious bandido. In November 1873, a large Fresno County sheriff's posse tracked Vasquez and his men from the site of a robbery into the Coast Range. In a canyon west of the modern-day town of Coalinga, they found Mariana living in a small adobe house with a Californio named Fernando Linares. She and Linares welcomed the ten travel-worn manhunters and allowed them to spend the night at their adobe. One of the posse, however, did not trust either Mariana or Linares. He stayed awake all night, on guard, while the rest slept soundly. At daybreak Mariana cooked them a breakfast of *tasajo*, or beef jerky, tortillas, and hot coffee. Then Linares—contrary to the posseman's fears—mounted his horse and guided the posse safely out of the mountains.[2]

Several weeks later, the California governor appointed Alameda County's famous sheriff, Harry N. Morse, as head of a state-funded posse to track down Tiburcio Vasquez and his gang. Morse chose his friend Tom Cunningham, the equally capable sheriff of San Joaquin County, as his lieutenant. Because Mariana was well known in the San Joaquin Valley as a consort of outlaws, Sheriff Morse decided to interrogate her. In March 1874, he and his posse, after making an exhausting horseback ride, found Mariana living with a sheepherder in his tent near Poso Chane. This spot, meaning the Well of the Chane Indians, was a notorious hideout for thieves and fugitives, located in the San Joaquin Valley about thirty miles due south of Cantua Creek.

The manhunters were intrigued by the notorious Mariana. "One drink of whiskey started her talking volubly in Spanish and a second filled her with animation," wrote a journalist who accompanied the posse. He added that Mariana was happy to tell of her relationship with Murrieta: "Scarcely less than her tongue do her eyes, head, and gracefully shrugged shoulders assist to convey her ideas, while under the exciting influence of her stories, her swinging arms, and her small feet stamping the earth, she gives strong emphasis to her assertions." Mariana claimed that she and Murrieta had a son together, also named Joaquin, who was then living in Mexico. She also admitted to the posse that she knew Tiburcio Vasquez and said that two of his gang, who had been wounded in a bandit raid, had visited her camp a few months previous.[3]

Mariana also needed no encouragement to spin a yarn about Joaquin. "Mariana Murietta says that when Joaquin was killed he was with five of his men," the newspaperman wrote. "They had gone into the Cantua canyon to secure a large amount of gold dust that they had secreted from time to time . . . The whole party were killed or wounded by Harry Love's company. Joaquin was so badly wounded, although able to escape into the hills, that he died in two days. The head taken to San Francisco and still exhibited there as the head of Joaquin, is that of Pedro Venda, one of the gang. It is that of a very dark, swarthy man, and this imposition has doubtless caused the belief that Joaquin is still alive. The hidden treasure has never been found." Of course, the severed head had been identified by scores of people, and was not that of a dark and swarthy man. And Mariana's claim that Joaquin buried gold in Cantua Canyon would soon be widely believed. Sheriff Morse arrested Mariana for harboring fugitives, but any charges against her were soon dropped. It is significant that Morse and Cunningham—two of the most renowned sheriffs of the Old West—acknowledged her as Joaquin's widow. Both lawmen had numerous informants, and they possessed a vast knowledge of California criminals. They were well positioned to know the truth. In the end, their manhunt for Tiburcio Vasquez was a success. Sheriff Morse got a tip that the bandit chieftain was hiding out in an adobe on what is now Melrose Place in West Hollywood. Los Angeles lawmen captured

Maria Ana Andrada, popularly known as Mariana Murrieta, the widow of Joaquin. This photo was taken about 1885. *William B. Secrest collection*

him, and in 1875 Vasquez was convicted of a triple murder and died on the gallows in San Jose.[4]

Within a few years, Mariana settled in an adobe house situated in a grove of cottonwood trees high in the Coast Range, about twenty miles southwest of Coalinga. There she supposedly found religion. A visitor to her home in 1878 said, "For a long time Mariana has been the mistress of a comparatively well-to-do ranchero, who kept her in a style which enabled her to preserve the dignity worthy the relict of so noble a consort, and her house was looked upon by her countrymen of the *caballero del camino* [knight of the road, or highway robber] stripe as a haven of hospitality, security, and peace . . . Mariana still clings to the glorious memories of the past with all the pride of a descendant of Montezuma. How she reconciles her antecedents and habits with her extreme piety I am unable to say, but she certainly has surrounded herself with the greatest profusion of crucifixes and emblems of her faith one will meet with outside of a cloister."[5]

Two years later, a census taker visited Mariana's modest adobe home. He did not find her living with the prosperous ranchero. Instead she had reunited with Fernando Linares, identified as a forty-eight-year-old laborer. She gave her name as Mariana Linares and told the census enumerator that she was his wife. Also living with them were four Mexican men, one of whom was twenty-eight years old. The Anglo census taker recorded his name phonetically as "Raphel Muriata." Although the proper spelling was Rafael Murrieta, it is unknown if he was the son whom Mariana claimed she and Joaquin had conceived. Either way, the fact that a Murrieta family member was living with Mariana supports her connection with Joaquin.[6]

Mariana's longtime craving for money, coupled with her newfound interest in religion, soon created a public furor. Late in 1882, she first heard of Father Magin Catala, a Spanish priest who came to California in 1793 and spent decades at the Mission Santa Clara near San Jose. Until his death in 1830, he worked to Catholicize Native Americans and made numerous trips into the San Joaquin Valley to convert its tribes. He also became well-known for supposed prophecies and miracles. Fifty years later, the Catholic church received requests that Father Magin—pronounced *Mahin*—be considered for canonization as a saint. In December 1882, the archbishop in San Francisco assigned a priest to travel through central California and interview people who had known Padre Magin. The investigation quickly made the long-dead missionary famous again. For Mariana, it also provided an opportunity that she could not pass up.[7]

By this time, Mariana was no longer living with Fernando Linares. She had moved north to an adobe house situated at the base of Las Tres Piedras, or the Three Rocks. This spot, now called Joaquin Rocks, was a 4,100-foot-high ridge, topped by three jagged peaks, located six miles due south of the mouth of Cantua Creek, where Joaquin had been slain. Las Tres Piedras was reached by a rough ten-mile trail from the San Joaquin

Valley into the Coast Range. Today, this remote area is largely uninhabited, but in that era, it was home to a number of cattle raisers and sheepmen. Each of the three massive rocks, about two hundred feet high, was made of sandstone. Today they can easily be seen from Interstate 5, towering over the San Joaquin Valley. Mariana's adobe was a large one, forty by sixty feet, and rested in a sloping meadow in the northeast shadow of Joaquin Rocks. A spring was nearby in the rocky hills, studded with willows and cottonwoods. Mariana, convinced that Murrieta had buried stolen treasure nearby, often hunted around the rocks, hoping to find it.

In late March 1883, a few months after she learned about Father Magin, Mariana made a startling announcement. She declared that while on one of her searches for Murrieta's gold, in a canyon near Joaquin Rocks, she encountered the long-dead Padre Magin. Mariana claimed that she had known him well and had worshiped in his church—a remarkable feat given that she was born the same year Father Magin died. Mariana quickly spread word that the padre had erected an altar made of stone, and she called on devout Catholics to visit the site and see the venerable priest. Soon people began flocking to Cantua Creek and trudging up the long trail to Joaquin Rocks, at the crest of the Coast Range. They were greeted by Mariana and several male companions, one of whom was an elderly Mexican with flowing white locks named Guadalupe Olivas. To all comers she announced that she was the Virgin Saint Mariana. While she prayed loudly and called the congregation together, Olivas, dressed in monk's garb, pretended to communicate with the spirit of Father Magin. Sometimes he would claim that he was Magin. He told the crowd that Padre Magin had transformed the Joaquin Rocks into a holy temple, and that each of the three rocks was a cathedral tower. He said that the world would end in three years, and all of earth except the Cantua Creek region would be destroyed. Olivas declared that only those who came

Joaquin Rocks, which overlooked the camp established by Mariana la Loca in 1883. *Bureau of Land Management*

to the stone temple would be spared. Those congregants who believed in the prophecy would see and hear Father Magin; nonbelievers would not.[8]

The news spread quickly, and within a few weeks, some four hundred Catholics—Latino, French, Portuguese, and Basque—had gathered at the site. They made camp on the flat just below Joaquin Rocks and lived in tents and brush huts. Mariana encouraged them to sell their worldly goods and bring their cattle and sheep to feed the multitude. The beef and other food was cooked and shared equally among the crowd. Many, at Mariana's urging, turned their money and jewelry over to her for safekeeping. All were overcome with religious fervor, and none questioned Mariana or her motives. One of the devotees declared that Father Magin "announces to the faithful that all mankind who do not respond to his invitation to locate in the

Coast Mountains, and obey the commands of God, will be destroyed by fire and flood within three years. He says for them to abandon everything and come there and he will provide for them and take care of them. He has with him tablets of stone containing the laws of God engraved on them. These he brought from the shores of Galilee, they having been engraved by mortal hands." The believer added that a young Mexican woman "saw the Virgin Mary pass from the presence of the holy man, and disappear into the solid rock" and that "a bedridden woman has by his magic touch has been restored to health and youthfulness."[9]

One of Mariana's most devout adherents was Angel Maria Chavoya, a fifty-four-year-old Californio who owned a prosperous cattle ranch on a creek six miles south of Joaquin Rocks. An Anglo settler called him "a half crazy Spaniard." Chavoya and his wife Maria had a large family, and they moved with several of their youngest children into the camp. Another pioneer recalled, "For about three months he killed a beef every day to feed the people at the Rocks, and sold nearly all the rest of the herd to get money for Mariana." Chavoya and his son Abraham, age eighteen, played an active role in the religious ceremonies. While it seems evident that Guadalupe Olivas, by masquerading as Padre Magin, knew that he was engaging in fraud, the Chavoyas were clearly true believers. But they would rue the day that they put their faith in Mariana la Loca.[10]

By mid-May 1883, five hundred people were camped in the shadow of Joaquin Rocks. An Anglo newspaper reporter from Fresno tried to ride up the trail, but he was turned back by armed guards who had been hired by Mariana. The journalist, after disguising himself in Mexican-style clothing and bribing the guards, managed to enter her camp. He found that Mariana had transformed her large house into a chapel. She stood before the crowd outside the adobe and addressed them in Spanish. "Brothers and sisters, I am here to receive you all with my arms open, by the order of Padre Magin and the order of the

Almighty. Sisters and brothers, this world is coming to an end, and I am here to save you all from the blazes of hell."

Men and women gathered around her, crying and praying for salvation. Mariana continued, "Brothers and sisters, all those who have appeared before me this 16th day of May shall see the new and coming world. And you shall have salvation after death, but that will be hundreds of years after you enter the new and coming world. You shall never grow any older, nor can you estimate the great length of time that you will live in the new world."

Mariana pointed to the towering rocks and clusters of scrub brush and declared, "Those rocks that you see there are not rocks, they are the three temples that were lost at Galilee. You can't see the temple, the rock that covers it is your sins, and all those rocks you see comprise the city of Galilee. Those trees and bushes you see are the fruit trees that are to appear in the garden of Eden of the new world."

According to the newspaperman, Mariana became more specific. "She then said that the San Joaquin River and Buena Vista [Tulare] lake would flood this valley and drown all that are in it. She said that the Pope of Rome was hid in the temple with Father Magin. She announced that a child had been born with a feather in its forehead; it was the child that was to burn up the world . . . She then ordered them to prepare their food, after which they were to go at half past four o'clock to hear Padre Magin preach. When the hour arrived the apostles arrived leading a large black stallion. The young maidens of the party were instructed by Mariana to tie silk handkerchiefs in his mane and tail, and a young man was placed on his back. He was then placed in the lead and the girls were placed on each side, they holding onto the handkerchiefs. The apostles then formed two and two behind, sister Mariana and the balance of the crowd in the rear. We went to the temple but could not find Padre Magin. Sister Mariana went to the door—a hole in the side of the rocks—in the center of which stands an oval rock which she represents to be St. Peter, and, having kissed it, the entire procession marched up and followed suit, after which they were marched out to the place where Padre Magin was expected. But he did not appear; he was not there and never had been. It was all a humbug. Early next morning Mariana was out again, crying and praying, and announced that the Almighty had called upon her and she was going to heaven at once. The others begged her not to go, but she said when she was called she had to obey. But when I left she was still there, waiting for her wings to grow so that she could fly to heaven, but I am afraid she will never get there. She is better suited for the Stockton Asylum than for heaven."[11]

Despite the failure of Padre Magin to appear, the faithful, now numbering almost seven hundred, stayed at Joaquin Rocks. Mariana claimed that she could cure the sick, and she regularly put on an elaborate charade. Accompanied by Guadalupe Olivas, Angel Chavoya, and his son Abraham, she would lead hundreds of her followers in a procession around Joaquin Rocks, loudly chanting prayers and invocations. Then, facing the middle rock, she had them all face west, kneel, and pray silently. Mariana, wearing a large cross around her neck, whispered to each of the sick disciples and called out the name of a saint whom she said could heal them. Next she declared that the saints, all of whom happened to be invisible, had suddenly arrived. According to an eyewitness, "Then the sick folks began their performance. Rising up, they embraced, kissed, and carried on an apparent conversation with their invisible visitors. All this time the widow and her two assistants were walking around the sick and the assumed circle of administering ghosts." Finally, as the spectator explained, "They got up and walked away with their friends, professing to be cured. Many persons claim to have been cured of Bakersfield malarial fever and its incidents. It is claimed by believers that men blinded by accident and children by disease have been restored to sight."[12]

Mariana's antics received widespread publicity, and reports were published in numerous California newspapers. Rumors began to spread that her camp had become a hideout for fugitives and thieves. A sheriff's posse, hunting for an escaped killer, visited Joaquin Rocks and found that the stories were false. The news of Mariana and her prophecies soon caught the attention of the Catholic archbishop in San Francisco. He issued a proclamation announcing that "the whole affair is a fraud, an imposition, and a witchcraft." But as a Fresno journalist remarked, "It is doubtful if the venerable Archbishop's letter will have much effect on the followers of Mariana and her prophet, as they are all too deeply impressed."

Another Fresno newspaperman who managed to enter Mariana's camp reported, "All property taken there is immediately turned over to Mariana, who seems to be the chief manager. One man turned over to her $1,600 in gold coin, besides several milk cows, horses, sheep, etc." He concluded by echoing the words of the archbishop, "The whole thing is a preposterous fraud," and called for the arrest of Mariana and her cohorts "for obtaining property under false pretenses." By this time Mariana's disciples were getting disillusioned and began drifting away. In mid-June a newspaper published a cynical, but racist, conclusion: "The excitement at Cantua Canyon is gradually dying out. Mariana's followers are becoming convinced that the whole scheme is a humbug, and are leaving her. It is estimated that she has already cleared several thousand dollars by her success in hoodwinking the ignorant natives and foreigners."[13]

A month later, newspapers announced, "Mariana Murieta, the Cantua canon prophetess, has skipped out for old Mexico with $1,500 belonging to the pilgrims who were duped to her shrine and who had deposited it with her for safe keeping." Though there is no doubt that Mariana had benefitted financially, she certainly did not flee to Mexico. She stayed in her adobe in the shadow of Joaquin Rocks with a handful of hardcore followers, among them Angel Chavoya, his wife Maria, and their younger children. They were all still at Joaquin Rocks two years later when they were joined by the Chavoyas' fifteen-year-old daughter, Elizabeth, her husband, Adolfo Corona, age twenty-five, and their infant daughter. Adolfo Corona became convinced that Mariana was a fraud, and he tried to persuade the Chavoya family to leave her camp. Mariana was furious. On July 1, 1885, she dramatically revealed to Maria Chavoya a new prophecy: within a short time, her son-in-law Corona, her daughter Elizabeth, or the couple's baby would face death. Mariana told Maria that she could pick which of the three should die. Maria Chavoya later admitted that she "told the prophetess that if one of the three had to die within a certain time she would rather let the child go to the angels."[14]

Adolfo Corona ignored the purported prophecy, and he left to attend to business in Fresno. Four days later, on July 5, he rode back to Joaquin Rocks, gathered up his wife, child, and their belongings, and prepared to leave the camp. Before they departed, Mariana declared, "You will come back crying."

Once again Corona paid her no heed, and they started off on horseback toward the San Joaquin Valley. Corona carried the child in his arms as he swayed in the saddle, following the dusty trail out of the Coast Range. They had only gone a mile when the infant suddenly broke into violent spasms. The Coronas wheeled their horses around and rushed back to Joaquin Rocks for help. But their efforts were in vain, for half an hour later, the baby died.

The sudden death of his grandchild brought Angel Chavoya to his senses. He and Adolfo Corona quickly concluded that Mariana had poisoned the infant in order to reestablish her reputation as a prophetess. They sent a horseback messenger who raced sixty miles to Fresno, where he reported the suspicious death. A deputy sheriff, accompanied by a doctor and the county coroner, proceeded to Joaquin Rocks. There an autopsy on the child's body was performed but proved inconclusive, so the doctor removed the stomach so that it could be analyzed more fully in Fresno. The deputy interviewed witnesses, and Corona swore out a warrant for Mariana, charging her with murder. The officer placed Mariana under arrest, and they returned to Fresno, where she was locked in jail.[15]

Mariana's preliminary hearing began on August 4, 1883. A reporter who was present observed, "The prophetess appeared in court dressed in a long drab colored gown, cut in the Mother Hubbard pattern, but belted in with a blue sash. Around her neck she wore a rosary to which was attached a crucifix. She had on a hat covered with a dark blue veil. She is quite stout and about five feet six inches high, and appears to be about fifty years old." The prosecuting attorney informed the judge that he had not yet received a report from the chemist who was analyzing the dead child's stomach. The hearing was continued for a week. Apparently the medical examination failed to reveal any traces of poison, and the judge then ruled that there was insufficient evidence of murder. Mariana was set free, much to the consternation—and even terror—of the Chavoya family.[16]

The widow of Joaquin was ecstatic. Reported a newspaperman, "After her release, in company with one of her apostles, who carried a long staff, she walked down Mariposa Street, smiling and chatting, evidently greatly pleased with the result of her trial. The prosecuting witnesses, when Mariana was discharged, seemed greatly alarmed, and wanted to know what they would do. They seem to be in great dread of the old hag." The dead child's father, Adolfo Corona, was a tough vaquero who, ironically, would later serve a short term in San Quentin prison for grand theft. Unlike the Chavoyas, he had no fear of Mariana. According to an old account, Corona returned to Joaquin Rocks and "dug a grave for her and vowed she would fill it if they ever caught her around their homes again."[17]

A 1900 prison mug photograph of Adolfo Corona. In 1885 he brought murder charges against Mariana, accusing her of poisoning his infant child.
California State Archives

Mariana wisely stayed away from Joaquin Rocks. For the next few years, she resided quietly in the San Joaquin Valley towns of Hanford and Visalia. A vaquero who knew her in Hanford recalled, "She lived in a rented house in the middle of town in an alley. It was a little house. They did not number the houses or the streets then." He said that Mariana invited him in for a drink and that he stayed with her for two months. She surfaced again in 1890 when the corpse of a huge man—supposedly petrified—was dug up in Cantua Canyon. The purported body, six and a half feet long and weighing four hundred pounds, was taken on display through many California towns. When Mariana heard of the discovery, she claimed that Joaquin had told her that he "once killed a very large Spaniard and buried his body in Cantua Canyon." She later viewed the supposed corpse and announced that it was the same man whom Murrieta had killed. But how she could identify someone she had never seen before, Mariana did not bother to say.[18]

By this time she had taken up with yet another lover. Antonio Bergara was a Mexican laborer twenty years her junior. He worked as a wood chopper on a ranch east of Visalia, and the couple lived there together in a small cabin. She asserted that they were married and called herself Mariana Bergara. In keeping with her claims that she had known Padre Magin personally before his death in 1830, Mariana added eighteen years to her age. On the evening of July 25, 1892, she and Bergara hosted a large celebration for Mariana's eightieth birthday, though in fact she was sixty-two. The guests were a diverse group: Latino, Anglo, and African American. The fiesta was accompanied by heavy drinking, and many of the guests stayed up all night in the crowded cabin, imbibing freely.

Antonio Bergara got roaring drunk, as did another ranch worker, Matias Neblina. Just before daybreak, Bergara and Neblina got into a petty quarrel over a watermelon. Then Neblina, with a whiskey glass in hand, stepped outside and rested his drunken frame against a wagon. Moments later Bergara, clutching a single-shot rifle, followed him out the door. Bergara cursed Neblina loudly and ordered him to leave the ranch. The latter simply raised his glass as if to toast—or antagonize—his adversary. Bergara stepped to within fifteen feet of Neblina and shouldered his rifle.

"I believe I will shoot you!" he roared. A split second later, Bergara pulled the trigger, and the heavy slug tore into Neblina's chest. Neblina dropped to the ground, and Bergara quickly reloaded his rifle. Before he could fire again, one of the crowd yanked the weapon from his grasp and smashed it over a tree stump, so hard that it bent the barrel. Several others then helped Neblina to his feet. Though desperately wounded, he pulled a knife from his pocket and staggered toward Bergara. The latter thrust his face and neck forward and declared, "Cut away!"

Neblina slashed Bergara across his cheek, but he was too weak to inflict more than a deep cut. He then collapsed to the ground in a pool of blood. Neblina lived until eleven that morning,

Antonio Bergara, the lover of Mariana. In 1892 he was sent to Folsom prison for killing a man at Mariana's birthday celebration.
California State Archives

when he succumbed to his wound. The county sheriff soon arrived at the ranch and arrested Bergara for murder. The next day he was taken from his cell in the Tulare County jail in Visalia to appear at the coroner's inquest. A reporter wrote that Bergara "was placed on the stand and testified in his own behalf. He had a frightened look and seemed to realize the gravity of his terrible crime. His face was bandaged, hiding from view the terrible cut on his cheek inflicted by Neblina after being shot." Bergara swore that before the shooting, he had left the cabin to avoid Neblina, who had threatened to kill him. But other witnesses testified that Neblina had made no such threat. Bergara's trial came up four months later. The jury convicted him of manslaughter, and he received a ten-year jolt in Folsom state prison. Mariana apparently attended court, for a newspaperman at the trial remarked, "Bergara's wife claims to be the former wife of Joaquin Murieta, the noted desperado years ago."[19]

Once again Mariana was on her own, at least for a time. The farming town of Visalia was then a hotbed for train robbers. America experienced an epidemic of train robbery in the

1890s, and Tulare County produced more railroad bandits than any community in the country. Those outlaws included the notorious Dalton brothers, as well as Chris Evans and his partner John Sontag, and the Tulare Twins, Ben and Dudley Johnson. One morning in January 1894, Mariana showed up at the county jail in Visalia and told the sheriff's officers that she had acquired inside information about a planned train robbery. She claimed that the bandits intended to bring her with them when they stopped the train. The lawmen did not take her seriously. As a local journalist reported, "Her vagaries are well known, however, and she was advised to return to her home." Not surprisingly, the alleged train holdup did not take place.[20]

Mariana, still something of a celebrity, was soon engaged as a featured attraction at California's Midwinter Fair of 1894, with a salary of $30 a month. This was a huge exhibition, intended to highlight the state's prospects and to draw visitors from throughout the country. It was set in San Francisco's Golden Gate Park, and some of the exhibits, such as the Japanese Tea Garden, exist to this day. The most popular attraction was a reenactment of an 1849 mining camp, and Mariana was to "participate in the reproduction of early California scenes." Whether she actually went through with the plan is unclear, for the San Francisco newspapers—which devoted extensive coverage to the fair—made no mention of her involvement.[21]

Mariana, with her lover Bergara in prison, moved in with Gabriel Saures, a wood chopper who lived in a cabin on the Kings River, eight miles northeast of Hanford. Saures was about the same age as Mariana and hailed from Brazil. He claimed that he had served as a Union soldier in a New York City regiment during the Civil War. Saures, despite his advanced years, worked regularly cutting wood along the river. Mariana, still hugely proud of her relationship with Joaquin, hung images of Murrieta and Tiburcio Vasquez on the walls of their cabin. As in her other relationships, she and Saures were not legally married. Saures later said that Mariana suffered from hearing loss, but she still enjoyed socializing and drinking.

On the afternoon of April 12, 1902, Mariana visited a neighbor and shared more than a bottle of wine. At four o'clock, she started home, and walked toward the Santa Fe Railroad crossing south of the town of Laton. Gabriel Saures was working in a patch of woods on the south side of the Kings River and he saw her approaching on foot. At the same time, a southbound Santa Fe train came into sight, and its engineer spotted Mariana stepping toward the tracks a half mile ahead. She was drunk, with a wine bottle clutched in one hand and a rebozo wrapped across her head. The engineer blew his steam whistle to warn her, but she did not hear it and continued walking forward, her head bent down. Oblivious to the onrushing train, Mariana staggered onto the tracks, then stopped between the two rails and looked around in a confused manner. The engineer frantically yanked the whistle, but it was too late. The locomotive slammed into Mariana at full speed, flinging her body forty feet through the air. She died instantly.

As a stunned Gabriel Saures looked on, the engineer brought his train to a grinding halt and backed it up. The crew carried the shattered body aboard and brought it into Hanford, where a coroner's inquest was held the next day. Saures and several of Mariana's friends were there. Apparently based on testimony from Saures, the coroner's jury found that Mariana's maiden name was Ana Andrada, she was about seventy years old, and she had been born in Mexico. The jurors also found that the railroad was not at fault for her death. The town newspaper provided a detailed, front-page account of the fatal accident, and reminded its readers, "She was the wife of Joaquin Murietta, the noted outlaw and bandit, who was killed in a fight at Joaquin Rocks."[22]

Mariana was buried in Hanford's Catholic cemetery. No tombstone marks the spot where she rests, but the story of her dramatic and troubled life is too intriguing to be forgotten in the shadows of the past.

CHAPTER 20

AN OUTLAW'S LEGACY: PROCOPIO MURRIETA

The suburban city of Rancho Cucamonga is nestled near the foothills of the towering San Gabriel Mountains, forty miles east of Los Angeles. Today its sprawling tracts of stucco houses with red tile roofs are home to almost two hundred thousand people. That is a far cry from the remote Rancho Cucamonga of the 1860s, which then consisted of the ranchero's hacienda and a handful of adobe jacales that housed vaqueros, laborers, and their families, all surrounded by lush vineyards and herds of grazing cattle. The rancho's single-story brick hacienda is still standing today, a popular historic site and museum. It was once the spacious home of ranchero John Rains and his young Californio-Anglo wife, Merced. In 1862, at this isolated, pastoral spot, a bloody saga began. It became one of Southern California's oldest murder mysteries, and introduced the nephew of Joaquin Murrieta into the annals of Western outlawry.

His name was Tomas Procopio Murrieta, born out of wedlock in the village of Ures in Sonora, Mexico, on April 28, 1843. Procopio's mother was Joaquin's older sister, Vicenta Murrieta, and according to family descendants, his father was Tomas Bustamante. When Procopio was eleven days old, his mother brought him to the pueblo's church to be baptized. Because Tomas and Vicenta were unmarried, he did not accompany her. Instead, two of Vicenta's relatives, Andres Murrieta and Luz Murrieta, went along. The priest duly recorded the infant's baptismal name and the fact that he was Vicenta's natural son, with no identified father. As part of the ceremony, Andres and Luz Murrieta promised to act as the child's godparents. If any boy ever needed the guiding hand of godparents, it was Procopio Murrieta.[1]

Tomas Bustamante was reportedly slain in an Indian attack in Mexico, and Vicenta then journeyed to California with her son during the gold rush. She was probably the same sister of Joaquin who lived in Marysville in 1853. Vicenta supposedly later settled in an adobe in Niles Canyon, near Mission San Jose in modern-day Fremont. Her son grew into a lanky, powerful young man, and he became an expert rider and vaquero. As Sheriff Harry Morse said, "Procopio was six feet tall, slim, a handsome face, brown-gray eyes, and, in general appearance, looked more like an American than a Mexican." By all accounts, Procopio took tremendous pride in his notorious uncle, and longed to follow in his footsteps. Yet, though his legal name was Procopio Murrieta, he often called himself Procopio Bustamante.[2]

By 1861 the eighteen-year-old Procopio had drifted south to Los Angeles County, where he began riding with a gang of horse thieves. The youth was no stranger to violence. At some point, he was wounded three times in an encounter with Indian warriors. He bore the scar of an arrow wound on his left arm and two more on his left breast. In January 1862, Procopio stole two mules from a Latino rancher in Cahuenga Pass, in what is now the Hollywood Hills. The ranchero tracked down the young horse thief and captured him with the mules and two other stolen horses. He also seized Antonio Rodriguez, a twenty-five-year-old Californio from Santa Barbara, who was with Procopio, and then brought the pair to jail in Los Angeles. Procopio's lawyer later said, "Upon the preliminary examination of these parties it was evident that the horses were stolen by Procopio, and the only suspicion of guilt attaching to Rodriguez was the circum-

Procopio Murrieta, also known as Procopio Bustamante. The nephew of Joaquin appears in an arrest photo taken in 1872.
John Boessenecker collection

stance of being in company with Procopio at the time the horses were found in his possession. I succeeded in getting Procopio released without a trial for the purpose of using his testimony in matters of graver importance." Procopio had apparently offered to testify against other members of the gang. Instead he disappeared, and Antonio Rodriguez was convicted of grand larceny and sentenced to ten years in San Quentin. A year later, due to the questions about his guilt, the governor pardoned Rodriguez. Procopio's narrow escape from the law only encouraged him to continue his newfound career of outlawry.[3]

One of Southern California's prominent rancheros was John Rains. The handsome, dark-bearded Rains was a Mexican War veteran who had married into wealth and acquired the vast Rancho Cucamonga, but he lost much of his money due to overspending and poor business acumen. On the morning of November 17, 1862, Rains bid goodbye to his twenty-three-year-old pregnant wife Merced and their four small children. He then stepped out of the rancho's brick hacienda, climbed into his expensive two-horse wagon, and started out alone on a business trip to Los Angeles. Rains had promised Merced that he would return in two days. At the appointed time, his horses trotted up to the hacienda, sans harness and wagon. At first Merced was not concerned, for her husband made frequent visits to Los Angeles. She recognized that he was a tough frontiersman who could return home afoot, with or without his wagon and team. But by the next day, he still had not arrived, and Merced grew frantic.

Her sister's husband, a well-known rancher named Bob Carlisle, began a long, exhaustive search. Rains's vaqueros and his many friends and neighbors, as well as Los Angeles County Sheriff Tomas Sanchez, joined the hunt. After scouring the countryside for three days, they finally discovered his wagon hidden in a deep ravine near the main road, midway between Rancho Cucamonga and Los Angeles. Two miles away, they found the harness hanging from the branch of a tree. Further searching revealed his overcoat and bloodstained hat. The searchers kept up the hunt, and five days later, they discovered John Rains's bullet-riddled body hidden in a clump of cactus four hundred yards from the road. He had been shot twice in the back, once in the left breast, and once in the right side. His mangled right arm had been torn from its socket, his clothes ripped to shreds, and one of his boots was missing. It was evident that he had been lassoed and dragged across the rough ground and into the brush.

News of the murder created a sensation in Southern California, rivaling that of the killings of General Joshua Bean in 1852 and Sheriff James Barton's posse in 1857. The *Los Angeles Star* called for calm and for citizens to refrain from vigilantism: "Let us have no uprising of a mob to execute punishment." Bob Carlisle, as brother-in-law of Rains, quickly offered a $250 reward for the killers and began an investigation. Suspicion soon rested on Jose Ramon Carrillo—the same man who had led the Californio militia that captured Thomas Cowie and George Fowler near Sonoma in the Mexican War. Many Anglos believed that Carrillo was responsible for their murders, when in fact Cowie and Fowler had been tortured and killed by Three Fingered Jack and Blas Angelino. Carrillo was the son of a distinguished Californio family. After the war, he settled in Southern California, married, and acquired a large rancho.

Despite his prominence in social and business circles, Carrillo was considered a desperado by some Anglos. As one said, "He was a rough and reckless fellow, often in bad company, but not regarded as a bad man by those who knew him best." Others claimed that Carrillo led a bandit gang; a Los Angeles journalist called him "the leader of this band of cutthroats." However, Romualdo Pacheco, a noted Californio who later served as governor of California, declared, "He was not a desperado . . . and possessed too high a sense of honor and self respect ever to have been associated with outlaws." Jose Ramon Carrillo and John Rains had been associated in a cattle raising operation, with Carrillo managing Rains's large herds. A few months before the murder, the pair had quarreled. According to Judge Ben Hayes, who investigated the Rains homicide, Rains and Carrillo "had high words some time ago, on the rancho, when it is said Rains insultingly discharged him from his employ." Soon after the killing, rumors spread that Carrillo had been involved. On hearing the reports, Carrillo immediately went into Los Angeles and appeared in the courtroom of Judge Hayes. He demanded a hearing, and because there was no evidence against him, Hayes ordered his release.[4]

By that time, Los Angeles peace officers had developed a vital clue. In that era, often a lawman's best source of information was the madam of a brothel. Thieves, after a raid, would get drunk, gamble, visit bordellos, and talk too much. Brothel keepers often acted as informants in exchange for police protection. In Los Angeles, an Indian woman known as Samantha ran a bagnio that was frequented by various desperadoes and, ironically enough, by John Rains himself. A few weeks after the

John Rains, murdered by Procopio Murrieta and four other desperadoes in 1862.
John Boessenecker collection

murder, Samantha told law officers that three of the Rains killers were Procopio Bustamante, a local desperado named Manuel Cerradel, and another known only as Juanito. Based on Samantha's information, the city marshal of Los Angeles tried to capture Manuel Cerradel, but he violently resisted arrest and managed to escape.

Procopio vanished, but a few months after the Rains murder, in early February 1863, the Los Angeles city marshal managed to recapture Cerradel and lodge him in the county jail. There he soon contracted smallpox, a contagious disease that was then often fatal. Cerradel, believing that he was going to die, made a full confession. He confirmed Samantha's information that he, with Procopio, Juanito, and two other desperadoes, Luis Sanchez and Eugenio Villa, were the killers. He said that Jose Ramon Carrillo had paid them $500 to do the deed. Cerradel admitted that on the day of the murder, they had ridden to the Rancho Cucamonga and surreptitiously watched the hacienda until they saw Rains leave in his wagon. They followed him down the road until one of the desperadoes trotted forward and asked Rains where he was going.

"To town," Rains said.

"I think not, we have got you now," the outlaw retorted.

Rains instantly whipped out a single-shot derringer and fired, slightly wounding the desperado. As Rains leaped down from his wagon, the other pistoleros galloped up, six-guns in hand. They fired a volley at Rains, riddling him with pistol balls. The ranchero was still alive and struggling, so Procopio and the others finished him off with their knives. They looped a lasso around him and dragged his body off the road. From Rains's corpse, the outlaws took his derringer, his watch, and $180 in cash. Then, after hiding the wagon and the corpse, the outlaws rode to Los Angeles.[5]

Based on Cerradel's confession, an arrest warrant was issued for Jose Ramon Carrillo, and a huge manhunt for Procopio and the other desperadoes swung into action. One posse, relying on information from Cerradel, captured Luis Sanchez in the San Gabriel Mountains. A week later, manhunters arrested Eugenio Villa in San Francisquito Canyon, north of Los Angeles. Both were held in the county jail. Newspapers then reported that Carrillo had fled to Mexico, but two months later, in April 1863, he rode into Los Angeles and surrendered. Under the law, then and now, uncorroborated statements of one codefendant cannot be used to convict a partner in crime. Because Manuel Cerradel was the sole witness against Carrillo, Judge Hayes once again set him free. A Los Angeles newspaper commented, "The whole proceedings may have been perfectly legal and correct, but we do think the discharge a rather hasty one."[6]

Carrillo then wrote a letter to his brother, explaining that he also had appeared before the Los Angeles vigilance committee. He declared that he "removed the false impressions the villains and cowards had circulated against me," and insisted the allegations against him had all been engineered by Bob Carlisle, the brother-in-law of Rains. Carrillo claimed that Carlisle wanted him out of the way so that he could take over the Rainses' rancho. He included an ominous warning: "Now I will tell you, that if by bad luck I should happen to disappear mysteriously, Bob Carlisle will know, and be the cause of my disappearance, and he is the one whom you should prosecute." Finally Carrillo closed his letter by saying that he was helping the widow, Merced Rains, who had rehired him as a ranch foreman: "I am resolved to protect her, if it costs me my life. It is for her interest that I am taking care of the property."[7]

Lawmen could not find Procopio. Meanwhile Manuel Cerradel, Luis Sanchez, and Eugenio Villa languished in jail for most of the year, when the murder charges against them were dropped for lack of evidence. Cerradel recovered from smallpox and was tried for attacking the city marshal when he had first tried to arrest him. A jury found Cerradel guilty of attempted murder, and he received a ten-year term in San Quentin prison. On December 9, 1863, Sheriff Tomas Sanchez took Cerradel and several other prisoners to the San Pedro harbor. While they were boarding the steamer, a band of men—vigilantes and friends of John Rains—rushed forward and overpowered the sheriff. Then they looped a rope around Cerradel's neck and swung him from the yardarm. After letting him hang for twenty minutes, they cut him down, tied heavy rocks to his feet, and tossed his body overboard. The same violent fate awaited Jose Ramon Carrillo. Less than six months later, on May 21, 1864, he was riding along the road through Rancho Cucamonga. An assassin, concealed in a grove of trees, fired a single rifle shot. The slug slammed into his chest and tore him out of the saddle. Carrillo died several hours later. Though his killer was never identified, he was probably one of Rains's many friends.[8]

The mystery of who killed John Rains has confounded everyone from the authorities in frontier Los Angeles to modern-day journalists and historians. Many later writers did not recognize the name Procopio Bustamante and did not know who he was. As a result, a number of suspects have been suggested, most notably Bob Carlisle, who reportedly lusted after the Rancho Cucamonga, and even Merced Rains, who supposedly wanted her husband out of the way because she lusted after Jose Ramon Carrillo. But no credible evidence supports such theories. The fact is that whether it was a murder for hire or a simple highway robbery, there can be little doubt that Procopio and his compadres were guilty. The reason is that Manuel Cerradel's confession, like that of Reyes Feliz in 1852, was inherently reliable. Cerradel, by squealing on the killers, placed his life in double jeopardy—first from the ever-aggressive Los Angeles vigilantes, and even worse, from the desperadoes themselves. The idea that Cerradel would admit his own guilt, falsely accuse the nephew of Joaquin Murrieta, and thereby sign his own death warrant is more than implausible.

By the time of the killings of Manuel Cerradel and Jose Ramon Carrillo, Procopio was fast following in his uncle's bloody footsteps. After murdering John Rains, he and his compadre Juanito rode north to the San Joaquin Valley. The pair split up, and Juanito tried to steal a horse from a Native American at Firebaugh's Ferry on the San Joaquin River. The Indian resisted, so Juanito fired at him but missed. That was a fatal mistake. The Indian shot back, putting three bullets into Juanito, and then slashed him to death with his knife. Meanwhile Procopio continued on to the Livermore Valley, where he joined up with two notorious bandidos, Narciso Bojorques and Chano Ortega.

On January 29, 1863, the trio nudged their horses east into Corral Hollow, a long, winding canyon that cuts through the Coast Range. Their target was the cattle ranch of Aaron Golding, a Cherokee Indian, situated near the spot where Corral Hollow meets the San Joaquin Valley, thirty miles southwest of Stockton. It was evening when Procopio and his partners burst into the ranch house. Inside they found Golding, his Mexican wife, their thirteen-year-old adopted son, and their vaquero. They pistol-whipped the three males, crushing their skulls. Then the bandidos bound Mrs. Golding with rope, looted the cabin, and set it on fire. Neighbors later found the cabin burned to the ground with the four charred bodies in the ruins. Narciso Bojorques and Chano Ortega were arrested on suspicion, but both were released for lack of evidence because the witnesses were all dead.[9]

Following the butchery of the Golding family, Procopio loitered about the nearby Livermore Valley for several months. Several small settlements had sprung up in the valley, after the raids of Claudio Feliz a decade earlier. Procopio frequented the monte parlors, fandango halls, and bordellos of the villages of Livermore, Little Mexico, and Alisal (now Pleasanton). In early July 1863, he and Narciso Bojorques were suspected of stealing a herd of cattle in the Livermore Valley and driving them west across the coastal hills to village of Alvarado, on the east side of San Francisco Bay and now part of Union City. Constable Orlo B. Wood of Alameda County obtained an arrest warrant and rode into Alvarado. From an Alvarado butcher, he learned that Procopio had made arrangements to sell the cattle. He was expected to arrive at the butcher's shop that afternoon, July 9, to receive his payment.

Constable Wood concealed himself in the rear of the shop and waited for the outlaw to arrive. Soon Procopio's lanky form appeared in the doorway. He glanced cautiously up and down the street, then lit a cigarette and took a few puffs. He stepped inside, and the butcher welcomed him and invited him to the back room where he kept his cash. As Procopio did so, Wood stepped out of hiding and barked, "Hold up your hands!"

Procopio, only twenty, had the same coolness as Joaquin Murrieta. He calmly raised his hands and said, "I surrender. I am unarmed."

Constable Wood foolishly lowered his six-gun and holstered

it. At that, Procopio whipped out his own pistol and began retreating toward the door. Wood, with more courage than sense, charged at the desperado, hoping to seize his weapon. Procopio pulled the trigger, and his bullet slammed into the constable's arm. He then burst out the door and fled on foot up the street toward a drawbridge that spanned Alameda Creek, on the outskirts of Alvarado. The bridge, no longer standing, was located on what is now Union City Boulevard, a few hundred yards north of Smith Street. Several citizens heard the gunfire and ran after him, but he held them off by flourishing his six-shooter. As Procopio reached the bridge, he saw that it was blocked by more townsfolk who had been alerted by the gunshot, and that some were armed with pistols and shotguns. He veered away from the bridge and raced down into the muddy creek bed. Clenching his six-gun in his teeth, the bandido plunged into the water and swam to the opposite bank. Several townsmen opened fire, but Procopio dodged the bullets, climbed out of the creek, and ran west toward the salt marshes that bordered San Francisco Bay.

By this time, even more armed citizens had joined the pursuit. They managed to surround the desperado, and a shootout erupted. Procopio traded gunfire with the manhunters until he ran out of bullets. Finally he surrendered, and the possemen loaded him into a buggy and drove him into Alvarado. There a crowd of citizens surrounded the buggy, yelling, "Lynch him! Lynch him!"

One man looped a rope around Procopio's neck and tried to hoist him up, but a bystander shoved his arm inside the noose to prevent a lynching. Several others then dragged the prisoner to safety inside a store and pleaded for calm. Finally the mob dispersed, and Procopio was lodged in the county jail. He was soon joined behind bars by Narciso Bojorques and a boy whom they had hired to help drive the herd of stolen cattle. In court, Procopio assumed full responsibility and claimed that the other two did not know that the herd was stolen. His accomplices were released, but Procopio was convicted of grand larceny and sentenced to nine years in San Quentin. Probably because he had been accused of murdering John Rains, he insisted that his name was Tomas Redondo, and under that alias, he was booked into prison. He was never charged with killing Rains, because the sole eyewitness, Manuel Cerradel, was dead. Narciso Bojorques, unfazed by his narrow escape, continued down the outlaw trail. He was later wounded in a gunfight with Sheriff Harry Morse and managed to escape. Bojorques died in a shootout with a fellow desperado in 1867.[10]

Procopio's new home held about six hundred convicts, watched over by just twenty-three guards, known as freemen. San Quentin now had an outer wall, topped with gun towers, and the prisoners were crammed into three long cellblocks. Many of them worked in the brickyard, located just outside the wall, while others labored in workshops inside the prison. Their food was meager, consisting of bread, beans, and a little meat. Convicts who violated prison rules were subject to flogging with a rawhide whip. Procopio, however, served out his time in San Quentin quietly. Because of his bloody reputation, Anglo convicts nicknamed him "Red Dick." On one occasion, Harry Morse, then the newly elected sheriff of Alameda County, visited the notorious outlaw in his cellblock. Morse's visit was, as he later said, "for the purpose of studying his features for future identification."[11]

Procopio made a number of friends in the prison, among them the notorious bandit leader Tiburcio Vasquez. Another was Juan Soto, a ferocious, cross-eyed desperado who later became known as "the human wildcat." Procopio received credits for good behavior, and he was released in March 1871. He promptly returned to his old haunts in the Livermore Valley and spent the next month celebrating his freedom in the bordellos and fandango halls. Then, needing cash, Procopio stole a cow and sold it to Juan Camargo, a local *tapadera*, or fence. The cow's owner tracked it to Camargo's adobe and had him

Procopio Murrieta as he looked in 1883.
John Boessenecker collection

arrested. Because there was no jail in the Livermore Valley, two deputy sheriffs guarded the ironed Camargo in a hotel in Pleasanton. That night, under the cover of blackness, a mob of fifty vigilantes entered the hotel, overpowered the two deputies, and dragged the prisoner to a bridge. They hoisted Camargo up and choked him, demanding a confession. After he gasped that Procopio had stolen the cow, the vigilantes let him go.[12]

Procopio wasted no time in fleeing the Livermore Valley. He rode south to San Juan Bautista, where he met Tiburcio Vasquez, who, with Juan Soto, had also been released from San Quentin. On May 5, 1871, Procopio, accompanied by Vasquez and another bandido, held up and robbed a stagecoach south of San Juan Bautista. Before riding off, they sarcastically told the stage driver to give their regards to the Wells Fargo agent in San Juan. Then they headed to the Saucelito Valley, situated high in the Coast Range twelve miles south of Pacheco Pass. In that remote valley, they hid out with Juan Soto and other desperadoes in several adobes owned by Mexican and Californio herders. But

Procopio and Soto soon got into a bitter quarrel, and on May 9, just four days after the stage holdup, Soto challenged Procopio to fight. Tiburcio Vasquez, who later had his own falling out with Procopio, recalled, "I was there. Soto made Procopio go down into his boots. If Procopio had not left like a coward Soto would have killed him."[13]

Vasquez and Procopio then rode out of the Saucelito Valley together, leaving Juan Soto and several other desperadoes at the bandit camp. It was the luckiest decision of their lives. A day earlier, Sheriff Harry Morse had learned that Soto, who was wanted for murder, was hiding out in the Saucelito Valley. Morse helped raise a large posse and wasted no time in riding to the outlaws' camp. There, on May 10, Sheriff Morse tried to arrest Soto in an adobe house, and the bandido opened fire. The two exchanged pistol shots at close quarters. Then Soto fled toward his horse picketed in the distance. Sheriff Morse grabbed his Winchester carbine and, at a range of 150 yards, put a bullet into the killer's shoulder. The enraged bandit wheeled around and raced headlong at Morse with a five-shooter in each hand. At a range of more than one hundred yards, Morse squeezed the trigger again. The heavy .44-caliber slug struck Juan Soto just above the eyes, tearing off the top of his head. The dramatic encounter was featured in newspapers nationwide and became known as one of the West's most famous outlaw-lawman gun duels.[14]

Procopio and Vasquez returned to San Juan Bautista. Due to his status as the nephew of Joaquin Murrieta, Procopio was well-known in the Latino community, feared by some and admired by others. Due to his good looks and tall, powerful frame, he had no trouble attracting the little pueblo's senoritas. Soon an ex-convict who had known both Procopio and Vasquez in San Quentin joined them in their hidden camp. As he recalled years later, "Procopio was six feet tall and an exceptionally handsome man. His Castilian birth, too, set him above Vasquez and he was regarded with favor by the women." The two bandidos had a falling out, as the ex-convict explained: "Procopio and Vasquez drew pistols over a woman, and though neither of them was seriously injured, the affray led to the disruption of the camp. I was amazed at the fairness in the division of goods that followed. If there was any honor among these thieves it was the first display I had witnessed, but the loot was evenly apportioned among them, the band of stolen horses exactly distributed, and every member of the band drove off with a goodly number . . . Procopio added the woman of the dispute to his loot."[15]

Procopio disappeared for a few months. Then in September 1871, newspapers trumpeted his death in a wild gun battle near Santa Cruz. In fact, the slain outlaw turned out to be another man, a member of the Tiburcio Vasquez gang. Soon after, Procopio was spotted in the San Fernando Valley, north of Los Angeles. One newspaper even reported, "He is said to have a wife near San Fernando." If true, Procopio did not remain with her long, for by the winter, he was in San Francisco, enjoying the company of prostitutes. He frequented the bordellos of Morton Street, a two-block-long alley that ran between Union Square and Kearny Street. Today, Morton Street is, ironically, renamed Maiden Lane, a center of fashionable galleries and upscale shops. But then it was one of the most notorious streets in San Francisco.[16]

On February 9, 1872, San Francisco police got a tip, likely from a prostitute or madam, that Procopio had been regularly visiting a Morton Street bagnio. They immediately sent a wire to Sheriff Harry Morse, across the bay in Alameda County. Morse had a warrant for Procopio, charging him with stealing the cow that he had sold to Juan Camargo almost a year before. He and a deputy boarded a ferry. That night, with two police detectives, they set up surveillance of the bordello. They watched the place until the following afternoon, but Procopio failed to appear. Finally Morse learned—probably from the same informant—that the bandido had been inside the brothel the whole time. The officers made a hasty plan. While the deputy and detectives prepared to enter the front door, Morse would guard the rear to stop Procopio from escaping.

As the sheriff walked to the back of the house, he peered into a window and spotted Procopio eating at a table while keeping an eye on the front door. Moments later the three officers stepped inside, but a bevy of prostitutes rushed forward to block them and give Procopio a chance to escape. The outlaw saw the ruckus and jumped to his feet, at the same time reaching for a pistol in his trouser pocket. But it was too late. During the commotion, Morse quietly slipped through the back door and stepped behind him. Just as Procopio drew his revolver, the muscular sheriff seized him by the throat and rammed the muzzle of his cocked six-gun into the bandido's right ear.

"Put up your hands, Procopio," Morse said evenly. "You're my man."

The desperado knew he was dead if he did not comply. In an instant, the other officers had him in handcuffs. A stunned Procopio asked Morse why he had been arrested, and the sheriff responded that the charge was for stealing a cow.

"Only one cow?" he asked incredulously.

"Yes," Morse answered.

"That's not much," was Procopio's retort.[17]

Morse and his deputy took their prisoner across San Francisco Bay and lodged him in the Alameda County jail. News of the capture created a sensation and was printed in newspapers throughout the country. The accounts included the details of his bloody career and his family connection to Joaquin Murrieta. Even the *New York Times* featured a detailed story, headlined "Procopio, the Bandit." These reports caught the eye of Ned Buntline, a famous author of dime novels. His blood-and-thunder stories were hugely popular. Three years earlier, he had written a dime novel about Buffalo Bill Cody, which made the army scout nationally famous and led to the creation of Buffalo

Bill's Wild West show. Buntline quickly cranked out a story, entitled "Red Dick, the Tiger of California," published a few months later in New York City. Though rank fiction, it made Procopio even more notorious.[18]

Meanwhile Procopio was tried and convicted of grand larceny—for theft of the cow—and sentenced to seven years in San Quentin. Once again he behaved himself in prison. Despite his countless faults, cowardice was not one of them. In February 1876, a massive fire broke out in the prison workshop, a huge building located across the prison yard from the cellblocks. The workshop held the prison shoe factory and furniture manufactory, where many inmates were required to work. Procopio was one of several hundred convicts who, instead of using the chaos as cover for an escape, formed a bucket brigade and battled the flames. At the same time, guards sent out emergency telegrams, and San Francisco firemen, police, and militia rushed across the bay to San Quentin. However, by the time they arrived hours later, the prisoners and guards had extinguished the fire. A few months later, the California governor issued commutations of sentences to numerous convicts for "meritorious conduct" during the fire. Among them was Procopio, whose prison term was reduced by one year.[19]

He was released from San Quentin in June 1877 and managed to keep out of the clutches of the law for a few months. Then in October, Procopio and a desperado named Avelino Tesca stole sixty-nine head of cattle from a rancher in the Livermore Valley. They drove the herd thirty miles north to Martinez and sold them to a pair of crooked butchers. After dividing the money, Procopio rode south into the San Joaquin Valley. Tesca foolishly went to San Francisco, where the city's police captured him in a bordello. He was returned to Contra Costa County, convicted of grand larceny, and sentenced to almost four years in San Quentin.[20]

Procopio then raised a band of five outlaws and prepared to

raid the tiny farming settlement of Grangeville in what is now Kings County in the San Joaquin Valley. Some of the gang spent a few days scouting the village, home to less than two hundred people and served by a hotel, saloon, and general store. At nine o'clock on the night of November 12, 1877, Procopio and his men hitched their horses in the brush just outside town. Donning masks, they walked to the general store and burst inside. The bandidos seized the store clerk, tied his hands behind his back, and bent him over the counter, face down. While one of the robbers held a cocked pistol to his head, the others spotted the storekeeper rushing toward a back bedroom. As they raced after him, the merchant reached his bed and pulled a revolver from underneath his pillow. He turned to fire, but one desperado leaped forward and swung his knife, slashing the storekeeper's arm. Procopio and his gang overpowered him, scooped up $250 in coin, and backed out of the store with their pistols drawn. They ran across the street and into the brush, then mounted their horses and galloped away. The townsfolk spread the alarm to nearby villages, and armed posses rode out in pursuit, but the robbers had vanished.[21]

Procopio's notoriety as a bandido and as the nephew of Murrieta prompted a number of other Mexicans and Californios to join his gang. Among them were Antonio Maron, Francisco Encinas, Miguel Elias, Fermin Eldeo, and Vicente Ruiz, all of whom would rue their rash decision. A month later, at dusk on December 16, Procopio and about ten of his band rode into the railroad stop of Caliente, 120 miles south of Grangeville. Caliente, located on the Southern Pacific Railroad in the Tehachapi Mountains south of Bakersfield, boasted a train depot, Wells Fargo office, hotel, and general store. Procopio and his riders first trotted up to a livery stable and stole five valuable saddle horses. Then, while six of them held the animals in the street, the others rushed toward the general store, which also housed the town post office. As they forced their way inside, waving their pistols, the postmaster instantly swept up all the cash and tossed it into a waste basket. The bandidos never saw his furtive movement. They looted the store, taking clothing and provisions, but missed the greenbacks in the trash. Next Procopio and his men crossed the street and entered the train depot and express office. The Wells Fargo agent, however, had spotted them as they robbed the general store. He threw all the money and valuables into the safe, locked it, and ran for the nearby hills.[22]

Procopio and his band gathered up their loot, mounted their horses, and thundered out of Caliente. The gang soon separated. Procopio and several others started north, while Maron, Encinas, Elias, Eldeo, and Ruiz rode south toward Tejon Pass, headed for Los Angeles. A posse from Bakersfield took to the trail of the five robbers who fled south. On the morning of December 19, three days after the raid, they caught up with the bandits in Tejon Pass. All five surrendered without a fight. They were riding the horses stolen in Caliente and had pocket watches and other valuables taken from the general store. The posse brought their prisoners by horseback to Bakersfield, arriving on the evening of December 21. They turned the five—Maron, Encinas, Elias, Eldeo, and Ruiz—over to the sheriff, who lodged them in the Kern County jail. The jail and sheriff's office was located inside a newly constructed courthouse.[23]

News of the arrests spread rapidly. Citizens were outraged, for during the previous two years the county had seen much crime, including horse and cattle theft, stage robberies, and attacks by arsonists who burned several buildings in Bakersfield, including the new schoolhouse. The undersheriff soon heard rumors of a planned lynching. That night he locked all the jail cells, placed the keys in the sheriff's safe, and went home to bed, leaving one jailer in charge. At 1:00 a.m., a mob of a hundred men, who did not bother to wear masks, gathered at the entrance to the courthouse. They ordered the jailer to turn over the keys, but he said that they were in the safe and that only the undersheriff knew its combination. The mob then proceeded to the undersheriff's house, called him outside, and demanded that he go with them and open the safe. The officer adamantly refused, so the vigilantes returned to the courthouse, this time armed with axes, chisels, crowbars, and sledgehammers.

The entrance to the jail was a heavy wooden door inside the sheriff's office. The vigilantes set to work with their axes, and it took them several hours to hack through the door. Then they used chisels to open the cell doors and forced Maron, Encinas, Elias, Eldeo, and Ruiz to accompany them to a courtroom on the second floor. The vigilantes held a summary trial, with twelve of them acting as purported jurors. Though one of the prisoners proclaimed his innocence, the others admitted that all five had taken part in the Caliente raid. Then, despite the fact that California by this time had a well-established criminal justice system and a secure state prison, and that armed robbery was not a capital crime, the vigilante "jurors" voted to hang the five men. They took the prisoners into the yard behind the courthouse. While some of the mob prepared hanging ropes and bound each man's hands behind him, others hung a long wood beam between two trees. Then, without ceremony, the mob hanged three of the men from the beam and the other two from one of the trees.

At daybreak crowds of people flocked to the courthouse yard to view the lynched men. A town photographer set up his bulky camera and took a tintype image of Maron, Encinas, Elias, Eldeo, and Ruiz dangling from ropes. To this day, it remains one of the earliest known photographs of a lynching in the Old West. The editor of the Bakersfield newspaper condemned the hanging but paradoxically declared that the vigilantes should have lynched only one or two of the band's leaders. Latinos in Bakersfield were deeply angered. They believed, with good reason, that the men had been hanged due to their race. In response, the newspaper editor declared, "It would have made no difference had the highwaymen been Americans." That was hardly true,

The 1877 lynching of five members of Procopio's gang in the yard behind the Bakersfield courthouse. *John Boessenecker collection*

for numerous Anglo felons had been convicted by Kern County juries and merely sentenced to prison. But the fact that the dead men were members of Procopio's gang surely contributed to the vigilantes' decision to hang them.[24]

Five days after the lynching, on the night of December 27, 1877, Procopio and three of his men, all masked, rode into the village of Hanford, ninety miles north of Bakersfield. Hanford, now the seat of Kern County, was then a small farm town of about two hundred people. The bandidos dismounted in front of the general store, then forced their way inside and captured the two clerks at gunpoint. The outlaws forced one clerk to open the safe, then tied them both with rope. After stealing $300 in cash and another $300 in pocket watches and clothing, they mounted up and rode off into the night.[25]

Alarmed citizens tried to organize a pursuit, but due to the darkness and heavy tule fog—common then and now in the San Joaquin Valley—they had to wait until morning. At daybreak, five townsmen, including Solomon "Sol" Gladden, started in pursuit. The thirty-year-old Gladden was a harness maker who had served in the Union Army during the Civil War. The posse tracked the bandits southwest for eight miles until they reached the upper end of Tulare Lake. It was getting dark, so they dismounted and prepared to rest for the night. Their camp was not far from the spot where, twenty-four years earlier, Antonio Lopez, while prisoner of the California Rangers, had drowned with his horse in the Tulare Slough. The posse suddenly spotted a man walking toward them in the dusk, carrying a saddle on his back. The stranger was Procopio, and he had evidently lost his horse. One of the manhunters called for him to halt, but he threw down the saddle and broke into a run, disappearing in the tule fog.

At dawn Sol Gladden and his comrades mounted their horses and cut the outlaw's sign. At some point, Procopio managed to borrow or steal a mustang, and the possemen tracked him twenty-five miles west to Poso Chane. This was the notorious outlaw hideout, located six miles east of modern-day Coalinga, which was home, off and on, to Mariana Andrada. It consisted of a batch of adobe jacales and a general store. The manhunters arrived at four in the afternoon on December 28 and learned that their quarry was sound asleep in one of the adobes. The posse slipped into the house, woke him, and announced, "You are our prisoner!"

Sitting up in his bed, Procopio responded, "All right. I suppose you will let me dress myself."

"Of course," one of the manhunters responded. While a poseman stepped outside to find Procopio's horse, the outlaw casually pulled on his boots. Next he donned his jacket, and finally he turned his back to the posse while he put on a long winter overcoat. He then spun around, whipping out a pair of six-guns concealed in the coat pockets.

"Get out of here, you sons of bitches!" Procopio shouted. At the same time, he opened fire with both pistols. The manhunters immediately shot back, but Procopio dove to the floor, and the bullets whizzed above him. Sol Gladden jumped for cover in one corner of the adobe while the other four possemen fled out the door. Procopio leaped into the doorway. Pistols blazing, he sent several shots at the fleeing posse. As he ducked back inside, he realized that Gladden was still in the house. Raising one six-shooter, Procopio fired once. Gladden fell, horribly wounded. Then the bandido grabbed Gladden's revolver, rushed back out the door, and shoved his way past the posse's mounts hitched in front of the adobe. The four manhunters had taken cover nearby and several emptied their six-guns at him. One of the posse fired at Procopio with his Henry rifle but missed and killed one of their horses.

Sol Gladden suddenly staggered out of the adobe. A posseman later said that he looked as if he was smiling, but he must have been grimacing in pain. After taking a few steps, he collapsed into the winter mud, dead. At the same time, Procopio raced toward a creek one hundred yards distant, with the posse in pursuit. The desperado splashed across the stream, then stumbled and dropped one of his pistols. Picking it up, he yelled at the manhunters, "Why don't you shoot, you sons of bitches!"

The posse obliged, and for more than an hour, they took potshots at Procopio whenever they caught sight of him in the brush. The outlaw shot back, and in the exchange of fire, another of the posse's horses was killed. When the manhunters ran out of ammunition, they raced back into Poso Chane and reloaded their guns in the general store. Meanwhile Procopio fled up the creek to the adobe home of a Mexican couple. According to the posse, he covered the man with his pistols "and demanded his horse and saddle or his life." Procopio kept the Mexican covered and ordered his wife to saddle the horse. The outlaw then leaped onto the animal and galloped away. By this time it was dark, and the dispirited posse rode back to Hanford with the dead body of Sol Gladden draped across his saddle.[26]

Procopio rode twenty miles southwest to the adobe home of Mariana Andrada. She was happy to harbor him for several days before he rode across the Coast Range to San Luis Obispo County. By this time, a small posse led by a deputy sheriff from Fresno was on his trail. They tracked the fugitive to a Mexican settlement on the coast and recovered his worn-out horse. Finally they caught up with him at night near San Luis Obispo. Procopio leaped from his mustang, took cover behind a rail fence, and demanded to know why they were following him.

"Hold up your hands!" was the deputy's answer. Procopio leveled his pistol and fired one shot, striking the officer in the hand. A posseman responded with two blasts from his double-barrel shotgun, but Procopio dashed off into a heavy thicket and disappeared. At daylight the manhunters tried to find him, but a driving rain washed away his tracks. They returned to Fresno empty-handed, save Procopio's horse, which, not surprisingly, turned out to be stolen.[27]

The governor issued a $500 reward for his arrest, but Procopio did not linger in California. He fled across the line to Baja California, where he became the head of a gang of horse and mule thieves. In August 1878, Mexican officials publicly identified the band's leader as Procopio Murrieta and sent a troop of cavalry in pursuit. They captured five of the gang plus twenty-nine stolen horses, but once again Procopio managed to escape. He fled back north across the border to San Diego, where a month later he was spotted in Old Town, which today is a state park studded with historic adobe buildings. By the time Procopio left, three horses and a saddle were found to be missing. Rumors had the bandido drifting around Los Angeles, where he had a number of friends, but he seems to have returned to his old home in Hermosillo, Mexico.[28]

A year later, Procopio again made newspaper headlines in California. Mrs. Belle Paul, wife of a justice of the peace in Mountain View, north of San Jose, reported that she had overheard a group of Mexican desperadoes plotting to kidnap a state senator and hold him for ransom. She identified one of the men as Procopio. One journalist called the plot "the grandest exploit ever attempted in California." The county sheriff made an intensive investigation, but he could find no trace of Procopio. Six months later, on April 24, 1880, Belle Paul reported that a masked Mexican had barged into her home while her husband was gone. He angrily threatened to kill her for revealing the kidnapping scheme. Then, drawing a revolver, he fired one shot, which grazed her hip. Belle claimed that the masked man was Procopio, but detectives who investigated the incident concluded that her story "has been concocted to gain notoriety." It turned out that she was an expert equestrian, and soon adopted the name "Miss Belle Cook" and began touring the country, competing in horse races. Well before the advent of Buffalo Bill's Wild West show, she received extensive publicity as the "champion lady rider of the world." The detectives were right, for she had made up the whole Procopio story.[29]

During the next few years, Procopio managed to stay out of the limelight. He reportedly served for a time as a police officer in Hermosillo. On July 31, 1882, Procopio was carousing in a bordello in the Pacific port town of Guaymas, eighty miles south of Hermosillo. He got into a quarrel with an actor, Aurelio Cantabrana. Pulling his six-shooter, the pistolero shot Cantabrana dead. Procopio was arrested the same day, and newspapers reported that, pursuant to an order of the governor, he was executed by firing squad. But that was hardly true. Within a few months, Procopio was riding at the head of a gang of cattle thieves along the Arizona-Mexico border. They stole cattle in Mexico and drove them north, selling the herds to dishonest

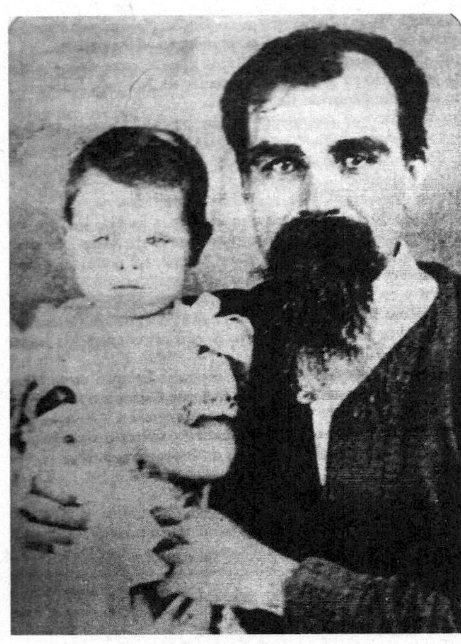

Procopio and his daughter in a photograph taken in Mexico about 1887.
William B. Secrest collection

butchers in Arizona. In November 1883, newspapers reported that he was finally captured near Tucson, but it turned out to be a case of mistaken identity.[30]

Three months passed, and in February 1884, Procopio married a young woman named Juana Bernal in Hermosillo. Two years later, they welcomed their first child, a baby daughter. Marriage and fatherhood seem to have transformed him. He acquired a ranch at Buenavista, on the Yaqui River, about one hundred seventy miles southeast of Hermosillo. Despite his narrow escape from a firing squad in Guaymas, he often visited the port town. The US consul in Guaymas later said, "Procopio was well known and liked in that section, was well behaved and a good citizen, and was frequently in Guaymas for trade, and bore nothing there of the bad character he does in California." During the next few years, Procopio and his wife had three more children, two boys and a girl. They moved back to Hermosillo and settled on a small ranch just outside the town.[31]

According to folklore, Procopio met his end in a shootout in Hermosillo in the early 1890s. The truth is far less dramatic. He spent his last Christmas in peace with his wife and children. A few days later, on December 30, 1891, he was riding his horse on his little rancho when the animal bucked and threw him from the saddle. He fell to the ground, fatally injured. By the time one of Juana's relatives found him, Procopio was dead. He was forty-eight years old. Procopio's death was reported to a local judge, who found that there was no evidence of foul play. Juana and her family doubtless sought to avoid publicity, for not a word of his demise appeared in the press. Nonetheless, proof of his passing is preserved in the official death records of Hermosillo. For the nephew of Joaquin Murrieta, it was a sudden and bloodless demise of one of the Old West's most dangerous outlaws.[32]

CHAPTER 21

FROM JOAQUIN TO ZORRO: THE LAUNCHING OF LEGENDS

Joaquin Murrieta rides boldly out of the fog of history and legend, his eyes flashing, his horse foaming with sweat, his pistol and poniard ever at the ready. Joaquin's youth, his daring, and his violence created a drama for the ages, and to this day his myth lives on in the public imagination. Murrieta has legions of admirers and aficionados, many of whom see him as one of the Wild West's greatest outlaws. Many more view him as a rebel, El Patrio, El Famoso, the Robin Hood of the gold rush, and perhaps most notably as Zorro. Because he died so early in the frontier era, before the advent of the telegraph and of rapid communication, it was difficult for pioneer journalists to obtain accurate and up-to-date information about his life and career. That vacuum was quickly filled in with folklore and fiction, first with the false newspaper reports that claimed that he had not been killed, followed by John Rollin Ridge's historical novel, and finally by the ensuing seventeen decades of fable and fabrication. As a result, no Western outlaw—not even Jesse James, Billy the Kid, or Butch Cassidy—has had so many false tales told about them as Joaquin Murrieta.

During the gold rush, many Latinos doubted the gang's murderous raids and saw Joaquin as a folk hero. Some sang corridos—folk ballads—about him and his exploits. Others believed that he was a revolutionary, striking back against the conquering Yankees. General Mariano Vallejo, the Californio leader, explained how Murrieta became an idol to his countrymen who had lost their land to Anglos: "Some of the Californios who were robbed dedicated themselves to useful enterprises. In one way or another they found a way to support themselves and their families. But the majority of the young people who had been plundered so unjustly had a thirst for revenge, so they left to swell the ranks of Joaquin Murrieta. Under the leadership of that dreaded bandit, they were able to retaliate, to a degree, for the wrongs the North American race had inflicted on them. A great many of those gullible people, who despised wise advice and tried to seek revenge by illegal and reprehensible means, have failed miserably. Some received passports for the other world through the actions of Judge Lynch and today they rest in tombs dug by the *aguaciles* [constables]. Others have ended up in San Quentin."[1]

However, contrary to Vallejo's assertions, only a handful of Californios joined the ranks of Joaquin Murrieta's gang. Yet there is no question that many Latinos in gold rush California considered him a heroic figure, and not without reason. Californios, Mexicans, and other Spanish-speaking people were often deprived of their land, their mining claims, their employment, and their civil liberties. When people are oppressed, they will reach out for anything that gives them hope. Latinos desperately needed a man whom they could exalt and admire as an avenger who sought to resist the Anglos who had marginalized them. Thus they embraced the fictional Joaquin, the rebel who sought to avenge Anglo injustice, the man who, like Robin Hood, surely stole from the rich and gave to the poor.

During the ensuing century and a half, two Joaquin Murrietas came to the forefront in literature, folklore, and film. One was the real Joaquin, whose true story was partially told in a handful of books, published from the 1960s onward and based largely on nineteenth century records and newspaper accounts. Those books were either privately printed or released by small publishers, and they received relatively little attention. The other Joaquin garnered extensive publicity. He was the Joaquin Murrieta of fiction and fable, the Joaquin of ballads, novels, movies, and television. In more recent years, the mythical and fictional Joaquin attracted the attention of many more writers, including scholars in the fields of history, sociology, philosophy, and literature. The two Joaquins—one real, one not—became conflated, and numerous authors and commentators came to believe that the fictional Joaquin created by Ridge was the Joaquin of fact and history. As a result, these writers inadvertently created even more legends and false narratives about Murrieta.

The Joaquin myths began almost immediately after his death, with the politically motivated attacks in the San Francisco *Alta California* that claimed that Harry Love and the California Rangers had killed the wrong man. The newspaper's spurious reports ignited a controversy that exists to this day. Even though the *Alta California* retracted its claims in 1854, in March 1855 the newspaper published a letter from a correspondent in Baja California who insisted that Joaquin "is alive, and promises to give the people of Los Angeles County another call." The writer said that Murrieta "was seen about a month ago at a ranch about fifty miles this side of the line, in company of eleven men, all well armed and masked. He stated to a friend of mine that he had returned from Sonora, and was going to the upper country for the sole purpose of revenging the death of a poor devil called Gregorio Lopez, who, having some slight resemblance to him, had fallen a victim to Love's thirst for the reward offered for Murieta's head." The unidentified correspondent signed his name as "H."[2]

Harry Love, needless to say, was furious when he read the letter in the *Alta California*. He wrote a detailed response that the *Alta*, to its credit, published in full. Love insisted, "Now, this is to state to the said 'H,' whoever he may be, that Harry Love knew Joaquin Murieta, and knows he is dead—which fact is certified to by some of the most reliable men in the State—

Joaquin Murrieta by Charles Christian Nahl, published in the California Police Gazette in 1859. *John Boessenecker collection*

and that Harry Love never thirsted for the reward offered for Murieta's head, and is ready to answer for his intentions to 'H' or anyone else." The exasperated Love was guilty of exaggeration when he said that he "knew Joaquin," for his personal acquaintance with the bandit chieftain lasted only the few frantic minutes before the rangers gunned him down.[3]

Love's statements, and the numerous affidavits he and the rangers had collected, were not enough to convince many Latinos that Joaquin was dead. In 1856 a Santa Cruz newspaper reported that a band of horse thieves was raiding in the county. "The native Californians say that the band are under the direction of the celebrated robber chieftain Joaquin Murietta, who has returned from Mexico," its editor wrote. "As to Joaquin we give the story for what it is worth. It is however proper to state that nearly or quite all of the native population believe that he is still alive, and that he paid a dollar to see the head exhibited as his at San Francisco." The story that Joaquin had forked over money to view his own head would be repeated for the next century and a half.[4]

As the years went by, unsubstantiated rumors that Joaquin was alive continued to circulate. An 1879 newspaper report came from Alfred A. Green, a well-known pioneer. He claimed that in 1857, a Catholic priest in Southern California had told him in confidence that Joaquin was then alive. The cleric had said, "About one month ago I was in the city of Los Angeles. While there I was called upon to marry a young man, named Murieta. Struck by the name, I said to him, 'Are you any relation of the famous outlaw, Joaquin Murieta?' 'Yes, Senor Padre,' he responded. 'I am his brother.' 'Is it true that the Americans got the head of your brother?' 'No, Senor Padre, but read for yourself.' With that he took a letter from his pocket and handed it to me. I took the letter and read it; it was from Joaquin Murieta, dated only about a month earlier at Magdalena, Sonora, Mexico." According to Green, the priest explained that in his letter, Joaquin asked that his family in California confirm that the head was indeed his, so as to discourage any manhunts for him in Mexico. Green also claimed that in 1879, Murrieta was living in Mexico.[5]

Green's account was widely republished, and five days later, the *Sacramento Union* printed a letter from another pioneer that purportedly confirmed Murrieta had survived. The writer asserted, "Some time after his reported death I saw and talked with his brother-in-law, who told me that Joaquin was in Mexico, with his relatives. I also talked with one of his dulcineas [sweethearts], who told me that the people of California were fooled, and that Joaquin was safe at home. An American, who was once his partner, showed me a letter that he received from Joaquin some two months after his reported death. In that letter he reported himself alive and well." But the accounts from Green and the *Sacramento Union*'s correspondent had two fatal defects. First, vital statistics records show that no man named

Murrieta, or with any similar surname, was married in Los Angeles in the 1850s. Second, and most significantly, Murrieta could neither read nor write.[6]

A week after the second report was published, a gold rush journalist named Oliver P. Stidger provided an even more detailed story. Stidger had been editor of the *Marysville Herald* when Harry Love and his rangers visited the town to display the severed head and hand. Stidger recalled, "I was at that time a resident of Marysville, and pretty well known by all of the then inhabitants of that famous city, among whom was a sister of the bandit Joaquin Murieta. Captain Love placed the head, with a hand of Three Fingered Jack, on exhibition in a room at the corner of D and Second streets, and gave me an invitation to come and view the head and hand of the two famous outlaws. I accepted the invitation, and on the day I visited the place the sister of Joaquin also came, in company with a Mexican gentleman and lady. Knowing her to be a sister of the bandit, I had some curiosity to learn how she would be affected by the sight of her brother's head, and consequently I placed myself in a position to watch her every movement. She smiled but said nothing, until she was accosted by the gentleman who accompanied her, who asked in Spanish, 'Is that your brother's head?' She answered in a very low tone of voice, but loud enough for me to collect the words, 'No, sir, it is not; it is the head of Joaquin Gonzales. But say nothing; let them think it to be my brother's head if they want to." Soon after making these remarks she left the room, and I repeated her words to Captain Love. His reply was, 'I know this to be the head of Joaquin Murieta, and she says it is not because she is too proud to own it.' Soon after this I interviewed the lady at her residence, and she then informed me that her brother had made his escape from the State and had gone to Mexico. She laughed heartily at the hoax practiced upon the people by Captain Love, and again repeated that the head was that of Joaquin Gonzales. From that day to this I never had any doubt about the matter, feeling convinced that the head was not that of the famous bandit. Consequently, I was well prepared in mind to believe Mr. Green's statement."[7]

Because Stidger's story was firsthand and not hearsay like the other two accounts, it was widely believed by readers and was reprinted in other newspapers. Although the bandido's sister, probably Vicenta, indeed had lived in Marysville at the time of Joaquin's death, Stidger's account had a fatal flaw. He forgot what he had published in 1853 when he was editor of the *Marysville Herald*: "There can be no doubt that the head on exhibition is that of Joaquin Murieta." Stidger had manufactured his story out of whole cloth. Perhaps not surprisingly, in later years numerous writers and historians swallowed Stidger's yarn and used it to support their claims that Joaquin was not killed by the California Rangers.[8]

Yet another fable attained much publicity beginning in 1893, when an old forty-niner and newspaperman claimed that Bill Byrnes had admitted that the rangers had slain the wrong man. Supposedly, during the early 1860s, he had told friends in Virginia City, Nevada, "Joaquin would have to be killed once more to entitle him to burial." Byrnes also allegedly said, "One pickled head was as good as another, if there was a scar on the face and no one knew the difference." But the story was far from true. Not only did Byrnes point out Murrieta to the other rangers at Cantua Creek, he had signed the sworn affidavit confirming that they had killed Joaquin. And for the next twenty years, he told his friends that the California Rangers had slain Murrieta and Three Fingered Jack.[9]

The reason for the many stories that Joaquin survived is simple: famous outlaws die hard. Popular myth insists that no mere mortal could kill a legendary folk bandit. Many fervently believe that Billy the Kid was not killed by Sheriff Pat Garrett in 1881, and instead survived to old age. Nor could Jesse James possibly have been slain by the coward Robert Ford in 1882. Butch Cassidy and the Sundance Kid never died at the hands of Bolivian troops in 1908, but returned to the US and lived happily ever after. Even John Dillinger could never have been shot to death by FBI agents in Chicago in 1934, despite the fact that bystanders saw him killed and photographs of his dead body were numerous. The same is true of Joaquin Murrieta. In folklore, he was too romantic, too daring, and too heroic to have ever been shot down like a common criminal resisting arrest.

Like Joaquin himself, his severed head also became the subject of controversy. The head and the hand of Three Fingered Jack, with several dozen supporting affidavits, had been kept by Lieutenant Edward Connor of the California Rangers. Connor either sold or gave the relics to a man in San Francisco, who soon went into debt. In 1855 the county sheriff, to satisfy a court judgment, seized the head and hand. In one of America's most bizarre auctions, held on the front steps of the San Francisco courthouse, the sheriff sold them to the highest bidder—for all of $36. The buyers were a banker and a former justice of the California Supreme Court. A local newspaperman reported, "When next heard of, these trophies will be in the cabinet of some museum in London, Paris, or New York, as it is, we understand, the intention of the purchasers to present them to an institution of the kind." But they did no such thing. Within a few days, they sold them to Andrew "Natchez" Taylor, San Francisco's best-known gunsmith. Taylor promptly put the head and hand on display in the front window of his gun shop and shooting gallery. One San Francisco journalist remarked sarcastically, "Poor Joaquin! He never dreamed his head would come to this."[10]

During the next few years, Natchez Taylor stirred controversy by providing and loading pistols used in several infamous formal duels and grudge shootings. In September 1858, his career came to a sudden end. Taylor forgot that one of the Colt revolvers in his display case was loaded. He cocked and handed it to a customer, who began examining the weapon. As the man turned it over in his hand, one finger brushed against the trigger. A deafening roar swept through the shop, and Taylor dropped dead with a bullet in his brain. But Joaquin's sightless eyes were not present for this final bit of bloodshed. By that time, Taylor had sold the head and hand to a San Francisco businessman. "He intends exhibiting them through the interior cities of the United States, and wintering in New York," reported one of the city's newspapers. "He confidently expects to realize $50,000 by his speculation. We shall probably next hear of this noted *cabeza* in Europe, exciting the wonder of Cockneys, Parisians, and invalids at Bath and Baden-Baden."[11]

The head and hand, however, never left San Francisco. During the next ten years, they were exhibited in various San Francisco saloons. By 1866 the grisly relics were on display in a "scientific" exhibition hall in the city's downtown, run by a man who called himself Dr. Louis J. Jordan. Shortly after Christmas, a local journalist was walking down Montgomery Street when he encountered a huckster standing on the sidewalk.

"Here, gentleman and ladies," the showman cried out, but there was only one boy and one man with earshot. He then called on them to step inside and see a "learned pig, who will tell you the time of day with accuracy; will beat you five times out of six at seven-up; will tell your age; will count, calculate, and demonstrate."

As if that was not enough of an attraction, he declared, "Also, the head of Joaquin, the bloody murderer, whose terrific deeds struck terror to the hearts of the early settlers of California. I've got his head in a pickle, a beautiful evidence of the ability of man to preserve, for scientific means, for the edification of the rising generation." Then he announced the price of a ticket: "Only two bits for the entire exhibition."[12]

The place was called the Pacific Museum of Anatomy and Natural Science. Despite its high-sounding name, the museum was a freak show and Jordan a quack doctor. In addition to the head of Joaquin and the hand of Three Fingered Jack, Dr. Jordan

Louis Jordan's horror museum in San Francisco, about 1870. The head of Joaquin and the hand of Three Fingered Jack were displayed there for forty years. *John Boessenecker collection*

displayed more than nine hundred grotesque oddities: skeletons, Egyptian mummies, a "Cyclops child" with one eye, and diseased body parts, especially those showing signs of syphilis and gonorrhea. Horrified visitors, after viewing the displays, would then be urged to see Dr. Jordan. He invariably diagnosed them with exotic diseases and tried to peddle his snake-oil treatments.[13]

Dr. Jordan displayed the head and hand for more than three decades, and they were viewed by many visitors. In 1868 the noted San Francisco artist Charles Christian Nahl produced his now famous oil painting of Joaquin Murrieta. It shows the outlaw on horseback, racing along a mountainside, his hair flowing and dagger in hand. Nahl's depiction of Joaquin's facial features is almost identical to that of the sole image of the severed head. Given that Nahl's studio was not far from Jordan's museum, it seems likely that the artist had viewed Joaquin's head. In 1895 an artist for the *Overland Monthly*, a magazine published in San

Francisco, visited Jordan's museum and made a drawing of the head. It was published as an engraving in the *Overland Monthly* to illustrate a story about Joaquin Murrieta. This rendering, the only one known of the severed head, matches exactly the description published by the *San Francisco Herald* in 1853: "The hair—of a beautiful light brown with a golden tint—is long and flowing; the nose high and straight, and the eyebrows, which meet in the middle, dark and heavy . . . The face tapers off to the chin—upon which, and on the upper lip, there is a thin beard like that of a young man who had never shaved." During the 1920s and later, a number of people claimed that they had seen the head in Jordan's museum, and it was that of a dark-complected Indian and not Joaquin Murrieta. Either their memories were bad or they recalled seeing a different severed head, of which Jordan displayed at least half a dozen.[14]

In June 1902, two men from Hanford made a visit to San Francisco, where they happened upon Jordan's museum. They were fascinated by the collection, especially one exhibit that they said showed an old woman's head and a severed hand. According to the pair, a placard identified the relics as those of Mariana Murrieta, the widow of Joaquin, and displayed with them was a newspaper clipping about her fatal encounter with a railroad train a few weeks earlier. On the men's return to Hanford, they told the county coroner what they had seen. Grave robbery was common in that era, with human remains often being sold to unsuspecting medical schools. The alarmed coroner, fearing that he would be accused of peddling the relics, sought the assistance of the county sheriff. Then they, with two other officers, proceeded to the Catholic cemetery in Hanford. After notifying the church sexton, they shoveled the dirt from the top of Mariana's grave and lifted the coffin lid.

"There was the body with the head and both hands attached just as it was placed on the grave," a Hanford journalist reported. "The old Mexican grave digger, who knew the deceased for the past thirty years, said, 'That is Mary Anna.'" The reporter concluded that Dr. Jordan "is deceiving the people for the few dollars he can get out of it, and every paper in the State ought to brand him as an imposter." If the story was true, San Francisco's dailies, then in the heyday of sensationalist "yellow journalism," would have gleefully reported it. Yet they printed not a word. The two visitors had merely seen the head of Joaquin and the hand of Three Fingered Jack, and their imaginations got the better of them.[15]

Four years later, in 1906, the great earthquake and fire swept through San Francisco, destroying much of the city and killing more than three thousand people. Dr. Jordan's museum, then located at 1051 Market Street, was obliterated, along with the head and hand. Yet even that holocaust was not enough to bury Joaquin Murrieta, and many devotees continued to insist that his head survived. Those nonsensical claims reached a nadir in 1968 when a gun collector in Sonoma, California, displayed the purported head of Joaquin in a large glass jar. He was interviewed by numerous journalists. The bottled head was photographed and published in newspapers and magazines, and more recently, on internet websites. This despite the fact that the head was a wax fake that, beginning in 1957, had been exhibited as a prop at the Old Town Museum in San Jose. The gun collector, convinced that it was real, had purchased the wax head for $2,000 after the museum closed. Then, in 1985, a Jesuit priest in San Francisco who was fascinated with Joaquin Murrieta convinced himself that the prop was real. He began a campaign to have the alleged head buried with full Catholic funeral rites. Naturally the cost-conscious collector refused to comply, and to this day, aficionados devoutly believe that the head of Joaquin survives.[16]

Just as controversial as Murrieta's head is the claim that there were five different Joaquins. That story was widely believed from 1853 to this day. Numerous writers and historians insist that the many robberies and murders by Murrieta's men in 1853 were committed by five separate men named Joaquin. Some even concocted a new name for the band: The Five Joaquins Gang. However, as early as 1854, John Rollin Ridge pointed out, "There were two Joaquins, bearing the various surnames of Murieta, O'Comorenia, Valenzuela, Botellier, and Carillo—so that it was supposed that there were no less than five sanguinary devils ranging the country at one and the same time. It is now fully ascertained that there were only two, whose proper names were Joaquin Murieta and Joaquin Valenzuela." Many subsequent writers and scholars chose to ignore Ridge's accurate statement. Some, unfamiliar with the facts and the geography of the mining region, even insisted that it was impossible for one outlaw gang to have committed all the raids in the early months of 1853. Instead, they have claimed that due to public hysteria, the forays were all simply attributed to a generic outlaw named Joaquin. But as we have seen, not only were the raids perpetrated by a single gang, they took place one after another, and close together, as the band rampaged across the Mother Lode region.[17]

Like everything else connected with Joaquin Murrieta, the identity of Three Fingered Jack has long been disputed. Ridge incorrectly called him Manuel Garcia, and that name has been used in almost all books and articles ever since. Such chroniclers were unaware that multiple government documents and newspaper accounts from 1846 to 1853 identified him as Bernardino Garcia. In 1906 a newly published book about Marin County's colorful history reported that Bernardino Garcia was Three Fingered Jack. Garcia's grandchildren, prominent residents of Mill Valley, were shocked and dismayed by the book's account. Three Fingered Jack's daughter, Carmelita Garcia Boyle, had donated the land for the town park, which bears her married name to this day. In that era, families rarely talked about their black sheep, and Garcia's grandchildren were unaware of his bloody history. They contacted local newspapers and told reporters,

"Mr. Garcia was not of Murieta's band; on the contrary he was one of our most law abiding citizens." They insisted, "Never at any time was his name connected with any but honorable actions, and far from being a law breaker, he was one of Marin's foremost defenders of law and order." Finally, the grandchildren claimed that Garcia had died in 1852 of natural causes and was buried in the Mission Dolores cemetery in San Francisco. Not only were their stories false, the records of Mission Dolores—still extant—show that no one named Bernardino Garcia was ever buried, or had funeral services, at the mission.[18]

Over the years, every rusty gun found inside a cave, a crumbling adobe, or an abandoned mine shaft was proclaimed to be Joaquin Murrieta's. Treasure hunters scoured the hills looking for Joaquin's buried gold, even though he, like all bandits, undoubtedly spent it. By the 1920s, every aging mining town in the Sierra Nevada boasted a building, cellar, tunnel, or nearby cave that was proudly identified as Joaquin's hideout. One of the best known of these is the historic mining camp of Hornitos, situated seventeen miles west of Mariposa. Joaquin had indeed visited Hornitos on March 4, 1853, where he shot and wounded the two manhunters, William Prescott and Henry Crowell, in a large fandango tent. That sole incident gradually inflated into a scenario in which the bandido frequently hid out in Hornitos. One of the town's popular tourist attractions is the ruins of an old stone fandango hall that supposedly served as headquarters for Joaquin and his gang. At the rear, still visible, is the "Murrieta tunnel." It was reportedly constructed as a secret exit, and whenever manhunters approached, Joaquin and his compadres would escape through it. For more than a hundred years, visitors have marveled at the Murrieta tunnel, unaware that the stone building was erected after Joaquin's death and that the tunnel was built to roll wine barrels into the fandango hall.

One of the most popular and oft-repeated stories about Murrieta held that during the manhunt for him in Calaveras County,

I am Joaquin by Charles Christian Nahl, 1859. *John Boessenecker collection*

he boldly visited a crowded gambling hall in Mokelumne Hill. While sitting at a monte table, he overheard an Anglo bragging that he hoped he would encounter Joaquin, and he "would kill him as quick as he would a snake." Overhearing that, Murrieta leaped on top of the monte table in front of the whole house. Drawing his six-gun, he shouted, "I am Joaquin! If there is any shooting to do, I am in." Then he strode outside, mounted his horse, and galloped away. This account first appeared in Ridge's book, and was retold countless times over the years. As the story became inflated, it supposedly took place everywhere from Jackson to Marysville, and from Napa to San Jose. The artist Charles Christian Nahl even prepared a dramatic rendering, showing Joaquin atop the table, six-gun in hand and baring his breast in defiance. As compelling as the story is, it was not mentioned in any contemporary account and certainly would have received extensive notice if it had actually occurred.[19]

As we have seen, the literary legend of Joaquin originated in 1854 with the publication of Ridge's *The Life and Adventures of Joaquín Murieta.* Soon after its release, a San Francisco newspaper printed a negative review and concluded, "The book may serve as very amusing reading for Joaquín Murieta, should he get hold of it, for notwithstanding all which has been said and published to the contrary, we have little faith in his reported death at the hands of Love's party." Ridge promptly responded by letter, complaining about the reviewer and his claims. "I require him to prove it," Ridge declared. "I require him to travel over the state as I did, to consult laboriously the files of the different papers which have published well authenticated accounts of Joaquin, and to converse with those who personally knew this individual, and then to compare my work with the facts he has thus obtained, before I will allow him arrogantly to come forward, and say or intimate, that I have written untruths."[20]

What Ridge failed to add was that his book was a combination of fact and fantasy. He had indeed read the 1853 newspaper reports and had also obtained various details from eyewitnesses whom he interviewed. However, to fill out the story, he included a great deal of fiction, plus fabricated dialogue. His ninety-page paperback sold well in California, well enough to prompt the editor of the *California Police Gazette* to publish a plagiarized version. The *California Police Gazette*, founded in 1859, was a San Francisco weekly newspaper that specialized in crime news. In the fall of that year, it released a serial entitled *The Life of Joaquin Murieta, the Brigand Chief of California.* It was followed by a soft-cover book of the same name, illustrated by Charles Christian Nahl.

Ridge was enraged by the release of the *Police Gazette*'s story, which substantially copied his own book. He declared that "a spurious edition has been foisted upon unsuspecting publishers and by them circulated, to the infringement of the author's copyright and the damage of his literary credit—the spurious work, with its crude interpolations, fictitious additions, and imperfectly designed distortions of the author's phraseology, being by many persons confounded with the original performance." But Ridge, apparently lacking the funds to hire a lawyer, never sued for breach of his copyright. In 1864 he and his wife moved to the gold rush mining camp of Grass Valley, where he worked as a journalist and struggled financially. He acquired an interest in the town newspaper, the *Grass Valley National*. One of its editors was a cousin of Bill Byrnes, and from him Ridge apparently obtained additional details about Murrieta that were included in an 1871 edition of his novel. That revised edition proved very popular, but John Rollin Ridge never lived to see its success. He died of illness in Grass Valley in 1867 at the age of forty. [21]

Because Ridge's book was published only a year after Joaquin's death, it quickly colored the memories of pioneers. For several succeeding generations, old-timers loved to tell newspapermen their purported recollections of Murrieta and his gang. But in most cases, they simply repeated the many yarns that they had read in Ridge's novel. The reason was that most readers in that era believed his book was factual, a work of history. Even California's two most prominent historians of the nineteenth century, Hubert Howe Bancroft and Theodore H. Hittell, failed to recognize that much of the book was fiction. In their published works, which are still standard sources today, they included detailed accounts of Joaquin's career that are based largely on Ridge's novel. For the next century, unsuspecting historians and authors blindly followed the false information published by Bancroft and Hittell.

During the late nineteenth century, Joaquin's name was kept alive by the popular poet Cincinnatus Hiner Miller. In 1870 he adopted the pen name Joaquin Miller to honor the legendary outlaw. He became widely known as the "Poet of the Sierras" and in 1871 authored an epic poem, "Joaquin Murietta." His rustic home still stands in Joaquin Miller Park in the hills of Oakland, California. At the same time, a number of dime novels about Murrieta appeared. Among the bloodcurdling titles were *Joaquin, the Terrible*; *Joaquin, or The Marauder of the Mines*; and *The Pirate of the Placers, or, Joaquin's Death Hunt*. Yet another dime novel was published in Chile in 1902 and titled *El Bandido Chileno, Joaquin Murieta en California*. It was a plagiarized version of Ridge, and made Joaquin a native of Chile. Not surprisingly, this created a myth that Murrieta was Chileno, culminating in the popular 1967 play *Splendor and Death of Joaquin Murieta* by Chile's Nobel Prize–winning poet, Pablo Neruda.

In 1932, bestselling author Walter Noble Burns released his epic biography *The Robin Hood of El Dorado*. Burns, a newspaperman, had authored the enormously successful books *The Saga of Billy the Kid*, published in 1926, and *Tombstone*, an account of Wyatt Earp, in 1927. To research Joaquin Murrieta, he visited California, toured the Mother Lode region, and read sources at the California State Library in Sacramento. But just as he did with his prior two books, Burns sacrificed historical truth for a good story. He followed Ridge's novel, mixing in more detail plus invented dialogue, and produced a highly entertaining blend of fact and fiction. *The Robin Hood of El Dorado* was serialized in newspapers nationwide and then released as a big-budget film of the same name in 1936, starring Warner Baxter as Joaquin Murrieta.[22]

The many myths contained in *The Robin Hood of El Dorado* rankled Joseph Henry Jackson, a San Francisco literary critic and avocational historian. In his influential 1949 book *Bad Company*, he included a detailed chapter on Joaquin. Jackson did excellent work in analyzing the Murrieta literature and in tracing most of the previous accounts to the original Ridge book. However, he concluded that Ridge's work was all fiction and that Joaquin Murrieta was a mythical person. Jackson was unfamiliar with the early newspaper reports about the Murrieta gang. He failed to recognize that Ridge based his story on them, and that many of the events described in his book actually took place. Jackson's ill-considered conclusion was accepted by many Western historians, thus discouraging research on the real Joaquin Murrieta for several decades.

During the next thirty years, Murrieta's mythical status as a folk hero grew exponentially, reaching a pinnacle during the Chicano movement of the 1960s and '70s. Numerous historians and other scholars began to describe Joaquin Murrieta as a so-called "social bandit." The social banditry concept was first developed in the 1950s and purportedly represents a type of protest against poverty and oppression, a quest for vengeance against the rich and the oppressors, and a righting of individual wrongs. The theory posits three types of social bandits: the "noble robber" or Robin Hood, the primitive rebel, and the terrorist avenger. Proponents of this concept argue that Joaquin Murrieta and many other Latino bandits of the Old West were not criminals, but instead were victims of Anglo injustice, striking back at the Yankee conquerors, and were forced into lives of banditry in order to survive. Yet this analysis fails to recognize that the vast majority of Latinos in the frontier regions were honest miners, ranchers, farmers, and vaqueros who never robbed anyone. Most of these scholars failed to research the real Joaquin Murrieta in the primary sources of the 1850s: newspapers, diaries, and court records. As a result, they were unaware that Joaquin and his band robbed and killed men of every ethnicity—white, black, Latino, and Asian. And Murrieta and his men certainly did not steal from the rich and give to the poor. They robbed for plunder, not for social justice. The man whom these historians concluded was a social bandit was the fictional Joaquin created by John Rollin Ridge and his many adherents, and not the Joaquin of history.[23]

Then in 1980, Frank F. Latta, a retired schoolteacher and collector of California folklore, released a 685-page hardcover book on the life of Murrieta. Titled *Joaquin Murrieta and His Horse Gangs*, Latta's massive volume was based on fifty years of research that he began in the 1920s. It was quickly accepted as the bible on Joaquin, and for years thereafter was relied on as a principal source by many writers, scholars, and historians. Latta claimed that his book revealed the bandit chieftain's full story for the first time. Although Latta's tome included copies of pertinent historical documents and newspaper reports, most of it was based on the oral recollections of old-timers whom Latta interviewed. Based on their stories, Latta created a scenario in which Murrieta led a highly organized band of more than sixty men, headquartered in the Coast Range. Most of Joaquin's riders, instead of robbing and murdering in the Mother Lode, rounded up wild horses and drove them for sale in Sonora, Mexico. Latta, however, never explained why the animals would be driven almost one thousand miles across the desert to Mexico when they could have been sold at much higher prices at local California horse markets. Such fatal weaknesses in logic permeated the book.

Frank Latta's main informant was an old vaquero named Avelino Martinez who said that he had been a member of Murrieta's gang from 1851 to 1853. In interviews during the 1930s, he told Latta that he was born in 1824, he was more than one hundred years old, and he had come to California in the gold rush. Martinez provided voluminous information and many dramatic stories about the band and its activities. He said that he rode with Joaquin Valenzuela and even once had an encounter with Harry Love. Martinez claimed that he was with several of the gang near Cantua Creek at the time of the gun battle with the California Rangers, and that he helped bury the slain outlaws. But there were several problems with Martinez's accounts.

First, voting registers and census records show that he was born in 1845, and he was therefore eight years old when Joaquin died. Most damning is that Latta, in his book, omitted any mention of a newspaper interview he had conducted with Martinez in 1935. In that news story, Latta questioned Martinez's purported age of 110 years and said that Martinez told him that he had once met Joaquin Murrieta in 1877—twenty-four years after the bandit's death. Latta added that Martinez was "always glad to spin a few yarns about the old days." Neither Martinez nor Latta said a word about his alleged association with the Murrieta gang. Despite the fact that Latta had questioned Martinez's credibility in 1935, he based the bulk of his book on the old vaquero's bogus stories.[24]

Latta's other principal informant was Teodora Arredondo, whom he interviewed at her home in Madera, California, not long before her death in 1931. She told Latta that she was born in Mexico in 1831 and was then one hundred years old. She said that she had come to California in 1847 with her first husband, who in 1849 or 1850 became a mule packer for Joaquin Murrieta and his gang. Mrs. Arredondo said that she had known Joaquin personally, as well as his wife Rosa and several others whom she claimed were members of the Murrieta family. She provided Latta with intimate details about the band and how they operated, including descriptions of almost thirty purported members of Joaquin's gang. But Latta, as was customary with his interviewees, never asked for written evidence to support her claims, or for proof of her age. In fact, census records and her obituary show that she was born between 1840 and 1842. Teodora Arredondo was less than seven years old when she supposedly married and came to California, and was no older than ten when her husband allegedly began working for Joaquin. She was also obviously unaware that in 1849 and 1850, Joaquin was not a robber and had no need for a pack train. The stories that Teodora Arredondo told Latta were wild fabrications and folktales.[25]

Frank Latta collected oral traditions from numerous other old-timers. Strong evidence of their unreliability is that neither Latta nor any of his informants knew the names of many of the most well-documented members of the gang, among them Claudio Feliz, Bernardino Garcia, Salomon Pico, Pancho Daniel, Domingo Hernandez, Robert Scott, Antonio Valencia, Pedro Sanchez, and Jose Barrillo. Despite the fact that most of the people whom Latta interviewed were not even alive in the 1850s, he published their spurious yarns as gospel. Unable to reconcile their conflicting folktales, Latta concluded that there were no less than four different Joaquin Murrietas who rode with the gang. He also visited northern Mexico several times between 1936 and 1972 and interviewed numerous people surnamed Murrieta, all of whom were eager to claim that they were related to Joaquin. It is certainly possible that some were relatives, because one was unquestionably the daughter of Procopio Murrieta. But with that sole exception, Latta obtained from them no written documents or baptismal records as proof of any blood relationship. As a result, he recorded their many unreliable stories about Joaquin's life and included those in his book. Finally Latta, in a mortal sin for a historian, gave short shrift to primary sources like newspapers, diaries, and court records in favor of folklore and third-degree hearsay. The result is that Latta's book, short on facts and long on fiction, created countless myths and muddied the Joaquin Murrieta story almost beyond comprehension.

At the time Frank Latta began his research in the 1920s, a new and even more powerful legend about Joaquin began to appear. One of the most popular pulp fiction writers of that era was Johnston McCulley, who ended up authoring more than a hundred novels. In 1915 the thirty-two-year-old Midwesterner arrived in Los Angeles, already a seasoned newspaper reporter and creator of magazine adventure stories. He soon went to work as a drama critic for the *Los Angeles Times* and immersed himself in the history and culture of Southern California. In 1919 McCulley wrote "The Curse of Capistrano," published as a magazine serial in five parts. Set in Spanish-era California, its hero is a masked, rapier-wielding avenger called Zorro who battles corrupt officials and poses as a rich, harmless dandy named Don Diego Vega. He is elusive and sly, hence his nickname, Zorro the Fox. Because he came from the mission pueblo of San Juan Capistrano, his enemies call him the Curse of Capistrano.[26]

McCulley's Zorro is a California Robin Hood, and the governor offers a reward for him, dead or alive. As a lovestruck senorita tells Zorro, "No man knows your face, and if you take off your mask, none will ever know your guilt. I know why you have stolen—to avenge the helpless, to punish cruel politicians, to aid the oppressed. I know that you have given what you have stolen to the poor." By the end of McCulley's story, Don Diego, alias Zorro, wins the senorita's heart and defeats the wicked Spanish soldiers.[27]

"The Curse of Capistrano" proved so popular that in 1920, it was released as a bestselling novel and adapted as a silent film. *The Mark of Zorro*, starring Douglas Fairbanks, proved a major hit and made Zorro a household name. Then, in 1927, *The Gay Defender*, a motion picture about Joaquin Murrieta, appeared. Based on Ridge's novel, it featured silent film stars Richard Dix as Joaquin and Thelma Todd as his lover. Joaquin is depicted as an aristocratic young Spaniard who turns to banditry during the gold rush to avenge the wrongs done to him by forty-niners. Following its release, a number of film reviewers believed that *The Gay Defender* was inspired by *The Mark of Zorro*. That appears to be the first time anyone suggested a connection between Joaquin and Zorro. Two years later, in 1929, Harry Carr, a feature writer for the *Los Angeles Times*, wrote that Joaquin Murrieta "was the real hero of Douglas Fairbanks's 'The Mark of Zorro.'" Carr undoubtedly knew Johnston McCulley, for the two had worked together at the *Los Angeles Times* in 1916. But whether Carr had been told of this connection by McCulley, or he was simply speculating, is unknown.[28]

Johnston McCulley was interviewed by a journalist in 1923, who wrote, "McCulley created the character of Zorro in 'The Curse of Capistrano.' He studied the old California mission empire for years, and has written several stories dealing with mission times. Zorro was intended to express the spirit of the caballero of the time, and to everyone's satisfaction he did. Douglas Fairbanks made his greatest screen success with Zorro." While is it certainly possible, perhaps even probable, that McCulley had read or heard about Murrieta, he said nothing about that in the interview. Nor is there any evidence that McCulley ever stated that Zorro was based on Joaquin. His most obvious inspiration was Baroness Orczy's novel *The Scarlet Pimpernel*, published in 1905. Like Zorro, the hero of *The Scarlet Pimpernel* poses as a foolish fop. He runs a secret organization that saves aristocrats from the guillotine during the French Revolution.[29]

The success of Zorro during the 1920s was only the beginning. Johnston McCulley wrote more short stories and novels about him, and several sequel films were released. Then in 1940, *The Mark of Zorro* appeared in theaters. A remake of the 1920 motion picture and a box office smash, it starred Tyrone Power as Zorro and Basil Rathbone as his foe, a sadistic Spanish army captain. Many critics in 1940 preferred the original silent version, but today the Tyrone Power movie is viewed as a masterpiece of film making. In 1957 Walt Disney released the classic television series *Zorro*, starring Guy Williams. A huge success, *Zorro* aired for two years, and then for decades afterward it delighted audiences in television reruns. In several episodes of *Zorro*, two characters are named "Murrietta," and another is called Joaquin. This was the first time that Joaquin and Zorro were linked together on film.[30]

The first explicit connection of the two figures surfaced in the 1990s during production of the blockbuster film *The Mask of Zorro*. Two published books, as well as Hollywood press releases, declared that Zorro was based on Murrieta. *The Mask of Zorro*, released in 1998, starred Antonio Banderas as the swashbuckling superhero. It not only was a major commercial success but also brought Joaquin Murrieta and Three Fingered Jack into the story of the masked avenger. Zorro is depicted as Alejandro Murrieta, the fictitious brother of Joaquin, and the villain is Captain Harrison Love, loosely based on Harry Love. Captain Love captures Joaquin, but Alejandro and Three Fingered Jack manage to escape. When Love is about to kill Joaquin, the bandido shoots himself. Alejandro Murrieta then goes on to become Zorro and defeat Captain Love and the other evil officials. Based almost entirely on the publicity surrounding the film, Joaquin is now widely believed to be the basis for Zorro. This transition—of Murrieta into Zorro—is a modern example of how myths are created. And due to the undying popularity of the *Zorro* films, Joaquin is now inexorably linked to the masked swordsman.

Today, in addition to appearing on the silver screen, the name of Joaquin Murrieta graces a public park in Tucson, Arizona, as well as streets in several California cities. A monument to him has been erected in Trincheras, a village in northern Mexico that, according to local folklore, was once the bandido's home. Even an upscale residential community in the foothills of Sacramento County is named after him. Rancho Murieta was first developed in the late 1960s, but the community and its public agencies no longer seem to promote the origins of its misspelled name. And in Riverside County in Southern California is the bedroom city of Murrieta, home to 110,000 people. But contrary to myth, it is not named in honor of Joaquin. The town was founded in the 1880s and is instead named after Juan Murrieta, a local Californio ranchero.

In 1854, John Rollin Ridge closed his epic tale by saying, "Briefly, and without the aid of ornament, the life and character of Joaquin Murieta have been sketched. His career was short, for he died in his twenty-second year; but in the few years which were allowed him he displayed qualities of mind and heart which marked him as an extraordinary man, and leaving his name impressed upon the early history of this State, he also leaves behind him the important lesson that there is nothing so dangerous in its consequences as *injustice to individuals*—whether it arise from prejudice of color or any other source; that a wrong done to one man is a wrong to society and to the world." Though Ridge was describing the fictional Joaquin, almost two centuries later his judgment about injustice remains just as truthful and compelling.[31]

In the end, we are left with the two Joaquin Murrietas. The Joaquin of legend, folklore, and fiction is one man. The actual, authentic Joaquin is quite another. Joaquin Murrieta's innermost thoughts, the intricacies of his personality, his hopes, his dreams, and his aspirations, are all lost to history. We are left to judge the real man solely by his deeds. Was he a Robin Hood, a rebel, a horseback avenger who battled injustice and fought for the rights of Latinos in the Wild West? Perhaps the ghosts of twenty slaughtered Chinese miners can best answer that question.

ACKNOWLEDGMENTS

I have collected information about Joaquin Murrieta since the 1970s. Over the years I have accumulated research debts to many people. First and foremost I owe thanks to my great friend, the late William B. Secrest, the leading authority on the outlaws and lawmen of frontier California. Bill authored numerous books on the topic, including a biography of Harry Love, *The Man from the Rio Grande*. Bill's work was invaluable in helping uncover the true story of Murrieta. It is fitting that this book is dedicated to his memory. I also owe a special word of gratitude to my friend Paul Hutton, author and professor of history at the University of New Mexico. Ten years ago, over a couple of beers at a Wild West History Association meeting in Texas, Paul urged me to write a biography of Joaquin Murrieta. At first I resisted the idea due to the difficulty in separating the story's myth from fact, but eventually I came around and followed Paul's advice.

I extend my thanks to many more folks who helped me: John M. Cahoon of the Seaver Center, Natural History Museum of Los Angeles County; Sven Crongeyer; Andrew Galvan, curator, Mission Dolores, San Francisco; Mark Hall-Patton; Donna Harrell; Ray Iddings; Kristopher Mandell, Executive Director, Calaveras County Historical Society; Andrew Mattos, County of Tuolumne Carlo De Ferrari Archives; Cate Mills, History San Jose; Alison Moore, California Historical Society; the late Kevin J. Mullen; Allan Ochs, History Center of San Luis Obispo County; Pat Perry; Joseph P. Samora; Paul R. Spitzzeri, Workman and Temple Family Homestead Museum; the late Troy

Tuggle; Sue Tyson, California State Library; and Shannon Van Zant, Calaveras County Archives.

Special thanks to the staffs of the California State Archives and the Bancroft Library, University of California, Berkeley, for their assistance over the years. Credit also goes to the staff of the California Digital Newspaper Collection, which has made countless historic newspapers available online. This book could not have been written absent their work. My gratitude also goes out to the members of the Wild West History Association for their fellowship and support. The journal and annual rendezvous of the WWHA are highly recommended. Anyone interested in the history of the Old West is encouraged to join this organization.

To my agent, Claire Gerus, and my editors, Peter Joseph and Eden Railsback, and also copy editor Jennifer Stimson, I extend my heartfelt appreciation for all their work.

Last but certainly not least, I owe a huge debt of gratitude to my wife, Marta S. Diaz, for her advice, support, proofreading, and Spanish-language translations.

NOTES

CHAPTER 1

1. Baltimore (MD) *Niles' National Register*, August 3, 1839; James W. Parins, *John Rollin Ridge: His Life and Works*, Lincoln, NE: University of Nebraska Press (1991), pp. 12–30; John R. Ridge, *Poems*, San Francisco, CA: Henry Payot & Co. (1868), p. 7.
2. Parins, *John Rollin Ridge*, pp. 30, 37, 44, 53-54.
3. Van Buren (AR) *Arkansas Intelligencer*, May 26, 1849; Boston (MA) *Liberator*, August 10, 1849; Parins, *John Rollin Ridge*, pp. 62–77, 102–104.
4. Parins, *John Rollin Ridge*, pp. 92, 103–104.
5. John Rollin Ridge, *The Life and Adventures of Joaquín Murieta, The Celebrated California Bandit*, Norman, OK: University of Oklahoma Press (reprint, 1955), pp. 8–14.
6. The Murrieta family background is from an interview with family descendant Robert J. Richards in the San Francisco (CA) *Call-Bulletin*, April 28, 1934. Also see William B. Secrest, *The Man from the Rio Grande: A Biography of Harry Love*, Spokane, WA: Arthur H. Clark Co. (2005), p. 50; and Lori Lee Wilson, *The Joaquin Band: The History Behind the Legend*, Lincoln, NE: University of Nebraska Press (2011), pp. 41–42, 277 n85.
7. Ridge, *The Life and Adventures of Joaquín Murieta*, p. 8; San Jose (CA) *Evening News*, July 18, 1891.
8. On the Feliz family, see San Francisco (CA) *Daily Alta California*, September 4, 1852; Secrest, *The Man from the Rio Grande*, pp. 50–51; and the confession of Reyes Feliz in the San Francisco (CA) *Alta California*, December 15, 1852, wherein he stated that he "was born at the Real de Bayareca [Baroyeca], state of Sonora."
9. Cave J. Couts, quoted in Secrest, *The Man from the Rio Grande*, pp. 49–50.

CHAPTER 2

1. Joseph Warren Revere, *A Tour of Duty in California*, New York, NY: C.S. Francis & Co. (1849), p. 25.
2. Dale L. Walker, *Bear Flag Rising: The Conquest of California*, New York, NY: Forge Press (1999), p. 128.
3. San Francisco (CA) *Daily Alta California*, July 30, 31, 1853; Sacramento (CA) *Daily Union*, September 10, 1853; Marie E. Northrup, *Spanish-Mexican Families of California*, Burbank, CA: Southern California Genealogical Society (1984), vol. 2, p. 94; Hubert Howe Bancroft, *History of California*, San Francisco, CA: The History Company (1886), vol. 4, p. 667.
4. Affidavit of M.G. Vallejo, February 9, 1854, in *United States vs. Heirs of Juan Reed*, case no. 184, Northern District of California (1852), Bancroft Library, University of California, Berkeley; San Joaquin (CA) *Republican*, August 6, 1853; New York (NY) *Daily Herald*, September 17, 1853; Sausalito (CA) *News*, December 8, 1906; Northrup, *Spanish-Mexican Families of California*, vol. 2, p. 94; Hubert Howe Bancroft, *Pioneer Register*, Los Angeles, CA: Dawson's Book Shop (1964), p.752; Bancroft, *History of California*, vol. 5, p. 370; Rose Marie Beebe and Robert M. Senkewicz, eds., Mariano Guadalupe Vallejo, *Recuerdos: Historical and Personal Remembrances Relating to Alta California*, Norman, OK: University of Oklahoma Press (2023), p. 1257. As explained in Chapter 21, Three Fingered Jack is usually, and incorrectly, identified as Manuel Garcia.
5. Beebe and Senkewicz, eds., *Recuerdos: Historical and Personal Remembrances Relating to Alta California*, p. 1257.

6. Monterey (CA) *Californian*, September 12, 1846, June 5, 1847; San Francisco (CA) *Daily Alta California*, July 24, 1852; Los Angeles (CA) *El Clamor Público*, October 4, 1856; Vallejo, *Recuerdos*, p. 1257; Bancroft, *History of California*, vol. 5, pp. 160–164; *History of Marin County, California*, San Francisco, CA: Alley, Bowen & Co. (1880), pp. 74–76. On the numerous conflicting accounts of this affair, see Jeff Elliott, "The Many Deaths of Cowie and Fowler," at www.santarosahistory.com.
7. Letters from Captain John B. Montgomery, in *Message from the President of the United States*, Washington, DC: Wendell and Van Benthuysen (1848), pp. 1029–1032.
8. Stockton (CA) *San Joaquin Republican*, August 6, 1853; Lieutenant Henry Watson to Captain John Montgomery, October 3, 1846, in *The Journals of Marine Second Lieutenant Henry Bulls Watson, 1845–1848*, Washington, DC: U.S. Marine Corps (1990), pp. 219, 412.
9. Captain Ward Marston to Captain Joseph B. Hull, December 9, 14, 21, 1846, in *The Journals of Marine Second Lieutenant Henry Bulls Watson*, pp. 404, 407, 411; Marius Duvall, *A Navy Surgeon in California, 1846-1847: The Journal of Marius Duvall*, San Francisco, CA: John Howell (1957), p. 72.

CHAPTER 3

1. Dale L. Morgan and James R. Scobie, eds., *Three Years in California: William Perkins' Journal of Life at Sonora, 1849-1852*, Berkeley, CA: University of California Press (1964), p. 92.
2. J.D. Borthwick, *Three Years in California*, London, England: W. Blackwood and Sons (1857), p. 56.
3. Herbert O. Lang, *A History of Tuolumne County, California*, San Francisco, CA: B.F. Alley (1882), pp. 5–6.
4. Perkins, *Three Years in California*, pp. 161–162.
5. California State Census, 1852, San Joaquin County and Calaveras County; U.S. Census, 1850, Campo Seco, Tuolumne County; Margaret Hanna Lang, *Early Justice in Sonora*, Sonora, CA: Mother Lode Press (1963), pp. 56–57, 59, 77.
6. Christman, *One Man's Gold*, pp. 171–172.
7. Susanna Bryant Dakin, *A Scotch Paisano: Hugo Reid's Life in California, 1832-1852*, Berkeley, CA: University of California Press (1939), p. 164.
8. Hinton Helper, *Dreadful California*, New York, NY: The Bobbs-Merrill Co. (1948), p. 55.
9. San Francisco (CA) *Weekly Alta California*, July 2, 1849.
10. Edwin A. Beilharz and Carlos U. Lopez, eds., *We Were 49ers! Chilean Accounts of the California Gold Rush*, Pasadena, CA: Ward Ritchie Press (1976), p. 104.
11. Sister M. Colette Standart, O.P., "The Sonora Migration to California, 1848-1856: A Study in Prejudice," *Historical Society of Southern California Quarterly*, vol. 58, no. 3 (Fall 1976), pp. 335–338, 342.
12. San Francisco (CA) *Examiner*, November 29, 1879; San Jose (CA) *Herald*, December 17, 1879; San Francisco (CA) *Chronicle*, February 6, 1881, April 21, 1907; Lang, *A History of Tuolumne County*, p. 208.
13. San Francisco (CA) *Herald*, April 18, 1853; San Francisco (CA) *Examiner*, November 29, 1879. On Henderson's acquaintance with Joaquin Murrieta, see Mariposa (CA) *Gazette*, March 3, 10, 1883.
14. Sacramento (CA) *Daily Union*, June 20, 1851; San Francisco (CA) *Herald*, August 4, 1853; San Francisco (CA) *Chronicle*, February 6, 1881.
15. U.S. Census Population Schedules, Mariposa County, 1850; Mariposa (CA) *Gazette*, March 3, 1883.
16. Carlo M. De Ferrari, ed., *Annals of Tuolumne County*, Sonora, CA: The Mother Lode Press (1963), pp. 82–85, 87; Lang, *A History of Tuolumne County*, pp. 13–14.
17. William Hubert Burgess, "Anecdotes of the Mines," *Century Magazine*, vol. XLII, no. 1 (May 1891), p. 270.
18. Stockton (CA) *Independent*, September 24, 1856.
19. On the development of the sluice box, see Nevada City (CA) *Journal*, April 19, 1851.
20. Borthwick, *Three Years in California*, pp. 313–314.

21. Sacramento (CA) *Daily Union*, February 15, 1853; Effie Enfield Johnston, "Wade Johnston Talks to His Daughter," *Las Calaveras: Quarterly Bulletin of the Calaveras County Historical Society*, vol. XVIII, no. 1 (October 1969), p. 1; Rollin M. Daggett in San Francisco (CA) *Call*, November 5, 1893.
22. Affidavit of William Byrnes, August 8, 1853, Affidavit of Henry V. McCargar, August 11, 1853, both in California State Archives; Stockton (CA) *Evening Mail*, June 14, 1893; San Francisco (CA) *Examiner*, December 17, 1893. Henry Vaughn McCargar later left the gold fields, married, and returned to his native New York, where he died at age thirty-eight in 1862.
23. Borthwick, *Three Years in California*, pp. 60–61.
24. Friedrich Gerstaecker, *Narrative of a Journey Round the World*, New York, NY: Harper and Brothers (1854), p. 200.
25. Journal of Leonard W. Noyes, typescript, pp. 46, 48, Calaveras County Historical Society collection. Several writers have insisted that Byrnes was never in Murphys Camp in 1850 and therefore could not have met Joaquin there. That is not correct, as set forth in Noyes's journal.

CHAPTER 4

1. San Francisco (CA) *Daily Alta California*, June 3, 1850; New York (NY) *Daily Herald*, July 8, 1850.
2. Lang, *A History of Tuolumne County*, pp. 24, 28–32; De Ferrari, *Annals of Tuolumne County*, pp. 131–138.
3. San Francisco (CA) *Alta California*, July 19, 1850; De Ferrari, *Annals of Tuolumne County*, p. 138, n4; Christman, *One Man's Gold*, pp. 174–178; Perkins, *Three Years in California*, pp. 169–172; Lang, *A History of Tuolumne County*, pp. 39–44; Edna Bryan Buckbee, *The Saga of Old Tuolumne*, New York, NY: Press of the Pioneers (1935), pp. 38, 345–350. The foregoing accounts of this affair are somewhat conflicting but agree in the major details.
4. Sonora (CA) *Herald*, December 21, 1850, quoted in Lang, *Early Justice in Sonora*, p. 12. The homicide count is from the author's examination of various contemporary sources, including diaries, court records, and newspaper reports.
5. Sacramento (CA) *Daily Union*, February 24, April 8, 1852; Baltimore (MD) *Sun*, May 18, 1852; John Boessenecker, *Gold Dust and Gunsmoke: Tales of Gold Rush Outlaws, Gunfighters, Lawmen, and Vigilantes*, New York, NY: John Wiley & Sons (1999), pp. 23–37.
6. Stockton (CA) *San Joaquin Republican*, August 6, 1853; Robert Scott, *Confession, History, and Life of Robert Scott, Executed at Auburn, California, March 31, 1854 for the Murder of Andrew King*, San Francisco, CA: Placer Times and Transcript Steam Presses (1854), p. 6. Some of the crimes Scott describes in his confession do not appear in chronological order.
7. John Boessenecker, *Bandido: The Life and Times of Tiburcio Vasquez*, Norman, OK: University of Oklahoma Press (2010), pp. 37–38.
8. San Francisco (CA) *Daily Alta California*, September 14, 1850; Boessenecker, *Bandido: The Life and Times of Tiburcio Vasquez*, p. 44.
9. Auburn (CA) *Placer Herald*, October 22, 1853; Sacramento (CA) *Daily Union*, February 15, 1854; Scott, *Confession, History, and Life*, pp. 3–4.
10. Sacramento (CA) *Daily Union*, February 15, 1854; Scott, *Confession, History, and Life*, pp. 5–6. On Joaquin and Jesus Valenzuela, see Los Angeles (CA) *El Clamor Público*, June 5, 1858; Los Angeles (CA) *Star*, June 12, 1858; San Luis Obispo (CA) *Tribune*, October 27, November 17, 1877.
11. Scott, *Confession, History, and Life*, p. 6.
12. Benicia (CA) *Gazette*, February 21, 1852; Scott, *Confession, History, and Life*, p. 6; Harvey L. Carter, "The Divergent Paths of Fremont's 'Three Marshalls,'" *New Mexico Historical Review*, vol. 48, no. 1 (January 1973), pp. 5–18.
13. Sacramento (CA) *Transcript*, October 29, 1850; San Francisco (CA) *Daily Alta California*, March 21, 1851; Benicia (CA) *Gazette*, February 21, 1852; Stockton (CA) *San Joaquin Republican*, August 6, 1853; Scott, *Confession, History, and Life of Robert Scott*, p. 6; Albert Shumate, *Francisco Pacheco of Pacheco Pass*, Stockton, CA: University of the Pacific (1977), pp. 12–13, 21–22.

CHAPTER 5

1. Fall River (MA) *Monitor*, February 16, 1850.
2. Borthwick, *Three Years in California*, pp. 57–50.
3. *People v. Joaquin Muliati*, case no. 35, San Joaquin County Court of Sessions, in Carlo M. De Ferrari, "A Time of Terror," *Chispa, the Quarterly of the Tuolumne County Historical Society*, Vol. 42, No. 3 (January–March 2003), pp. 1514–1515. This rare court file was located in the late 1950s in the old San Joaquin County courthouse in Stockton by historian Carlo M. De Ferrari.
4. Sacramento (CA) *Transcript*, December 24, 1850.
5. John Marsh to General Persifor F. Smith, December 5, 1850, published in San Francisco (CA) *Daily Pacific News*, December 7, 1850.
6. San Francisco (CA) *Daily Pacific News*, December 14, 1850; Sacramento (CA) *Transcript*, December 24, 1850; Benicia (CA) *Gazette*, February 21, 1852; James F. Varley, *The Legend of Joaquin Murrieta*, Twin Falls, ID: Big Lost River Press (1995), pp. 16–17; George D. Lyman, *John Marsh, Pioneer*, New York, NY: Charles Scribner's Sons (1931), pp. 304–305, 318–323.
7. San Francisco (CA) *Daily Pacific News*, December 14, 1850.
8. Boessenecker, *Bandido: The Life and Times of Tiburcio Vasquez*, pp. 38–39.
9. San Francisco (CA) *Daily Alta California*, December 18, 20, 1850; San Francisco (CA) *Daily Pacific News*, December 19, 1850; Estate of Digby B. Smith, deceased, Santa Clara County, CA, and Will of Digby B. Smith, Middlesex County, New Jersey, both accessed on www.ancestry.com; Frederic Hall, *The History of San Jose*, San Francisco, CA: A.L. Bancroft and Co. (1871), p. 235. The role of Claudio Feliz in these bandit raids is detailed in the confession of Teodor Vasquez, first published in the San Jose (CA) *Visitor*, then republished in the Benicia (CA) *Gazette*, February 21, 1852, and finally reprinted in Varley, *The Legend of Joaquin Murrieta*, pp. 174–179. Varley's book contains groundbreaking research and much previously unpublished information, but unfortunately, his analysis of events strays far from the facts, and his resulting conclusions are frequently faulty or otherwise unreliable. On Domingo Hernandez's involvement in the triple murder on Los Gatos Creek, see Sacramento (CA) *Daily Union*, July 28, 1852.
10. San Francisco (CA) *Daily Alta California*, December 20, 1850, February 14, 1851; San Jose (CA) *Daily Argus*, January 29, 1851; San Francisco (CA) *Daily Pacific News*, February 14, 1851; Sacramento (CA) *Transcript*, February 15, 1851; Benicia (CA) *Gazette*, February 21, 1852.
11. San Francisco (CA) *Daily Pacific News*, February 18, 1851; Varley, *The Legend of Joaquin Murrieta*, pp. 17, 179. Teodor Vasquez's published confession referred to Jesus Sanate as "Jesus Chanate," an error by the transcriber. Benicia (CA) *Gazette*, February 21, 1852.
12. U.S. Census Population Schedules, Contra Costa County, 1850, 1860; California State Census, Contra Costa County, 1852; San Francisco (CA) *Daily Alta California*, February 24, 1851; Northrup, *Spanish-Mexican Families of Early California*, vol. 1, p. 268.
13. Scott, *Confession, History, and Life*, pp. 6–7.
14. Sacramento (CA) *Democratic State Journal*, September 16, 1853; San Francisco (CA) *Daily Evening Bulletin*, June 30, 1858.

CHAPTER 6

1. San Francisco (CA) *Daily Pacific News*, March 3, 1851; Sacramento (CA) *Transcript*, March 5, 1851; De Ferrari, "A Time of Terror," p. 1515. The old Stockton jail burned down in 1873. Sacramento (CA) *Daily Union*, September 24, 1873.
2. U.S. Army, Register of Enlistments, 1846-1850, Noah James, on www.ancestry.com; Sacramento (CA) *Daily Union*, December 10, 1851; Stockton (CA) *Journal*, reprinted in New York (NY) *Tribune*, December 30, 1851; Santa Cruz (CA) *Weekly Sentinel*, August 31, 1872; Hubert Howe Bancroft, *California Inter Pocula*, San Francisco, CA: The History Company (1888), p. 58.
3. San Francisco (CA) *Daily Alta California*, March 17, 18, 1851; San Francisco (CA) *Daily Pacific News*, April 24, 1851; Perkins, *Three Years in California*, pp. 223–224; Hubert Howe Bancroft, *Popular Tribunals*, San Francisco, CA: The History Company (1887), vol. 1, pp. 449–451.

4. San Francisco (CA) *Daily Alta California*, reprinted in York (PA) *Gazette*, July 29, 1851; San Francisco (CA) *Daily Alta California*, October 24, November 30, 1851; San Joaquin (CA) *Republican*, June 4, November 29, 1851; Sacramento (CA) *Daily Union*, December 10, 1851; San Quentin Prison Register, inmate no. 27, Jerome Boland. The U.S. Army Mexican War service records show no service by Frederick Salkman under any of the seven different spellings of his surname that appeared in the gold rush newspaper accounts.
5. Affidavit of Hilaria Sanchez de Reed, August 25, 1865, in *United States vs. Heirs of Juan Reed; Hilaria Sanchez v. United States*, case no. 185, Northern District of California (1853), Bancroft Library, University of California, Berkeley; House of Representatives, 32nd Congress, Miscellaneous no. 22 (1853), pp. 108, 114; *Reed v. Ring*, 93 California Supreme Court Reports (1892), pp. 96, 101.
6. Affidavit of Dominique Blaive, August 11, 1853, California State Archives; Varley, *The Legend of Joaquin Murrieta*, p. 197 n. 48.
7. Hanford (CA) *Sentinel*, April 17, June 19, 1902; Ridge, *The Life and Adventures of Joaquín Murieta*, p. 159.
8. Angel Sanchez to John Peabody Harrington, 1930, courtesy the late Patsy Ludwig. A slightly different version is reprinted in Ray Iddings, *Joaquin Murrieta: The True Story from News Reports of the Period*. Published by author (2016), p. 197 n48.
9. Angel Sanchez to John Peabody Harrington; Iddings, *Joaquin Murrieta*, p. 197; Fresno (CA) *Bee*, October 7, 1935.
10. San Francisco (CA) *Chronicle*, May 17, 1874.
11. San Joaquin (CA) *Republican*, June 20, 1851; San Francisco (CA) *Daily Alta California*, August 12, 1851; Perkins, *Three Years in California*, pp. 221–224.
12. San Francisco (CA) *Argonaut*, June 29, 1878; Diary of Joseph Warren Matthews, May 15, 1883, quoted in Raymund F. Wood, *Mariana la Loca: Prophetess of the Cantua and Alleged Spouse of Joaquin Murrieta*, Fresno, CA: Fresno County Historical Society (1970), p. 51.
13. San Francisco (CA) *Daily Alta California*, June 10, July 2, 1851; Stockton (CA) *San Joaquin Republican*, June 11, July 2, 1851; Benicia (CA) *Gazette*, February 21, 1852; Perkins, *Three Years in California*, pp. 231–232. Some contemporary accounts refer to David Hill as Jim Hill. Campo Seco in Tuolumne County is not to be confused with the town of the same name in Calaveras County.
14. San Francisco (CA) *Daily Alta California*, July 2, 1851; Stockton (CA) *San Joaquin Republican*, July 2, 1851; Enos Christman, *One Man's Gold: The Letters and Journal of a Forty-Niner*, New York, NY: Whittlesey House (1930), pp. 189–194; Perkins, *Three Years in California*, pp. 231–235. For the confession of David Hill, see Mary Floyd Williams, *Papers of the San Francisco Committee of Vigilance of 1851*, Berkeley, CA: University of California Press (1919), pp. 162–163.
15. San Francisco (CA) *Daily Alta California*, December 15, 1852; Benicia (CA) *Gazette*, February 21, 1852.
16. Sacramento (CA) *Daily Union*, October 11, 1851; San Francisco (CA) *Telegram*, quoted in Marysville (CA) *Daily National Democrat*, December 8, 1858.
17. San Francisco (CA) *Daily Alta California*, October 10, 15, 1851; Sacramento (CA) *Daily Union*, October 11, 1851; Kevin J. Mullen, *Dangerous Strangers: Minority Newcomers and Criminal Violence in the Urban West, 1850-2000*, New York, NY: Palgrave Macmillan (2005), pp. 37, 40.
18. San Francisco (CA) *Daily Alta California*, December 16, 1851; Benicia (CA) *Gazette*, February 21, 1852.

CHAPTER 7

1. San Francisco (CA) *Daily Alta California*, July 13, 1852.
2. Baptismal record of Tomas Procopio Murrieta, May 9, 1843, at www.familysearch.org; Marysville (CA) *Express*, reprinted in Sacramento (CA) *Democratic State Journal*, September 16, 1853; *History of Yuba County, California*, Oakland, CA: Thompson & West (1879), p. 261.
3. Franklin A. Buck, *A Yankee Trader in the Gold Rush*, New York, NY: New York, Houghton Mifflin Co. (1930), pp. 96–97.

4. Sacramento (CA) *Daily Union*, November 13, 18, 1851; Benicia (CA) *Gazette*, February 21, 1852.
5. San Francisco (CA) *Examiner*, October 21, 1888.
6. Sacramento (CA) *Daily Union*, November 13, 18, 1851; San Francisco (CA) *Daily Alta California*, November 12, 1851; Benicia (CA) *Gazette*, November 15, 1851, February 21, 1852; Varley, *The Legend of Joaquin Murrieta*, pp. 18–19.
7. Sacramento (CA) *Daily Union*, November 13, 1851; Sacramento (CA) *Daily Democratic State Journal*, June 15, 1855; *A Memorial and Biographical History of Northern California*, Chicago, IL: The Lewis Publishing Co. (1891), pp. 174, 283–284. The Kentucky Ranch visited by the gang south of Wyandotte in Butte County should not be confused with the mining camp of the same name near Dobbins in Yuba County.
8. Benicia (CA) *Gazette*, February 21, 1852; Marysville (CA) *Herald*, reprinted in Nevada City (CA) *Journal*, November 15, 1851; San Francisco (CA) *Daily Alta California*, November 15, 1851.
9. Benicia (CA) *Gazette*, February 21, 1852; Sacramento (CA) *Daily Union*, December 17, 1851.
10. Benicia (CA) *Gazette*, November 15, 1851.
11. Marysville (CA) *Herald*, reprinted in Nevada City (CA) *Journal*, November 15, 1851; Marysville (CA) *Express*, reprinted in San Francisco (CA) *Daily Alta California*, November 19, December 4, 1851; Benicia (CA) *Gazette*, February 21, 1852; Stockton (CA) *San Joaquin Republican*, March 2, 1853; Marysville (CA) *Daily Herald*, September 14, 1853.
12. Marysville (CA) *Herald*, reprinted in San Francisco (CA) *Daily Alta California*, November 16, 1851; W.J. Organ, "A Pioneer in the Land of the Setting Sun," *The Grizzly Bear*, vol. 8, no. 4 (February 1911), p. 10.
13. Marysville (CA) *Herald*, reprinted in San Francisco (CA) *Daily Alta California*, November 16, 1851.
14. Benicia (CA) *Gazette*, February 21, 1852.
15. Marysville (CA) *Express*, reprinted in San Francisco (CA) *Daily Alta California*, December 16, 1851; Sacramento (CA) *Daily Union*, December 17, 18, 1851. The four arrested men were Antonio Flores, Enrique Artraya, Jose Jesus Pera, and Carlos Camplido.
16. Sacramento (CA) *Daily Union*, November 18, 1851; Varley, *The Legend of Joaquin Murrieta*, p. 24.
17. San Francisco (CA) *Daily Alta California*, November 24, 1851; Stockton (CA) *San Joaquin Republican*, November 19, 26, 1851, January 29, 1853.

CHAPTER 8

1. Benicia (CA) *Gazette*, February 21, 1852.
2. San Francisco (CA) *Daily Alta California*, April 9, 1853.
3. Benicia (CA) *Gazette*, February 21, 1852; San Francisco (CA) *Daily Pacific News*, March 14, 1851; San Francisco (CA) *Daily Alta California*, October 19, 1851.
4. San Francisco (CA) *Daily Alta California*, October 8, 1851; Stockton (CA) *San Joaquin Republican*, October 8, 1851; Sacramento (CA) *Daily Union*, October 11, 1851.
5. San Francisco (CA) *Alta California*, December 16, 1851; Benicia (CA) *Gazette*, February 21, 1852.
6. Benicia (CA) *Gazette*, February 21, 1852; Sacramento (CA) *Daily Union*, February 26, 1857. Teodor Vasquez was also known in San Jose by the surname Velasquez.
7. San Francisco (CA) *Daily Alta California*, December 16, 1851. In Vasquez's confession, which appears in the Benicia (CA) *Gazette*, February 21, 1852, Cheverino's name is phonetically misspelled as "Sefarino."
8. Benicia (CA) *Gazette*, February 21, 1852; Sacramento (CA) *Daily Union*, May 24, June 12, July 13, 14, 1852.
9. San Francisco (CA) *Daily Alta California*, December 27, 1851; Benicia (CA) *Gazette*, February 21, 1852.
10. Benicia (CA) *Gazette*, February 21, 1852. On the leaky San Jose jail, see San Francisco (CA) *Daily Alta California*, December 31, 1850, and San Francisco (CA) *Daily Pacific News*, December 31, 1850.

11. People v. Theodoro Velasquez, Court of Sessions, Santa Clara County, Docket Book, pp. 89, 91–93, Bancroft Library collection, Berkeley, CA.
12. San Francisco (CA) *Daily Alta California*, December 27, 1851, January 1, February 7, April 5, 1852.
13. Benicia (CA) *Gazette*, February 21, 1852; San Francisco (CA) *Daily Alta California*, April 5, 1852.
14. People v. Pedro Montemayor, Santa Clara County Court of Sessions, case no. 203, March 4, 1852, History San Jose collection; Sacramento (CA) *Daily Union*, March 8, 1852; Wilson, *The Joaquin Band*, p. 26; Ridge, *The Life and Adventures of Joaquín Murieta*, pp. 20–21.
15. Sacramento (CA) *Daily Union*, April 13, 21, 1852; Stockton (CA) *San Joaquin Republican*, April 14, May 1, 1852; Jesse D. Mason, *History of Amador County, California*, Oakland, CA: Thompson & West (1881), pp. 67, 286–287.
16. Sacramento (CA) *Daily Union*, April 10, 1852; Walter Van Tilburg Clark, ed., *The Journals of Alfred Doten: Book No. 6*, Reno, NV: University of Nevada Press (1973), p. 124; Lang, *A History of Tuolumne County*, p. 214–215; Varley, *The Legend of Joaquin Murrieta*, pp. 26, 32–33; Margaret Lang, *Early Justice in Sonora*, pp. 77–83.
17. Lang, *A History of Tuolumne County*, p. 214.
18. California State Census, Mariposa County, 1852; Allen Ruddle to James Ruddle, May 12, 1850, reprinted in Oakland (CA) *Tribune*, December 2, 1934; Sacramento (CA) *Daily Union*, May 3, 1852; Stockton (CA) *San Joaquin Republican*, February 6, 1854; John Outcalt, *A History of Merced County, California*, Los Angeles, CA: Historic Record Co. (1925), pp. 106, 379–380.
19. Carvel Collins, *Sam Ward in the Gold Rush*, Stanford, CA: Stanford University Press (1949), pp. 168–169.
20. Stockton (CA) *San Joaquin Republican*, May 5, 1852; San Francisco (CA) *Daily Alta California*, May 15, 1852; Varley, *The Legend of Joaquin Murrieta*, pp. 26–27, 38.
21. Stockton (CA) *San Joaquin Republican*, May 15, 1852.
22. Stockton (CA) *San Joaquin Republican*, May 26, 1852, June 4, 1853; San Francisco (CA) *Daily Alta California*, May 29, 1852; Sacramento (CA) *Daily Union*, May 26, 1852, June 8, 1853; Secrest, *The Man from the Rio Grande*, p. 129. Contemporary accounts also spell Barrillo's surname as Borella and Carello.
23. San Francisco (CA) *Daily Alta California*, June 26, December 15, 1852; Los Angeles (CA) *Star*, June 12, 1852; Benjamin Hayes, *Pioneer Notes from the Diaries of Judge Benjamin Hayes*, Los Angeles, CA: McBride Printing Co. (1929), p. 96.

CHAPTER 9

1. On Harry Love as a tracker, see Teresa Griffin Vielé, *Following the Drum: A Glimpse of Frontier Life*, New York, NY: Rudd & Carleton (1858), p. 229.
2. Los Angeles (CA) *Star*, June 19, 26, 1852; *Tennessee v. Garner* (1985) 471 U.S. 1; Varley, *The Legend of Joaquin Murrieta*, pp. 30–31; Secrest, *The Man from the Rio Grande*, pp. 97–98.
3. Los Angeles (CA) *Star*, July 3, 1852, reprinted in San Francisco (CA) *Herald*, July 11, 1852. On Harry Love's identification of Joaquin Murrieta as the killer of Captain Wilson, see Stockton (CA) *San Joaquin Republican*, August 11, 1853.
4. *People v. Claude Felice* [sic], 1852, Court of Sessions Minutes, Book A, p. 90, Tuolumne County Archives, Sonora, CA; Lang, *A History of Tuolumne County*, pp. 214–215.
5. San Francisco (CA) *Daily Alta California*, July 22, 1852; San Francisco (CA) *Daily Placer Times and Transcript*, April 19, 1854; Heckendorn and Wilson, *Miners and Businessmen's Directory*, Columbia, CA: Clipper Office (1856), p. 74.
6. Lang, *A History of Tuolumne County*, pp. 210–211.
7. Sacramento (CA) *Union*, July 15, 1852; San Francisco (CA) *Daily Alta California*, July 22, 1852; Heckendorn and Wilson, *Miners and Businessmen's Directory*, p. 75.
8. Stockton (CA) *San Joaquin Republican*, July 14, 1852; San Francisco (CA) *Daily Alta California*, July 16, 1852; Heckendorn and Wilson, *Miners and Businessmen's Directory*, p. 75.

9. San Francisco (CA) *Daily Alta California*, July 22, 1852; Sonora (CA) *Herald*, reprinted in Sacramento (CA) *Daily Union*, September 7, 1852.
10. San Francisco (CA) *Daily Alta California*, August 31, 1852.
11. Sonora (CA) *Herald*, reprinted in Sacramento (CA) *Daily Union*, September 7, 1852.
12. Stockton (CA) *San Joaquin Republican*, September 4, 1852.
13. Stockton (CA) *San Joaquin Republican*, September 11, 1852.
14. San Francisco (CA) *Daily Alta California*, September 4, 1852; Monterey County Jail Register, 1851–1872, California History Room Archives, Monterey Public Library.
15. San Francisco (CA) *Daily Evening Picayune*, December 1, 1851; San Francisco (CA) *Daily Alta California*, January 17, 1852; San Francisco (CA) *Herald*, September 18, 1852.
16. John Kottinger's account of this raid is in the Pleasanton (CA) *Times*, January 17, 1891.
17. San Francisco (CA) *Herald*, September 18, 1852. On James Anthony, see U.S. Census, city of Monterey, 1850; California State Census, Monterey County, 1852; Bancroft, *Pioneer Register*, p. 38; San Andreas (CA) *Independent*, July 10, 1858.
18. On Anastacio Garcia, see Boessenecker, *Bandido*, pp. 42–51, 54–68, 393–394.
19. Allan Ochs, History Center of San Luis Obispo County, to author, August 2, 2023.
20. San Francisco (CA) *Herald*, September 18, 1852; Stockton (CA) *San Joaquin Republican*, September 29, October 27, 1852; Sacramento (CA) *Union*, June 2, 1874; Monterey County Jail Register, prisoner no. 127, Manuel Espinosa, and prisoner no. 128, Mateo Andrade; San Quentin Prison Inmate Register, prisoner no. 117, Mateo Andrade.
21. San Francisco (CA) *Daily Alta California*, September 18, 1852; Stockton (CA) *San Joaquin Republican*, September 29, 1852; San Francisco (CA) *Herald*, September 18, 1852.

CHAPTER 10

1. Horace Bell, *Reminiscences of a Ranger*, Santa Barbara, CA: Walter Hebberd (reprint, 1927), p. 10. Bell's book, the first to be published in Southern California, is filled with colorful portraits and anecdotes, but it has many weaknesses and errors as set forth in this chapter.
2. Bell, *Reminiscences of a Ranger*, p. 12.
3. Boessenecker, *Gold Dust and Gunsmoke*, p. 323.
4. Bell, *Reminiscences of a Ranger*, pp. 12–13.
5. Los Angeles (CA) *Star*, December 4, 1852, reprinted in San Francisco (CA) *Daily Alta California*, December 15, 1852; Iddings, *Joaquin Murrieta*, pp. 19–20. Online genealogical data banks and baptismal records fail to show any person named Ana Benites, or with any similar name, who was born in, or lived in, New Mexico in the 1830s or 1840s.
6. San Francisco (CA) *Daily Alta California*, April 29, 1851; Nevada City (CA) *Journal*, June 12, 1852; *Boessenecker, Bandido: The Life and Times of Tiburcio Vasquez*, pp. 40–42.
7. Boessenecker, *Gold Dust and Gunsmoke*, pp. 63–64; Boessenecker, *Bandido: The Life and Times of Tiburcio Vasquez*, p. 44.
8. Los Angeles (CA) *Star*, November 13, 1852; Jack Skiles, *Judge Roy Bean Country*, Lubbock, TX: Texas Tech University Press (1996), pp. 2–4.
9. Sacramento (CA) *Daily Union*, June 4, 1851; San Francisco (CA) *Daily Alta California*, June 17, 1851; Boessenecker, *Gold Dust and Gunsmoke*, pp. 60–63.
10. Los Angeles (CA) *Star*, November 13, 1852.
11. Los Angeles (CA) *Star*, November 13, 1852.
12. Los Angeles (CA) *Star*, November 20, 1852, reprinted in San Francisco (CA) *Daily Alta California*, November 30, 1852; Dakin, *A Scotch Paisano*, pp. 34, 107, 192–193. Felipe Reid's wife was one of the sisters of Patricio Ontiveros. See Northrup, *Spanish-Mexican Families of California*, vol. 2, pp. 190–191. Horace Bell in *Reminiscences of a Ranger*, p. 8, is the sole source for the claim that Felipe Reid was one of the arrested suspects. His claim is not supported by any contemporary source.
13. Los Angeles (CA) *Star*, November 13, 20, 1852, February 26, 1853; San Francisco (CA) *Daily Alta California*, November 30, 1852. Several later writers asserted that the suspect who surren-

dered and established an alibi was Felipe Reid, but the reports in the *Los Angeles Star* of November 13 and 20, 1852, make it evident that this man was actually Patricio Ontiveros, whose name the *Star* misspelled as Patricio Ontivera.

14. Doyce B. Nunis, Jr., ed., Antonio Coronel, *Tales of Mexican California*, Santa Barbara, CA: Bellerophon Books (1994), p. 70. On vigilantism in Los Angeles, see John Mack Faragher, *Eternity Street: Violence and Justice in Frontier Los Angeles*, New York, NY: W.W. Norton & Co. (2016).
15. Los Angeles (CA) *Star*, November 27, 1852.
16. Los Angeles (CA) *Star*, November 20, 1852, reprinted in San Francisco (CA) *Daily Alta California*, November 30, 1852.
17. Los Angeles (CA) *Star*, December 4, 1852, reprinted in San Francisco (CA) *Daily Alta California*, December 15, 1852. The *Star*'s account has an apparent printer's error in which the word *knue*, which has no meaning, is used instead of *duende*.
18. Los Angeles (CA) *Star*, November 27, 1852; Los Angeles (CA) *Herald*, January 23, 1899.
19. Los Angeles (CA) *Star*, December 4, 1852, reprinted in San Francisco (CA) *Daily Alta California*, December 15, 1852.
20. Coronel, *Tales of Mexican California*, pp. 70–71; Los Angeles (CA) *Star*, December 4, 1852, reprinted in San Francisco (CA) *Alta California*, December 18, 1852.
21. Coronel, *Tales of Mexican California*, p. 71; Francisco (CA) *Daily Alta California*, July 27, August 18, 1853; Los Angeles (CA) *Star*, September 17, 1853. Coronel, in his memoirs, dictated in 1877, mistakenly referred to Ana as Antonia la Molinera, meaning "Antonia, the miller woman." His error was repeated by historian Hubert Howe Bancroft in 1888 and in turn by various writers ever since.
22. Los Angeles (CA) *Star*, December 4, 1852, reprinted in San Francisco (CA) *Alta California*, December 18, 1852.
23. Los Angeles (CA) *Star*, December 4, 1852, reprinted in San Francisco (CA) *Alta California*, December 18, 1852.
24. Los Angeles (CA) *Star*, December 4, 1852, reprinted in San Francisco (CA) *Alta California*, December 18, 1852; Sacramento (CA) *Daily Union*, December 16, 1852; Bell, *Reminiscences of a Ranger*, pp. 27–28.
25. Coronel, *Tales of Mexican California*, pp. 70–71.
26. Stockton (CA) *San Joaquin Republican*, December 18, 1852; San Francisco (CA) *Daily Alta California*, Volume 3, December 31, 1852; burial record of Cipriano Sandoval, Benito Lopez, and Yginio Barumas, December 5, 1852, accessed on findagrave.com; John W. Moore, *Moore's Historical, Biographical, and Miscellaneous Gatherings*, Concord, NH: Republican Press Association (1886), p. 549; Bell, *Reminiscences of a Ranger*, p. 29.
27. Bell, *Reminiscences of a Ranger*, p. 9.
28. Los Angeles (CA) *Star*, October 11, 1853; Los Angeles (CA) *El Clamor Público*, February 21, 1857. A correspondent in Los Angeles incorrectly reported that "Cipriano, while under trial, confessed to being an accomplice in the murder." See San Francisco (CA) *Herald*, December 16, 1852. In fact, it was Ana who claimed that Sandoval confessed to her; the only suspects who made confessions were Reyes Feliz and Benito Lopez. Another account claims that Felipe Reid confessed on his deathbed that he had killed Bean. There is no proof to support that story, either.
29. Most of those who have written about Joaquin Murrieta over the years have been unaware that Reyes Feliz and Claudio Feliz were brothers, and that they were also Joaquin's brothers-in-law, despite the fact that this family connection was described by multiple California newspapers in 1853.

CHAPTER II

1. San Francisco (CA) *Chronicle*, May 17, 1874.
2. Sacramento (CA) *Daily Union*, February 19, June 8, 10, 1853; San Francisco (CA) *Daily Alta California*, February 10, 21, 1853; Affidavit of N.B. Hubbell, August 12, 1853, California State Archives; Varley, *The Legend of Joaquin Murrieta*, p. 49. Some accounts claim that the notorious

Jack Powers, an Irishman who came to California with the Regiment of New York Volunteers, was one of the gang. That is impossible, for during early months of 1853, Powers was engaged in a legal battle—which turned deadly—over his ranch in Santa Barbara County. See Dudley T. Ross, *Devil on Horseback: A Biography of the Notorious Jack Powers*, Fresno, CA: Valley Publishers (1975), pp. 46–61.

3. San Francisco (CA) *Argonaut*, June 29, 1878.
4. Stockton (CA) *San Joaquin Republican*, January 26, 1853, December 25, 1857; San Francisco (CA) *Placer Times and Transcript*, January 29, 1853.
5. San Joaquin (CA) *Republican*, January 29, 1853.
6. San Francisco (CA) *Daily Alta California*, November 1, 1852. Ellis's surname is also spelled Ellas in contemporary accounts. On Jeff Gatewood's participation in the manhunt for Joaquin Murrieta, see John Daggett, "Early Day Reminiscences of Well Known Pioneer of California," n.d., Daggett Scrapbooks, vol. 4, p. 4, California State Library; San Andreas (CA) *Independent*, February 20, 1858; Sacramento (CA) *Bee*, May 27, 1882; and Sacramento (CA) *Record-Union*, September 22, 1889.
7. San Francisco (CA) *Placer Times and Transcript*, January 28, 1853; San Francisco (CA) *Daily Alta California*, January 31, 1853; San Joaquin (CA) *Republican*, January 29, February 2, 1853. Various writers have confused the location of the Phoenix Quartz Mill. For the correct location, as given here, see David Shorr, "A Quartz Mine, a Bar and Gulches," unpublished ms. (2012), Calaveras Historical Society collection.
8. San Francisco (CA) *Pacific*, June 11, 1852.
9. San Joaquin (CA) *Republican*, January 29, February 2, 1853; Mokelumne Hill (CA) *Calaveras Chronicle*, reprinted in San Francisco (CA) *Herald*, February 8, 1853; Varley, *The Legend of Joaquin Murrieta*, p. 46.
10. San Joaquin (CA) *Republican*, January 29, 1853; Clark, ed., *The Journals of Alfred Doten: Book No. 7*, p. 140.
11. San Joaquin (CA) *Republican*, January 29, February 2, 1853, December 25, 1857; San Francisco (CA) *Herald*, February 8, 1853; San Francisco (CA) *Daily Alta California*, February 8, 1853.
12. San Joaquin (CA) *Republican*, January 29, February 2, 1853, December 25, 1857.
13. San Joaquin (CA) *Republican*, January 29, 1853.
14. Elias S. Ketchum diary, 1853, Huntington Library, quoted in Ronald H. Limbaugh and Willard P. Fuller, Jr., *Calaveras Gold: The Impact of Mining on a Mother Lode County*, Reno, NV: University of Nevada Press (2004), p. 124.
15. Stockton (CA) *San Joaquin Republican*, February 2, 5, 8, 12, 1853; Sacramento (CA) *Daily Union*, February 8, 1853, March 14, 1856; Varley, *The Legend of Joaquin Murrieta*, p. 48. On David C. Cady (1810–1866), see California State Census, Calaveras County, 1852; Providence (RI) *Evening Bulletin*, September 25, 1866; and Military Service Records, Mexican War, 1845–1848, at www.ancestry.com.
16. San Francisco (CA) *Daily Placer Times and Transcript*, February 5, 1853; Varley, *The Legend of Joaquin Murrieta*, p. 49.
17. San Francisco (CA) *Daily Placer Times and Transcript*, February 5, 1853.
18. Affidavit of N.B. Hubbell, August 12, 1853. On Hubbell, see Gold Hill (NV) *Daily News*, October 21, 1863.
19. San Francisco (CA) *Daily Placer Times and Transcript*, February 8, 1853.
20. California State Census, Calaveras County, 1852; Ruby City (ID) *Owyhee Avalanche*, December 16, 1876; Boise (ID) *Idaho Statesman*, April 3, 1883.
21. Mokelumne Hill (CA) *Calaveras Chronicle*, March 19, 1853; Varley, *The Legend of Joaquin Murrieta*, p. 50; Wilson, *The Joaquin Band*, p. 135–136.
22. Stockton (CA) *San Joaquin Republican*, February 16, 1853.
23. On William McMullen (1827-1880) see Sacramento (CA) *Daily Union*, February 15, 1853, August 13, 1860; Santa Cruz (CA) *Weekly Sentinel*, February 21, 1863; Santa Fe (NM) *New Mexican*, October 30, 1880; *Reports from the Court of Claims*, Washington, DC: Government Printing Office (1861), vol. 1, pp. 108–112; Darlis A. Miller, *The California Column in New Mexico*, Albuquerque, NM: University of New Mexico Press (1982), p. 137.

24. Sacramento (CA) *Daily Union*, February 15, 1853.
25. San Francisco (CA) *Daily Alta California*, February 14, 1853; Sacramento (CA) *Daily Union*, February 15, 1853.
26. Sacramento (CA) *Daily Union*, February 15, 1853.
27. Sacramento (CA) *Daily Union*, February 15, 1853; Stockton (CA) *San Joaquin Republican*, February 19, 23, 1853.

CHAPTER 12

1. Stockton (CA) *San Joaquin Republican*, June 28, 1851; Sacramento (CA) *Daily Union*, April 24, 1852.
2. San Andreas (CA) *Calaveras Chronicle*, March 19, 1853.
3. San Francisco (CA) *Daily Alta California*, June 23, 1853; William Speer, *The Oldest and the Newest Empire: China and the United States*, Cincinnati: National Publishing Co. (1870), 595–597.
4. Sacramento (CA) *Daily Union*, February 15, 20, 1853; San Francisco (CA) *Daily Alta California*, February 16, 1853; Stockton (CA) *San Joaquin Republican*, February 16, 1853; San Francisco (CA) *Placer Times and Transcript*, February 16, 1853; San Francisco (CA) *Daily Evening Journal*, February 22, 1853.
5. Sacramento (CA) *Daily Union*, February 15, 1853; Stockton (CA) *San Joaquin Republican*, February 16, 1853.
6. Stockton (CA) *San Joaquin Republican*, February 16, 19, 1853; Sacramento (CA) *Daily Union*, February 17, 19, 1853; Coloma (CA) *Miners' Advocate*, February 19, 1853; San Francisco (CA) *Daily Evening Journal*, February 22, 1853. The plaque marking the location of Jackson's hanging tree is in the sidewalk in front of 26 Main Street; it was placed there in 1937.
7. San Francisco (CA) *Daily Alta California*, February 14, 1853.
8. Quoted in San Francisco (CA) *Daily Alta California*, February 16, 1853.
9. Stockton (CA) *San Joaquin Republican*, February 16, 1853; Sacramento (CA) *Daily Union*, February 22, 1853.
10. San Francisco (CA) *Daily Whig*, reprinted in Sacramento (CA) *Daily Union*, February 14, 1853.
11. San Francisco (CA) *Golden Era*, March 27, 1853.
12. Stockton (CA) *San Joaquin Republican*, February 19, 1853.
13. San Francisco (CA) *Placer Times and Transcript*, February 19, 1853; Sacramento (CA) *Daily Union*, February 19, 1853; San Francisco (CA) *Daily Alta California*, February 21, 1853.
14. Stockton (CA) *San Joaquin Republican*, February 23, March 2, 1853; Sacramento (CA) *Daily Union*, February 24, 27, 1853; Shasta (CA) *Shasta Courier*, March 26, 1853.
15. Daggett, "Early Day Reminiscences of Well Known Pioneer of California."
16. San Francisco (CA) *Daily Alta California*, February 21, 1853. On Charles A. Clarke, see Stockton (CA) *Independent*, February 9, 1863, and John Boessenecker, *When Law Was in the Holster: The Frontier Life of Bob Paul*, Norman, OK: University of Oklahoma Press (2012), pp. 27–29 and chs. 2–4.
17. Stockton (CA) *San Joaquin Republican*, March 2, 1853.
18. Stockton (CA) *San Joaquin Republican*, March 2, 1853; San Francisco (CA) *Daily Alta California*, February 24, 1853; Sacramento (CA) *Daily Union*, February 24, 1853. Some accounts refer to the gang's raid at Rich Gulch as separate from a raid near Liberty Hall Ranch. They were the same incident.
19. Stockton (CA) *San Joaquin Republican*, February 26, March 2, 1853.
20. Stockton (CA) *San Joaquin Republican*, March 2, 1853.
21. Stockton (CA) *San Joaquin Republican*, February 26, 1853.

CHAPTER 13

1. Journals of William Hubert Burgess, California Historical Society, San Francisco, CA.
2. San Francisco (CA) *Alta California*, February 24, 1853; Nevada City (CA) *Journal*, March 4, 1853.

3. Stockton (CA) *San Joaquin Republican*, February 23, March 2, 1853.
4. Stockton (CA) *San Joaquin Republican*, March 2, 1853.
5. San Francisco (CA) *Daily Placer Times and Transcript*, March 9, 1853.
6. Stockton (CA) *San Joaquin Republican*, March 12, 1853.
7. San Francisco (CA) *Daily Alta California*, March 11, 1853; Stockton (CA) *San Joaquin Republican*, March 12, 18, 1853. On William Prescott, see Sacramento (CA) *Daily Union*, March 3, 1868; Stockton (CA) *Evening Record*, December 18, 1926. Most accounts have William Prescott's first name as Willis, which is incorrect. He later served briefly in the California Rangers. On the origin of the name Hornitos, see Oroville (CA) *Weekly Butte Record*, June 27, 1857.
8. Sonora (CA) *Union Democrat*, reprinted in Petaluma (CA) *Weekly Argus*, August 2, 1866; Outcalt, *A History of Merced County*, p. 109.
9. San Francisco (CA) *Daily Alta California*, April 9, 10, 1853.
10. San Francisco (CA) *Daily Alta California*, April 10, 1853; Stockton (CA) *San Joaquin Republican*, July 16, 1853.
11. San Francisco (CA) *Daily Alta California*, April 27, 1853; San Francisco (CA) *Daily Evening Journal*, April 23, 1853, reprinted in Iddings, *Joaquin Murrieta*, p. 120.
12. San Francisco (CA) *Herald*, April 18, 1853.
13. Stockton (CA) *San Joaquin Republican*, May 4, 1853.
14. Varley, in *The Legend of Joaquin Murrieta*, p. 69, doubts the story because the man identified as Joaquin reportedly "carried *four* six-shooters, no less." However, numerous men in the gold rush carried two sidearms and two revolvers in pommel holsters.
15. Stockton (CA) *San Joaquin Republican*, April 23, 1853.
16. Sacramento (CA) *Sacramento Union Steamer Edition*, April 22, 1853.
17. Stockton (CA) *San Joaquin Republican*, April 23, June 4, 1853; Sacramento (CA) *Daily Union*, April 21, June 8, 1853.
18. George H. Tinkham, *History of San Joaquin County, California*, Los Angeles, CA: Historic Record Co. (1923), pp. 276–277. The Gnekow block was a commercial building at 725 East Main Street, Stockton.

CHAPTER 14

1. Donna Harrell, authority on Jesse James, to author, July 20, 2023.
2. San Francisco (CA) *Daily Alta California*, March 11, 1853.
3. San Francisco (CA) *Daily Alta California*, April 1, 1853; *Journal of the Fourth Session of the Legislature of the State of California*, San Francisco, CA: George Kerr, State Printer (1853), pp. 344, 351, and Appendix, Document No. 49, pp. 3–4.
4. Petitions from the citizens of Mariposa County, 1853, California State Archives; Secrest, *The Man from the Rio Grande*, p. 119.
5. Stockton (CA) *San Joaquin Republican*, May 4, 1853; Secrest, *The Man from the Rio Grande*, p. 119.
6. Sacramento (CA) *Daily Union*, May 16, 1853; *The Statutes of California, Passed at the Fourth Session of the Legislature*, San Francisco, CA: George Kerr, State Printer (1853), p. 194.
7. Los Angeles (CA) *Star*, June 4, 1853.
8. Stockton (CA) *San Joaquin Republican*, May 21, 1853.
9. Captain Elijah S.C. Robertson, discharge paper for H. Love, January 11, 1843, Texas State Archives; Santa Cruz (CA) *Weekly Sentinel*, July 4, 1868; Denver (CO) *Statesman*, January 27, 1900; Secrest, *The Man from the Rio Grande*, pp. 20–32.
10. Secrest, *The Man from the Rio Grande*, pp. 32–36.
11. Vielé, *Following the Drum*, p. 227; Helen Chapman to her mother, August 19, 1849, quoted in Secrest, *The Man from the Rio Grande*, p. 46.
12. New Orleans (LA) *Crescent*, October 21, 1848; Secrest, *The Man from the Rio Grande*, pp. 36-38.
13. Matamoros (Mexico) *American Flag*, October 9, 1848, reprinted in Charleston (SC) *Daily Courier*, October 31, 1848; Secrest, *The Man from the Rio Grande*, pp. 38–40.
14. Secrest, *The Man from the Rio Grande*, pp. 43–45.

15. San Francisco (CA) *Daily Alta California*, December 12, 1850; Secrest, *The Man from the Rio Grande*, pp. 48, 63–71.
16. Sacramento (CA) *Daily Union*, February 28, 1852; Secrest, *The Man from the Rio Grande*, pp. 121–123.
17. Jill L. Cossley-Batt, *The Last of the California Rangers*, New York, NY: Funk & Wagnalls Co. (1928), p. 181; William B. Secrest, *Showdown! Lionhearted Lawmen of Old California*, Fresno, CA: Craven Street Books (2010), p. 3.
18. Stockton (CA) *San Joaquin Republican*, June 8, 1853; San Francisco (CA) *Examiner*, December 17, 1893.
19. Brigham D. Madsen, *Glory Hunter: A Biography of Patrick Edward Connor*, Salt Lake City, UT: University of Utah Press (1990), pp. 3–20.
20. San Francisco (CA) *Daily Alta California*, April 17, 1850; Sacramento (CA) *Transcript*, April 20, 1850; Madsen, *Glory Hunter*, pp. 20–27.
21. Stockton (CA) *San Joaquin Republican*, June 21, 1853; San Francisco (CA) *Daily Alta California*, April 7, 1854; Madsen, *Glory Hunter*, pp. 27–29.
22. Affidavit of William Byrnes, August 8, 1853, California State Archives; Sacramento (CA) *Daily Union*, June 1, 1872, March 28, 1873; Los Angeles (CA) *Herald*, June 18, 1893; San Francisco (CA) *Examiner*, December 17, 1893; William B. Secrest, *Lawmen and Desperadoes*, Spokane, WA: Arthur H. Clark Co. (1994), p. 70.
23. Sacramento (CA) *Daily Union*, June 1, 1872, March 28, 1873; Journal of Leonard W. Noyes, typescript, p. 48; Robert W. Ellison, *Territorial Lawmen of Nevada, Volume One*, Minden, NV: Hot Springs Mountain Press (1999), pp. 12–13; Charles W. Haskins, *The Argonauts of California*, New York, NY: Fords, Howard & Hulbert (1890), p. 156. Haskins, at pp. 335–336, claimed that Byrnes took part in the lynching of a black man named Bartlett near Placerville in 1851, but no reports of such an event appeared in the California press. In 1892, Byrnes's daughter, Nellie J. Abbott (1857–1918), gave a fictional account of her father's life to a San Francisco journalist. She falsely claimed that her father had studied for the priesthood in Missouri, then served as a Texas Ranger, and had even befriended Joaquin Murrieta during the war in Mexico. See San Francisco (CA) *Call*, April 3, 1892. Byrnes himself stated that he first met Joaquin in California in the spring of 1850. See Affidavit of William Byrnes, August 8, 1853, California State Archives.
24. Ellison, *Territorial Lawmen of Nevada*, pp. 9–10, 13–14, 17.
25. U.S. Census Population Schedules, Mariposa County, 1850; California State Census, Mariposa County, 1852; California Great Register, Kern County, 1866, Madera County, 1878; Mariposa (CA) *Gazette*, March 3, 1883; Santa Cruz (CA) *Sentinel*, November 21, 1895.
26. Secrest, *The Man from the Rio Grande*, pp. 123–124.
27. U.S. Census Population Schedules, Woodford County, Kentucky, 1850, and Mariposa, CA, 1850; Stockton (CA) *San Joaquin Republican*, September 10, 1851; Santa Cruz (CA) *Sentinel*, February 25, 1885; Mabelle Eppard Martin, ed., "From Texas to California in 1849: Diary of C. C. Cox," *Southwestern Historical Quarterly*, Vol. 29, No. 1 (July 1925), p. 134; Secrest, *The Man from the Rio Grande*, pp. 126–127, 225–226; Varley, *The Legend of Joaquin Murrieta*, pp. 83, 88–90, 182–183.

CHAPTER 15

1. Stockton (CA) *San Joaquin Republican*, May 4, 1853; Sacramento (CA) *Daily Union*, June 18, 1853.
2. Affidavit of Susan Banta, August 8, 1853; Myron Angel, *History of San Luis Obispo County, California*, Oakland, CA: Thompson & West (1883), p. 305.
3. Los Angeles (CA) *Star*, June 11, 1853.
4. Los Angeles (CA) *Star*, June 18, 1853; San Francisco (CA) *Daily Alta California*, July 3, 15, 1853.
5. Los Angeles (CA) *Star*, June 18, 1853.
6. Los Angeles (CA) *Star*, June 25, 1853.
7. Los Angeles (CA) *Star*, June 18, 1853.

8. San Francisco (CA) *Daily Alta California*, July 15, 1853.
9. San Francisco (CA) *Daily Alta California*, July 27, 1853; Stockton (CA) *San Joaquin Republican*, July 28, 1853.
10. San Francisco (CA) *Daily Alta California*, August 10, 1853; San Francisco (CA) *Herald*, August 19, 1853; San Francisco (CA) *Daily Placer Times and Transcript*, August 23, 1853.
11. San Francisco (CA) *Daily Alta California*, May 1, 1853; Sacramento (CA) *Daily Union*, May 2, July 29, 1853; Nevada City (CA) *Journal*, May 6, 1853.
12. Sacramento (CA) *Daily Union*, June 10, 13, 1853; San Francisco (CA) *Daily Alta California*, June 14, 1853. Leyba's name is given in some accounts as Teba, which is not a Spanish surname.
13. Stockton (CA) *San Joaquin Republican*, June 16, 1853; San Francisco (CA) *Herald*, July 16, 1853.
14. Sacramento (CA) *Daily Union*, June 7, 1853; Stockton (CA) *San Joaquin Republican*, June 8, 1853; San Francisco (CA) *Daily Alta California*, June 12, 1853.
15. Stockton (CA) *San Joaquin Republican*, June 8, 1853.
16. Stockton (CA) *San Joaquin Republican*, June 21, 1853; San Francisco (CA) *Herald*, June 24, 1853.
17. San Francisco (CA) *Daily Alta California*, June 20, 24, 1853; Boessenecker, *Gold Dust and Gunsmoke*, pp. 212–214.
18. Stockton (CA) *San Joaquin Republican*, May 4, July 12, 1853. Edward Connor wrote regular letters to the *Republican*.
19. San Francisco (CA) *Daily Alta California*, July 18, 1853.
20. Stockton (CA) *San Joaquin Republican*, July 16, 1853; Cossley-Batt, *The Last of the California Rangers*, p. 186.
21. Stockton (CA) *San Joaquin Republican*, July 16, 1853; Harry Love to Governor John Bigler, July 12, 1853, California State Archives.
22. Stockton (CA) *San Joaquin Republican*, July 16, 19, 21, 28, 30, August 2, 1853; Stockton (CA) *Journal*, reprinted in Nevada City (CA) *Journal*, July 29, 1853; Sacramento (CA) *Daily Union*, July 29, 1853.
23. Love to Governor Bigler, July 12, 1853. Love's letter has been misinterpreted by numerous writers, who have relied on several 1853 newspapers that garbled the contents of the letter and incorrectly reported that Love's prisoner was Joaquin's brother, instead of his brother-in-law, and that he had written his letter from San Jose instead of San Juan Bautista. See, for example, San Francisco (CA) *Daily Placer Times and Transcript*, July 18, 1853.
24. Stockton (CA) *San Joaquin Republican*, July 23, 1853.
25. Harry Love to Governor John Bigler, August 4, 1853, California State Archives; Stockton (CA) *San Joaquin Republican*, August 11, 1853; San Francisco (CA) *Commercial Advertiser*, reprinted in Niles (MI) *Democrat*, September 17, 1853; Sacramento (CA) *Democratic State Journal*, August 13, 1853; Fresno (CA) *Expositor*, November 12, 1879; Mariposa (CA) *Gazette*, March 3, 1883; Stockton (CA) *Evening Mail*, June 14, 1893.

CHAPTER 16

1. Love to Governor Bigler, August 4, 1853; Stockton (CA) *San Joaquin Republican*, August 6, 11, 1853; San Francisco (CA) *Commercial Advertiser*, reprinted in Niles (MI) *Democrat*, September 17, 1853; Merced (CA) *Merced County Sun*, May 20, 1892; Secrest, *The Man from the Rio Grande*, pp. 149–151.
2. Love to Governor Bigler, August 4, 1853; Stockton (CA) *San Joaquin Republican*, August 11, 1853; San Jose (CA) *Evening News*, July 18, 1891.
3. Stockton (CA) *San Joaquin Republican*, July 30, August 6, 11, 1853.
4. San Francisco (CA) *Evening Journal*, July 29, 1853; Sacramento (CA) *Daily Union*, August 4, 1853; Stockton (CA) *San Joaquin Republican*, August 6, 11, 1853.
5. Love to Governor Bigler, August 4, 1853.
6. Court record, Mariposa County, August 5, 1853, California State Archives.
7. Stockton (CA) *Journal*, quoted in Sacramento (CA) *Daily Union*, August 2, 1853. Several newspapers incorrectly reported that Love had not been present at the Cantua Creek fight and that

Bill Byrnes had been in command. Lieutenant Connor promptly refuted that claim. See Nevada City (CA) *Journal*, August 5, 1853; Stockton (CA) *San Joaquin Republican*, August 6, 1853.

8. San Francisco (CA) *Daily Alta California*, August 1, 4, 1853.
9. San Francisco (CA) *Daily Placer Times and Transcript*, July 30, 1853.
10. California State Census, San Luis Obispo, CA, 1852; affidavits of William Byrnes, Susan Banta, Juliet G. Thorp, Pedro Manta, Jose Maria Vega, John Green, Henry C. Long, and Stephen Bond, August 7, 8, 1853, California State Archives.
11. Stockton (CA) *San Joaquin Republican*, August 6, 1853.
12. Stockton (CA) *San Joaquin Republican*, August 6, 11, 1853; Sacramento (CA) *Daily Union*, August 12, 1853; Auburn (CA) *Placer Herald*, August 13, 1853.
13. Affidavits of Dominique Blaive, Henry V. McCargar, August 11, 12, 1853, California State Archives.
14. Affidavits of Clemente Morales, Jose Maria Rivera, Francisco Rivera, Bernardo Reyna, and G.W. Havens, August 12, 1853, California State Archives.
15. Stockton (CA) *Journal*, reprinted in San Francisco (CA) *Daily Alta California*, August 13, 1853.
16. San Francisco (CA) *Herald*, August 18, 1853.
17. San Francisco (CA) *Herald*, August 4, 1853, quoted in Sacramento (CA) *Daily Union*, August 17, 1853.
18. San Francisco (CA) *Daily Alta California*, August 16, September 1, 1853.
19. San Francisco (CA) *Herald*, August 19, 1853.
20. San Francisco (CA) *Daily Alta California*, August 23, 1853.
21. San Francisco (CA) *Herald*, August 26, 1853.
22. San Joaquin (CA) *Republican*, August 11, 1853.
23. San Jose (CA) *Register*, August 25, 1853, reprinted in Sacramento (CA) *Daily Union*, August 29, 1853; San Francisco (CA) *Bulletin*, December 3, 1899; California State Prison Register, 1853–1854; Order of Governor John Bigler, August 27, 1853, California State Archives.
24. Sacramento (CA) *Daily Union*, September 9, 10, 1853.
25. Sacramento (CA) *Daily Union*, September 12, 1853; Marysville (CA) *Daily Herald*, September 14, 1853.
26. Marysville (CA) *Express*, reprinted in Sacramento (CA) *Democratic State Journal*, September 16, 1853.
27. The daguerreotype of Norton, Love, and Henderson was lost for some 150 years. In 2006 it appeared for sale on eBay as a photo of three unidentified armed civilians from the 1850s. John McWilliams, a California image collector and antiques dealer, immediately recognized the distinctive man in the center as Harry Love, and the man on the right as Billy Henderson. The Henderson solo image—plainly taken in the same sitting—had not been lost and had previously been published several times. The daguerreotype of the three California Rangers is in the collection of the Nelson-Atkins Museum of Art in Kansas City, Missouri.
28. Marysville (CA) *Daily Herald*, September 17, 1853.
29. Marysville (CA) *Daily Herald*, September 17, 1853; Pioche (NV) *Record*, July 7, 1877.
30. Auburn (CA) *Placer Herald*, September 24, 1853; Marysville (CA) *Daily Herald*, September 26, 1853; Sacramento (CA) *Democratic State Journal*, October 17, 1853; *The Journals of Alfred Doten* quoted in Secrest, *The Man from the Rio Grande*, p. 169.
31. Sacramento (CA) *Democratic State Journal*, October 28, 1853; Stockton (CA) *San Joaquin Republican*, November 1, 1853.
32. Columbia (CA) *Gazette*, reprinted in Sacramento (CA) *Daily Union*, October 24, 1853; Stockton (CA) *San Joaquin Republican*, October 20, 1853.
33. Marysville (CA) *Daily Herald*, October 21, 1853; Stockton (CA) *San Joaquin Republican*, October 25, 1853. Harry Love gave Governor Bigler the first sixteen affidavits that he collected, which are now in the California State Archives. These do not include the large number of affidavits he gathered on his subsequent tour through the mining region. Those affidavits, with the exception of the one signed by Ignacio Lisarraga in San Francisco, are now lost
34. San Francisco (CA) *Herald*, reprinted in Nevada City (CA) *Journal*, November 25, 1853.
35. San Francisco (CA) *Daily Alta California*, April 30, 1854.

CHAPTER 17

1. San Francisco (CA) *Herald*, September 5, 1852; Los Angeles (CA) *Star*, September 17, 1853; Merced (CA) *Merced County Sun*, May 20, 1892; Stockton (CA) *Evening Mail*, June 14, 1893; San Francisco (CA) *Bulletin*, December 3, 1899.
2. San Francisco (CA) *Daily Alta California*, September 24, 1853; Sacramento (CA) *Daily Union*, September 26, 1853; Los Angeles (CA) *Star*, October 8, December 10, 1853.
3. Los Angeles (CA) *Star*, October 8, 1853.
4. San Francisco (CA) *Daily Alta California*, October 11, 1853; Sacramento (CA) *Daily Union*, October 13, 1853; Los Angeles (CA) *Star*, October 8, 22, 1853. Horace Bell claimed that he was one of the Los Angeles Rangers involved in these events. However, his account is so wildly inaccurate that his participation seems improbable. Bell, *Reminiscences of a Ranger*, pp. 147–150.
5. San Francisco (CA) *Herald*, October 24, 1853; Los Angeles (CA) *Star*, December 10, 1853.
6. Los Angeles (CA) *Star*, December 10, 1853.
7. Auburn (CA) *Placer Herald*, October 22, 29, 1853, April 1, 1854; Sacramento (CA) *Daily Union*, February 15, 1854; Scott, *Confession, History, and Life*, p. 8.
8. Los Angeles (CA) *Star*, December 10, 1853; San Francisco (CA) *Daily Alta California*, December 13, 1853.
9. Stockton (CA) *San Joaquin Republican*, February 22, 1854; San Francisco (CA) *Examiner*, January 1, 1893; San Francisco (CA) *Call*, May 4, 1901.
10. People v. Atanacio Moreno, District Court, Los Angeles County, 1854, in Seaver Center, Natural History Museum of Los Angeles County; Los Angeles (CA) *Star*, January 21, 28, February 11, 1854; San Francisco (CA) *Vestkusten*, December 22, 1904; San Quentin Prison registers, Atanacio Moreno, convict nos. 362, 2651; Benjamin C. Truman, *Life, Adventures, and Capture of Tiburcio Vasquez*, Los Angeles, CA: Los Angeles Star (1874), pp. 31–33. Horace Bell provides a garbled account of these events in *Reminiscences of a Ranger*, pp. 155–162.
11. U.S. Census Population Schedules, Santa Clara County, 1860, Sebastian Flores; Great Register, Alameda County (1867), no. 1802, Sebastian Flores; J.M. Scanland, "Joaquin Murrieta," *Overland Monthly*, vol. 26 (November 1895), p. 538; Northrup, *Spanish-Mexican Families of Early California*, vol. 1, p. 297; Bancroft, *History of California*, vol. 7, p. 204.
12. San Francisco (CA) *Daily Alta California*, October 22, 1854; San Jose (CA) *Semi-Weekly Tribune*, October 24, 1854; Sacramento (CA) *Daily Union*, October 30, 1854; Newport (RI) *Herald of the Times*, December 7, 1854.
13. San Jose (CA) *Telegraph*, reprinted in Sacramento (CA) *Daily Union*, September 20, 1856; San Jose (CA) *Tribune*, reprinted in Petaluma (CA) *Sonoma County Journal*, September 26, 1856.
14. San Francisco (CA) *Daily Alta California*, October 22, 1854; San Jose (CA) *Patriot*, October 18, 1872, January 10, 11, August 15, 1873; San Jose (CA) *Mercury-News*, May 10, 11, November 11, 12, 1873; Oakland (CA) *Daily News*, August 18, 1873; Oakland (CA) *Alameda County Gazette*, August 23, 1873; San Quentin prison register, convict no. 5795, Sebastian Flores.
15. San Jose (CA) *Tribune*, January 8, 1858.
16. San Quentin prison register, convict no. 779, Juan Antonio Valenzuela; Governor's pardon file, Juan Antonio Valenzuela, California State Archives.
17. San Jose (CA) *Tribune*, July 9, 1856; Sacramento (CA) Daily Union, August 11, 1856; San Francisco (CA) *Herald*, February 20, 1857; San Francisco (CA) *Daily Alta California*, January 5, 1858; San Jose (CA) *Telegraph*, reprinted in Sacramento (CA) *Daily Union*, January 12, 1858; San Francisco (CA) *Evening News*, October 27, 1917.
18. San Quentin Prison Register, convict no. 613, Juan Flores; Los Angeles (CA) *Star*, January 31, 1857; Los Angeles (CA) *El Clamor Público*, January 24, 31, 1857; San Diego (CA) *Herald*, January 31, 1857; Boessenecker, *Gold Dust and Gunsmoke*, pp. 117–118.
19. Los Angeles (CA) *Star*, January 31, 1857; Los Angeles (CA) *El Clamor Público*, January 31, 1857; Boessenecker, *Gold Dust and Gunsmoke*, pp. 118–119. In 2024 a marker commemorating the murdered officers was erected near Barton Mound.

20. Los Angeles (CA) *Star*, January 31, 1857; Los Angeles (CA) *El Clamor Público*, January 24, 1857.
21. Boessenecker, *Gold Dust and Gunsmoke*, pp. 119–130.
22. San Jose (CA) *Tribune*, January 1, 8, 1858; San Francisco (CA) *Daily Alta California*, January 5, 1858; Los Angeles (CA) *El Clamor Público*, January 23, 1858; Boessenecker, *Gold Dust and Gunsmoke*, pp. 130–131.
23. San Francisco (CA) *Daily Evening Bulletin*, August 27, 1858.
24. Los Angeles (CA) *Star*, November 27, 1858; San Francisco (CA) *Bulletin*, December 6, 1858; San Francisco (CA) *Daily Alta California*, December 11, 1858; Boessenecker, *Gold Dust and Gunsmoke*, pp. 130–131. Horace Bell's account of the Juan Flores–Pancho Daniel band, in *Reminiscences of a Ranger*, at pp. 401–410, has been relied on by many writers during the past century. Unfortunately, Bell's story is riddled with errors and fabrications. Bell even claimed that Flores and Daniel had a gang numbering fifty men and tried to start a revolution in Southern California, a yarn Bell invented out of whole cloth. See Faragher, *Eternity Street*, pp. 343–344. On the Lookout Lynching case, see John Boessenecker, *Badge and Buckshot: Lawlessness in Old California*, Norman, OK: University of Oklahoma Press (1988), ch. 12.
25. Los Angeles (CA) *Star*, September 17, 1853; San Francisco (CA) *California Chronicle*, March 31, 1854; Boessenecker, *Bandido: The Life and Times of Tiburcio Vasquez*, pp. 40–42.
26. Dictation of Alfred A. Green, 1878, Bancroft Library; San Diego (CA) *Herald*, August 29, 1857; San Francisco (CA) *Daily Evening Bulletin*, September 12, 1857; Los Angeles (CA) *El Clamor Público*, September 12, 1857.
27. Los Angeles (CA) *Star*, May 5, 12, 1860; Sacramento (CA) *Daily Union*, May 15, 31, 1860; Hayes, *Pioneer Notes*, p. 198.
28. Bell, *Reminiscences of a Ranger*, p. 45. On Jack Powers see Ross, *Devil on Horseback*.
29. John Boessenecker, "Pio Linares: Californio Bandido," *The Californians, the Magazine of California History*, vol. 5, no. 6 (Nov.–Dec. 1987), pp. 34–44; Boessenecker, *Gold Dust and Gunsmoke*, pp. 103–113.
30. Death Warrant of Joaquin Valenzuela, History Center of San Luis Obispo County; San Francisco (CA) *Daily Evening Bulletin*, June 30, 1858.
31. Joaquin Valenzuela to David W. Alexander, May 21, 1858, History Center of San Luis Obispo County; San Francisco (CA) *Daily Evening Bulletin*, June 14, 1858.
32. Los Angeles (CA) *El Clamor Público*, June 5, 1858; San Francisco (CA) *Daily Evening Bulletin*, June 30, 1858.

CHAPTER 18

1. Washington (DC) *Evening Star*, May 8, July 16, 17, 22, 26, 1856; Varley, *The Legend of Joaquin Murrieta*, p. 156.
2. Sacramento (CA) *Daily Union*, October 8, 1853; Sacramento (CA) *Daily Union*, June 1, 1872; Ellison, *The Territorial Lawmen of Nevada*, p. 19; *Annual Report of the State Controller*, Sacramento, CA: State Printer (1855), Report on State Prison, p. 23.
3. Boessenecker, *Bandido: The Life and Times of Tiburcio Vasquez*, pp. 54–69.
4. U.S. Census Population Schedules, Monterey County, 1860 and 1870; Robert F. Heizer and Theodora Kroeber, eds., *Ishi, the Last Yahi: A Documentary History*, Berkeley, CA: University of California Press (1979), p. 18; Secrest, *Lawmen and Desperadoes*, p. 74.
5. Shasta (CA) *Courier*, September 3, 1859; Red Bluff (CA) *Beacon*, September 21, October 26, December 14, 1859.
6. Sacramento (CA) *Daily Union*, June 7, 1860, June 1, 1872; Marysville (CA) *Daily Appeal*, June 26, 1860; Sacramento (CA) *State Capital Reporter*, February 29, 1868; San Francisco (CA) *Chronicle*, November 13, 1869; San Rafael (CA) *Marin Journal*, November 20, 1869.
7. U.S. Census Population Schedules, Stockton, CA, 1880; California State Hospital commitment register, 1873, inmate no. 5664, William Byrnes; Sacramento (CA) *Daily Union*, March 28, 1873; San Francisco (CA) *Bulletin*, January 12, 1874.
8. Los Angeles (CA) *Star*, July 16, 23, 1859.

9. Los Angeles (CA) *Star*, July 30, August 8, 1859, March 31, April 7, 14, 21, 1860; Los Angeles (CA) *El Clamor Público*, September 17, 1859; Sacramento (CA) *Daily Union*, April 14, 1860.
10. Los Angeles (CA) *Daily News*, November 23, 1863; San Francisco (CA) *Daily Alta California*, November 24, 1863.
11. Sacramento (CA) *Daily Union*, September 9, 1857; Los Angeles (CA) *Star*, July 16, 1870; San Diego (CA) *Union*, March 17, 1875; Santa Cruz (CA) *Sentinel*, August 12, 1876, November 16, 1895; San Jose (CA) *Herald*, December 17, 1879; Merced (CA) *Sun-Star*, January 4, 1883; Nathan C. Sweet, "William T. Henderson," *The Madera County Historian*, vol. 4, no. 1 (January 1964), pp. 4–6, 8.
12. Sacramento (CA) Daily Union, December 22, 1860; Charles Kelly and Hoffman Birney, *Holy Murder: The Story of Porter Rockwell*, New York: Minton, Balch & Co. (1934), p. 197. Some accounts incorrectly give his alias as Joachim Johnston.
13. Sacramento (CA) *Daily Union*, December 22, 1860; Kelly and Birney, *Holy Murder: The Story of Porter Rockwell*, p. 189.
14. Los Angeles (CA) *Star*, January 28, 1860; Salt Lake City (UT) *Deseret News*, April 18, 25, 1860; Salt Lake City (UT) *Mountaineer*, April 21, 1860.
15. Salt Lake City (UT) *Deseret News*, May 23, 1860; Sacramento (CA) *Daily Union*, December 22, 1860; Kelly and Birney, *Holy Murder: The Story of Porter Rockwell*, p. 198.
16. Secrest, *The Man from the Rio Grande*, pp. 171–172.
17. Salt Lake City (UT) *Deseret News*, September 17, December 10, 1862; Salt Lake City (UT) *Evening Democrat*, March 29, 1887; Madsen, *Glory Hunter*, pp. 30–87.
18. Madsen, *Glory Hunter*, chs. 7–18.
19. Secrest, *The Man from the Rio Grande*, pp. 175, 183–185.
20. San Jose (CA) Mercury-News, January 29, 1882; David J. Langum, *Quite Contrary: The Litigious Life of Mary Bennett Love*, Lubbock, TX: Texas Tech University Press (2014), p. 89.
21. Shasta (CA) *Courier*, September 9, 1854.
22. Stockton (CA) *Republican*, May 19, 1854; Secrest, *The Man from the Rio Grande*, pp. 187–191.
23. President Franklin Pierce to Secretary of War, Jefferson Davis, at www.raabcollection.com; Philadelphia (PA) *Pennsylvanian*, June 30, 1854; Washington (DC) *Sentinel*, March 21, 1855; Washington (DC) *Evening Star*, April 9, 1856; San Francisco (CA) *Weekly Bulletin*, June 7, 1856.
24. Secrest, *The Man from the Rio Grande*, pp. 231–251. Most accounts incorrectly spell Iverson's surname as Eiverson. On Christian Iverson, see San Mateo County Great Register of Voters (1874), p. 14, and San Francisco (CA) *Examiner*, January 22, 1900.
25. San Francisco (CA) *Examiner*, July 9, 1868.
26. San Francisco (CA) *Examiner*, July 9, 1868; Secrest, *The Man from the Rio Grande*, pp. 252–261. Mary Love is buried in the Pioneer Cemetery in Watsonville, California. The location of Harry Love's grave was lost until 1988 when the author and the late William B. Secrest visited Mission City Memorial Park in Santa Clara. We examined the old typescript list of burial plots, which showed no grave for Harry Love, but one for a Mary Love. We then asked to see the original handwritten ledger, and sure enough, the typist had misread "Harry" as "Mary." In 2003 Love's grave was finally marked with a headstone erected by E Clampus Vitus, a California history organization.
27. U.S. Census Population Schedules, 1860, Santa Cruz County, CA; Santa Cruz (CA) *Sentinel*, February 25, 1885; Stockton (CA) *Daily Evening Herald*, October 28, 1868; Stockton (CA) *Independent*, December 13, 1869; Boessenecker, *Gold Dust and Gunsmoke*, pp. 196–197.
28. Stockton (CA) *San Joaquin Republican*, May 6, 1855; Cossley-Batt, *The Last of the California Rangers*, pp. 104–108.
29. Sacramento (CA) *Daily Union*, July 24, 26, 1882; Stockton (CA) *Evening Mail*, July 25, 1882; Merced (CA) *Express*, October 28, 1882; Merced (CA) *Sun-Star*, February 15, 1883; Secrest, *Showdown!*, pp. 28–42.
30. On Howard's accounts of the Rangers, see Mariposa (CA) *Gazette*, March 10, 1883; Merced (CA) *Sun*, May 20, 1892; Stockton (CA) *Evening Mail*, June 14, 1893; San Francisco (CA) *Examiner*, December 17, 1893; Omaha (NE) *Daily Tribune*, January 23, 1900; San Francisco (CA)

Chronicle, April 21, 1907; Sacramento (CA) *Daily Union*, April 30, 1922; Cossley-Batt, *The Last of the California Rangers*, pp. 187–191.

31. Stockton (CA) *San Joaquin Republican*, July 26, 1853; Secrest, *The Man from the Rio Grande*, p. 140; Secrest, *Showdown!*, pp. 1–2.

CHAPTER 19

1. San Francisco (CA) *Chronicle*, May 17, 1874; Diary of Joseph Warren Matthews, May 15, 1883, quoted in Wood, *Mariana la Loca*, pp. 51–52.
2. San Francisco (CA) *Daily Alta California*, July 18, 1868; Fresno (CA) *Expositor*, November 26, 1873; Lilbourne A. Winchell, *History of Fresno County and the San Joaquin Valley*, Fresno, CA: Arthur H. Cawston (1933), p. 95.
3. Stockton (CA) *Evening Mail*, March 30, 1882; San Francisco (CA) *Chronicle*, May 17, 1874.
4. Stockton (CA) *Evening Mail*, March 30, 1882; Boessenecker, *Bandido: The Life and Times of Tiburcio Vasquez*, ch. 18.
5. Fresno (CA) *Republican*, September 14, 1878.
6. U.S. Census Population Schedules, 1880, Fresno County, CA.
7. Wood, *Mariana la Loca*, pp. 23–24; Zephyrin Engelhardt, *The Holy Man of Santa Clara: Father Magin Catalá*, San Francisco, CA: James H. Barry Co. (1909), pp. 18, 44–46, 66.
8. Fresno (CA) *Weekly Expositor*, March 28, 1883; San Francisco (CA) *Examiner*, June 6, 1883; Santa Barbara (CA) *Morning Press*, June 14, 1883.
9. Fresno (CA) *Weekly Expositor*, April 30, 1883.
10. Santa Barbara (CA) *Morning Press*, June 14, 1883; Wood, *Mariana la Loca*, pp. 51, 56; Rosanne Gonzales-Hardy, "The Chavoya Family," accessed on www.somosprimos.com.
11. Fresno (CA) *Daily Expositor*, May 22, 1883.
12. San Francisco (CA) *Chronicle*, May 22, 1883.
13. Fresno (CA) *Daily Expositor*, June 2, 1883; San Francisco (CA) *Examiner*, June 5, 1883; Santa Barbara (CA) *Morning Press*, June 14, 1883; Hollister (CA) *Advance*, reprinted in San Jose (CA) *Mercury News*, June 26, 1883.
14. Fresno (CA) *Daily Expositor*, July 10, 17, 1883; Ventura (CA) *Signal*, July 21, 1883; Hanford (CA) *Daily Journal*, June 30, 1906.
15. Fresno (CA) *Daily Expositor*, July 17, 21, 1883.
16. Fresno (CA) *Daily Expositor*, August 4, 8, 13, 1885.
17. Fresno (CA) *Daily Expositor*, August 13, 1885; Hanford (CA) *Daily Journal*, June 30, 1906; San Quentin prison register, convict no. 18601, Adolf Corona.
18. Iddings, *Joaquin Murrieta*, p. 197; San Jose (CA) *Herald*, December 15, 1890; Fresno (CA) *Weekly Expositor*, December 17, 1890; San Francisco (CA) *Call*, July 29, 1891; San Francisco (CA) *Bulletin*, August 13, 1891.
19. Visalia (CA) *Daily Delta*, July 27, 28, November 16, 17, 1892; Tulare (CA) *Register*, July 27, 1892; Visalia (CA) *Daily Times*, July 26, November 15, 1892; Folsom prisoner register, convict no. 2772, Antonio Begara.
20. Visalia (CA) *Daily Times*, January 15, 1894.
21. Oakland (CA) *Tribune*, December 23, 1893; Visalia (CA) *Daily Delta*, December 20, 1883; Visalia (CA) *Daily Times*, January 31, 1894.
22. Visalia (CA) *Daily Delta*, April 13, 1902; Hanford (CA) *Sentinel*, April 14, 17, 1902; Wood, *Mariana la Loca*, pp. 63–68. A search of the National Park Service online database fails to show a Civil War soldier named Gabriel Saures, under that or any similar spelling.

CHAPTER 20

1. Baptismal record of Tomas Procopio Murrieta, May 9, 1843, at www.familysearch.org; Delfina Colby, great granddaughter of Procopio Bustamante, to author, December 22, 2006.

2. John Boessenecker, *Lawman: The Life and Times of Harry N. Morse*, Norman, OK: University of Oklahoma Press (1998), p. 31.
3. San Quentin Prison Register, convict no. 2603, Thomas Redondo, and no. 2334, Antonio Rodriguez; Governor's Pardon files, Antonio Rodriguez, California State Archives; Los Angeles (CA) *Daily News*, January 24, February 28, 1862; Los Angeles (CA) *Star*, March 1, 15, 1862, January 24, 1863; Sacramento (CA) *Union*, January 1, 1864.
4. Benjamin Hayes to Cave J. Couts, December 10, 1862, Huntington Library, San Marino, CA; Los Angeles (CA) *Star*, November 29, December 13, 1862; Sacramento (CA) *Daily Union*, December 4, 1862, June 9, 1864; Los Angeles (CA) *News*, December 2, 1863; Bancroft, *Pioneer Register*, p. 746; Esther Boulton Black, *Rancho Cucamonga and Dona Merced*, Redlands, CA: San Bernardino County Museum Association (1975), pp. 69–73.
5. Hayes to Couts, December 10, 1862; Robert S. Carlisle to Cave J. Couts, March 8, 1863, Huntington Library, San Marino, CA; Los Angeles (CA) *News*, February 11, 1863; Los Angeles (CA) *Star*, February 14, 1863; Sacramento (CA) *Daily Union*, February 27, 1863.
6. Los Angeles (CA) *Star*, February 14, 21, 1863; Sacramento (CA) *Daily Union*, February 27, 1863; Los Angeles (CA) *News*, April 15, 1863; Los Angeles (CA) *Star*, April 18, 1863.
7. Los Angeles (CA) *News*, June 23, 1864.
8. Los Angeles (CA) *News*, May 13, 1863, May 24, 1864; Los Angeles (CA) *Star*, November 21, December 12, 1863, May 28, 1864; San Francisco (CA) *Alta California*, November 23, 1863.
9. Shasta (CA) *Courier*, February 7, 1863; Santa Cruz (CA) *Sentinel*, February 7, 1863; Sacramento (CA) *Bee*, April 7, 1863; Boessenecker, *Lawman: The Life and Times of Harry Morse*, pp. 32–33, 70.
10. San Francisco (CA) *Alta California*, September 5, 6, 1863; Monterey (CA) *Republican*, August 21, 1871; Oakland (CA) *Tribune*, August 19, 1882; San Quentin Prison Register, convict no. 2603, Thomas Redondo; Boessenecker, *Lawman: The Life and Times of Harry Morse*, pp. 34–36.
11. Monterey (CA) *Republican*, August 21, 1871.
12. Boessenecker, *Lawman: The Life and Times of Harry Morse*, pp. 157–159.
13. Boessenecker, *Bandido: The Life and Times of Tiburcio Vasquez*, pp. 134–135.
14. Boessenecker, *Lawman: The Life and Times of Harry Morse*, pp. 159–169.
15. Boessenecker, *Bandido: The Life and Times of Tiburcio Vasquez*, pp. 145–149.
16. Los Angeles (CA) *Star*, September 21, 1871; San Francisco (CA) *Alta California*, September 21, 29, 1871.
17. Boessenecker, *Lawman: The Life and Times of Harry Morse*, pp. 175–179.
18. New York (NY) *Times*, February 27, 1872.
19. San Quentin commitment records, convict no. 5247, Tomas Redondo, California State Archives; San Francisco (CA) *Alta California*, February 29, March 1, 1876.
20. Oakland (CA) *Tribune*, November 16, 1877; San Francisco (CA) *Alta California*, January 14, 1878; San Francisco (CA) *Pacific Rural Press*, November 24, 1877; San Quentin Prison Register, convict no. 8106, Avelino Tesca.
21. Visalia (CA) *Weekly Delta*, November 17, 1877.
22. San Francisco (CA) *Chronicle*, December 18, 1877; Oakland (CA) *Tribune*, December 19, 1877; Bakersfield (CA) *Courier Californian*, December 20, 1877.
23. San Francisco (CA) *Chronicle*, December 23, 1877; Bakersfield (CA) *Courier Californian*, December 27, 1877.
24. San Francisco (CA) *Chronicle*, December 23, 1877; San Francisco (CA) *Examiner*, December 24, 1877; Bakersfield (CA) *Courier Californian*, December 27, 1877.
25. San Francisco (CA) *Chronicle*, December 28, 1877; Merced (CA) *Express*, January 5, 1878.
26. Merced (CA) *Express*, January 5, 1878; Visalia (CA) *Weekly Delta*, January 5, 1878; Oakland (CA) *Daily Evening Tribune*, January 19, 1878; San Francisco (CA) *Bulletin*, January 22, 1878.
27. San Francisco (CA) *Bulletin*, January 29, 1878; San Francisco (CA) *Daily Alta California*, November 11, 1883.
28. Documento Numero 95, Secretario de Estado y el Despacho de Gobernacion, August 31, 1878, accessed at www.uanl.mx; San Diego (CA) *Union*, August 27, September 4, October 1, 1878; Mexico City (Mexico) *La Voz de México*, January 1, 1879.

29. San Luis Obispo (CA) *Tribune*, October 25, 1879; San Jose (CA) *Mercury News*, April 27, 1880, February 27, 1883; Sacramento (CA) *Daily Union*, April 28, 1880.
30. Tucson (AZ) *Daily Star*, August 3, 1882; Mexico City (Mexico) *El Siglo Diez y Nueve*, August 28, 1882; John Boessenecker, *When Law Was in the Holster: The Frontier Life of Bob Paul* Norman, OK: University of Oklahoma Press (2012), pp. 226–229.
31. Marriage, birth, and death records, Hermosillo, Mexico: Procopio Bustamante and Juana Bernal, on www.familysearch.org; San Jose (CA) *Mercury News*, February 20, 1886.
32. Death Records, Hermosillo, Mexico, Tomas Bustamante, December 31, 1891, on www.familysearch.org.

CHAPTER 21

1. Rose Marie Beebe, Robert M. Senkewicz, eds., Mariano Guadalupe Vallejo, *Recuerdos: Historical and Personal Remembrances Relating to Alta California*, Norman, OK: University of Oklahoma Press (2023), p. 1342.
2. San Francisco (CA) *Daily Alta California*, March 26, 1855.
3. San Francisco (CA) *Daily Alta California*, March 28, 1855.
4. Santa Cruz (CA) *Sentinel*, reprinted in Sacramento (CA) *Union*, October 29, 1856.
5. San Francisco (CA) *Daily Alta California*, November 10, 1879.
6. Sacramento (CA) *Union*, November 15, 1879.
7. San Jose (CA) *Herald*, November 25, 1879; *History of Yuba County, California*, Oakland, CA: Thompson & West (1879), p. 126.
8. Marysville (CA) *Daily Herald*, September 14, 1853.
9. Sacramento (CA) *Daily Union*, June 1, 1872; San Francisco (CA) *Call*, November 5, 1893.
10. San Francisco (CA) *Alta California*, April 25, September 26, 1855; Stockton (CA) *San Joaquin Republican*, April 27, 1855; San Francisco (CA) *Daily Placer Times and Transcript*, September 22, 25, 1855; San Francisco (CA) *Golden Era*, September 30, 1855; Los Angeles (CA) *Star*, October 13, 1855.
11. Sacramento (CA) *Daily Union*, September 25, 1858; New York (NY) *Daily Herald*, March 14, 1856.
12. Sacramento (CA) *Daily Union*, December 31, 1866.
13. Louis J. Jordan, *Hand-book and Descriptive Catalogue of the Pacific Museum of Anatomy and Natural Science*, San Francisco, CA: Bruce's Printing House (circa 1872), pp. 43–44; William B. Secrest, "Love and the Bandit's Head," at www.historynet.com.
14. San Francisco (CA) *Herald*, August 4, 1853; Mokelumne Hill (CA) *Calaveras Chronicle*, September 12, 1868; San Francisco (CA) *Report*, reprinted in Auburn (CA) *Placer Argus*, December 23, 1892; J.M. Scanland, "Joaquin Murrieta, A Californian Fra Diavolo," *Overland Monthly*, vol. xxvi, no. 155 (November 1895), p. 553.
15. Hanford (CA) *Daily Journal*, June 12, 1902; Hanford (CA) *Sentinel*, June 19, 1902.
16. Oakland (CA) *Tribune*, August 28, 1891; Cotati and Rohnert Park (CA) *World*, July 10, 1968; Los Angeles (CA) *Times*, May 4, 1999; William B. Secrest, *The Return of Joaquin*, Fresno, CA: Saga-West Publishing Co. (1973), pp. 36–39; Richard Rodriguez, "The Head of Joaquin Murrieta," *California*, vol. 10, no. 7 (July 1985), pp. 62, 89; Secrest, *The Man from the Rio Grande*, p. 264. Numerous writers have asserted that Joaquin's head was not incinerated in the fire, claiming that Jordan's museum was then located on McAllister Street, outside the fire zone. That is incorrect, for city directories show that in 1906 the museum was actually at 1051 Market Street, which was destroyed.
17. Ridge, *The Life and Adventures of Joaquín Murieta*, p. 7.
18. Sausalito (CA) *News*, December 8, 1906; San Rafael (CA) *Independent*, reprinted in Petaluma (CA) *Courier*, December 14, 1856; Andrew Galvan, curator, Mission Dolores, to author, October 25, 2023.
19. Ridge, *The Life and Adventures of Joaquín Murieta*, p. 31; Scanland, "Joaquin Murrieta," p. 534; Marysville (CA) *Daily Appeal*, January 14, 1904; San Francisco (CA) *Call*, June 29, 1920, July 28, 1921.

20. San Francisco (CA) *California Chronicle*, August 7, 1854; San Francisco (CA) *Daily Placer Times and Transcript*, August 25, 1854.
21. Grass Valley (CA) *Morning Union*, January 23, 1870; Parins, *John Rollin Ridge*, pp. 107, 195, 220.
22. The voluminous research files of Walter Noble Burns, including his work on Joaquin Murrieta, are in Special Collections, University of Arizona, Tucson.
23. For examination of the voluminous myths and folklore surrounding Joaquin Murrieta, see Bruce Thornton, *Searching for Joaquin: Myth, Murieta and History in California*, San Francisco, CA: Encounter Books (2003); and Wilson, *The Joaquin Band*, chs. 1 and 6.
24. U.S. Census Population Schedules, Kern County, CA, 1920; Great Registers, Tejon, CA, 1884, and Tehachapi, CA, 1900; Fresno (CA) *Bee*, September 15, 1935; Frank F. Latta, *Joaquin Murrieta and His Horse Gangs*. Santa Cruz, CA: Bear State Books (1980), pp. 29, 121–122, 560–569.
25. U.S. Census Population Schedules, Madera, CA, 1900 and 1910; Fresno (CA) *Bee*, May 14, 1931; Latta, *Joaquin Murrieta and His Horse Gangs*, pp. 28–29, 141–142.
26. Los Angeles (CA) *Times*, November 25, 1958; Stephen J.C. Andes, *Zorro's Shadow: How a Mexican Legend Became America's First Superhero*, Chicago, IL: Chicago Review Press (2020), p. 109.
27. Johnston McCulley, *The Mark of Zorro*, New York, NY: Grosset & Dunlap (1924), p. 107.
28. Kansas City (MO) *Star*, October 2, 1927; Akron (OH) *Beacon Journal*, January 14, 1928; Baltimore (MD) *Sun*, January 15, 1928; Los Angeles (CA) *Times*, December 29, 1929.
29. Oakland (CA) *Tribune*, May 20, 1923; Andes, *Zorro's Shadow*, p. 107.
30. Andes, *Zorro's Shadow*, pp. 200–203.
31. Ridge, *The Life and Adventures of Joaquín Murieta*, p. 7.

INDEX

Note: Illustrations are indicated by italic page numbers.

A

Abbott, Nellie J., 475n23
Acklin, William M., 41, 94, 95
Adams & Company Express, 280–281, 289, 290
Agapito (Mexican horseman), 158, 159, 163, 164
Alexander, David W., 356–360, *359*
Alvitre, Juan, 159, 160, 162, 163
American Camp. *See* Columbia
Andrada, Maria Ana (Mariana)
  alias used by, 169, 389
  appearance of, 93, 96, *392*
  arrest by Osburn, 178
  background of, 91–92, 169
  on Bean murder, 178–181, 186, 189, 471n28
  Bergara and, 402–405
  Daniel and, 183, 190, 349, 351
  death and burial of, 406, 444
  disposition of, 92, 96, 389
  infidelity to Murrieta, 93–94, 183, 190
  Joaquin Rocks site and, 393–402
  Linares and, 390, 393
  Lopez informed on by, 182
  maroma attended by, 171–172, 179
  at Midwinter Fair, 405
  Murrieta's violence against, 94–96
  at New Idria quicksilver mine, 389–390
  Procopio harbored by, 430
  Saures and, 405–406
  on severed head of Murrieta, 391
Andrade, Mateo, 154, 160, 162–164
Angelino, Blas, 24–26, 29, 338–341, 411
Angels Camp, 200, 203, *204*, 227, 282
Anthony, James, 158–159, 339, 340, 342, 470n17
Anthony, John, 339, 340
Anthony, Mary, 339–340
Anza, Juan Bautista de, 16, 17
Apaches, 47–48, 173, 259–261, 266–267, 366
Arapaho people, 375
Armstrong, Thomas, 249, *250*
Arredondo, Teodora, 454
Artraya, Enrique, 468n15
Ashmore, Nicholas L., 270, 369–372
Auburn gold town, 322, 332–333

B

Baker, Charles K., 345–346
Baker, Charlie, 93–94
Bancroft, Hubert Howe, 450, 471n21
Banderas, Antonio, 458
Banta, Susan, 273, 309
Barber, Edgar, 77–79
Barrillo, Jose, 136–137, 191, 250–251, 455, 469n22
Barton, James, 170, 335–337, 345–346, 348, 350, 352–353, 410
Barton Mound, 346–347, 478n19
Barumas, Yginio, 186, 187
Bassett, Charles, 42–44, 52
Baxter, Warner, 451
Bay State Ranch, 194, 195, 197
Bean, Joshua H., 172–190, *181*, 257, 315, 316, 471n28
Bean, Roy, 172
Bear Flag Revolt (1846), 20–21, 23–27, 64, 118, 338
Bear River Massacre (1863), 374–375
Beatty, Elwood T., *205*, 205–207
Beckwourth, Jim, 266
Belcher, Lewis F., 363
Bell, Alexander, 176–177
Bell, Horace
  claim of being part of Los Angeles Rangers, 478n4
  on frontier Los Angeles, 167–169

Bell, Horace (*cont.*)
lynchings attended by, 187–188
on Powers as gambler, 354
on Reid as Bean's killer, 175
Reminiscences of a Ranger, 470n1, 470n12, 478n10, 479n24
on trial of Reyes Feliz, 184–185
Bellamy (ruffian), 104, 121–122, 124
Benites, Ana. *See* Andrada, Maria Ana
Bennett, Mary. *See* Love, Mary
Bennett, Samantha, 381
Bergara, Antonio, 402–405, *404*
Bidwell Bar gold camp, 107–110, *108*
Big Bar mining camp, 206–208, 211, 223, 229
Big Bill (desperado), 192, 200, 201
Bigler, John
as Democrat, 262
establishment of California Rangers, 255
failure to renew rangers' commissions, 318
Love's reports to, 291, 305, 476n23
opposition to, 286, 307, 308, 315
prejudice against Chinese miners, 216
reward for Murrieta issued by, 238–239, 243
Billy the Kid, 434, 440
Bingham, Ned, 377–378
Bishop, Sam, 302–304, *303*
Black, Lafayette, 270, 313, 383
Blaive, Dominique, 91, 311, 312, 317
Bludworth, Charley, 270, 294, 383–384
Blue Tent tavern and store, 79–80, 84, 123
Bojorques, Narciso, 415–418
Boland, Jerome, 88–89
Botero, Jose, 144–146, 256
Bowen, Ike, 110, 113–114
Boyle, Carmelita Garcia, 446
Breen, Patrick, 291
Brewer, Myron, 372
Bridger, Jim, 26, 64
Buchanan, Robert "Buck," 110, 113–114, 116–118, 228, 319
Buena Vista, Battle of (1847), 264, 270
Buntline, Ned, 422–423
Burgess, William, 234–235, *236*
Burgos, Luis, 335–338
Burns, Walter Noble, 451
Burroughs, Charles, 27
Bustamante, Procopio. *See* Murrieta, Tomas Procopio
Bustamante, Tomas, 106, 407, 408
Byrnes, Mike, 49
Byrnes, William W.
alcoholism of, 363–366
appearance of, 265–266, *266*
as California Ranger, 265, 268, 293, 294, 296, 299–304, 362, 440
death of, 365
decapitation of Murrieta and Three Fingered Jack, 299–301, 326, 366
in El Dorado Indian War, 267
in gun battle at Cantua Creek, 296, 477n7
marriage and children, 363
in Mexican War, 47–48, 266
monte and, 47, 49, 265, 267
in Murphys Camp, 49, 267, 465n25
relationship with Murrieta, 47–49, 265, 309, 475n23
as scalp hunter, 47–48, 266–267, 365, 366
as volunteer militia captain, 363–364

C

Cady, David C., 202–203
Cahuillas, 173–174
Calaveras Guards, 220–221, 228, 238
California. *See also* vigilantes and vigilantism; *specific cities*
Bear Flag Revolt in, 20–21, 23–27, 64, 118, 338
criminal justice system in, 57–58, 426
Donner Party's journey to, 85, 291
Mexican land grants in, 19, 21–22, 58–59, 73, 90–91, 377, 379
Midwinter Fair in (1894), 405
Spanish settlement of, 17–19
US annexation and statehood, 26, 29, 37, 178
California Column (Civil War), 207
California gold rush. *See also* fandango halls; gambling; *specific mining camps*
beginnings of, 29
communication delays in era of, 133, 165
firearms of, 71–72, *72*, *86*
fire destruction in camps, 106
geographical region of, 30–31
journey to gold fields, 6, 15–16, 30, 32
methods of finding gold, 31, 45–46, *46*
Murrieta as miner in, 1, 7–9, 33, 35–36, 41–42, 45–47, 53, 241, 248
Murrieta's raids on mining camps, 1, 7, 12, 192–199, 203, 206–212, 218–223, 230–233, 241
racism and, 38–40, 55
California Rangers
disbanding of, 318, 320, 372
Feliz's cooperation with, 289–292, 301

in gun battle at Cantua Creek, 296–298, 305, 368, 387–388, 453, 476–477n7
headquarters of, 268–269, 284, 288
hunt for Murrieta, 283–298
Love as leader of, 255–257, *256*, 262–263, 265, 283–295, 301, 304–306, 317–318
Murrieta shot and killed by, 298–300, *298*, 300
Ochovo's cooperation with, 300–301, 326
petition for establishment of, 254–255
political attacks against, 286–287
recruits for, 263, 265, 268–270, 474n7
rewards paid to, 318, 324–325, 373
toughness of, 362
calzoneras, *56*, 105, 172
Camargo, Juan, 418–419, 421
Camplido, Carlos, 468n15
Camp Opera, 206, 221, 230
Campo Seco (Calaveras County), 104, 117, 205–207, 224, 230
Campo Seco (Tuolumne County), 35, 96–100, 154, 205
Canavan, Edward, 289–290
Cantabrana, Aurelio, 431
Cantua Creek
geography of, 292–294, *295*
gun battle at, 296–298, 305, 327, 368, 387–388, 453, 476–477n7
Murrieta's death at, 298, *298*, *300*
Carlisle, Bob, 410, 413–415
Carly, Joseph, 132
Carr, Harry, 456–457
Carrillo, Joaquin. *See* Murrieta, Joaquin
Carrillo, Jose Ramon, 23–25, 410–415
Carrillo, Juan, 13, 312
Carson, Kit, 20, 24, 26, 64, 266
Carson, Moses, 24–25
Carson, Robert, 266
Carter, Henry A., 128–129
Carter, John, 197
Cassidy, Butch, 434, 440–441
Castro, Francisco, 356, 357
Castro, Jose, 353, 354
Catala, Magin, 393–398, 403
Catholic Church, 13–14, 17–18, 91, 166, 171, 393
Cerradel, Manuel, 412–415, 418
Chabolla, Antonio, 80, 81, 84, 123
Champlain (prospector), 384, 385
Chavoya, Abraham, 396, 398
Chavoya, Angel Maria, 396, 398, 400
Chavoya, Elizabeth, 400
Chavoya, Maria, 396, 400
Cheatham, Benjamin F., 98, *100*, 100–101
Cherokees, 4–6, 12, 415
Cheverino, Jose, 79, 80, 123–124, 209, 222, 468n7
Cheyennes, 375
Chicano movement, 13, 452
Chinese miners and mining camps
arrival in gold fields, 32, 215
gold claims worked by, 215, *217*
language barrier and, 216, 236
money raised for California Rangers, 324–325
Murrieta's head recognized by, 323, 324
racism experienced by, 215–216
raids on, 151–152, 193–195, 198, 203, 206, 208–209, 216–223, 230–233
Civil War (1861–1865), 98, 207, 262, 362, 373–374, 383, 405, 428
Clark, James, 128–130, 133, 229
Clarke, Charles A., 221, 228–233, 238
Cocanour, John, 243
Cocks, Henry, 158–164, 206, 246, 363
Cody, Buffalo Bill, 422–423
Columbia (American Camp)
Anglo march on, 52–53
gambling in, 51, 57
militia march to Sawmill Flat, 149–151
murders in, 131, 282
posses formed in, 131–132
severed head and hand displayed in, 323–324
Comanches, 178, 182, 259–260, 297
Conejo Mountain, 142–143, *143*, 184, 273, 346
Connor, Patrick Edward
affidavits collected by, 310–311
appearance of, *264*
Bear River Massacre and, 374–375
as California Ranger, 263, 265, 284–287, 289–291
in Civil War, 262, 373–374
death of, 376
letters to Stockton newspaper by, 284–287, 476n18
marriage and children, 373, *375*
in Mexican War, 262–265
Powder River Expedition led by, 375
severed head and hand in possession of, 311, 441
as Stockton Blues captain, 373, *375*
as undersheriff of San Joaquin County, 324, 372
Corcoran, James, 129, 130
Corona, Adolfo, 400–401, *402*
Coronel, Antonio, 177, 182, 183, 186–187, 471n21
Covarrubias, Jose M., 253–254

Cowie, Thomas, 21, 24–26, 64, 118, 338, 410–411
Crowell, Henry, 241–242, 254, 447
Cunningham, Tom, 390–391
"The Curse of Capistrano" (McCulley), 456, 457

D

Daggett, John, 227, 228
daguerreotypes, *6*, *23*, *56*, *108*, *222*, *269*, 299, 320, *320*, 477n27
Daimwood, Boston "Boss," 368
Dalton brothers, 405
dance houses. *See* fandango halls
Daniel, Bernardo, 122–123, 171, 272, 327–332, 342–343
Daniel, Francisco "Pancho"
  Andrada and, 183, 190, 349, 351
  appearance of, 122, 183, 343, 351
  Bell on, 479n24
  boasting of crimes by, 123, 342
  death of, 351–352
  injuries to, 344, 346, 349
  murder trial of, 350–351
  Murrieta and, 123, 351
  in Pico's gang, 171
  in San Juan Capistrano, 344–345
  in San Luis Obispo, 272
  Vasquez and, 122, 123, 125, 343
Davis, David, 195, 197
Davis, Jefferson, 378
Dawson (desperado), 279–281, 289–290, 307–308
Denver, James W., 286
Dickens, Charles, 377
Dillinger, John, 441
Dix, Richard, 456
Dixon, Maynard, *92*
Dodson, William "Pink," 385–387
Donner Party, 85, 291
Dorsey, Caleb, 40, 131–133, *132*, 146, 147
Douglass, David F., 289
Dublin Jack, 280

E

El Camino Real, 18, 61–62, 170, 271, 356
Eldeo, Fermin, 424–426
El Dorado Indian War (1850–1851), 267
Elias, Miguel, 424–426
Ellis, Charles H., 195–197, 227, 472n6
Encinas, Francisco, 424–426
Espinosa, Cayetana, 328, 329
Espinosa, Manuel, 159–160, 162–164
Espinosa, Ramon, 328–330
Evans, Chris, 405
Evans, George, 269–270, 383

F

Fairbanks, Douglas, 456, 457
fandango halls
  in Auburn, 332
  Dixon's depiction of, *92*
  in Hornitos, 241, 447
  in Livermore Valley, 416, 418
  in San Andreas, 45
  in San Francisco, 102
  in San Jose, 76, 77, 120–122, 127
  in San Luis Obispo, 272
  in Santa Margarita, 356
  in Sawmill Flat, 147
  in Sonoran Camp, 106–107
  in Sonorian Camp, 33, 36
  in Stockton, 136–137, 191, 250
Feliz, Claudio
  appearance of, 42, 73, 164
  bandido mentors of, 58, 64, 66
  boasting of exploits by, 58, 66, 74, 102, 109, 113, 119, 124–125
  Chinese miners attacked by, 151–152
  death and burial of, 161, 163–165, 190, 191, 206, 246, 288, 339, 363
  gang led by, 71–80, 84, 102–123, 148, 151–161, 338
  as gold miner, 33, 35, 43–44
  Hill and, 96, 98, 99, 102
  imprisonment of, 44, 122, 124–125, 133, 135, 146, 149
  injuries to, 131–133, 135, 146, 147, 152, 164
  journey to California, 16
  on Pacheco robbery, 65, 66
  ranchero dress of, 105
  revenge as motive of, 121, 147
  Vasquez and, 122–127, 133
  weapons carried by, 71
  Yuba County murders, 107–116, 118, 124
Feliz, Jesus
  cooperation with California Rangers, 289–292, 301
  as gold miner, 33, 35
  imprisonment of, 282–283, 288, 476n23
  journey to California, 16
  in Murrieta's gang, 191, 279
  release by Love, 304
Feliz, Reyes
  Bean murder and, 177, 182–185, 189, 257, 471n28

Calle de los Negros and, 168, 182
capture and escape of, 131–132, 149
Chinese miners attacked by, 151–152
death of, 185, 190, 288, 349
family background, 463n8
as gold miner, 33, 35
injuries to, 138–139, 148
journey to California, 16
Marias murder by, 102, 184
in Pico's gang, 169, 171
ranchero dress of, 105
Ruddle murder, 135–136, 142
rumors of imprisonment of, 160
in Tejon Pass attack, 137–138
Yuba County murders, 107–110, 118, 124
Feliz, Rosa, 15–16, 30, 40, 47, 91, 454
Fiddletown, 212–214, *213*, 218
firearms, 71–72, *72*, *86*
Flores, Antonio, 468n15
Flores, Juan, 344–349, 479n24
Flores, Sebastian, 338–339, 341, 342
Ford, Robert, 440
Foreign Miners' Tax Act (1850), 39–40, 51–52, 215, 217
Foreman, David, 194, 231
Forsyth, A. H., 282–283
Fowler, George, 24–26, 64, 118, 338, 410–411
Freeman, Frank, 279, 280, 289–290
Fremont, John C., 20, 26, 29, 64

G

Gabriel (desperado), 104
gambling. *See also* monte
atmosphere of gambling dens, 68
in Bidwell Bar, 107
in Columbia, 51, 57
in Hornitos, 241
in Los Angeles, 168–169
in Marysville, 105
in Mokelumne Hill, 44
in Murphys Camp, 49–50
in San Andreas, 45–47
social classes of gamblers, 69
in Sonorian Camp, 33–36, *34*, 47, 51, 57, 119
in Stockton, 67–69
Garcia, Anastacio, 159, 363, 470n18
Garcia, Bernardino (Three Fingered Jack)
adobe home of, *28*, 90
death of, 296
in gun battle at Cantua Creek, 296
marriage and children, 22–23, 29, 90, 91, 191, 380
Mexican War and, 21, 23–29, 90, 338, 411
misidentification of, 446–447, 463n4
Mountain Jim and, 85–86, 90
murder method used by, 118
Murrieta and, 17, 90, 191, 203–204, 218, 244, 272, 278
Nahl's depictions of, *191*
Ridge on murder of Chinese miners by, 237
severed head of, 309–310, *311*, 313–314, 317–323, 439, 441–445
severed hand of, 300–304
Garcia, Francisco "Negro," 338–342, 350
Garcia, Hilaria Sanchez, 22–23, *23*, *28*, 29, 90–91, 191, 380
Garcia, Manuela, 339, 342
Garcia, Miguela, 158
Gardner, John, 112, 113, 245
Garrett, Pat, 440
Gatewood, William Jefferson, 195–197, *196*, 472n6
The Gay Defender (film), 456
Gaylord, J. W., 273
Gilbert, Edward, 286
Gladden, Solomon "Sol," 428–430
Gleason, George, 96, 98
Godey, Alexis, 26, *63*, 64–65
Golding, Aaron, 415–416
gold rush. *See* California gold rush
Gonzales, Pedro, 135–139, 142–144, 184, 254, 262, 273, 279, 346
Grant, Ulysses S., 20
Green, Alfred A., 438, 440
Guadalupe Hidalgo, Treaty of (1848), 29, 36
Guerra, Pablo de la, 255
guns, 71–72, *72*, *86*

H

Hall, John, 195, 197
Hall, William Otis, 170
Harrington, William, 75
Harvey, Walter, 270, 284
Haskill, N. R., 268
Haskins, Charles W., 475n23
Havens, George W., 312
Hayes, Benjamin, 170, 177, 367, 411, 413
Henderson, William T. "Billy"
appearance of, 268, *269*
as California Ranger, 268, 293–295, 297–298, 300, 369
daguerreotype with Norton and Love, 320, *320*, 477n27
death and funeral of, 369
on disposition of Murrieta, 42

Henderson, William T. "Billy" (*cont.*)
general store owned by, 42, 241
in gun battle at Cantua Creek, 297–298, 368
shooting of Murrieta by, 298, 300, 369
on stories told about Murrieta, 40–41
tour of mining region with severed head and hand, 318–320, 322
Herbert, Philemon T. "Phil," 252–255, 262, 270, 361–362
Hernandez, Domingo, 76–78, 170, 291, 455, 466n9
Hernandez, Mariano, 58–61, 64, 76, 170
Herndon, William H., 85
Higuera, Anastacio, 328–330
Hill, David, 96–103, 467n13
Hipolito, Eduviges, 13, 312
Hittell, Theodore H., 450
Hope, Alexander W., 174, 176–177, 182, 186
Hornitos mining camp, 241–243, *242*, 254, 447
Horsley, John, 210
Horton, Belle, 385, *386*
Howard, Dela, 386–387
Howard, Thomas, 262, 268–270, 285, 384, 385
Howard, William J.
Buena Vista Ranch, 262–263, 268–269, 288, 326, 384–385
California Rangers and, 262–263, 268–270, 285, 288–289, 387–388
death of, 388
feud with Dodson, 385–387
marriage and children, 385, *386*
Ochovo transported and guarded by, 326–327
on severed head delivered to Bigler, 318
on stories told about Murrieta, 40
Hubbell, Noble B., 203–204, 311

I

Indian John (Paiute), 370–372
Indian Juan (desperado), 339, 341, 342
Irving, John "Red," 172–173
Iverson, Christian, 380–382, 480n24

J

Jackson, Joseph Henry, 451–452
Jackson Gate gold camp, 47, 209–212
Jackson gold camp, 124, 209–211, *210*, 219–223, *222*, 226, 322, 473n6
James, Jesse, 252, 434, 440
Janes, William W., 137, 191, 250
Jarauta, Celedonio Dómeco de, 225, 249
Jesus Maria mining camp, 202
Jinkerson, Andrew, 112, 113, 245
Joaquin Murrieta and His Horse Gangs (Latta), 453–455
Joaquin Rocks, 393–402, *395*, 406
Johnson, Ben and Dudley, 405
Johnson, Joseph W., 245
Jordan, Louis J., 442–445, *443*, 483n16
Juanito (desperado), 412, 415
Juarez, Reyes, 193–194
Julian (Californio), 122, 126–127

K

Keating, Patrick, 362
Keating, Thomas, 361–362
Kell, David, 5–6
Kemble, Edward C., 286
Kibbe, William C., 363–364
King, Andrew, 332–333
Kirk (deputy US Marshal), 371, 372
Kop, Ah, 193, 194, 236
Kottinger, John, 155–157, *156*, 470n16
Kottinger, Maria Bernal, 155–157, *156*

L

Lake, Joseph, 219, 220
Lane, Tom, 321–322
Latta, Frank F., 453–455
Leary, John, 131–133, 146, 152, 161, 164, 282
Lelong, Josefa Alanis, 336, 337
Lelong, Martin, 335–338
Leyba, Albino, 281–282, 476n12
The Life and Adventures of Joaquín Murieta (Ridge), 4, 7–13, 40, 449–452, 459
Linares, Fernando, 390, 393
Linares, Pio, 272, 355–357
Lincoln, Abraham, 20, 85
Lippincott, Charles, 96–98
Lisarraga, Ignacio, 313, 477n33
Little, William H., 345–346
Lookout Lynching case (1901), 352
Lopez, Antonio, 278, 296, 301, 302, 304, 428
Lopez, Benito, 171, 178, 182–183, 185, 187, 189, 471n28
Los Angeles
Andrada in, 91, 92, 169, 178–183, 389
Anza Trail and, 17
Bean murder in, 174–190, 257, 316, 471n28
Calle de los Negros in, *168*, 168–169, 181–182, 185

Catholic Church in, 166
Fort Moore Hill in, 185–187, *186*, 349
gambling in, 168–169
gold rush and, 30, 166
horse markets at, 137
Irving's gang in, 172–173
jail in, 155, 182, 337, 349, *352*, 368
Mexican settlement of, 18
Native American camp near, 144–145
Pico's gang in, 169–171
vigilantism in, 58, 176–177, 181–187, 189, 328–329, 349–352, 368, 413–415
violent crime in, 167–168, 174, 334–335
wagon roads to, 59, 138, 140
Los Angeles Rangers, 176, 328, 335–337, 478n4
Love, Harry
affidavits collected by, 309–312, 437, 477n33
appearance of, 140, *141*, *256*, 257–258, *378*
background of, 140–141, 254, 255, 257–262
as California Ranger, 255–257, 262–263, 265, 283–295, 301, 304–306, 317–318
as civilian express rider for US Army, 258–261
daguerreotype with Norton and Henderson, 320, *320*, 477n27
death and burial of, 382, *382*, 383, 480n26
Gonzales captured and killed by, 142–144, 184, 254, 262, 273, 346
in gun battle at Cantua Creek, 476–477n7
marriage of, 377, 379–381
Murrieta identified by, 144, 146, 256, 469n3
reports written to Bigler, 291, 305, 476n23
Ruddle killers apprehended by, 141–142, 144, 254, 262
sawmill purchased by, 376, 377, 379
tour of mining region with severed head and hand, 319–324, 439
as tracker, 140–141, 258, 469n1
trip to Washington, DC, 377–379
weapons carried by, 140
Love, Mary, 376–377, 379–383, 480n26
Luches, Miguel, 71, 77–78, 102–103

M

Maldonado, Ignacio, 327–328, 330, 331
Manta, Pedro, 309
Marcelino (desperado), 102–103
Mardis, Benjamin, 96–98
Marias, Anselmo, 102, 184
Marietto, Felipe, 35
The Mark of Zorro (film), 456, 457
maromas (Mexican circus), 169, 171–172, 174, 179, 188
Maron, Antonio, 424–426
Marsh, John, 72–75, *74*, 77, 155
Marshall, James, 29, 86
Martinez, Avelino, 453–454
Martinez (desperado), 60, 61, 82–83
Martinez (mining camp), 53–54, 57, 70, 81, 146–147, 281, 326–327, 423
Marvin, John G., 153–154
Mary (escaped enslaved woman), 178
Marysville
fire destruction in, 106
gambling in, 105
horse markets at, 122, 136
posses formed in, 110, 114–116
severed head and hand displayed in, 319–322, 439
as trading center, 105, *115*
Tremont House hotel in, 7
The Mask of Zorro (film), 13, 458
Mather, George, 111–113, 245
May, Charles. *See* Hill, David
Mazuca, Rafael, 275
McCargar, Henry V., 47, 311, 312, 465n22
McCulley, Johnston, 455–457
McLean (horse thief), 279, 282–283
McMullen, William, 207–209, 211–214, 218
McRae, Ira, 147–151
McWilliams, John, 477n27
Melones Camp gun battle, 94–96
Mendez, Salvador. *See* Ochovo, Jose Maria
mesteneros (mustang hunters), 136, 142–143, 285, 288–289, 292, 293
Mexican War (1846–1848). *See also specific battles*
Alabama Volunteers in, 258
Bear Flag Revolt and, 20–21, 23–27, 64, 118, 338
Bennett's actions during, 377
Fort Moore Hill and, 185
Jarauta as guerrilla leader in, 225, 249
Missouri Mounted Volunteers in, 266
New York Volunteers in, 192, 334, 336, 354
prisoners held during, 26–29
Texas Volunteers in, 253, 263–265
Three Fingered Jack and, 21, 23–29, 90, 338, 411
veterans of, 47–48, 76, 90, 98, 172, 176, 185, 195–196, 202, 207, 221, 229, 262–269, 409
Mier Expedition, 229
Miller, Cincinnatus Hiner, 450–451
Mission San Gabriel, 17, 171–172, 174, *175*
Mitchell, Hyman and Levi, 69

Mokelumne Hill, 44, 148, 194–195, 220–230, 233, 240, 322, 448
monte (card game)
  Byrnes and, 47, 49, 265, 267
  description of game, *34*, 48
  in Livermore Valley, 416
  McLean and, 282–283
  Murrieta and, 9–10, 47–51, 57, 69, 95, 103–104, 119, 147, 190, 209, 241, 248, 309, 448
  popularity of, 33, 35, 36, 106
Montemayor, Pedro, 127–128
Moore, B. F., 129–130
Morales, Clemente, 312
Moreno, Atanacio, 335–338
Moretta, Jose, 35
Moretto, Rafaela, 35
Moretto, Ygnacio, 202
Mormons, 278, 369–372, 374–376
Morse, Harry N., 390–391, 408, 418, 420–422
Murphy, John, 349–350
Murphys Camp, 44, 48–49, 51, 267, 465n25
Murrieta, Andres, 407–408
Murrieta, Jesus, 13, 16, 30, 33, 35, 40, 191, 203, *204*
Murrieta, Joaquin
  appearance of, 7, 10, 41, 47, 225, 239, 246, 272, 310
  Armstrong's depiction of, 249, *250*
  Bean murder, 177, 183, 184, 188–190, 257, 316
  birth and early life, 13–15, *14*
  as Botero, 144–146, 256
  Calle de los Negros and, 168
  Daniel and, 123
  death of, *298*, 298–300, *300*, 307, 315, 369
  disposition of, 7, 9, 10, 14–15, 42, 190, 246, 310
  doubts as to existence of, 276, 277, 287, 307, 451
  family background, 13, 463n6
  Feliz's gang and, 103–118
  as folk hero, 1, 276, 434–435, 452
  as gold miner, 1, 7–9, 33, 35–36, 41–42, 45–47, 53, 241, 248
  in gun battle at Cantua Creek, 296–298, 305
  imprisonment of, 70–71, 83–85
  journey to California, 15–16
  manhunts for, 193–214, 219–221, 226–233, 241–245, 253, 274–275, 283–298, 447, 472n6
  maroma attended by, 171–172, 174, 179
  mistreatment by Anglos, 8, 10, 40, 42, 49, 190, 247, 249, 271
  monte and, 9–10, 47–51, 57, 69, 95, 103–104, 119, 147, 190, 209, 241, 248, 309, 448
  as Montemayor, 127–128
  Nahl's depictions of, *191*, *283*, *437*, 443, 448, *448*
  Pico and, 123, 169, 171, 178
  raids on mining camps, 1, 7, 12, 192–199, 203, 206–212, 218–223, 230–233, 241
  ranchero dress of, 105
  recruitment of gang members, 190–192
  revenge as motive of, 1, 10–12, 40, 190, 197, 247, 276
  rewards offered for, 223, 226, *238*, 238–240, 243, 248–249, 253–254
  Robin Hood and, 1, 13, 434–435, 451–452, 456, 459
  Ruddle murder, 135–136, 142
  rumors and myths regarding, 206, 223–225, 244, 436–441, 451
  in San Luis Obispo, 271–273, 309
  severed head of, 299–324, *307*, *311*, 313–314, *314*, 391, 437–439, 441–445, 483n16
  social banditry of, 1–2, 452
  in Tejon Pass attack, 137–138
  Three Fingered Jack and, 17, 90, 191, *191*, 203–204, 218, 244, 272, 278
  violence against women, 94–96, 128
  weapons carried by, 72, 130, 246, 474n14
  Willow Springs murders, 129–130, 133
  Ybarra attack and robbery, 274, 277
  Yuba County murders, 107–116, 118
  Zorro and, 1, 13, 434, 456–458
Murrieta, Jose M., 35
Murrieta, Juan, 458
Murrieta, Juana Bernal, 432, 433
Murrieta, Luz, 407–408
Murrieta, Mariana. *See* Andrada, Maria Ana
Murrieta, Rafael, 393
Murrieta, Tomas Procopio
  alias used by, 418
  appearance of, 408, *409*, *419*, 420
  birth and early life, 407–408
  Caliente raid, 424–425
  death of, 433
  Golding raid, 415–416
  Grangeville raid, 424
  Hanford raid, 427–428
  as horse and cattle thief, 408–409, 416–419, 421–423, 430–432
  imprisonment of, 417–418, 423
  manhunts for, 427–430
  marriage and children, *432*, 432–433

Rains murder, 412–415, 418
rewards offered for, 430
stagecoach robbery, 419
uncle Joaquin as idol to, 106, 408
Murrieta, Vicenta, 13, 106, 312, 407–408, 440

N

Nahl, Charles Christian, *191*, *283*, *437*, 443, 448, *448*, 449
Native Americans. *See also specific groups of people*
Bear River Massacre of, 374–375
at Buena Vista ranch, 269
Catholic Church and, 17–18, 171, 393
El Dorado Indian War, 267
peon game played by, 144–145
punitive expeditions against, 59
reservations for, 364
as trackers, 226, 347
Trail of Tears and, 4
uprisings by, 172
Natividad, Battle of (1846), 27
Neblina, Matias, 403–404
Neruda, Pablo, 451
New Almaden quicksilver mine, 120–121
Newhall Incident (1970), 346
New Idria quicksilver mine, 389–390
Northrup, Sarah Bird, 4
Norton, Jim, 318–320, *320*, 322, 477n27
Noyes, Leonard, 49, 465n25
Nuttall, John, 313–314, 316–317

O

Ochovo, Jose Maria, 278, 296, 300–301, 304–306, 326–327
Olivas, Guadalupe, 394–396, 398
Olivas, Jose, 366–368, *369*
Olivas, Manuel, 328–330
Ontiveros, Patricio, 175, 176, 470–471nn12–13
Ortega, Chano, 415–416
Osburn, William, 177–179, 181–183, 187
Overstreet, J. T., 176–177
Owen, Billy, 87–89, 94–96

P

Pacheco, Antonio, 81–82
Pacheco, Francisco, 65–66, *66*, 123
Pacheco, Jose, 81
Pacheco, Romualdo, 411
Pacheco Pass, 62–65, 81, 419
Padilla, Juan N., 23–25
Paiutes, 370–371
Patton, Joseph, 365
Paul, Belle, 431
Pena, Manuel, 105–110, 118, 119
Pera, Jose Jesus, 468n15
Phoenix Quartz Mill, 197–200, 227, 472n7
Pico, Andres, 58, 278–279, 329, 343, 347–349, *348*
Pico, Pio, 19–20, 58
Pico, Salomon
Bean murder and, 177
execution of, 354
family background, 58, 353
Feliz brothers and, 58, 64, 66, 76, 169, 171
hometown of, 291
injuries to, 170, 352
as Mexican War veteran, 59
Murrieta and, 123, 169, 171, 178
revenge as motive of, 59
in San Luis Obispo, 272
Pierce, Franklin, 377, 378
Polk, James, 32
Possum Bar mining camp, 207–208, 211
Powder River Expedition, 375
Powell, Abraham, 306
Power, Tyrone, 457
Powers, Jack, 354–357, 360, 472n2
Pray, Isaac, 113, 245
Prescott, William, 241–242, 254, 270, 447, 474n7
Price, Sterling, 266

R

racism, 38–40, 55, 95, 147, 215–216, 399
Rains, John, 407, 409–415, *412*, 418
Rains, Merced, 407, 409–410, 414, 415
Ramirez, Juanito, 275
Rathbone, Basil, 457
Reed, Hilaria Sanchez. *See* Garcia, Hilaria Sanchez
Reed, John, 22, 23, 91
Reid, Felipe, 175–176, 188, 189, 470–471nn12–13, 471n28
Reid, Hugo, 175–176
Requena, Manuel, 177
Reyna, Bernardo, 312
Reynolds Ferry, *232*, 232–233
Rich Gulch mining camp, 230–231, 473n18
Rico, Jesus, 171, 174, 179, 180
Rico, Juanito, 171, 177, 179
Ridge, Elizabeth Wilson, 5, 6

Ridge, John, 4
Ridge, John Rollin
  on Chinese miners murdered by Three Fingered Jack, 237
  daguerreotype of, *6*
  death of, 450
  on departure of Rosa Feliz, 91
  family background, 4
  The Life and Adventures of Joaquín Murieta, 4, 7–13, 40, 449–452, 459
  marriage and children, 5, 6
  on Montemayor's arrest, 127
  murder of Kell by, 5–6
  trauma experienced by, 3–5
  on two Joaquins, 446
Rivera, Francisco, 312
Rivera, Jose Maria, 312
Roach, William F., 363
Robin Hood, 1, 13, 434–435, 451–452, 456, 459
The Robin Hood of El Dorado (film), 13, 451
Rockwell, Orrin Porter, 370, 372, *373*
Rodriguez, Antonio, 408–409
Ruddle, Allen, 133–136, *135*, 139, 141–142, 144, 252, 254, 262
Ruddle, John, 133, 134
Ruiz, Vicente, 424–426

S

Sacramento
  butcher markets in, 157
  horse markets at, 136
  jail in, 102, 290
  severed head and hand displayed in, 318–319
  Sutter's Fort in, 20–21
  theft of horses from, 87
  wagon roads to, 128
Salazar, Juan, 355
Salinas River, 158–165, *162*, 246, 271, 339, 342
Salkman, "Dutch Fred," 86–91, 125, 467n4
Samantha (brothel keeper), 411–412
San Andreas mining camp
  danger in, 44
  fandango halls in, 45
  gambling in, 45–47
  Murrieta as miner in, 45–47
  pioneer journalists in, 41
  posses formed in, 195–197
  raids on, 192, 223
  severed head and hand displayed in, 322–323
  vigilantism in, 202, 228
Sanate, Jesus, 80, 334–338, 466n11
Sanchez, Hilaria. *See* Garcia, Hilaria Sanchez
Sanchez, Luis, 412–414
Sanchez, Pedro, 191, 279, 281–282
Sanchez, Tomas, 347, 368, 410, 414
Sandoval, Cipriano, 177, 179–181, 185–189, 471n28
San Francisco
  butcher markets in, 157
  fandango halls in, 102
  fire of 1850 in, 205
  fire of 1906 in, 445, 483n16
  gold rush and, 32, 42, 90, 265
  Mexican settlement of, 18
  in Mexican War, 26–27
  Midwinter Fair in (1894), 405
  Morton Street in, 421
  Murderers' Alley in, 102, 103
  police department in, 87, 103
  presidio (military fort) in, 21, 22
  rumors of Murrieta's presence in, 244
  severed head and hand displayed in, 313–314, *314*, 321, 437, 441–445
  theft of horses from, 87
San Jacinto, Battle of (1836), 228–229
San Jose
  business street in, *126*
  fandango halls in, 76, 77, 120–122, 127
  Hernandez in, 59–60, 64
  jail in, 122–125, 161, 165, 341, 468n10
  Mexican settlement of, 18
  murders in, 77–79, 102, 127–128
  posses formed in, 78–79, 120–121, 128, 245
  social life in, 119–120
San Juan Bautista, 123, 290–293, 327, 419–420
San Juan Capistrano, 277, 344–345
San Luis Obispo
  fandango halls in, 272
  Mexican settlement of, 18
  mission in, 271, 272, 330, *332*
  outlaws in, 271–273, 309, 328, 330–331, 355–357
  rumors of Reyes Feliz's imprisonment in, 160
  vigilantism in, 164, 329–331, 357–358
San Pasqual, Battle of (1846), 58
San Quentin prison, 338, 342–344, 363, 401, 409, 414, 418–420, 423, 435
Santa Anna, Antonio López de, 264
Saures, Gabriel, 405–406, 481n22
Savage, Jim, 270
Sawmill Flat, 53–54, 57, 70, 131, 146–151
The Scarlet Pimpernel (Orczy), 457

Scott, Robert
appearance of, 60
camaraderie with Valenzuela, 83, 279
Coarse Gold Gulch murder, 82–83
El Camino Real attacks by, 61–62
execution of, 333–334
murders confessed to by, 58, 332–334
Pacheco Pass and hacienda attacks, 62–66
separation from Murrieta's gang, 280
Seabough, Samuel, 40, 41
Secrest, William B., 480n26
Sherman, William, 259–260
Shoshones, 374–375
Silva, Esteban Alvarado, 154–155, 160, 162–164
Sioux people, 375
Smith, Ann, 83
Smith, Charles H. "Buckskin," 127–128, 144, 252
Smith, Digby, 77–78, 102
Smith, Volney, 210
Snelling, William, 383
social banditry, 1–2, 452
Soliz (desperado), 104
Sonoran Camp (Northern Mines), 106–107, 110, 113–114
Sonora/Sonorian Camp (Southern Mines)
description of, 31, *39*
eviction of foreigners from, 56–57
fandango halls in, 33, 36
gambling in, 33–36, *34*, 47, 51, 57, 119
homicide rate in, 57, 465n4
jail in, 98, 133, 135, 146, 154
Murrieta as miner in, 33, 35–36, 41, 53
posses formed in, 52, 54, 55, 152
racism within, 38–39, 55
severed head and hand displayed in, 324
theft of horses from, 87–88
vigilantism in, 54, 57–58, 97–101, 133
wagon roads to, 151, 153
Sontag, John, 405
Sosa (Comanche), 178, 182
Soto, Juan, 418–420
Soto, Lorenzo, 274–275
spoils system, 262
Stacey, William, 148–151
Starr (owner of Blue Tent tavern), 79–80
Stidger, Oliver P., 439–440
Stockton
butcher markets in, 157
Catholic Church in, 91
fandango halls in, 136–137, 191, 250
gambling in, 67–69
horse markets at, 136
jail in, 84, 290, 466n1
Murrieta's imprisonment in, 70–71, 83–85
severed head and hand displayed in, 310–312, *311*, 316
theft of horses from, 87
as trading center, 35, 67, *68*
vigilantism in, 88–89
wagon roads to, 138
Walsh murder suspect in, 289
Sundance Kid, 441
Sutherland, Jack, 211
Sutter, John, 20–21, 29, 218
Sydney Ducks, 58, 60, 64–65, 172
Sylvester, John, 270, 294, 301–304, 366–368

T

Taliaferro, Theophilus W., 202
Taylor, Andrew "Natchez," 441–442
Taylor, Zachary, 258, 264
Tejon Pass, 63, 137–138, 140–142, 184, 288, 356, 366, 425
Tejon people, 138, 184
Tesca, Avelino, 423
Texas Rangers, 172, 202, 229, 254, 258, 380, 475n23
Texas Revolution (1835–1836), 202, 228–229
Thorp, Juliet G., 309
Three Fingered Jack. *See* Garcia, Bernardino
Tinkham, George, 251
Todd, Thelma, 456
Trail of Tears, 4
Treaty of Guadalupe Hidalgo (1848), 29, 36
Trinidad (desperado), 104, 121–122, 124
Turnersville gold camp, 117–118
Twain, Mark, 200

V

Valdez, Pablo, 160, 162–164
Valencia, Antonio, 191, 218, 220–223, 226
Valenzuela, Antonio, 159, 160, 162, 163
Valenzuela, Jesus, 60, 61, 82, 191, 272, 355–357
Valenzuela, Joaquin
camaraderie with Scott, 83, 279
capture and escape of, 355
Coarse Gold Gulch murder, 82–83
death and burial of, 358, 360
El Camino Real attacks, 61–62
false accounts regarding, 316
Feliz and, 58, 66
in Murrieta's gang, 191, 357, 359
nicknames for, 60, 191, 256–257, 272, 354, 357

Valenzuela, Juan Antonio, 343
Vallejo, Mariano, 21–25, 435
Varley, James F., 466n9, 474n14
Vasquez, Teodor, 122–127, 133, 343, 466n9, 466n11, 468nn6–7
Vasquez, Tiburcio, 159, 390–392, 405, 418–421
Vega, Jose Maria, 309
Venda, Pedro, 391
Vergara, Manuel, 183
vigilantes and vigilantism
  Bean murder and, 176–177, 181–189
  committees formed by, 57–58, 98–99, 113, 176–177, 183–187, 228, 329, 413
  lynchings by, 37, 54, 57–58, 99–101, 124, 133, 164, 170, 177, 185, 187, 199–203, 221–223, 228, 329–331, 349–352, 357–358, 368, 426, *427*
  during Mexican War, 27
  Mountain Jim and, 88–89
  Ochovo and, 326, 327
  opposition to, 97, 189, 201–202
  Pacheco theft and, 81–82
  Rains murder and, 413–415
  trials held by, 57, 98, 184–187, 228, 268, 328–329, 426
Villa, Eugenio, 412–414
Vining, Leroy "Lee," 241–242, 254

W

Walsh, James, 244–246, 280, 284, 289, 317
Ward, Ned, 98
Ward, Sam, 134–135
Warren, R., 282–283
Whalen, Jack, 334–336
White, John, 294, 297–298, 300
Whitman, George N., 120–122
Wilburn, Robert, 370, 372
Williams, Guy, 457
Willow Springs, 128–130, 133, 229
Wilson, Noah James "Mountain Jim," 85–91, 94, 96, 125
Wilson, William, 144–146, 252, 256, 469n3
Winter's Bar gold camp, 206–207, 230
Wood, Orlo B., 416–417
Woodbeck, Peter, 198, 199
Wood (cook at Marsh ranch), 77–78
Wool, John E., 264
Work, George, 51–52, 54–55, 97–101

Y

Yaqui Camp, 193–195, 197, 200–201, 227, 236–237
Yaqui people, 38, 54–55, 193
Ybarra, Andres, 274, *274*, 277
Young, Brigham, 376
Young, James A. "Coho," 270, 284
Yuma Massacre (1781), 18

Z

Zapatero, Jose, 138, 142, 184, 279
Zorro, 1, 13, 434, 456–458